Functional
Programming
in
Kotlin
by Tutorials

by Massimo Carli

Functional Programming in Kotlin by Tutorials

Massimo Carli

ISBN: 978-1-950325-67-2

Table of Contents

Book License

By purchasing *Functional Programming in Kotlin by Tutorials*, you have the following license:

- You are allowed to use and/or modify the source code in *Functional Programming in Kotlin by Tutorials* in as many apps as you want, with no attribution required.

- You are allowed to use and/or modify all art, images and designs that are included in *Functional Programming in Kotlin by Tutorials* in as many apps as you want, but must include this attribution line somewhere inside your app: "Artwork/images/ designs: from *Functional Programming in Kotlin by Tutorials*, available at www.raywenderlich.com".

- The source code included in *Functional Programming in Kotlin by Tutorials* is for your personal use only. You are NOT allowed to distribute or sell the source code in *Functional Programming in Kotlin by Tutorials* without prior authorization.

- This book is for your personal use only. You are NOT allowed to sell this book without prior authorization, or distribute it to friends, coworkers or students; they would need to purchase their own copies.

Before You Begin

This section tells you a few things you need to know before you get started, such as what you'll need for hardware and software, where to find the project files for this book, and more.

What You Need

To follow along with this book, you'll need the following:

- **IntelliJ IDEA Version 2022 or higher**: This book uses IntelliJ IDEA Version 2022. While you can use other editors, this book shows examples using this editor. You can download IntelliJ IDEA 2022 or higher from the JetBrains website (https://www.jetbrains.com/idea/download/).

- **Android Studio Bumblebee or higher**: There are a couple of chapters in Section III that use an Android app for real-world examples. For those chapters, this book expects you to open and build the project using Android Studio. Download Android Studio Bumblebee (2021) or higher from the Android developer website (https://developer.android.com/studio).

- **Kotlin 1.6**: If you're using IntelliJ IDEA and Android Studio, the editor comes bundled with Kotlin already. If you're choosing another editor, you can download Kotlin at KotlinLang.org. This book assumes you have basic knowledge of Kotlin. If you're unfamiliar with Kotlin, start with Kotlin Apprentice (https://www.raywenderlich.com/books/kotlin-apprentice/).

- **A readiness to learn!** This book assumes you're here to learn some exciting things. Dive right in . :]

Book Source Code & Forums

Where to download the materials for this book

The materials for this book can be cloned or downloaded from the GitHub book materials repository:

- https://github.com/raywenderlich/fpk-materials/tree/editions/1.0

Forums

We've also set up an official forum for the book at https://forums.raywenderlich.com/c/books/functional-programming-in-kotlin. This is a great place to ask questions about the book or to submit any errors you may find.

"To my family who's always here for me."

— Massimo Carli

About the Author

 **Massimo Carli** is the author of this book. He's been working with Java since 1995 when he co-founded the first Italian magazine about this technology (http://www.mokabyte.it). After many years of creating Java desktop and enterprise applications, he started to work in the mobile world. In 2001, he wrote his first book about J2ME. After many J2ME and Blackberry applications, he then started to work with Android in 2008. The same year he wrote the first Italian book about Android; a bestseller on amazon.it. That was the first of a series of 12 books. He's also the author of *Dagger by Tutorials*. He worked at Yahoo, Facebook, Spotify and he's currently a Software Engineer at WhatsApp. He's a musical theatre lover and a supporter of the soccer team S.P.A.L.

About the Editors

 **Martyn Haigh** is the tech editor of this book. Martyn is a seasoned software engineer, currently working at Meta. He started hacking on Android way before it was cool, and has the scars to prove it. When not working he loves coffee, traveling without a plan, snowboarding, good food and his gorgeous family.

 **Emily Wydeven** is the editor of this book. Emily is an avid scavenger of typos and grammatical errors. She has worked extensively in the tech industry and was managing editor of an online tech magazine for several years. She is a nerd for technology, cats, medical history, and comic books (among many other things). While her favorite comic book characters are Deadpool and Squirrel Girl, the character with whom Emily most closely identifies is Nancy Whitehead.

 **Victoria Gonda** is the final pass editor for this book. They are a software engineer who primarily works with Android. After having studied both dance production and computer science, they focused their career on software because of its potential to help people in a meaningful way. This is visible in their passion for accessibility. In their spare time, Victoria enjoys playing board games and curling up with a good book. You can connect with them on Twitter at @TTGonda.

Introduction

Functional programming is a paradigm for writing your code. It's an alternative to object-oriented programming that focuses more on functions and composition than objects and classes. Rather than writing your code to say *how* to do something, you declare *what* to do.

In many contexts, learning functional programming can feel like an academic exercise. The point here is to show you how to use it in your everyday app development work. In this book, you'll take a hands-on approach to apply functional programming in a practical way. You'll build on knowledge you already have while approaching these new topics.

You'll take a pragmatic approach to learn how to make your code more:

- Declarative

- Robust

- Error-proof

You'll learn this and much more in Chapter 1. By the end of this book, you'll know how to apply pure functions, immutability and composition to simplify your complex logic!

How to read this book

This book is written to be read linearly. That said, functional programming is a vast topic, and chapters often call back to previous chapters. It's expected that you'll end up rereading chapters as you progress through the book and learn about related concepts.

This book is split into four main sections:

Section I: Functional Programming Fundamentals

This is the very start of your functional programming journey. Here, you'll learn what functional programming is and why it's useful as well as its fundamental concepts. Using hands-on examples every step of the way, you'll discover pure functions, higher-order functions, composition and so much more!

Section II: Data Types & Typeclasses

In this section, you'll learn some of the types you see when using functional programming. You'll see concepts you likely already know, like "List" and "Optional", while discovering some of their very important properties as they relate to functional programming.

Section III: Functional Programming in Practice

Time to put all that knowledge to work. In this section, you'll use all the principles you've learned so far to see the functional programming way for handling errors and managing state changes. You'll also meet some libraries you can use in your projects to quickly introduce functional programming.

Appendix

This book has many exercises and challenges throughout. In this appendix, you'll find solutions to all exercises and challenges, along with additional explanations about the answers.

Section I: Functional Programming Fundamentals

This is the very start of your functional programming journey. Here, you'll learn what functional programming is and why it's useful as well as its fundamental concepts. Using hands-on examples every step of the way, you'll discover pure functions, higher-order functions, composition and so much more!

Chapter 1: Why Functional Programming

When you approach a topic like functional programming, the most common questions are:

- Why do you need it?

- What are the benefits of using it?

- Is knowledge of all the theory supporting it necessary?

- Isn't object-oriented programming enough for writing good quality code?

In this chapter, you'll answer these and other questions about functional programming. But first, consider these three main points:

- This might surprise you, but you don't need to know functional programming to write your code. Many professional engineers have been writing code for years without using any functional programming techniques, which is totally fine. But in this chapter, you'll learn that when you use functional programming, your code will be more readable, robust, reusable and testable.

- Functional programming isn't all or nothing. Gang of Four design patterns (https://en.wikipedia.org/wiki/Design_Patterns) you use with the object-oriented approach are still completely valid.

- Believe it or not, you're probably already using some functional programming tools. If you write your code in Kotlin, you've probably already invoked `map` or `flatMap` on a `List<T>`. You're also using `Result<T>` to handle errors. Some functional programming concepts are already there, and this is the approach most standard libraries follow.

But what exactly does "better code" mean? The answer is complex, but in this first chapter, you'll get a taste of some of the principles that are the pillars of functional programming:

- Declarative approach

- Higher-order functions

- Composition

- Pure functions and testability

- Exception handling

You'll also have the chance to solve some fun and interesting exercises.

Using a declarative approach

Readability is one of the most important properties that all your code should have. The ability to return to your code after some time and still understand it is vital. If your code is readable, that means other engineers should be able to understand it. And *that* means they won't bother you with questions you might not even remember how to answer.

Moving from an imperative approach to a declarative one can drastically improve the readability of your code. This is a book about *real-world programming*, so an example can be helpful:

Suppose you have a list, List<String>. Some list elements are numbers, like "123". Others are normal Strings, like "abc". You want to implement a function, stringSum, which returns the sum of all the values you can convert from String to Int.

For instance, given the following input:

```
val input = listOf(
  "123", "abc", "1ds", "987", "abdf", "1d3", "de1", "88", "101"
)
```

In this case, the Strings you can convert to Ints are:

```
"123", "987", "88", "101"
```

And the sum would then be:

```
123 + 987 + 88 + 101 = 1299
```

You can create a first solution to the problem and write it in the **Declarative.kt** file in this chapter's material:

```kotlin
fun imperativeSum(list: List<String>): Int { // 1
  var sum = 0 // 2
  for (item in input) { // 3
    try {
      sum += item.toInt() // 4
    } catch (nfe: NumberFormatException) { // 5
      // Skip
    }
  }
  return sum // 6
}
```

In this code, you:

1. Define imperativeSum as a function accepting a List<String> as input and returning an Int.

2. Initialize the initial value to 0 for the sum to return as the result.

3. Use an enhanced for to iterate over all the values in List<String>. item contains the current value at every iteration.

4. Try to convert the String to Int using toInt, adding it to the sum if you can.

5. If it isn't possible to convert the String, you catch a NumberFormatException without doing anything. This is very bad practice, and it's even considered an anti-pattern called "Head in the sand".

6. Return the sum.

To test this solution, just add and run the following code using the list declared above:

```kotlin
fun main() {
  println("Sum ${imperativeSum(input)}")
}
```

As expected, you get:

```
Sum 1299
```

This is an **imperative** approach because *you're telling the program exactly what to do* and you're doing this *in its own language*. Now, imagine you want to solve the same problem, but explain it to a friend of yours in plain English. You'd just say:

1. Take a list of `Strings`.

2. Filter out the ones that don't contain numbers.

3. Convert the valid `Strings` to their corresponding `Ints`.

4. Calculate their sum.

This logic is closer to how you think, and it's much easier to explain and remember. But how can you translate it into code?

Add this in the same **Declarative.kt** file:

```
fun declarativeSum(list: List<String>): Int = list // 1
    .filter(::isValidNumber) // 2
    .map(String::toInt) // 3
    .sum() // 4
```

In this code, you:

1. Define `declarativeSum` as a function accepting a `List<String>` as input and returning an `Int`, exactly as `imperativeSum` did.

2. Use `filter` to remove the values that can't convert to `Ints` from the `List<String>`.

3. Convert the `String` you know is valid to an `Int`, getting a `List<Int>`.

4. Use the predefined `sum` of `List<Int>`.

This code won't compile because you still need to define `isValidNumber`, which is a function you can implement like this:

```
fun isValidNumber(str: String): Boolean =
    try {
        str.toInt()
        true
    } catch (nfe: NumberFormatException) {
        false
    }
```

Here, you just try to convert the `String` to `Int` and return `true` if successful and `false` otherwise.

Now, add and run this code:

```
fun main() {
  // ...
  println("Sum ${declarativeSum(input)}")
}
```

Which gives you the same result:

```
Sum 1299
```

You might argue that in the declarative solution, you still use that ugly way of testing whether String can be converted to Int. If String can be converted, you also invoke toInt twice. You'll come back to this later, but at the moment, what's important to note is that:

- declarativeSum is written in a way that's closer to how *you* think and not to how *the compiler* thinks. If you read the code, it does exactly what you'd describe in plain English. Filter out the Strings you don't want, convert them to Ints and calculate the sum. The code is noticeably more readable.

- Good code is also easier to change. Imagine you have to change the way you filter Strings. In imperativeSum, you'd need to add if-elses. In declarativeSum, you just add a new filter, passing a function with the new criteria.

- Testability is a *must* in the modern software industry. How would you test imperativeSum? You'd create different unit tests, checking that the function's output for different input values is what you expect. This is true for declarativeSum as well. But what you'd need to test is just isValidNumber, as filter, map and sum have already been tested. You really just need to test that the function isValidNumber does what you expect.

Functional programming means programming with functions, and the declarative approach allows you to do it very easily. In declarativeSum, this is obvious because of the use of isValidNumber and String::Int, which you pass as parameters of functions like map and filter. These are examples of a particular type of function you call a **higher-order function**.

Exercise 1.1: Implement the function `sumInRange`, which sums the values in a `List<String>` within a given interval. The signature is:

```
fun sumInRange(input: List<String>, range: IntRange): Int
```

Give it a try, and check your answer with the solution in Appendix A.

Higher-order functions

In this chapter's introduction, you learned that the functions `map` and `flatMap` — which you're probably already using — are implementations of some important functional programming concepts. In Chapter 11, "Functors", you'll learn about `map`, and in Chapter 13, "Understanding Monads", you'll learn about one of the most interesting concepts: monads. Monads provide implementations for the `flatMap` function.

At this stage, it's important to note how `map` and `flatMap` are examples of a specific type of function: They both accept other functions as input parameters. Functions accepting other functions as input parameters — or returning functions as return values — are called higher-order functions. This is one of the most significant concepts in functional programming. In Chapter 5, "Higher-Order Functions", you'll learn all about them and their relationship with the declarative approach.

As a very simple example, create a function called `times` that runs a given function a specific number of times. Open **HigherOrder.kt** and add the following code:

```
fun main() {
  3.times { // 1
    println("Hello") // 2
  }
}
```

This code doesn't compile yet, but here, you:

1. Invoke `times` as an extension function for the `Int` type. In this case, you invoked it on 3.

2. Pass a lambda containing a simple `println` with the "Hello" message.

Running this code, you'd expect the following output:

```
Hello
Hello
Hello
```

The code prints the "Hello" message three times. Of course, to make the `times` function useful, you should make it work for all code you want to repeat. This is basically a function accepting a lambda that, in this case, is a function of type `() -> Unit`.

> **Note:** The previous sentence contains some important concepts, like *function type* and *lambda*, you might not be familiar with yet. Don't worry — you'll come to understand these as you work your way through this book.

`times` is a simple example of a higher-order function because it accepts another function as input. A possible implementation is the following, which you should add to **HigherOrder.kt**:

```
fun Int.times(fn: () -> Unit) { // 1
  for (i in 1..this) { // 2
    fn() // 3
  }
}
```

In this code, you:

1. Define `times` as an extension function for `Int`. You also define a single parameter fn of type `() -> Unit`, which is the type of any function without input parameters and returning `Unit`.

2. Use a `for` loop to count the number of times related to the receiver.

3. Invoke the function `fn` you pass in input.

Now, you can run `main`, resulting in exactly what you expect as output: "Hello" printed three times.

Like it or not, this implementation works, but it's not very, *ehm*, functional. The `IntRange` type provides the `forEach` function, which is also a higher-order function accepting a function of a slightly different type as input. Just replace the previous code with the following:

```
fun Int.times(fn: () -> Unit) =
```

```
(1..this).forEach { fn() }
```

forEach iterates over an Iterable<T>, invoking the function you pass as a
parameter using the current value in input. In the previous case, you don't use that
parameter, but you might've written:

```
fun Int.times(fn: () -> Unit) =
    (1..this).forEach { _ -> fn() } // HERE
```

As mentioned, you'll learn everything you need to know about this in Chapter 5,
"Higher-Order Functions".

> **Exercise 1.2**: Implement chrono, which accepts a function of type () ->
> Unit as input and returns the time spent to run it. The signature is:

```
fun chrono(fn: () -> Unit): Long
```

> Give it a try, and check your answer with the solution in Appendix A.

Composition

As mentioned, functional programming means programming using functions in the
same way that object-oriented programming means programming with objects. A
question without an obvious answer could be: Why do you actually need functions?
In Chapter 2, "Function Fundamentals", and Chapter 3, "Functional Programming
Concepts", you'll have a very rigorous explanation using category theory. For the
moment, think of functions as the unit of logic you can compose to create a program.
Decomposing a problem into smaller subproblems to better understand them is
something humans do every day. Once you've decomposed your problem in
functions, you need to put them all together and compose them in the system you've
designed.

> **Note**: This also happens with objects. You use the classes as a way to model
> the different components that collaborate to achieve a specific task.

The most important part of functional programming involves composition.

Open **Composition.kt** in this chapter's material and add the following code:

```
fun double(x: Int): Int = 2 * x // 1

fun square(x: Int): Int = x * x // 2
```

These are two very simple functions:

1. double returns the double of the Int value in input.

2. square returns the square of the Int value in input.

Both the functions map Ints to Ints, and you can represent them as functions of type (Int) -> Int.

Composing double with square means invoking the first function and then passing the result as input for the second. In code, this is:

```
fun main() {
    val result = double(square(10)) // HERE
    println(result)
}
```

Here, you invoke square by passing 10 in input. Then, you use the result to invoke double. In that case, the output will be:

```
200
```

The question at this point is different. Because square and double are both functions of type (Int) -> Int, you can assume that a third function exists: squareAndDouble. It's of the same type, (Int) -> Int, and does the same as invoking square first and then double. Here, the input value doesn't matter anymore. You're thinking in terms of functions. A simple — and obvious — way to implement that function is the following:

```
fun squareAndDouble(x: Int) = double(square(x))
```

This isn't very interesting, though. In the previous section, you learned what a higher-order function is. So now, the question is: Can you implement a higher-order function that, given two functions as input, returns a third function that's the composition of the two? Yes, you can! Of course, the two functions need to be compatible, meaning the output type of the first needs to be compatible with the input type of the second. Besides that, you want a new function that creates the composition of the other two functions.

In Chapter 8, "Composition", you'll learn all about this. At the moment — *spoiler alert* — you can define compose like the following, which you should add in **Composition.kt**:

```
infix fun <A, B, C> ((A) -> B).compose(
    g: (B) -> C
): (A) -> C = { a ->
    g(this(a))
}
```

> **Note**: Don't worry if you don't understand the previous definition. Teaching how to write functions like this is the goal of the following chapters! :]

Now, update main like this:

```
fun main() {
    // ...
    val squareAndDouble = ::square compose ::double // HERE
    println(squareAndDouble(10))
}
```

squareAndDouble is a function that's the composition of square and double. You can simply invoke it like any other function. Also note that compose works for every pair of functions that are *composable*, which means the output of the first must be a type that's compatible with the input of the second.

That's nice, but do you really need a compose function? Why not just invoke functions the same way you did with square and double? The answer is that functional programming is *magic*. In this book, you'll learn the main concepts of category theory. You'll also prove that using a functional programming approach will make your code more robust, reusable and even more efficient.

Unfortunately, not all functions are like double and square. Other functions aren't so easy to compose and are **impure**. Functional programming is about **pure** functions. But what are pure functions, and why are they so important?

Pure functions and testability

In Chapter 3, "Functional Programming Concepts", you'll learn all about pure functions.

Just to give you an idea, they're functions whose work only depends on the input parameter, and the function doesn't change the world outside the function itself when invoked. `double` and `square` are pure functions. They return a value that depends *only* on the input value and *nothing else*. The following, which you can add in **Pure.kt**, isn't pure:

```kotlin
var count = 0 // 1

fun impure(value: Int): Int { // 2
  count++ // 3
  return value + count // 4
}
```

This is impure for different reasons. Here, you:

1. Define a global variable `count`.

2. Create `impure` as a function of type `(Int) -> Int`.

3. Increment `count`.

4. Use `count` and the input parameter `value` to calculate the value to return.

`impure` isn't pure because the output doesn't depend only on the input parameter. Invoking `impure` multiple times with the same input parameter will return different values.

Another example of an impure function is the following, which you can add to the same file:

```kotlin
fun addOneAndLog(x: Int): Int { // 1
  val result = x + 1 // 2
  println("New Value is $result") // 3
  return result // 4
}
```

In this case, you:

1. Define `addOneAndLog` of type `(Int) -> Int`, which just returns the value it gets in input and adds 1.

2. Calculate the incremented value and store it in `result`.

3. Use `println` to write a log message on the standard output.

4. Return the `result`.

If you invoke `addOneAndLog` multiple times with the same value in input, you'll always get the same value in output. Unfortunately, `addOneAndLog` isn't pure because the `println` changes the state of the world outside the function itself. This is a typical example of a side effect. Impure functions are difficult to test because you need to somehow replicate — using mocks or fakes — the external world, which impure functions change. In the case of `addOneAndLog`, you'd need to abstract the standard output, introducing complexity.

Now, you have bad news and good news. The bad news is that all the great principles of functional programming you'll learn in this book are only valid for pure functions. The good news is that you'll also learn how to make impure functions pure.

How can you make `addOneAndLog` pure, then? A classic way is to move the effect to become part of the result type. Replace the existing `addOneAndLog` implementation with the following:

```
fun addOneAndLog(x: Int): Pair<Int, String> { // 1
  val result = x + 1
  return result to "New Value is $result" // 2
}
```

The changes you made from the previous implementation are:

1. Making the return type `Pair<Int, String>` instead of `Int`.

2. Returning a `Pair` of the `result` and the message you were previously printing.

Now, `addOneAndLog` is a function of type `(Int) -> Pair<Int, String>`. More importantly, it's now pure because the output only depends on the value in input, and it doesn't produce any side effects. Yes, the responsibility of printing the log will be that of some other component, but now `addOneAndLog` is pure, and you'll be able to apply all the beautiful concepts you'll learn in this book.

But, there's a "but"...

The first implementation of addOneAndLog had type (Int) -> Int. Now, the type is (Int) -> Pair<Int, String>. What happens if you need to compose addOneAndLog with itself or another function accepting an Int in input? Adding the effect as part of the result type fixed purity but broke composition. But functional programming is all about composition, and it must have a solution for this as well. Yes! The solution exists and is called a monad! In Chapter 13, "Understanding Monads", you'll learn everything you need to know about monads, solving not just the problem of addOneAndLog, but all the problems related to the composition of functions like that.

Exception handling

Exceptions are a typical example of side effects. As an example you should be familiar with, open **ExceptionHandling.kt** and add the following code:

```
fun strToInt(str: String): Int = str.toInt()
```

As you know, this function throws a NumberFormatException if the String you pass as a parameter doesn't contain an Int.

Even if it's not visible in the function's signature, the exception is a side effect because it changes the world outside the function. Then, strToInt isn't pure. In the previous section, you already learned one way to make this function pure: Move the effect as part of the return type. Here, you have different options. The simplest is the one you get with the following code:

```
fun strToIntOrNull(str: String): Int? = // 1
  try {
    str.toInt() // 2
  } catch (nfe: NumberFormatException) {
    null // 3
  }
```

In this code, you:

1. Define strToIntOrNull, which now has the optional type Int? as its return type.

2. Try to convert the String to Int, but do it in a try block.

3. Return null in the case of NumberFormatException.

This function now is pure. You might argue that the try/catch is still there, so it's the exception. It's crucial to understand that functional programming doesn't mean *removing* side effects completely, but it means being able to *control* them. strToIntOrNull now returns the same output for the same input, and it doesn't change anything outside the context of the function.

In the case of strToInt, the information you want to bring outside is minimal: You just want to know if you have an Int value or not. In another case, you might need more information like, for instance, what specific exception has been thrown. A possible, idiomatic Kotlin alternative is the following:

```
fun strToIntResult(str: String): Result<Int> =
  try {
    Result.success(str.toInt())
  } catch (nfe: NumberFormatException) {
    Result.failure(nfe)
  }
```

Here, you encapsulate the Int value or the error in a Result<Int>.

You'll learn all about error handling in a functional way in Chapter 14, "Error Handling With Functional Programming". What's important now is understanding how even the existing Kotlin Result<T> is there as a consequence of the application of some fundamental functional programming concepts a model engineer should know to create high-quality code.

Key points

- While object-oriented programming means programming with objects, **functional programming** means programming with functions.

- You decompose a problem into many subproblems, which you model with functions.

- **Higher-order functions** accept other functions as input or return other functions as return values.

- **Category theory** is the theory of composition, and you use it to understand how to compose your functions in a working program.

- A **pure function's** output value depends only on its input parameters, and it doesn't have any side effects.

- A **side effect** is something that a function does to the external world. This can be a log in the standard output or changing the value of a global variable.

- Functional programming works for pure functions, but it also provides the tools to transform impure functions into pure ones.

- You can make an impure function pure by moving the effects to make them part of the return value.

- Functional programming is all about **composition**.

- Error handling is a typical case of side effects, and Kotlin gives you the tools to handle them in a functional way.

Where to go from here?

Great! In this chapter, you had the chance to taste what functional programming means. In this book, you'll learn much more using both a pragmatic method and a theoretical and rigorous one. You'll also have the chance to see where these concepts are already used. You'll be able to recognize them and apply all the magic only math can achieve. You've got a lot of learning ahead of you!

Chapter 2: Function Fundamentals

In Chapter 1, "Why Functional Programming", you learned that **functional programming** means programming with **functions** in the same way that **object-oriented programming** means programming with **objects**.

Objects and functions are very different beasts. Objects, at first sight, probably look closer to what you see and interact with every day. Think of your car, for instance. It has some properties like brand, color, engine and size. You use property values to distinguish a Ferrari from a Fiat 500. When you write your code, you model objects using **classes**. For instance, you define a Car class like this:

```
class Car(
  val brand: String,
  val color: Color,
  val engine: Engine,
  val size: Int,
  var speed: Int
) {

  fun drive() {
    // Driving code
  }

  fun accelerate() {
    speed += 1
  }
}
```

The state of an object is the set of its properties' values. Objects also interact, sending messages to each other. This interaction happens by invoking something called **methods**.

You can interact with a Car instance by invoking the accelerate method to increase its speed, which then changes its state.Classes allow you to define what the methods are. The concept of a class is just the first tool you have to describe your application in terms of objects. Many other concepts and tools help define what object-oriented programming is, such as interface, inheritance, polymorphism and aggregation.

But what about functions? Are functions also close to what you see and interact with every day? What does it really mean to program with functions? Is there something similar to the concept of a class with functional programming?

Unfortunately, you can't answer all these questions in a single chapter. To understand it, you need to really understand what a function is, which requires the knowledge of some fundamental concepts of **category theory**. This chapter will give you that knowledge! What you'll learn in this chapter will give you a strong foundation for the rest of the book.

In this chapter, you'll learn:

- What **category theory** is.

- How a **category** is related to the concept of a **function**.

- The useful concepts of **initial and terminal objects**, using logic as a fun example of a category.

- What the relationship is between category theory and functional programming.

- What the concept of **type** has to do with **sets**.

- Where the Kotlin Nothing and Unit types come from.

- What it means for an object to be an element of a set in the context of category theory, and therefore, functional programming.

These are all very theoretical concepts, but you'll see some practical examples using the Kotlin language.

> **Note**: If you're not confident with Kotlin, our Kotlin Apprentice (https://www.raywenderlich.com/books/kotlin-apprentice) book is the best place to start.

Note: The concepts in this chapter might look theoretical and, sometimes, not very intuitive. Don't worry! It's perfectly normal, and even expected, to read this chapter multiple times to digest the content that will help you to better understand many other concepts of functional programming in this book.

What is a function?

You might already have an initial idea about what a function is from the math you learned in school. You may remember that a function is a way to describe how to calculate an output given an input value, like in Figure 2.1:

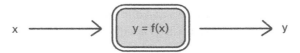

Figure 2.1: A mathematical function

For instance, the function:

```
fun twice(x: Int) = 2 * x
```

Returns an output value that's double the value you pass in as an input. That's a representation of a **mathematical function**.

In the context of functional programming, a function is something more abstract that's not necessarily related to computation. A function is a way to *map some values to others*. The **bunch** of all the values a function accepts as input is the **domain** of the function. The bunch of all the values the function returns as output is the **range** of the function. Domain and range can also be the same **bunch of values**.

Note: It's important at this point to emphasize the term **bunch of values**. This is because the term **set**, as you'll see soon, is something that gives some kind of rules to that bunch. For instance, a set can include an object or not, and it can't include the same object more than once.

Figure 2.2 better represents what a function is:

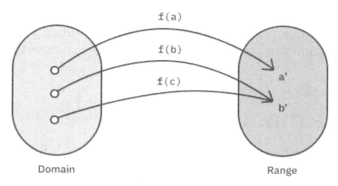

Figure 2.2: A function definition

- For each value in the domain, there's *one and only one* value in the range. This implies that the function always returns a value for inputs in its domain.

- The function f can map multiple values in the domain to the same value in the range.

- By definition, the function has meaning for each value in the domain, as you'll see later. This might seem obvious, but it's a crucial concept to understand.

> **Exercise 2.1**: Can you write an example of a function mapping distinct values in the domain to non-distinct values in the range, like f(b) and f(c) in Figure 2.2?
>
> Give it a try, and afterward, check the challenge project for a solution to see how you did. You can find hints and an explanation of the solution in Appendix B, "Chapter 2 Exercise & Challenge Solutions".

Functions like twice mapping distinct values in the domain to distinct values in the range have some interesting properties. As you'll see later, the most significant is that they have an **inverse function**. An inverse function maps the values in the range back to the domain.

> **Exercise 2.2**: Can you write the inverse function of twice? What are the domain and range for the inverse function? Check out the challenge project and Appendix B for the solution.

Another simple and useful exercise is to define the domain and range for `twice` in the previous example:

```
fun twice(x: Int) = 2 * x
```

In that case, you have what's shown in Figure 2.3:

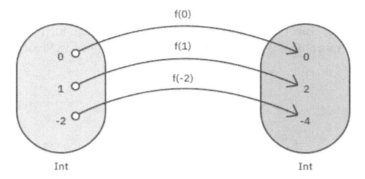

Figure 2.3: Twice domain and range

In this exercise, you've done something that's not as obvious as it appears because you used the set of all the `Int` values as the domain and range for the function `f`. But what is `Int`? What's the relation of the `Int` type with the bunch of things mentioned earlier?

To really understand all this, it's time to introduce **category theory**.

> **Note**: If you've heard category theory is intimidating, don't be scared. This book is here to help. :] Soon, you'll realize how understanding what a category is will help you assimilate many critical concepts about functional programming. Again, feel free to read this chapter multiple times to make this process easier. This book will go over only what you really need, and it'll be a lot of unexpected fun.

Introduction to category theory

Category theory is one of the most abstract branches of mathematics, and it's essential here because programming is one of its main applications. It's also important to start with the definition of **category**.

A category is a **bunch of objects** with connections between them called **morphisms**. Categories follow three rules:

• Composition

• Associativity

• Identity

You can picture an object like a dot with no properties and no further way to be decomposed. A morphism is *an arrow between two objects* like in Figure 2.4:

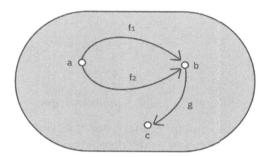

Figure 2.4: Objects and morphisms

In this image, you:

• Have objects named a, b and c.

• Define two morphisms between a and b and one morphism between b and c.

• Assign the names f1 and f2 to the morphisms between a and b and the name g to the morphism between b and c.

Objects and morphisms are the primitive tools you can use to describe every possible concept about category theory.

As mentioned earlier, objects and morphisms need to follow some rules that will lead you to other fundamental functional programming concepts. It's time to study them in detail.

Composition

A bunch of objects and arrows don't make a category; they also need to follow some important rules, and **composition** is probably the most significant.

Look at Figure 2.5:

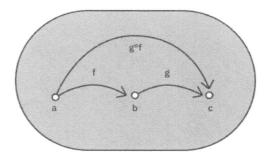

Figure 2.5: Composition

In this image, you have:

- The objects a, b and c.

- The morphism f from a to b.

- The morphism g from b to c.

The composition rule says that for every object a, b and c and every morphism f and g, as shown in Figure 2.5, the category *must have* a morphism from a to c. You represent this as g∘f between a and c, which is the composition of f and g. You read g∘f as "g after f", where the small circle ∘ represents the composition.

For a Kotlin example, if f is your twice and g is triple, then g∘f might look like:

```
val `g∘f`: (Int) -> Int = { triple(twice(it)) }
```

Note: An analogy with LEGO® makes the definition of the composition property for a category easier to understand. Imagine an object of a category is a LEGO® brick. Being able to attach a LEGO® brick to another is equivalent to having a morphism between them. In this case, composition means you can attach one LEGO® to another to get another LEGO® component that is the composition of the two bricks.

Associativity

The **associativity** rule is similar to the one you studied back in school about addition or multiplication. Look at the following image:

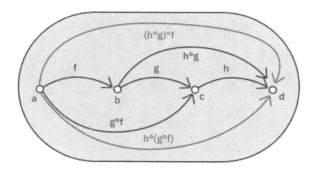

Figure 2.6: Associativity

Here, you have:

- The objects a, b, c and d.

- The morphism f from a to b.

- The morphism g from b to c.

- The morphism h from c to d.

The associativity rule says that for every object a, b, c and d and morphism f, g and h (like in Figure 2.6), the following equivalence must be true:

$$(h \circ g) \circ f \;=\; h \circ (g \circ f)$$

Figure 2.7: Associativity equivalence. (h∘g)∘f = h∘(g∘f)

This means that if you do the composition of f, g and h, it doesn't matter if you first compose f to g or g to h. Looking at Figure 2.6, this also means that, with those objects and morphisms, there must be a morphism from a to d, which you can obtain by either composing f with h∘g or composing g∘f with h.

Continuing with the previous example and quadrupling h, this means:

```
twice(triple(quadruple(x))) == quadruple(twice(triple(x)))
```

Because these are equal, it conforms to associativity.

> **Note**: The LEGO® analogy helps simplify the understanding of the associativity property too. Imagine you have three different LEGO® bricks you call **A**, **B** and **C**. If you attach **A** and **B** first and then **C**, you get a component that is exactly the same as what you'd get by attaching **B** and **C** first and then **A**. What you get is basically another LEGO® component you can use like the others.

Identity

Identity is the last rule, but it's no less important than the other two. Consider the smiling diagram in Figure 2.8:

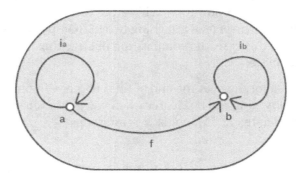

Figure 2.8: Identity

The identity property says that *every object* in a category must have at least one morphism to itself. This is why, in Figure 2.8, you have:

- The objects a and b.

- A morphism f from a to b.

- A morphism ia from a to itself.

- A morphism ib from b to itself.

This must be true for all the objects in the category.

An example of ia might be `timesOne` or `{ x * 1 }`:

```
timesOne(x) == x
```

It's interesting to use the identity with the previous properties. You can easily prove that, in a category, the following equivalence is true:

$$i_b \circ (f \circ i_a) \ = \ (i_b \circ f) \circ i_a$$

Figure 2.9: Identity, composition and associativity. (ib∘f)∘ia = ib∘(f∘ia)

> **Note**: Understanding why a category needs identity might not be very intuitive, and there's not a plausible way to visualize identities using LEGO®. If a morphism in this analogy means to attach a LEGO® brick to another, it's quite difficult to represent how to attach a piece to itself. On the other hand, you could think of the inverse of attaching two LEGO® pieces as the action of detaching them. In this case, the composition of attaching and detaching leads you to the initial piece.
>
> The concept of isomorphism at the end of this chapter will probably help, but don't worry — everything will be clearer when you get to Chapter 11, "Functors", and Chapter 12, "Monoids & Semigroups".

Now that you know what a category is, it's time for some fun — you'll give some meaning to objects and morphisms. Always remember that what's true for a category will also be true when you give objects and morphisms specific meanings.

Category and logic

As mentioned, a category is a very abstract concept, but giving objects and morphisms some specific meanings makes everything closer to what you use every day.

In the context of **logic**, assume that objects are **propositions** and morphisms are **entailments**. Consider, then, Figure 2.10:

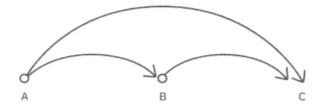

Figure 2.10: Category and logic

Using the symbol ⇒ to represent entailment, you have:

- The propositions A, B and C.

- An arrow from A to B, meaning that A ⇒ B.

- Another arrow from B to C, meaning that B ⇒ C.

To prove it's a category, you need to verify the three important rules:

- Composition

- Associativity

- Identity

It's time to have some fun!

Proving composition

As you know, composition is the property that allows you to compose a morphism from A to B and one from B to C into a single morphism from A to C. In this case, if A ⇒ B and B ⇒ C, is it also true that A ⇒ C? Try to use the following propositions:

- A = Alice drives to work every day.

- B = Alice has a driver's license.

- C = Alice is at least 18 years old.

The fact that Alice drives to work every day entails she has a driver's license. That Alice has a driver's license entails she's at least 18. You then need to prove the following: Is the fact that Alice drives to work every day entailing she's at least 18 years old? This is true, and this *proves composition*.

> **Note:** In this example, you're assuming Alice is in a place where you need to be 18 years old to drive a car and vote. You might also object that this works just for the previous propositions. In this case, you have two options: You can just believe it or find a case where this isn't true. :]

Proving associativity

To prove associativity, you need a new proposition like:

- D = Alice can vote.

In this case, referring to Figure 2.10, you can use the following entailments:

- f = A $\Rightarrow$ B = Alice drives to work every day. $\Rightarrow$ Alice has a driver's license.

- g = B $\Rightarrow$ C = Alice has a driver's license. $\Rightarrow$ Alice is at least 18 years old.

- h = C $\Rightarrow$ D = Alice is at least 18 years old. $\Rightarrow$ Alice can vote.

From the definition of category, to prove associativity, you need to prove that:

$(h \circ g) \circ f = h \circ (g \circ f)$

You can break it down like this:

- $(h \circ g)$ = Alice has a driver's license. $\Rightarrow$ Alice can vote.

- $(g \circ f)$ = Alice drives to work every day. $\Rightarrow$ Alice is at least 18 years old.

- $(h \circ g) \circ f$ = Alice drives to work every day. $\Rightarrow$ Alice can vote.

- $h \circ (g \circ f)$ = Alice drives to work every day. $\Rightarrow$ Alice can vote.

Which proves the hypothesis.

Proving identity

The final property to prove is very interesting and funny. In logic, you basically need to prove that for every proposition A, you can say that A $\Rightarrow$ A. This is equivalent to saying that:

- Alice has a driver's license. $\Rightarrow$ Alice has a driver's license.

This actually has a name: **tautology**. :] This proves that logic is a category, and you'll use it to introduce two more crucial concepts: **initial and terminal objects**.

Category theory and the real world

Before introducing initial and terminal objects, it's valuable to stop for a second and think about an important aspect of category theory. In the introduction for this chapter, you read that object-oriented programming allows you to model your code using objects, which might seem closer to what you see and interact with every day. Can you say the same thing about a category?

A category has composition as a fundamental property. You can even say that *category theory is the science of composition*. Isn't decomposing concepts into smaller ones what you do every day? Humans' brains continuously decompose concepts to make them simpler to understand and memorize, and then recompose them. This might seem somewhat philosophical, but it's proof that category theory isn't something completely unrelated to reality.

At this point, an example might help. Suppose somebody asks you to solve the following addition problem:

```
7 + 10
```

Of course, you answer 17. When you do that, are you getting the result from your memory, or is your brain actually computing the addition of 7 with 10? Frankly, it could be either. With this simple addition, your brain has probably memorized the answer somewhere and is giving it as the answer.

Now, imagine somebody asks you to solve the following subtraction problem:

```
42 - 8
```

In this case, you probably don't have the answer memorized, so your brain needs to do some "computation". Because it's not an obvious answer, your brain might do something like this:

```
42 - 2 = 40
40 - (8-2) = 40 - 6 = 34
```

Putting it all together, you might mentally compute:

```
42 - 2 - (8 - 2) = 34
```

Your brain has decomposed the simple subtraction into multiple operations that are probably easier to calculate and then composed the results back into a single value. This is an example of composition!

Initial and terminal objects

You already learned that category theory explains everything in terms of objects and morphisms. Not all the objects and morphisms are the same, though. For instance, not all the objects are somehow connected with a morphism. For logic, this means that a proposition doesn't necessarily entail all the others. For the same reason, not all the propositions are entailments of another.

> **Note**: Using the LEGO® analogy, you represent this concept saying that not all the LEGO® pieces can be attached to any other piece.

To understand why this is, you need the definition of **uniqueness**. In this context, you can say that the morphism f between the objects A and B is **unique** if any other morphism g between the same objects cannot be different from f. In short, if this happens, f and g must be equal.

With this definition in mind, you can define an **initial object** as an object with *a unique outgoing morphism to every other object* in the category. A **terminal object** is an object with *a unique incoming morphism from any other object*. Figure 2.11 gives an idea of these concepts:

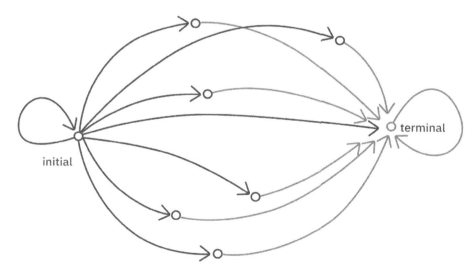

Figure 2.11: Initial and terminal objects

Not all categories have initial and terminal objects but, if they do, they are unique. In logic, the initial object has the name **False** and the terminal object **True**.

Category properties have funny implications on these objects:

- Each object has at least one identity morphism. This means that what is false is false, and what is true is true.

- Because there's always a morphism starting from the initial object to any other objects, there's also a morphism from the initial object to the terminal one. This means that a false assumption entails everything. Therefore, "Tom has wings" entails "Tom can fly", is a **counterfactual implication**.

You're probably wondering what all this has to do with functional programming — and Kotlin.

The good news is that *anything you see that's true for a generic category is also true for a specific one*. What's true in logic is also true in programming when you give a specific meaning to objects and morphisms. It's now time to be more pragmatic and start studying the most critical category for an engineer — *spoiler alert* — the category of types and functions.

> **Exercise 2.3**: Can you prove that using Set*s as objects* and *"is a subset of" as morphisms* results in a category? In other words, a morphism from set A to set B would mean that A is a subset of B. In that case, what are the initial and terminal objects?
>
> Don't forget to check out Appendix B for hints and solutions.

Category of types and functions

So far, you've learned what a category is, and you also had some fun with the category of propositions and entailments. That allowed you to introduce the properties of a category and define some significant concepts like initial and terminal objects. That's all good — but this is a book about programming, and you need something more pragmatic. You basically need to answer the following questions:

- What happens if objects are types and morphisms are functions?

- What's the meaning of composition, associativity and identity in the category of types and functions?

- What's the meaning of initial and terminal objects?

In the following paragraphs, you'll answer these questions using the Kotlin language, and you'll have some revelations about some of the most important Kotlin standard types. Here, using Kotlin, you'll:

- Prove that using types as objects and functions as morphisms, you define a category.

- See what initial and terminal objects mean when dealing with types and functions.

- Find out where the Kotlin types Unit and Nothing come from.

As mentioned, you'll do this using Kotlin.

Do types and functions define a category?

As a first step, you need to prove that by using types as objects and functions as morphisms, what you get is actually a category. You need to prove:

- Composition

- Associativity

- Identity

Proving each of the category properties is also a good exercise to review some interesting Kotlin concepts.

In the material for this chapter, you'll find the **starter project** with some empty files you'll fill in along the way. Start by opening the **Aliases.kt** file and write the following definition:

```
typealias Fun<A, B> = (A) -> B
```

This is a type alias that represents all the functions from a type A to B. If A and B are two objects of the category of types and functions, Fun<A, B> is a morphism.

This simple definition allows you to prove each of the properties for a category.

Proving composition

To prove composition, you need to prove that for any function f from A to B and any function g from B to C, there's an equivalent function: g∘f from A to C, which is the composition of the two.

This is nothing new to you because you're probably composing functions every day. Consider, for instance, the following code you can write in the **Main.kt** file:

```
fun twice(a: Int): Int = a * 2 // 1

fun format(b: Int): String = "Result is $b" // 2
```

These are very simple functions that:

1. Double the Int value it gets as input. The type of twice is Fun<Int, Int>.

2. Format the Int it gets as input to a String. The type is Fun<Int, String>.

You can compose twice and format in a very simple way, like this:

```
fun formatAfterTwice(x: Int) = format(twice(x))
```

You can prove this by adding the formatAfterTwice definition in the **Main.kt** file along with the following:

```
fun main() {
  println(format(twice(37)))
  println(formatAfterTwice(37))
}
```

When you run this code, you get the following output:

```
Result is 74
Result is 74
```

This is just an example, but proving that this works for any type and function requires something more.

Open the initially empty **Category.kt** file in the project for this chapter, and add the following definition:

```
inline infix fun <A, B, C> Fun<B, C>.after(crossinline f: Fun<A,
B>): Fun<A, C> =
  { a: A ->
    this(f(a)) // HERE
  }
```

> **Note**: In the previous code you use the Kotlin keywords `inline`, `infix` and `crossinline`. In this case, `infix` allows you to use a syntax like `g after f` instead of `g.after(f)`. The `inline` keyword, as you'll see in Chapter 4, "Expression Evaluation, Laziness & More About Functions", allows you to basically replace every `after` invocation with the expression it represents. Using `inline` then requires the use of `crossinline` for the input parameter, `f`, in order to allow *no-local returns* from the function `f` itself.
>
> For a full description of these keywords, please refer to Kotlin Apprentice (https://www.raywenderlich.com/books/kotlin-apprentice), which is the best place to start.

This is a code representation of the (g∘f) notation you were using before, where g represents `this` and f represents `f`.

The definition of `after` has many interesting things to note. It:

1. Is a generic function of the parameters types `A`, `B` and `C`.

2. Creates an extension function for the `Fun<B, C>` type.

3. Uses the `infix` and `inline` keywords.

4. Accepts a function `Fun<A, B>` as an input parameter and returns a function `Fun<A, C>` as output.

> **Note**: The last point asserts that `after` is a **higher-order function** because it accepts a function as an input parameter and returns a function as output. Don't worry — you'll learn about higher-order functions in Chapter 5, "Higher-Order Functions".

The definition of `after` looks more complicated than it actually is. Looking at its body, it does exactly what you've done with `formatAfterTwice` but in a more generic way. It:

• Returns a function with an input parameter `a` of type `A`.

• Uses the parameter `a` as input for the function `f`.

• Passes the result of `f(a)` as an input parameter for the function you use as the receiver, which in this case has type `Fun<B, C>`.

You can now use `after` with the previous example. Just add the following code to `main` in **Main.kt** with:

```
main() {
  // ...
  val f: Fun<Int, Int> = ::twice // 1
  val g: Fun<Int, String> = ::format // 2
  val formatTwice = g after f // 3
  println(formatTwice(37)) // 4
  // ...
}
```

> **Note**: In the previous code, you used `::` to reference a function using its name without calling it. For instance, `::twice` is a reference to `twice`.

Here, you:

1. Define f as a reference to `::twice` of type Fun<Int, Int>.

2. Initialize g as a reference to `::format` of type Fun<Int, String>.

3. Create `formatTwice` as a reference of type Fun<Int, String> to g∘f.

4. Invoke `formatTwice`, passing 37 as a value.

Build and run `main`, and you get the following additional output:

```
Result is 74
```

> **Exercise 2.4**: In this section, you defined `after`, which allows you to write expressions like:

```
val formatTwice = g after f
```

> Can you write `compose` instead, which would allow you to implement the same expression as:

```
val formatTwice = f compose g
```

> Again, give it a try and check the challenge project and Appendix B to see how you did.

It's fundamental to note here the fact that `after` compiles is proof that composition works for every type A, B and C and every function F<A, B> and F<B, C>.

Proving associativity

To prove that the category of types and functions follows the associativity property, you basically need to prove that:

```
(h after g) after f == h after (g after f)
```

Open **Main.kt** and add the following function:

```
fun length(s: String): Int = s.length
```

> **Note**: Here, you defined `length` explicitly, but you could use `String::length` instead.

It's a simple function that returns the length of the `String` you pass as an input parameter. Its type is Fun<String, Int>.

In the same **Main.kt** file, add the following code in `main`:

```
fun main() {
    // ...
    val h: Fun<String, Int> = ::length // 1
    val leftSide: Fun<String, Int> = (h after g) after f // 2
    val rightSide: Fun<String, Int> = h after (g after f) // 3
    println(leftSide(37) == rightSide(37)) // 4
}
```

In this code, you:

1. Define h as the reference to `length` as a function of type Fun<String, Int>.

2. Create `leftSide` as the left side of the equation you want to prove.

3. Define `rightSide` as the right side of the equation you want to prove.

4. Check that the two members are equal.

When you run `main`, you get the following additional output:

```
true
```

You might object again that this specific example doesn't prove anything — and you're right! What actually proves that associativity works for the category of types and functions is the successful compilation of `after`.

This is because it means that, given the types A, B and C and the functions f and g, you can always create a function that is their composition.

Another way to prove it is to replace the definition of `after` with its implementation. In this case, the left side of the equation is:

```
(h after g) after f =
  ({ b: B -> h(g(b))}) after f =
  { a: A -> { h(g(f(a)))}}
```

The right side is:

```
h after (g after f) =
  h after ({ a: A -> g(f(a))}) =
  { a: A -> { h(g(f(a)))}}
```

The two members are exactly the same.

> **Note**: In the last proof, you actually applied fundamental tools you'll learn about in detail in Chapter 3, "Functional Programming Concepts".

Proving identity

What does it mean to prove identity for the category of types and functions? It means to prove that, for every type A, there's always at least one function of type Fun<A, A>. To create such a function, open the **Category.kt** file and add this code:

```
fun <A> identity(value: A) = value
```

Although this function proves that identity exists, it's important to mention that it's not the only one. The function `twice` you created earlier, for instance, is an identity function because of type Fun<A, A>.

At this point, there's something interesting to say about identity. As mentioned earlier, twice is an example of a function that maps distinct values in the domain to distinct values in the range. This means that twice has an inverse function you can call half and define like this:

```
fun half(a: Int): Int = a / 2
```

But what does it mean to say that twice is the inverse of half? This means that:

```
half after twice = twice after half = identity
```

> **Note**: In this case, if you half a value and then double it, you get the same value. The same is true if you first double and then halve it.

When you have a function and an inverse function, you say that the functions are **isomorphisms**. This definition gives a first reason for the existence of the identity property. Of course, this isn't true for all the functions from a type A to a type B. Some functions don't have an inverse.

Anyway, it's noteworthy that an isomorphic function somehow makes identity obsolete because it would just be the composition of the function with its inverse.

> **Exercise 2.5**: Can you write an example of an isomorphic function f and its inverse g and prove they always compose to identity? When you're done, look at the solution in Appendix B.

This concludes the proof that types and functions creates a category. What, then, is the meaning of starting and terminal objects for the category of types and functions?

Initial and terminal objects

At this point, it's interesting to see what the meaning of initial and terminal object is in the category of types and functions.

The initial object

As you learned earlier, the starting point is an object with a *unique* morphism compared to all other objects in the category. With types and functions, it means that the initial point is a type you can use as input to a *unique* function to any other type. Said in other words, any function that you call with this initial type must always have the same result.

In Kotlin, this initial object is Nothing. You might argue that you could always write a function from Int to any other type, and this is true. The problem is that the function must be unique.

If Int were a starting point, the following two different functions of type Fun<Int, String>:

```
val f: Fun<Int, String> = { a: Int -> "2 * $a = ${2*a}"}

val g: Fun<Int, String> = { a: Int -> "$a * $a =  ${a*a}"}}
```

Would be the same function, but they aren't! Instead, for any type A you define:

```
fun <A> absurd(a: Nothing): A = a as A
```

This function's name is absurd because, if you want to invoke it, you need a value of type Nothing, which is impossible. IntelliJ gives you a hint for this:

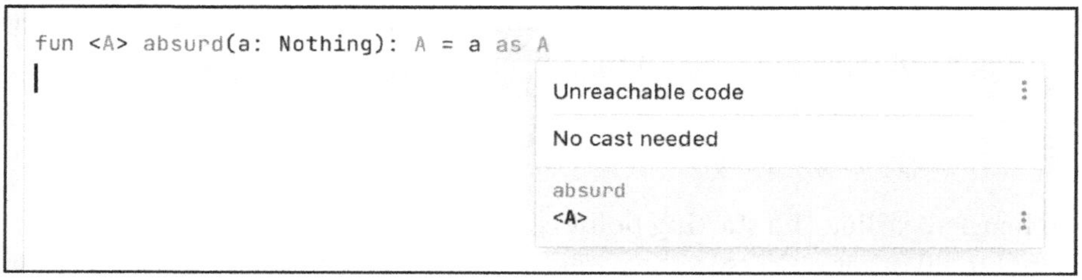

```
fun <A> absurd(a: Nothing): A = a as A

                                Unreachable code            ⋮

                                No cast needed

                                absurd
                                <A>                         ⋮
```

Figure 2.12: The absurd function

> **Note**: You might wonder why some of the functions have names like absurd and others are anonymous, like f and g in the last example. The reason is that anonymous functions cannot be generic.

You might try to invoke it like this, giving the Kotlin compiler some hint about the generic type, but the result would be the same.

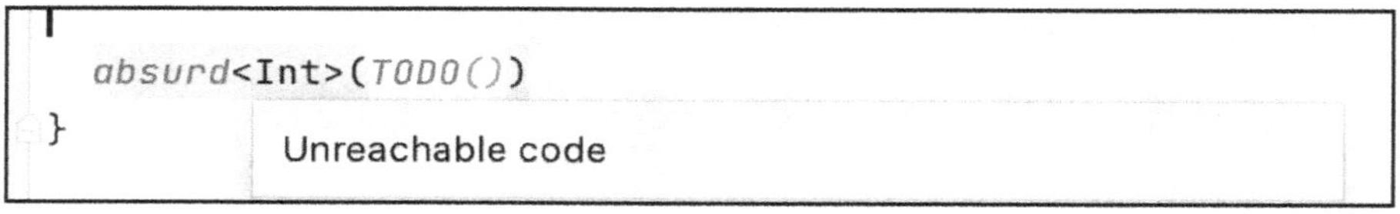

```
absurd<Int>(TODO())
}
        Unreachable code
```

Figure 2.13: Trying to use absurd

More importantly, because absurd is a function you can't invoke, it never returns, and this makes it unique. Any other function starting from Nothing to any other type A would do exactly the same, so it'd be the same as absurd.

The terminal object

In the previous section, you learned where the famous Nothing Kotlin type comes from. In the category of logic, you also learned that the terminal object is the counterpart of the initial object. A terminal object, if it exists, is an object with a unique incoming morphism from all other objects. In other words, all functions that return this type will return the same object.

In the category of types and functions, this means a terminal object is a type output of a unique function accepting an input parameter of any other type, Nothing included. In Kotlin, this is the Unit type.

For any type A, you can create the function:

```
fun <A> unit(a: A): Unit = Unit
```

Also, in this case, there are many significant things to note:

1. The unit function is generic with the type A, and it always returns something you represent with Unit.

2. For any type A, the function unit is unique.

3. Unit isn't just a type; it's also the only value of that type.

To disprove uniqueness, you might try to create the following function as a possible alternative. This wouldn't work:

```
fun <A> unit2(a: A): Unit {
    println("I'm different")
    return Unit
}
```

At the beginning of the chapter, you learned that the concept of function isn't strongly related to the concept of computation. A function is a way to map values in the domain to values in the range. In terms of mapping, unit and unit2 are the same function.

> **Note**: unit2 is actually a **bad** function because it hides a **side effect**, which is another fundamental concept you'll learn about in the next chapter.

The last point is also essential. You learned that with category theory, you can only use objects and morphisms. What does it mean to say that Unit is the only value for the Unit type? What does it mean that a is a value of type A? In general, what's the relationship between the concept of **type** and the probably more familiar concept of **set**?

Types and sets

In the previous section, you learned some interesting properties of the category where objects are types and morphisms are functions. But what is a type? What do you mean when you define a variable like this?

```
var a: Int = 10
```

You usually read this as "a is an Int", but what do you mean by Int? If you think about this, Int is just a name to represent the *set of all the integer values*. a is of type Int means that you can assign to a only values that are in the set you call Int.

> **Note**: To be accurate, Int represents the set of all the possible integers that you can represent using 4 bytes, so the whole numbers between -2,147,483,648 (-2^{31}) and 2,147,483,647 $(2^{31}-1)$.

In the same way, consider the following expression:

```
var s: String = "Hello"
```

In this case, you're defining the variable s of type String, which is a way to represent the set of all possible Strings. Again, you can assign to s only elements of the set you call String.

Thinking in terms of **sets** makes things easier. Consider the function twice that you've already met:

```
fun twice(a: Int): Int = a * 2
```

This is basically a way to map elements in the set of `Int` to other elements in the same set.

The function `format` is a way to map elements in the set of `Int` to elements in the set of `String`.

```
fun format(b: Int): String = "Result is $b"
```

The following image gives a more intuitive representation of the previous functions:

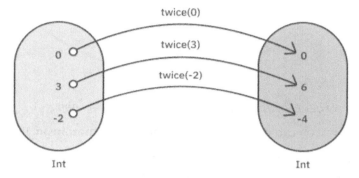

Figure 2.14: Representation of a function between Int values

Figure 2.14 can be a bit misleading, though, because it represents relations between elements of two `sets`, which in this case are both `Int`. But what does it mean to be an element of a set? How can you represent this using just objects and morphisms?

Definition of element

As you learned earlier, objects in category theory are like dots; they cannot be decomposed. This also means the morphisms are the only tool you can use to distinguish one object from the others.

In particular, category theory introduces the concept of **structure**, which you define using the incoming morphism. Because of this, the initial object has no structure. The terminal object, on the other hand, has a very clear and unique structure because there's exactly one and only one morphism from any other object. This property makes the terminal object unique.

Nobody said that a terminal object can't have outgoing morphisms. On the contrary, from the terminal object, you might have many morphisms to a given object A, like in Figure 2.15:

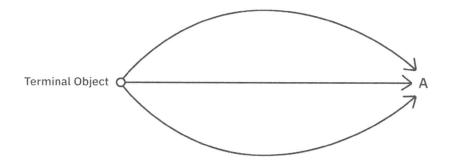

Figure 2.15: Final object with morphisms to object A.

More importantly, you can give a different name to each morphism, like x, y or z.

You need to understand what this means for the category of types and functions. This means that for a given type A, there are many functions of type Fun<Unit,A>, one for each value of type A.

As a simple example, consider the type Int. You can create a different function of each value of Int, like these you can add to the **Main.kt** file:

```
fun one(u: Unit): Int = 1
fun two(u: Unit): Int = 2
fun minusThree(u: Unit): Int = -3
// ...
```

A function for each element of the set you associate to the type Int and the name you give to that function is an element of the set A represents.

To see how to describe a simple invocation of a function using composition, just add the following code to main:

```
fun main() {
  // ...
  // twice 2
  val twiceTwo = ::twice after ::two // 1
  println(twiceTwo(Unit))   // 2
  // ...
}
```

In that code, you:

- Define `twiceTwo` as the composition of `two` and `twice`.

- Invoke `twiceTwo`, passing `Unit` as a parameter.

When you run that code, you'll get the expected output:

```
4
```

Initial and terminal objects using sets

Thinking in terms of sets makes things a little bit easier. The initial object, by definition, doesn't have any incoming morphisms. It's the type for a set without any elements. `Nothing` is like the **empty set**. If you consider the concept of subtype related to the concept of inheritance, you also understand why `Nothing` is a subtype of every other type in Kotlin. *This is because the empty set is a subset of every other set.* If you look at the source code for the `Nothing` type, you'll find this:

```
public class Nothing private constructor()
```

`Nothing` has a private constructor. This means that `Nothing` is a type, but you can't create any instances of it.

What about the terminal object? By definition, there's a unique morphism from any other type. This means there's a unique function from any other type. If you consider the terminal type to be a set, this means it's a set containing a single value that you know, in Kotlin, has the name `Unit`. Look at its source code, and you'll find this:

```
object Unit {
    override fun toString() = "kotlin.Unit"
}
```

This means that `Unit` is a type, but it's also the name for its unique instance.

Function types

In one of the previous paragraphs, you created the following definition:

```
typealias Fun<A, B> = (A) -> B
```

With Fun<A, B>, you wanted to represent the set of all the functions from A to B.

According to what you learned previously, this is exactly the concept of **type of a function**. You've already learned how the category of types and functions works. If the objects of that category are types of functions, what would the morphisms be? This is something you'll learn in the following chapter, and in particular, with the concept of **functor**.

Challenges

In this chapter, you learned some fundamental concepts about category theory and functional programming. It's now time to solve some challenges and have some fun. You'll find the solutions in Appendix B, and the code in the **challenge** project for this chapter.

Challenge 1: Functions and sets

How would you represent a specific Set using a function? For instance, how would you represent the set of even numbers with a function? After that, how would you print all the values in the set?

Challenge 2: Functions and sets again

How would you represent the intersection and union of two sets using functions? The intersection is the set of objects that belong to set A *and* set B, and the union is the set of all objects that belong to set A *or* set B.

Challenge 3: The right domain

Consider the following function:

```
fun oneOver(x: Int): Double = 1.0 / x
```

What's the domain and the range for this function? If you invoke oneOver(0), you get an exception. How can you be sure you only pass values in the domain as an input parameter?

Key points

- A **function** is a way to map things from a domain to things in a range.

- **Category theory** is necessary for understanding the fundamental concepts of functional programming.

- You define a category using **objects and morphisms**, which must follow the fundamental rules of composition, associativity and identity.

- **Logic** is a category that makes some concepts closer to the way humans think.

- The category of **types and functions** is the most important for a software engineer because it explains functional programming concepts.

- The **initial object** in a category has outgoing unique morphisms to all other objects.

- The **terminal object** in a category has incoming unique morphisms from all other objects.

- Not all categories have a terminal object.

- Initial and terminal objects explain the meaning of the Kotlin standard types `Nothing` and `Unit`.

- It's useful to think of a type for a variable as a way to represent the set of all the values that variable can reference.

- Understanding the relationship between types and sets simplifies some of the most critical functional programming concepts.

Where to go from here?

Congratulations! At this point, you have an idea of what a category is and why category theory is important in understanding functional programming. It might have been tough, but you don't have to worry if something isn't completely clear at this point. In the following chapters, you'll have the opportunity to see these concepts again in a more practical context. In the next chapter, you'll start to focus on pure functions.

> **Note:** The inspiration for this chapter comes from the excellent work of Bartosz Milewski in his YouTube video series Category Theory for Programmers (https://bit.ly/3raqxg6).

Chapter 3: Functional Programming Concepts

In the previous chapter, Chapter 2, "Function Fundamentals", you had a deep dive into what **category theory** is and how it relates to the concepts of **types** and **functions**, which are the pillars of functional programming. You touched on many things along the way. You learned:

- That a function is a way to map elements of a **domain** set into values of a **range** set.

- The relation between sets and types.

- The logic category.

- What the Kotlin `Nothing` and `Unit` types really are.

You also had the opportunity to learn the concept of **type of a function**. You defined the `typealias Fun<A, B>` to represent all the functions mapping values in A to values in B. For instance, `Fun<Int, String>` represents the set of all the functions from `Int` to `String`. On the other hand, not all functions are the same, and what you've seen so far is true for a specific type: **pure functions**. You'll learn more about this as you read on.

It's also important to mention that all the functions you use in programming contain some sort of computation, and the output is often calculated from the input as the result of expressions.

In this chapter, you'll learn some vital concepts about functions, and in particular:

- What a pure function is.

- What an **expression** is, and what **referential transparency** means.

- How to prove a function is pure using the **substitution model**.
- What a **side effect** is.
- How to handle side effects in a functional way.
- How side effects change the way you compose functions.

You'll learn all these concepts using the Kotlin language and a bunch of entertaining exercises and challenges.

Pure functions

In the previous chapter, you learned that a function is a way to map values from a set A to values in a set B. You use sets to represent values of a specific type. For functions from A to B, you defined the following typealias where A is the type for the domain, and B is the type for the range:

> **Note**: If you need a reminder about domain and range, skip back to Chapter 2, "Function Fundamentals".

```
typealias Fun<A, B> = (A) -> B
```

> **Note**: You'll find this definition already in the **Aliases.kt** file in this chapter's **starter** project.

Now, consider the following functions and add them to **Pure.kt** in the same starter project:

```
fun twice(x: Int): Int = x * 2

fun twiceAndLog(x: Int): Int {
  val result = x * 2
  println("2 * $x = $result")
  return result
}
```

In this code, `twice` and `twiceAndLog` have type `Fun<Int, Int>`, and you can prove this by adding the following code to the same file:

```
fun main() {
    var f: Fun<Int, Int> = ::twice // 1
    println("Executing twice(10)")
    f(10) // 2
    f = ::twiceAndLog // 3
    println("Executing twiceAndLog(10)")
    f(10) // 4
}
```

In this code, you:

1. Assign `twice`'s reference to a variable f of type `Fun<Int, Int>`.

2. Invoke `f(10)`.

3. Change the value of f, assigning the reference to `twiceAndLog`.

4. Invoke `f(10)`.

Compile the code and run it. It provides the following output:

```
Executing twice(10)
Executing twiceAndLog(10)
2 * 10 = 20 // HERE
```

Of course, the invocation of `twice` produced no log output but `twiceAndLog` did because of the `println` statement in its body, pointed out with "HERE". But in terms of functions, they should be exactly the same because they map the same input values to the same output values. So, what's the difference? The difference is that `twice` *is* a pure function and `twiceAndLog` *is not.* So, how would you define what a "pure function" is?

Pure function definition

A function f is pure if the following properties are *both true*:

1. f always maps the same input values to the same output values.

2. The *universe doesn't change* after each **invocation** of f.

The first point means that if you invoke the function f with specific input parameters, you'll always get the same output. In other words, the output of f depends only on the input parameters and nothing else. **Referential transparency** gives this concept a formal definition, and you'll learn all about it very soon.

The second property might look weird. If you consider the universe as a very big object with some properties, it has a state. You can think of the universe as everything else that exists outside the function's body. As mentioned in the introduction of Chapter 2, "Function Fundamentals", the state of an object is the set of all its property values — remember the Ferrari and Fiat 500?

If the execution of f changes the state of the universe, such as a property on one of those cars, then f is not pure. The formal definition says that, in this case, f has **side effects**. You'll learn a lot about side effects in this chapter as well as the following ones.

More formally, you can now say that a function is pure if:

1. Its body is a **referential transparent expression**.

2. It doesn't have any side effects.

As mentioned, you'll see what referential transparency and side effects are very soon. For right now, it's useful to see some examples and describe why pure functions are so important in functional programming.

> **Note:** The term "pure" comes from Lisp, a functional language that also allows side effects. Functions with side effects aren't considered to be good functions, and so are somehow **impure**. :]

Examples of pure and impure functions

Open the **Pure.kt** file of the **starter** project in the material for this chapter and look at twice, which you met earlier in the chapter:

```
fun twice(x: Int): Int = x * 2
```

This is a **pure function** because:

1. Every time you invoke twice with the same parameter value for x, you always get the same result, x * 2, in output.

2. It just returns an output value that is double the value you pass as input. Nothing happens to the universe outside the function body, no matter how many times it's called.

To get an idea of the first property, add the following code to **Pure.kt**:

```
fun main() {
    // ...
    println(twice(10))
    println(twice(10))
    println(twice(10))
    println(twice(10))
    println(twice(10))
}
```

> **Note:** The previous code just gives you an idea of referential transparency: that the same input always maps to the same output. To be rigorous, you should prove that the property is true for all the values in the domain of `twice` and not just for the value `10`. :]

Here, you invoke `twice(10)` five times and, with `println`, you can verify the result is always `20`. Run `main` and check the following output:

```
20
20
20
20
20
```

Now, follow the same process with `twiceAndLog` that you already wrote in the **Pure.kt** file:

```
fun twiceAndLog(x: Int): Int {
    val result = x * 2
    println("2 * $x = $result")
    return result
}
```

In this case, `twiceAndLog` is *not* pure. To understand why, check the aforementioned two properties:

1. Every time you invoke `twiceAndLog` with the same parameter x, you always get the same result, x * 2, as output. As said, from this point of view, `twiceAndLog` is the same function as `twice`.

2. Unfortunately, returning a result isn't the *only* thing this function does. It also *changes the universe* in the sense that the world now has some output messages the function has written using `println`. The state of the universe, specifically the standard output of your small program, is now different.

Exercise 3.1: Is inc a pure function?

```
var count = 0
fun inc(x: Int): Int = ++count + x
```

Try arguing your answer and check Appendix C to see how you did.

Now, consider the following example, and add it in **Pure.kt**:

```
fun randomInc(a: Int): Int = a + Random.nextInt()
```

This function adds a random integer to the value that was passed in. If you check the two properties for a pure function, you see that:

1. Invoking randomInc multiple times with the same input parameter, you get different output values because of the random value you get with Random.nextInt(). This alone allows you to say that randomInc isn't pure. It's worth checking the second property regardless.

2. Every time you invoke randomInc, you also change the universe. This isn't obvious because you don't have any println, and apparently, you're not changing anything outside the function's body. This actually isn't true because every time you invoke Random.nextInt(), you're changing the state of Random, the object responsible for generating random numbers. Random works as a global object, which is part of the universe.

You can easily prove the first point by adding the following code to main in **Pure.kt**:

```
fun main() {
  // ...
  println(randomInc(10))
  println(randomInc(10))
  println(randomInc(10))
  println(randomInc(10))
}
```

If you run main, you'll get different values like this as output:

```
424226219
-1433325033
-326412163
1941055914
```

Note: Of course, the values in your output will be different because of the randomness of `Random.nextInt()`.

In **Why are pure functions important?**, you'll learn how to recognize pure and impure functions with other examples. But *why* is it so important to understand if a function is pure?

Exercise 3.2: Is inc2 a pure function?

```
val count = 0
fun inc2(x: Int): Int = x + count + 1
```

Give it a try and check Appendix C to see how you did.

Why are pure functions important?

Understanding if a function is pure is a fundamental concept in functional programming. Pure functions provide many significant benefits, and in particular, they are:

- Easy to understand.
- Easy to test and debug.
- Composable in other pure functions.
- Easy to run in parallel.
- Idempotent and easy to recover.
- Memoizable.
- Able to be performed lazily.

It's worth going over each of these advantages with some small examples. You'll also have the chance to see each of these in depth in the rest of the book.

Pure functions are easy to understand

A pure function doesn't depend on anything other than its input parameters. This means you can understand it simply by following the logic path from the input to the output, which you define using the expression in the function body. If a pure function is too complex, you can decompose it into smaller functions and recompose them later into a final, single result. You don't need any knowledge of the universe because all you need is in the function body.

Add the following example to **Pure.kt**:

```
fun abs(x: Int) = if (x < 0) -x else x
```

This function checks if x is negative, changing its sign if it is. Because x is all you need, understanding what abs does is very simple. If this is too complex, you could replace it like this:

```
fun negate(x: Int) = -x // 1
fun identity(x: Int) = x // 2
fun abs(x: Int) = if (x < 0) negate(x) else identity(x) // 3
```

In this case, you define:

1. The pure function negate, which negates the input value.

2. The identity function, which is also pure.

3. abs, which applies some logic to understand if it should invoke identity or negate.

The complexity of a function is in the interaction with the external world. These interactions are called side effects. By definition, side effects aren't present in pure functions.

Pure functions are easy to test and debug

The absence of side effects also makes pure functions easier to test. Imagine you want to count how many times you invoke abs, which you defined earlier.

A possible approach is the following. Add it to **Counter.kt**:

```
var count = 0 // 1

fun countedAbs(x: Int): Int { // 2
  count++
```

```
    return abs(x)
}
```

In this simple code, you:

1. Define `count` and initialize it to 0.

2. Create `countedAbs` as a function, which increments the value of `count` and returns the output of `abs`.

From what you learned earlier, this is **impure** because it changes the state of the universe, and in particular, its property `count`, which is a mutable global variable.

You'll see in the rest of the book why this solution is far from being the best. But in this case, you just need to understand whether or not it's easy to test and debug. To test it, create a test using IntelliJ. Select the name `countedAbs` and press **OPTION+ENTER** to get the drop-down with a **Create test** option in Figure 3.1:

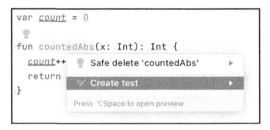

Figure 3.1: Create a unit test with IntelliJ

Select **Create test** and, after switching to **JUnit4** in **Testing Library**, you'll see the following dialog:

Testing library:	◀▶ JUnit4
💡 JUnit4 library not found in the module	Fix
Class name:	CounterKtTest
Superclass:	
Destination package:	com.raywenderlich.fp
Generate:	☐ setUp/@Before
	☐ tearDown/@After
Generate test methods for:	☐ Show inherited methods
Member	

?   Cancel   OK

Figure 3.2: Set up JUnit test

Select **OK** and choose the **test/kotlin** folder, like in Figure 3.3:

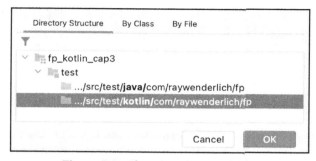

Figure 3.3: Choosing the test folder

Selecting **OK** for the last time, you'll end up at an initially empty **CounterKtTest.kt** file. In this file, write your first test like this:

```
class CounterKtTest {
  @Test
  fun test100Times() {
    100.invokeTimes { // 1
      countedAbs(it) // 2
    }
    assertThat(count).isEqualTo(100) // 3
  }
}
```

In this test, you simply:

1. Use invokeTimes, which is a simple utility method you'll find in **Util.kt**. This allows you to run the lambda you pass as a parameter the number of times you use as the receiver. In this case, you invoke the lambda 100 times.

2. Invoke countedAbs, passing the current execution number as a parameter. For this test, you don't really care about the input parameter for countedAbs.

3. You assert that the counter value is 100.

If you run test100Times, you'll get a green result, which means the test succeeded. So far, so good.

Now, suppose you add another test like the following to the same **CounterKtTest.kt** file:

```
class CounterKtTest {
  //...
  @Test
  fun test50Times() {
```

```
    50.invokeTimes {
       countedAbs(it)
    }
    assertThat(count).isEqualTo(50)
  }
}
```

If you now run the two tests, you'll get some problems. In particular, you'll get something like this:

```
value of: getCount()
expected: 100
but was : 150
value of: getCount()
expected: 100
but was : 150
   at
com.raywenderlich.fp.CounterKtTest.test100Times(CounterKtTest.kt
:47)
```

The specific test `test100Times` fails because you were expecting a count of `100`, but you get a count of `150` instead. The reason is obvious: The previous test, `test50Times`, *changed the universe* and you didn't run `test100Times` in isolation like every test should be. In this case, the problem is that you need to know what's already happened to the universe to predict the result of your function. What already happened depends on many things, like the number of times the same `countedAbs` was already executed, making the test difficult to implement.

You might argue that just resetting the value of `count` before each test, like the following, could fix the problem:

```
@Test
fun test100Times() {
  count = 0 // HERE
  100.invokeTimes {
    countedAbs(it)
  }
  assertThat(count).isEqualTo(100)
}
```

This is true, but only if all the tests aren't run concurrently. In that case, this fix wouldn't work because of the risk of resetting the value of `count` in the middle of the execution of another test.

How could you solve this problem, then? Would a pure version of `countedAbs` solve this testability problem?

Spoiler alert: A pure countedAbs

Remember, a pure function doesn't change the universe, and it has all it needs in the input parameters. You'll see these concepts again in the book, but to give you some idea, consider the following function and add it to **Counter.kt**:

```kotlin
fun countedAbs(count: Int, a: Int): Pair<Int, Int> =
    abs(a) to count + 1
```

As you see, countedAbs now has two parameters: count is the number of times the function has been invoked before this, and a is the input parameter for abs. The return type is now very interesting because it's a Pair<Int, Int>. The first value is the result of abs, and the second is the new value of count, which is the previous +1. You can easily verify that countedAbs is now a pure function:

* The output depends only on the input parameters.

* Invoking countedAbs doesn't change the universe. It also causes no side effects.

What about the test, then? Open **CounterKtTest.kt** and replace the existing tests with the following:

```kotlin
class CounterKtTest {
  //...
  @Test
  fun test50TimesAbs() {
    var c = 0  // 1
    50.invokeTimes {
      val (count, _) = countedAbs(c, it) // 2
      c = count // 3
    }
    assertThat(c).isEqualTo(50) // 4
  }

  @Test
  fun test100TimesAbs() {
    var c = 0  // 1
    100.invokeTimes {
      val (count, _) = countedAbs(c, it) // 2
      c = count // 3
    }
    assertThat(c).isEqualTo(100) // 4
  }
}
```

In this case, you:

1. Use a local variable c for the count, which you initialize at 0.

2. Invoke countedAbs 50 times in the first test and 100 in the second, passing the value you got from the previous execution for the count parameter.

3. Update the value of the local variable c.

4. Assert the value of c to check it's what you expected.

Now, run the tests, and everything will pass. Consider also that the tests run in complete isolation. Even if executed in a different thread, they'd be successful. In this case, all of the changes are local to the scope of a single test.

> **Note**: In the previous tests, you invoked countedAbs many times, but *one* invocation would've been enough to test that it works! This is because this version of countedAbs is pure. :]

Pure functions are composable

As you know, by definition, in a pure function, the output depends only on the input parameters, making the composition of pure functions pure as well. You might argue that you can combine impure functions in the same way you combine pure functions. This is true, but composition wouldn't fix their purity. Add the following functions to **Pure.kt**:

```
var sharedCount = 1 // 1

fun comp1(x: Int): String = "Hello ${x + sharedCount}" // 2

fun comp2(x: String): Int = x.length - sharedCount // 3
```

Here, you:

1. Initialize the global variable sharedCount to 1.

2. Define comp1 as Fun<Int, String>, which returns a formatted String using sharedCount. This is impure.

3. Define comp2 as Fun<String, Int>, which returns the length of the String as input minus sharedCount. This is also impure.

Both `comp1` and `comp2` are impure because their output doesn't depend just on the input parameters but also on `sharedCount`. You can now compose them like this using `after`, which you defined in the previous chapter and is found in **Category.kt**:

```
val comp2AfterComp1 = ::comp2 after ::comp1
```

Here, you defined `comp2AfterComp1`, which is still impure because its output doesn't depend just on its input but still on `sharedCount`. If you have instead composed two pure functions, the result would also be pure. In the rest of the book, you'll see many examples of pure functions composed of other pure functions.

Pure functions can run in parallel

As you'll see in Section III, thread safety is one of the big advantages of functional programming. This thread safety is mainly because of the use of pure functions.

As you've read many times now, the output of a pure function just depends on the input. Another way of saying this is that, with the input values, the function has all it needs to return an output value. Pure functions don't have any dependency with the external universe and don't share data with it. Pure functions can run in parallel.

Open the **Parallel.kt** file and add the following code:

```
fun square(x: Double): Double = x * x // 1

fun root(x: Double): Double = Math.sqrt(x) // 2

fun distance( // 3
  x0: Double,
  x1: Double,
  y0: Double,
  y1: Double
): Double {
  val s1 = square(x1 - x0) // 4
  val s2 = square(y1 - y0) // 4
  return root(s1 + s2) // 5
}
```

In this simple code, you define the following functions:

1. `square`, which calculates the square of the `Double` value you pass as input. This is a pure function.

2. `root`, which calculates the square root of the `Double` value you pass as input. This is a pure function.

3. `distance`, which calculates the distance between two points given their coordinates. This is also a pure function.

Look into the body of `distance`, and you'll see that you:

4. Calculate the square of the difference for the x coordinates first and then the square of the difference of y values and save them in `s1` and `s2`.

5. Return the square root of the sum of `s1` and `s2`.

The interesting thing here is that the order you use to calculate `s1` and `s2` doesn't matter. You could've calculated `s2` first and then `s1`. The important thing is that you invoke `sqrt` when you have both `s1` and `s2`. Because the order in which you calculate `s1` and `s2` doesn't matter, it means you could calculate them in parallel and then join the result when invoking `sqrt`. All the options in Figure 3.4 are valid:

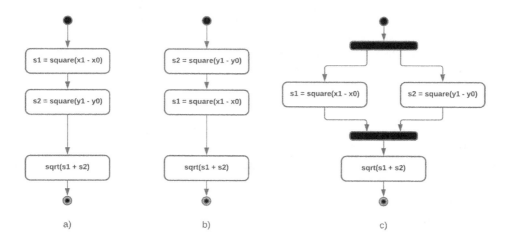

Figure 3.4: Pure function parallelism

It is possible because `square` is pure. If it wasn't pure and had side effects, the result of `square`'s two executions would depend on what's in the universe, which also depends on the execution order.

The chance to run pure functions in parallel is also essential in the case of distributed systems. You might run the functions on different machines, providing just the input parameters and collecting the result.

Race conditions and deadlocks are two of the main problems when you run functions in a concurrent environment. These especially happen when multiple threads share mutable data. If a function is pure, it has all it needs in its input parameters, so it doesn't need to share anything.

> **Note:** The code you execute as the body of a pure function must run in a single thread.

Pure functions are idempotent and easy to recover

Idempotent is a term you normally use in the context of a RESTful service in the case of requests using **PUT** or **DELETE** methods. The effect of an idempotent request is the same in the case of a single or multiple requests. A pure function is idempotent because it doesn't have side effects, so invoking the function once or multiple times doesn't make any difference. Another way of saying this is that *pure functions are safe*. You can execute them multiple times without any problems besides the CPU usage.

The execution of a function can fail for many reasons. Imagine a function that takes some time, and then, in the middle of the execution, the machine crashes. Because the output depends on the input, you can simply retry the function's execution, and you'll be sure to get the result you're expecting. If the result is very important, you could run the function on multiple machines and collect the result from the first one that completes.

Pure functions are easy to memoize

Like in the previous paragraph, imagine you have a function that takes some time to execute. If the function is pure, for the same input value, you'll always get the same output value. If the function takes some time and you already know the result for a given input, why would you repeat the computation?

You'd always get the same result. The best solution, then, is to save the previous result somewhere and return it if you invoke the function with the same input. This process is called **memoization**.

> **Note**: In Chapter 5, "Higher-Order Functions", you'll see how to implement a higher-order function for adding memoization to any other existing function.

Pure functions are lazily executable

There's a definition saying that "a function is a way to describe some code you can maybe run later". This definition is apt because it makes explicit that you can:

- Execute the function long after you've implemented it.

- Completely avoid the execution of the function, saving time and resources.

Because pure functions don't depend on the universe around them, you can execute them at any time, wait to execute them, or even never execute them if you never need the output value!

In the next chapter, Chapter 4, "Expression Evaluation, Laziness & More About Functions", you'll learn more about laziness and why it's an important feature of pure functions.

Referential transparency and the substitution model

In the previous part of the chapter, you learned why pure functions are important. You also learned that a pure function always returns the same output values when you provide the same input values. As previously mentioned, when you write the body of a pure function, you basically write an expression. You define **expression** as a combination of constants, variables, operators and functions that your computer computes, producing another **value**. The following are some basic examples of expressions:

```
val exp1 = 1 + 2 * 2  // 1
val exp2 = exp1 * 20 // 2
val exp3 = 2 * (expr2 - expr1) // 3
```

Here, you:

1. Define exp1 as the result of the sum of 1 and the result of the multiplication of 2 with itself.

2. Reuse the result from the previous expression, exp1, in a second one, expr2, which multiplies the previous value by 20.

3. Reuse both the previously calculated expressions, exp1 and exp2, for a third, slightly more complex exp3.

To get the result of exp3, you basically reduce all the other expressions until you get a single value. In the previous case, you calculate the result like this:

```
exp1 == 1 + 2 * 2 == 5
exp2 == exp1 * 20 = 5 * 20 == 100
exp3 == 2 * (expr2 - expr1) == 2 * (100 - 5) == 2 * 95 == 190
```

An expression like expr3 is **referentially transparent** if, in every place it's used, you can replace it with its final result. More formally, any program using the expression exp3 shouldn't change its behavior if you replace exp3 with 190.

A function f is pure if the expression f(x) is referentially transparent for all referentially transparent x. If an expression isn't referentially transparent, you say it's **referentially opaque**.

It's worth seeing some more examples.

Examples of referentially transparent expressions

Referential transparency is a mandatory property of pure functions. Keep reading for some more examples.

Consider the following expressions:

```
// 1
val a = expr
val (a1, a2) = a to a

// 2
val (a1, a2) = expr to expr
```

Is the definition in **1** equivalent to the one in **2**? The answer is yes, but *if and only if* expr is **pure**. To prove that, copy the following code into **ReferentialTransparency.kt**:

```
fun main() {
  val expr1 = { 3 * 10 } // 1
  val (a1, a2) = expr1() to expr1() // 2
  val expr1Eval = expr1() // 3
  val (a1Eval, a2Eval) = expr1Eval to expr1Eval // 4
  assertOrThrow("expr1 is not RT") { // 5
    a1 == a1Eval && a2 == a2Eval
  }
}
```

In this code, you:

1. Define the simple referentially transparent expression expr1, multiplying 3 and 10. Note how the expression is 3 * 10, but you put it as the body of a lambda for it to be evaluated later.

2. Create a Pair<Int, Int> evaluating expr1 for the first and second values.

3. Evaluate expr1 once in expr1Eval.

4. Create another Pair<Int, Int> using expr1Eval twice.

5. Assert that the two Pair<Int, Int> are the same. You find assertOrThrow in **Ext.kt** in the **util** package.

Run the code and see that there's no exception thrown. This means the two expressions are equivalent, so expr1 is referentially transparent. Can you do the same with a referentially opaque function? To verify that, just add the following code to main, which differs from the previous because it uses expr2, which isn't referentially transparent. It changes an outside count variable:

```
var count = 1 // 1
val expr2 = { 3 * 10 * ++count } // 2
val (b1, b2) = expr2() to expr2()
val expr2Eval = expr2()
val (b1Eval, b2Eval) = expr2Eval to expr2Eval
assertOrThrow("expr2 is not RT") {
  b1 == b1Eval && b2 == b2Eval
}
```

In this case, expr2 isn't referentially transparent because it returns different values every time you invoke it.

This is because it depends on the value of count it changes at every execution. When you run the code, you now get:

```
Exception in thread "main" java.lang.AssertionError: expr2 is
not RT
```

In this case, the number of times you execute expr2 changes its output, making it referentially opaque.

Exercise 3.3: Is expr3:

```
val expr3 = 42
val (a1, a2) = expr3 to expr3
```

The same as the following?

```
val (a1, a2) = 42 to 42
```

Give it a try and check Appendix C to see how you did.

Consider, now, the following expression:

```
val expr3 = { println("Hello World!") }
```

Is this referential transparency? The answer is no, but if you add and run the following code in **ReferentialTransparent.kt**, you don't get any errors:

```
val expr3 = { println("Hello World!") }
val (c1, c2) = expr3() to expr3()
val expr3Eval = expr3()
val (c1Eval, c2Eval) = expr3Eval to expr3Eval
assertOrThrow("expr2 is not RT") {
  c1 == c1Eval && c2 == c2Eval
}
```

So, what's wrong? The previous code just tests if the output of the expression is always the same for the given input. In this case, there's no input, and the output is the output of println, which is Unit. To understand why expr3 isn't pure, you need to check the definition.

Given:

```
val expr3 = { println("Hello World!") }
```

Is the program:

```
val (c1, c2) = expr3() to expr3()
```

Equivalent to the following?

```
val expr3Eval = expr3()
val (c1Eval, c2Eval) = expr3Eval to expr3Eval
```

The answer, again, is no. The first produces as output:

```
Hello World!
Hello World!
```

The second produces:

```
Hello World!
```

In the second case, you've replaced the expression's invocation with its result value, and the program has changed. This proves that expr3 isn't referentially transparent.

In the previous examples, you've basically replaced every invocation of a given expression with its result and checked if the resulting program was somehow different. This model of substituting values for expressions is called the **substitution model**.

Exercise 3.4: Suppose you have the following code:

```
val CounterIterator = object : Iterator<Int> {

  private var count = 0

  override fun hasNext(): Boolean = true

  override fun next(): Int = count++
}
```

Is the following expression referentially transparent?

```
val expr4 = { CounterIterator.next() }
```

Give it a try and check Appendix C to see how you did.

Referentially transparent expressions and Kotlin inline functions

You just learned that you can replace a referentially transparent expression with its result in every place it's used without breaking the related program. This is something that probably reminds you of the concept of **inline functions** in Kotlin. The question you want to answer now is: *Can a referentially transparent function always be inlined?*

To answer this question, add the following function to **Inline.kt**:

```
fun cube(x: Int): Int = x * x * x
```

This simple function calculates the cube of the input value. This is clearly a pure function, and its body contains an expression that's clearly referentially transparent. Now, add the following new function to the same file:

```
fun doubleCube(x: Int) = cube(x) + cube(x)
```

This is another simple pure function calculating the sum of the values you get from invoking cube twice. To calculate the result of doubleCube for 2, do the following:

```
doubleCube(2) ==
    cube(2) + cube(2) ==
    (2 * 2 * 2) + (2 * 2 * 2) ==
    8 + 8 ==
    16
```

You apply the substitution model and reduce the expression to the single value 16. Because the expression in the body of doubleCube is referentially transparent, you could replace every call to doubleCube(2) with the simple value 16.

Write and run the following code to verify that the result is 16:

```kotlin
fun main() {
  assertOrThrow("") {
    doubleCube(2) == 16
  }
}
```

It's interesting now to look at the code Kotlin generates from the previous code.

In the **Tools** menu, go to the **Kotlin** submenu and select the **Show Kotlin Bytecode** option, like in Figure 3.5:

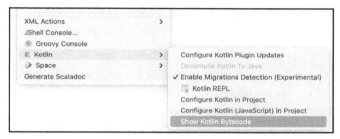

Figure 3.5: Show Kotlin Bytecode option

This will display some bytecode like in Figure 3.6.

```
Kotlin Bytecode                                              ⚙ —
 ( Decompile )   ☑ Inline  ☑ Optimization  ☑ Assertions  ☐ IR Target:
  1  // ================com/raywenderlich/fp/InlineKt.class ====
  2  // class version 52.0 (52)
  3  // access flags 0x31
  4  public final class com/raywenderlich/fp/InlineKt {
  5
  6
  7    // access flags 0x19
  8    public final static cube(I)I
  9      // annotable parameter count: 1 (visible)
 10      // annotable parameter count: 1 (invisible)
 11      L0
 12       LINENUMBER 35 L0
 13       ILOAD 0
 14       ILOAD 0
 15       IMUL
 16       ILOAD 0
 17       IMUL
 18       IRETURN
 19      L1
 20       LOCALVARIABLE x I L0 L1 0
```

Figure 3.6: The generated Kotlin bytecode

Reading Kotlin bytecode can be made simpler with the **Decompile** button, so press that now.

That leads to a more readable representation of the code the Kotlin compiler generates from your source code, like in Figure 3.7:

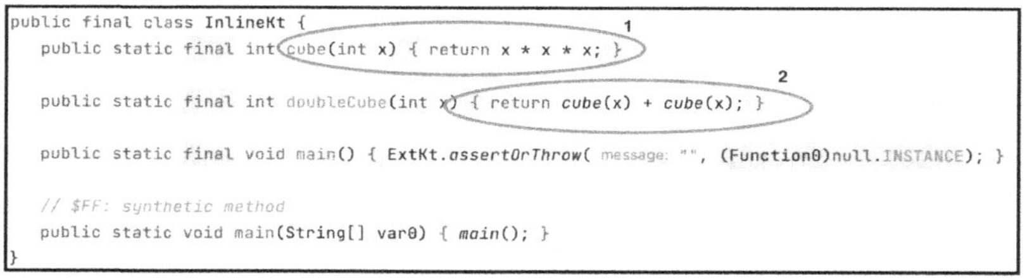

Figure 3.7: The generated Kotlin bytecode decompiled

> **Note**: Don't worry if you see some compilation errors in the decompiled code. What you see here isn't supposed to compile successfully, but it's useful to have an idea of how the Kotlin compiler works.

As you can see, the generated code isn't much different from the one you wrote initially. You still have:

1. The same definition of cube.

2. doubleCube, which still invokes cube twice.

As said, cube and doubleCube are pure functions, and the expressions in their bodies are referentially transparent. What about defining them as inline functions? Change the previous implementations to include the inline keyword. They should now look like this:

```
inline fun cube(x: Int): Int = x * x * x

inline fun doubleCube(x: Int) = cube(x) + cube(x)
```

The only difference is the use of the `inline` keyword. If you now repeat the process to get the Kotlin bytecode, this time removing what's not critical, you'll get something like Figure 3.8:

```
public static final int cube(int x) {
    int $i$f$cube = 0;
    return x * x * x;
}

public static final int doubleCube(int x) {
    int $i$f$doubleCube = 0;
    int $i$f$cube = false;          1
    int var10000 = x * x * x;
    $i$f$cube = false;               2
    return var10000 + x * x * x;
}
```

Figure 3.8: The generated Kotlin bytecode decompiled for inline functions

As you can see, the Kotlin compiler has replicated the expression you wrote in `cube` in every place where the same function has been invoked in `doubleCube`. If you look at the generated code, you also note that:

1. Kotlin generates a variable, `var10000`, with a copy of the expression in `cube`.

2. The return value of `doubleCube` reuses `var10000` and then another copy of the expression in `cube`.

For a correct application of the replication model, the return value would've been:

```
return x * x * x + x * x * x
```

You can say, then, that you can inline a pure function, but what's really happening isn't a complete application of the substitution model. In addition, when you look carefully at your source code, you'll see a warning from IntelliJ, like in Figure 3.9:

```
/** Cube of the value in input */
inline fun cube(x: Int): Int = x * x * x
```
> Expected performance impact from inlining is insignificant. Inlining works best for functions with parameters of functional types

Figure 3.9: Inline function warning message

The message basically says the benefit in performance you get by inlining a function like cube or doubleCube is insignificant and probably useless. The message also says the possible benefits happen when you have parameters of functional types. This means higher-order functions, which you'll learn about in detail in Chapter 5, "Higher-Order Functions".

Side effects

You know that a pure function returns output values, which depend only on the values you provide as input. The function calculates the output value, resolving the referentially transparent expression you define in its body. You also learned that a pure function doesn't change the state of the universe. This means you can run it an unlimited number of times without any external effect.

It's very easy to fall into the trap of thinking that *side effects are things you must avoid completely*. This isn't actually true because side effects are the reasons you create and run programs. For instance, if you want your app to persist some data in a database or fetch some data by accessing the network, you need to have some functions with side effects. Side effects are everywhere. So, what's the problem?

One of the problems you want to solve with functional programming is to *control side effects* or isolate and execute them safely. As said, you'll study side effects much more in the following chapters, but it's now important to give an example of what it means to have control of side effects. Open **SideEffects.kt**, and add the following code:

```
fun shiftLeft(x: Int) = x shl 1 // 1
fun not(x: Int) = x.inv() // 2
```

These are two basic pure functions that:

1. Shift the input value left by 1 position.

2. Negate the binary representation of the input value.

Using after, you can easily compose the two functions like this:

```
val shiftLeftAndNot = ::not after ::shiftLeft
```

You can test `shiftLeftAndNot` by running the following code:

```
fun main() {
  val comp1 = not(shiftLeft(10))
  val comp2 = shiftLeftAndNot(10)
  assertOrThrow("comp1 != comp2") {
    comp1 == comp2
  }
}
```

So far, so good! Now, suppose you want to log the operation you're executing in `shiftLeft` and `not`. How could you solve this problem in a functional way?

A first, impure, approach would be to use the following. Add it to **SideEffect2.kt**:

```
fun shiftLeftAndLog(x: Int): Int {
  println("Shift Left of $x") // 1
  return x shl 1
}

fun notAndLog(x: Int): Int {
  println("Negate $x") // 2
  return x.inv()
}
```

In this code, you:

1. Used `println` to print a message in the body of `shiftLeftAndLog`.

2. Did the same for `notAndLog`.

The new functions `shiftLeftAndLog` and `notAndLog` are not pure because they have side effects! Each function is changing the universe by writing something in the standard output. The side effects aren't under control, and it's like each function is firing its own effect in a different direction.

The first consequence involves testability. How can you test `shiftLeftAndLog` and `notAndLog`? Trying to improve testability is a reason to improve the previous example by introducing the `Logger` abstraction. Add the following code in **SideEffects3.kt**:

```
interface Logger { // 1
  fun log(msg: String)
}

val StdLogger = object : Logger { // 2
  override fun log(msg: String) {
    println(msg)
  }
}
```

```
}

fun shiftLeftWithLogger(logger: Logger, x: Int): Int { // 3
  logger.log("Shift Left of $x") // 4
  return x shl 1
}

fun notWithLogger(logger: Logger, x: Int): Int { // 3
  logger.log("Negate $x") // 4
  return x.inv()
}
```

In this code, you:

1. Define Logger as the abstraction for the object responsible for logging.

2. Provide StdLogger as a Logger implementation for the standard output.

3. Add Logger as an additional input parameter and create shiftLeftWithLogger and notWithLogger.

4. Use the Logger in the body of shiftLeftWithLogger and notWithLogger.

shiftLeftWithLogger and notWithLogger are impure, and they have side effects. However, they are — compared to the previous implementations — easier to test. You just need to provide a MockLogger implementation like the following:

```
class MockLogger : Logger {

  private val internalLog = StringBuilder()
  val log: String
    get() = internalLog.toString()

  override fun log(msg: String) {
    internalLog.append(msg)
  }
}
```

And test the previous functions by adding the following code to main in
SideEffects3.kt:

```
fun main() {
  val mockLogger1 = MockLogger()
  shiftLeftWithLogger(mockLogger1, 10)
  assertOrThrow("Problem testing shiftLeft()") {
    mockLogger1.log == "Shift Left of 10"
  }
  val mockLogger2 = MockLogger()
  notWithLogger(mockLogger2, 10)
  assertOrThrow("Problem testing not()") {
```

```
        mockLogger2.log == "Negate 10"
    }
}
```

Here, you're basically trying to put the result of the side effect into some sort of container, `MockLogger`, and verifying its content at the end of the test. Run `main` and check that everything is fine without any exceptions.

The biggest problem is that now `shiftLeftWithLogger` and `notWithLogger` aren't composable, like the original `shiftLeft` and `not` were in **SideEffects.kt**. The output of `shiftLeftWithLogger` has type `Int`, but the input of `notWithLogger` now needs two parameters: one of type `Logger` and one of type `Int`.

How can you implement the initial `shiftLeft` and `not` implementations with logging capabilities as pure functions, making them easier to test and compose?

A first look at composition with side effects

You'll learn how to handle side effects in great detail in the following chapters of this book, particularly in Chapter 8, "Composition". In this case, it's worth first seeing an example of how you can implement composition when you have a function with side effects.

In the previous examples, you implemented the side effect, invoking `println` in the body of `shiftLeftAndLog` and `notAndLog` or delegating to a `Logger` in `shiftLeftWithLogger` and `notWithLogger`. Now, use a different approach and write the following code in **SideEffects4.kt**:

```
fun shiftLeftWithEffect(x: Int): Pair<Int, String> { // 1
    return x shl 1 to "Shift Left of $x" // 2
}

fun notWithEffect(x: Int): Pair<Int, String> { // 1
    return x.inv() to "Negate $x" // 2
}
```

In this code, you:

1. Decorated the output value of `shiftLeftWithEffect` and `notWithEffect` with the information you want to use for the log.

2. Returned a `Pair<Int, String>` with the result of the original function as the first value and the log message as the second.

The idea is to include the *description of the side effect* in the return value of the function. Both `shiftLeftWithEffect` and `notWithEffect` are pure! Unfortunately *they aren't composable yet*. The input for `notWithEffect` is Int, but the output of `shiftLeftWithEffect` is Pair<Int, String>.

Again, you'll see these concepts in greater detail later, but now look at the previous functions and their signatures. Define the following `typealias`:

```
typealias Writer<A, B> = (A) -> Pair<B, String>
```

You can say the previous:

1. `shiftLeftWithEffect` has type `Writer<Int, Int>`.

2. `notWithEffect` has the same type `Writer<Int, Int>`.

You now have two functions of the same type, and you just have to define *how composition works* for them. In the same **SideEffects4.kt** file, add the following code:

```
infix fun <A, B, C> Writer<B, C>.after(
  w: Writer<A, B>
): Writer<A, C> = { a: A -> // 1
  val (b, str) = w(a) // 2
  val (c, str2) = this(b) // 3
  c to "$str\n$str2\n" // 4
}
```

In the higher-order function `after`, you:

1. Use `Writer<B, C>` as receiver and accept an input parameter of type `Writer<A, B>`. The output type is `Writer<A, C>`.

2. Invoke the `Writer<A, B>` you pass as a parameter on the input a of type A and, using Kotlin destructuring, save the result in two different local variables: b of type B and `str` of type `String`.

3. Invoke `Writer<B, C>` using b from the previous expression, and destructure the result in c of type C and `str2` of type `String`.

4. Implement the actual composition, returning a Pair<Int, String> where `first` is the value c you got from the previous instruction and `second` is the concatenation of the `String`s you got in the previous instruction.

Now, by adding the following code in the same file, you can test everything:

```
fun main() {
    val f: Writer<Int, Int> = ::shiftLeftWithEffect // 1
    val g: Writer<Int, Int> = ::notWithEffect // 2
    val shiftLeftAndNotWithEffects = g after f // 3
    println(shiftLeftAndNotWithEffects(10).second) // 4
}
```

In this example, you:

1. Save in f the reference to ::shiftLeftWithEffect, giving it the explicit type Writer<Int, Int>.

2. Do the same for g and ::notWithEffect.

3. Create shiftLeftAndNotWithEffects using after. This is a composition of f and g, which is the composition of shiftLeftWithEffect and notWithEffect.

4. Print second in the final result, which is the concatenation of the logs.

Run the previous code, and you'll get the following output:

```
Shift Left of 10
Negate 20
```

The new versions of shiftLeftWithEffect and notWithEffect are pure functions you can compose into another pure function, getting all the advantages you learned earlier.

> **Note**: Don't worry if this process isn't completely clear at this point. What you've done in this paragraph is anything but obvious, and you'll have many opportunities to revisit the same concepts in the following chapters of the book.

Lifting a function to a writer

Look again at the functions you created in **SideEffects4.kt** in a previous example:

```
fun shiftLeftWithEffect(x: Int): Pair<Int, String> {
  return x shl 1 to "Shift Left of $x"
}

/** A second version of not */
fun notWithEffect(x: Int): Pair<Int, String> {
  return x.inv() to "Negate $x"
}
```

These are two functions of type `Writer<Int, Int>`, but they're different from the original ones of type `Fun<Int, Int>` you defined in **SideEffects.kt**:

```
fun shiftLeft(x: Int): Int  = x shl 1

fun not(x: Int): Int = x.inv()
```

Is there a way to get the former version from the latter? Of course there is! Write the following function in **SideEffects5.kt**:

```
fun <A, B> Fun<A, B>.liftW(
  log: (A, B) -> String
): Writer<A, B> =
  { a: A ->
    val b = this(a)
    b to log(a, b)
  }
```

This is an extension function on the `Fun<A, B>` type, which creates a `Writer<A, B>`, adding a string as decoration in the resulting type. The log you use as decoration is the result of the function you pass as an input parameter from the input and output values of the receiver function.

> **Note**: `liftW` is another example of a higher-order function. Don't worry, you'll learn all about them in Chapter 5, "Higher-Order Functions".

As you'll see in Chapter 9, "Data Types", you're **lifting** a function to a different data type: in this case, `Writer<A, B>`. This allows you to start from a function f of type `Fun<A, B>` and lift it to a function of type `Writer<A, B>`. With `liftW`, you can now write the following code:

```
fun main() {
  val shiftLeftAndLog = ::shiftLeft.liftW { a, _ -> // 1
    "Shift Left $a"
  }
  val notAndLog = ::shiftLeft.liftW{ a, _ -> // 2
    "Negate $a"
  }
  val shiftLeftAndNotAndLog = notAndLog after shiftLeftAndLog //
3
  println(shiftLeftAndNotAndLog(10).second) // 4
}
```

In this code, you:

1. Define `shiftLeftAndLog`, lifting `shiftLeft` to a `Writer<Int, Int>`, passing a lambda containing the logic for the creation of the log in decoration.

2. Do the same for `negate`, creating `notAndLog`.

3. Get `shiftLeftAndNotAndLog` from the composition of `shiftLeftAndLog` and `notAndLog`.

4. Use `shiftLeftAndNotAndLog` and print the log in output.

When you run this code, you'll get exactly the same output you got earlier:

```
Shift Left 10
Negate 20
```

You did all this just using pure functions and composition!

> **Exercise 3.5**: The `Writer<A, B>` data type you defined earlier is a very important concept in functional programming. If you use types as objects and the functions `Writer<A, B>` as morphisms, you get a very special category: the **Kleisli category**.
>
> Can you prove that by using types as objects and `Writer<A, B>` as morphisms, you get a category? Look back at Chapter 2 if you need a reminder for how to prove this.
>
> Again, give it a try and check the solution in Appendix C to see how you did.

Challenges

In this chapter, you learned two of the most important concepts in functional programming: referential transparency and side effects. You also learned how to recognize a pure function. Now it's time for a few challenges:

Challenge 1: Pure or impure?

Is inc3 a pure function? Why or why not?

```
var count = 0
fun inc3(x: Int): Int {
  val result = x + ++count + 1
  println("Res: $result") // WHAT IF YOU REMOVE THIS?
  --count
  return result
}
```

What if you remove the println() with the comment?

Challenge 2: Pure or impure?

Is output a pure function? Why or why not?

```
fun output(x: Int): Unit = println("x = $x")
```

Challenge 3: Pure or impure?

Is randomAdd a pure function? Why or why not?

```
fun randomAdd(a: Int, b: Int): Int = a + b + Random.nextInt()
```

Key points

- A function f is **pure** if its body is a **referentially transparent** expression and it doesn't have **side effects**.

- A **pure function** always returns the same output values for the same input values.

- A pure function depends only on its input parameters and nothing else.

- Pure functions are easy to test and debug.

- You can run pure functions in **parallel**.

- Because the output of a pure function for a given input is always the same, you can evaluate its expression only once and **memoize** it for following invocations.

- Pure functions are **lazy**. You can defer their execution until you really need them.

- An expression is **referentially transparent** if replacing every occurrence in a program with its value doesn't alter the behavior of the program itself.

- The **substitution model** is a way to test if an expression is referentially transparent.

- An expression that isn't referentially transparent is **referentially opaque**.

- If the execution of a function *changes the state of the universe*, the function is **not pure**, and you have **side effects**.

- Side effects aren't a problem per se, but you need to control them to reduce the complexity of your program.

- The Writer<A, B> data type is an example of how you can control side effects.

- Using Writer<A, B> as morphisms and types as objects, you define the **Kleisli category**.

Where to go from here?

Wow, congrats! In this chapter, you did a lot of work and learned many fundamental concepts about functions and functional programming in general. You had the opportunity to see examples of pure and impure functions and learned how to recognize them using the substitution model. You've achieved a lot already because you've encountered side effects for the first time and, with `Writer<A, B>`, you've seen for the first time how to control and compose them.

You did a great job, but you've still got many concepts to learn — starting with the concepts of strictness, laziness, immutability and tail recursion. You'll learn about how they're related to functional programming and how they can help you create better code.

Chapter 4: Expression Evaluation, Laziness & More About Functions

In the previous chapters, you learned that you can define a function as "a bunch of code that might be executed later". You also learned several interesting points:

- As a software engineer, you write code and, more specifically, you write functions.

- If the functions you write are pure, their bodies are referentially transparent expressions.

- Executing a function means evaluating the expression in its body.

- "Executed later" means the expression of a function is evaluated at a time that isn't related to the position of the expression itself.

- It's possible that a function is never executed and the expression never evaluated.

Evaluation strategy is the relationship between the position where you define the expression in your code and the point when the expression is actually evaluated. In this chapter, you'll learn about two different evaluation strategies:

- Applicative-order evaluation

- Normal-order evaluation

These two evaluation strategies will lead you to other very important concepts in this chapter:

- The evaluation strategy for Kotlin.

- What **strictness** and **laziness** mean.

- How **lambda expressions** allow you to execute your code *later*.

- The Kotlin **lazy** function and how to use it to improve performance.

- How to implement **memoization** for pure functions in Kotlin.

- How to implement infinite Streams of data using lazy functions.

Again, all this uses Kotlin and many engaging exercises and challenges. Open up the starter project for this chapter to begin!

Expression evaluation order

As you know, you can write a pure function and execute it much later. Here's an example to help you understand how the position of an expression relates to the time it's evaluated.

Suppose you want to evaluate the following expression that calculates triple the average of two values:

```
3 * avg(x, y)
```

To represent this expression as a function, write the following code in the initially empty **Evaluation.kt** file in this chapter's material:

```
fun add(x: Int, y: Int): Int { // 1
  val result = x + y
  println("add") // 5
  return result
}

fun triple(x: Int): Int { // 2
  val result = add(add(x, x), x)
  println("triple") // 5
  return result
}

fun divide(x: Int, y: Int): Int { // 3
  val result = x / y
  println("divide") // 5
  return result
}

fun average(x: Int, y: Int): Int { // 4
  val result = divide(add(x, y), 2)
  println("average") // 5
  return result
}
```

In this code, you:

1. Create add, which returns the sum of the two input values.

2. Define triple, which uses add twice. This is possible because addition is associative, as are pure functions. You also know that pure functions and types create a category, which has associativity by definition.

3. Implement divide, which returns the division between the two input values. This is a division of Ints, so the result will always round down to a whole number. In this context, the precision of the function doesn't really matter, so that's OK. :]

4. Create average, which uses divide and add.

5. All these functions would be pure, but you added some println just to understand *how* and, more importantly, *when* they're evaluated. It's important to note how println follows the evaluation of the expression, giving evidence of the actual execution.

Now, write and run the following:

```
fun main() {
   triple(average(2, 4))
}
```

You get the output:

```
add
divide
average
add
add
triple
```

At first glance, you see that triple is the function evaluated last.

To understand why, apply the substitution model like this:

```
triple(average(2, 4)) // 1
triple(divide(add(2, 4), 2)) // 2
triple(divide(2+4, 2))
triple(divide(6, 2)) // 3
triple(6/2)
triple(3)
add(add(3,3), 3) // 4
add(3+3, 3)
add(6, 3) // 5
```

```
6+3
9
```

In the previous representation, you see that you always reduce the expression that allows you to give the leftmost function all the value it needs. In particular:

1. To resolve `triple`, Kotlin needs to resolve the expression you pass as an input parameter: `average`.

2. Next, you need to evaluate and give `divide` the value it needs as input: the sum of 2 and 4. This is why Kotlin evaluates `add(2, 4)` first.

3. At this point, `divide` has all the values it needs, and Kotlin starts the `divide` evaluation.

4. It's now time to evaluate `triple`, which needs to evaluate the `add` you have as the first input parameter.

5. Finally, you reduce everything to the value 9, which you can see by printing the result of the expression using this code:

```
fun main() {
  val result = triple(average(2, 4))
  println(result)
}
```

The previous example proves that in Kotlin, a function's arguments are evaluated *before* the function is applied, which is the definition of **applicative-order evaluation**. With applicative-order evaluation, a function executes only when all the expressions you pass as input parameters are evaluated, starting from the *leftmost* parameter.

> **Note**: Another name for Kotlin's applicative-order evaluation is **eager evaluation**.

But is this evaluation strategy good or bad? How would the same expression be evaluated in the case of **normal-order evaluation**, and what would the advantages be? Before exploring that, it's important to see some more examples.

Applicative-order evaluation examples

You just learned what applicative-order evaluation is, resolving a simple expression in Kotlin. To better understand what the consequences are, open the initially empty **ApplicativeOrder.kt** and write the following code:

```
fun greaterThan10(x: Int): Boolean { // 1
  println("greaterThan10") // 2
  return x > 10
}

fun main() {
  val inputValue = 3
  if (inputValue > 4 && greaterThan10(inputValue * 2)) { // 3
    println("OK") // 4
  } else {
    println("KO") // 4
  }
}
```

In this code, you:

1. Define `greaterThan10` as a simple function returning a `Boolean` stating whether the input value is greater than `10`.

2. Use `println` to give some evidence of the invocation of `greaterThan10`.

3. Define a simple test to check if the value of a local `inputValue` variable is greater than 4 and whether the result of `greaterThan10` passing `inputValue * 2` as input is `true`.

4. Print `OK` or `KO` if the test is `true` or `false`, respectively.

Run the previous code, and you'll get:

```
KO
```

This is because `inputValue` isn't greater than 4. The interesting part is that `greaterThan10` wasn't even invoked. The reason is the use of &&, which is a **short circuit** operator. When you resolve A && B, a `false` value of A makes the whole expression `false` and the evaluation of B would be irrelevant.

> **Note**: The same is true with the || operator. In the case of A || B, a true value for A would make the whole expression true. The evaluation of B would then be irrelevant.

Now, change the previous example like the following, assigning 30 to inputValue and passing it to greaterThan10:

```
fun main() {
    val inputValue = 30 // HERE
    if (inputValue > 4 && greaterThan10(inputValue)) {
        println("OK")
    } else {
        println("KO")
    }
}
```

Run the code and find:

```
greaterThan10
OK
```

In this case, inputValue > 4 evaluates to true and && requires the evaluation of greaterThan10(inputValue). This is why you see greaterThan10 as part of the output.

So far, so good. This is how && works. Now, change the previous code like this:

```
fun main() {
    val inputValue = 3 // 1
    val greater10 = greaterThan10(inputValue) // 2
    if (inputValue > 4 && greater10) { // 3
        println("OK")
    } else {
        println("KO")
    }
}
```

In this case, you:

1. Use 3 as the initial value for inputValue.

2. Invoke greaterThan10, passing inputValue as input.

3. Use greater10 in the condition for if.

This is equivalent to the very first example but, when you run the code, you get the following output:

```
greaterThan10
KO
```

The output contains KO, but greaterThan10 has been invoked anyway. This might look obvious because you evaluate greaterThan10 before the test, and you don't know yet if the if condition would require it or not.

However, is it possible to define the invocation of greaterThan10 in the same position as the last example but then execute it when you actually need it? The answer is yes, using **lazy evaluation** with **lambda expressions**.

Understanding lambda expressions

A lambda expression is simply an *anonymous function you can use as a value*. This basically means that:

- You can define a lambda expression on the fly, assigning it to a variable.

- As you'll see in detail in Chapter 5, "Higher-Order Functions", you can use a lambda expression as an input parameter or the result value of another function.

You define a lambda expression by adding a normal expression in a code block. The following is a perfectly valid lambda expression you can find in **Lambdas.kt** in this chapter's material.

```
val empty = {}
```

In the case of an input parameter, you define a lambda expression like the following:

```
{ a: Int, b: Int -> a + b }
```

In this case, you create an anonymous function that returns the sum of two input parameters of type Int. The result of evaluating a lambda expression is the value of the last expression in its body, in this case, the sum of a and b. You separate the input parameters list and the result expression with ->. It's important to note that both the input parameter and the result expression are optional, as you saw in the first example.

> **Exercise 4.1**: Can you write a lambda expression that calculates the distance between two points given their coordinates, x1, y1 and x2, y2? The formula for the distance between two points is distance = $\sqrt{(x2-x1)^2+(y2-y1)^2}$.
>
> Give it a try, and afterward, check the solution in Appendix D or this chapter's challenge project.

Lambda type inference

Type inference is the mechanism a compiler uses to understand the element types involved in an expression.

When the compiler can't get all the information it needs about types, you're supposed to help. You can give the compiler the information it needs in different ways. In the previous code, you helped the Kotlin compiler by adding explicit type information for a and b. The Kotlin compiler then understands that a and b are Ints, and the result of the lambda expression will also be Int because of the type of the result of a + b.

The following code would give a compilation error because the Kotlin compiler wouldn't know the types for a and b.

```
val lambda = { a, b -> a + b }
```

You can use a lambda expression as a normal value. This means you can assign it to a variable, like in the following example:

```
var operation = { a: Int, b: Int -> a + b }
```

In this case, you assign a lambda expression to a variable operation. The compiler infers for operation the type (Int, Int) -> Int, which is the type of any function with two input parameters of type Int returning another Int. Another way to give the compiler the information it needs is:

```
var operation: (Int, Int) -> Int = { a, b -> a + b }
```

By defining operation of type (Int, Int) -> Int, you're telling the Kotlin compiler the type of values you can assign to it. Because { a, b -> a + b } is compatible with the type of operation, the compiler infers an Int type for a and b and also verifies the return type. In this case, the Kotlin compiler inferred the type of the input parameters a and b from the type of operation you defined explicitly.

Exercise 4.2: What's the type for the lambda expression you wrote in Exercise 4.1?

Again, give it a try and check the solution in Appendix D or the challenge project.

The type of a **lambda expression** is then a **function type**, meaning the following code is perfectly legal:

```
typealias Fun<A, B> = (A) -> B

val multiplyBy2: Fun<Int, Int> = { x -> 2 * x }
```

Exercise 4.3: What are the types of the following lambda expressions?

```
val emptyLambda = {} // 1
val helloWorldLambda = { "Hello World!" } // 2
val helloLambda = { name: String -> "Hello $name!" } // 3
val nothingLambda = { TODO("Do exercise 4.3!") } // 4
```

Can you write an example of a lambda expression of the following type?

```
typealias AbsurdType = (Nothing) -> Nothing
```

In this case, can you show how to invoke it?

Try to answer without the support of IntelliJ, and check your solutions in Appendix D or the challenge project.

Lambda expression evaluation

A lambda expression allows you to define an expression without actually resolving it. Consider the following definition:

```
var operation = { a: Int, b: Int -> a + b }
```

Here, you're defining a lambda expression that *describes* how to calculate the addition of two Ints, but you're not actually running it. This is the beauty of lambda expressions: They allow you to describe code you'll execute later with the advantage that you can treat them as data. You can handle the value 2 and the lambda operation as values exactly the same way. You can treat them as input parameters and return values of functions.

Eventually, you might need to execute or resolve the lambda expression. How can you do that? And, in that case, what would the final result be?

As mentioned earlier, a lambda expression is a function type. This means you can execute it like any other function. For instance, in the previous example, add the following to **Lambdas.kt**:

```kotlin
fun main() {
  val result = operation(3, 4)
  println(result)
}
```

Running this code, you get:

```
7
```

You can achieve the same thing using invoke like this:

```kotlin
fun main() {
  val result = operation.invoke(3, 4)
  println(result)
}
```

The value you get resolving a lambda expression is the value of the last expression in its body. Consider the following code:

```kotlin
val testLambda = { a: Int ->
  val doubleA = a * 2
  if (doubleA > 10) "$doubleA is Greater than 10"
  else "$doubleA is Smaller or Equal to 10"
}
```

In this example, the if expression is the last in the body of testLambda.

> **Note**: You'll see much more about this in Chapter 5, "Higher-Order Functions".

More about lambda expressions

You'll see much more about lambda expressions in the following chapters of this book. Here, it's helpful to provide some useful and interesting information about:

- Lambda type inheritance

- Generic lambda expressions

Lambda type inheritance

In the previous paragraphs, you learned that the type of a lambda expression is a function type. In Chapter 2, "Function Fundamentals", you learned that a type is a way to represent the set of all possible values. For instance, with Int, you represent the set of all the possible integer values — or, at least, the ones you can represent in Kotlin. When you define operation like this:

```
var operation: (Int, Int) -> Int = { a, b -> a + b }
```

What are the actual lambdas you can assign to it? Only the ones of type (Int, Int) -> Int? In this case, the answer is yes. You can only assign functions of that type to operation because Int is final, but this isn't always the case.

> **Note:** Saying that Int is final means the Int class can't be extended.

Suppose you have the following types:

```
class A
class B
```

Now, suppose you define the following function type:

```
typealias LambdaType = (A) -> B
```

LambdaType is the type of generic function from A to B. This means you can write the following code, which is perfectly legal:

```
var lambda: LambdaType = { a -> B() }
```

Now, suppose you have the following new types:

```
class C
class D
```

What relation do these new types need to have with the previous A and B to make the following definition valid?

```
lambda = { c: C -> D() }
```

At the moment, the compiler is complaining because C isn't an A and D isn't a B. You basically need to make the function type (C) -> D a subtype of (A) -> B.

To fix this, you need to create the following relations you can visualize in Figure 4.1:

```
class A : C()
open class C
class D : B()
open class B
```

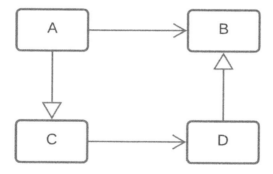

Figure 4.1: Lambda types inheritance

This means LambdaType is **contravariant** for the input type and **covariant** for the output type.

> **Note: Variance** is a crucial concept when working with generic types. Given a hierarchy relation between two types, A and B, it describes the relation between F<A> and F<B>. Here, F is a data type you represent using generic types like List<T>, Set<T> and others. Using this terminology:
>
> You have **covariance** when given B IS-A A entails that F<B> IS-A F<A>.

> When given B IS-A A entails that F<A> IS-A F<B>, you have **contravariance**.
>
> When given B IS-A A entails nothing about F<A> and F<B>, you have **invariance**.\
>
> To give a quick example, if Triangle IS-A Shape entails that List<Triangle> IS-A List<Shape>, you say that List<T> is **covariant**.

Generic lambda expressions

You might be wondering about the difference between a normal function and a lambda expression. For instance, what's the difference between the function:

```
fun add(a: Int, b: Int): Int = a + b
```

And the following lambda expression?

```
val sum = { a: Int, b: Int -> a + b }
```

Well, in this specific example, there's no difference — but consider the following case instead:

```
interface Combinable<A> { // 1
  fun combine(rh: A): A
}

fun <A : Combinable<A>> combine(lh: A, rh: A): A =
lh.combine(rh) // 2
```

In this case, you define:

1. The Combinable<A> interface, which defines combine. combine returns the combination of two objects of the same type A.

2. The combine function, which appends two input Combinable<A> objects into another Combinable<A>. This is a generic function in the type A with the constraint of considering only Combinable<A> objects.

How would you represent combine(lh: A, rh: A) using a lambda expression? Unfortunately, the following definition wouldn't work:

```
val combineLambda = { lh: A, rh: A -> lh.combine(rh) } // ERROR
```

You can't define a generic lambda expression the same way you do for a normal generic function. You might try to solve this problem with the following code:

```
typealias CombineLambdaType<A> =
  (Combinable<A>, Combinable<A>) -> Combinable<A> // 1

val combineLambda: CombineLambdaType<A> =  // 2
  { lh: A, rh: A -> lh.combine(rh) } // ERROR
```

In this case, you:

1. Define the typealias `CombineLambdaType<A>` as a function from two `Combinable<A>` to a single `Combinable<A>`.

2. Use `CombineLambdaType<A>`, trying to infer the parameter type to the lambda.

This doesn't work because you wouldn't be able to set the constraint on the type `A`.

In short, you can't define a lambda expression on a generic type. This is why expressing `combine(lh: A, rh: A)` using a lambda expression won't work. It's the consequence of the fact that lambda expressions are like values, and you can't define a value of a generic type `A`.

Lazy evaluation

Now that you know almost everything about lambda expressions in Kotlin, you can return to the following example you already wrote in **ApplicativeOrder.kt**. Next, copy it into **LazyEvaluation.kt**, using the same `greaterThan10`:

```
fun main() {
  val inputValue = 3
  val greater10 = greaterThan10(inputValue)
  if (inputValue > 4 && greater10) {
    println("OK")
  } else {
    println("KO")
  }
}
```

As you remember, if you run the code, you get:

```
greaterThan10
KO
```

How can you keep the same layout and evaluate `greaterThan10` only when you really need to? Now you know the answer: Use a lambda expression. Just replace the previous code with the following:

```
fun main() {
  val inputValue = 3
  val greater10 = { greaterThan10(inputValue) } // 1
  if (inputValue > 4 && greater10()) { // 2
    println("OK")
  } else {
    println("KO")
  }
}
```

In this code, you:

1. Replace `greaterThan10` with a lambda expression you saved in `greater10`.

2. Invoke `greater10` only if necessary.

Run the code, and you get:

```
KO
```

Running the same code after changing `inputValue`'s value to `30`, you get:

```
greaterThan10
OK
```

What you implemented using a lambda expression is called **lazy evaluation**. Lazy evaluation means resolving an expression only when you actually need it.

Exercise 4.4: Can you implement a function simulating the **short-circuit and** operator with the following signature without using &&? In other words, can you replicate the short-circuiting behavior of `left && right`:

```
fun shortCircuitAnd(left: () -> Boolean, right: () -> Boolean):
Boolean
```

Can you also write a test to prove that `right` evaluates only if `left` is false?

Try to answer without the support of IntelliJ, and check your solutions in Appendix D or the challenge project.

Kotlin lazy delegate

Kotlin allows you to implement lazy evaluation using the… **lazy** delegate. :] Before understanding how `lazy` works, it's useful to look at the by keyword. The Kotlin keyword by allows you to control the access to a variable, delegating **getters and setters** to the object you use as the target of the delegation: the **delegatee**. You call this **property delegation**.

To understand how it works, write the following code in **Lazy.kt**:

```kotlin
fun testDelegate() {
  var variable by object { // 1

    var localInt: Int? = null

    operator fun getValue( // 2
      thisRef: Any?,
      property: KProperty<*>
    ): Int? {
      println("Getter Invoked returning $localInt")
      return localInt
    }

    operator fun setValue( // 3
      thisRef: Any?,
      property: KProperty<*>,
      value: Int?
    ) {
      println("Setter Invoked with value $value")
      localInt = value
    }
  }
  variable = 10 // 4
  println("Reading $variable") // 5
}
```

In this code, you:

1. Use by to delegate `variable`'s access to a generic object.

2. Implement `getValue`, which is invoked every time you **access** `variable`.

3. Implement `setValue`, which is invoked every time you **set a value** to `variable`.

4. Assign the `10` value to `variable`.

5. Access `variable` and print its value.

This is why, running `testDelegate()`, you get the following output:

```
Setter Invoked with value 10
Getter Invoked returning 10
Reading 10
```

Now that you know how by works, just write the following code:

```
fun main() {
  val inputValue = 30
  val greater10 by lazy { greaterThan10(inputValue) } // 1
  if (inputValue > 4 && greater10) { // 2
    println("OK")
  } else {
    println("KO")
  }
}
```

In this code, note that you:

1. Use the Kotlin keyword by to delegate the access to the `greater10` variable to the object you get by invoking `lazy`. You pass to `lazy` the lambda function you want to eventually execute for `greater10` initialization.

2. Just access `greater10` in the `if` condition.

Running the previous `main`, you get:

```
greaterThan10
OK
```

Change the `inputValue` to 3, and you get:

```
KO
```

This is what you're expecting, but `lazy` gives you something more. Add the following code to **Lazy.kt**:

```
fun multiLazy() {
  val multiLambda by lazy { println("I'm MultiLambda") }
  multiLambda
  multiLambda
  multiLambda
  multiLambda
}
```

In this code, you:

1. Use `lazy` with a lambda expression containing the `println` of a message.

2. Access `multiLambda` multiple times.

When you run `multiLazy`, you get:

```
I'm MultiLambda
```

This is cool! The lambda expression you pass as a parameter to `lazy` is evaluated just once, and its result is reused when accessed again.

Of course, in this example, you use a `println` to prove that behavior, but if it doesn't have any side effects or the expression takes some time, `lazy` is very useful. In this way, you achieved **memoization**, which you'll learn about next.

> **Exercise 4.5**: Can you implement the function myLazy with the following signature, which allows you to pass in a lambda expression and execute it just once?

```
fun <A: Any> myLazy(fn: () -> A): () -> A // ???
```

> Try to answer without the support of IntelliJ, and check your solutions in Appendix D or the challenge project.

Memoization

In the previous chapter, you learned that a pure function always produces the same result for the same input values, a concept known as **referential transparency**. A pure function also doesn't have any side effects, and this makes it **idempotent**. Because of this, you don't need to run the same pure function multiple times! You simply run it once and store the result for later invocations, saving time at the cost of some memory. Of course, the advantage is bigger if the computation takes some time.

You already learned how to implement memoization with Kotlin using the `lazy` function. It would be a good exercise to implement memoization for any function of type Fun<A, B>. How would you implement it?

> **Note**: You can try to solve this problem on your own as a fun exercise before looking at the proposed solution. :]

Open the initially empty **Memoization.kt** file and write the following code:

```
fun <A, B> Fun<A, B>.memo(): Fun<A, B> { // 1
  val cache by lazy { mutableMapOf<A, B>() } // 2
  return { a: A ->  // 3
    val cached = cache[a] // 4
    if (cached == null) {
      cache[a] = this(a)
    }
    cache[a]!! // 5
  }
}
```

In this code, you:

1. Define memo as an extension function for Fun<A, B>. The return type is still Fun<A, B>. Remember Fun<A, B> is an alias of the type (A) -> B.

2. Use lazy to define MutableMap<A, B>, which will store the values to cache. In this case, lazy allows you to create just one instance of the cache in a lazy way.

3. Return a lambda accepting a parameter of type A. This is a lambda of type Fun<A, B>.

4. Check in the cache to see if you already have a result for the given input a. If not, you invoke the function and store the result.

5. Now you have the result, cached or not, to return.

To test this function, write this simple code:

```
fun main() {
  val testFunction = { a: Int -> println("Evaluating... $a"); a
* 2 } // 1
  println("Running testFunction 4 times")
  testFunction(2) // 2
  testFunction(2)
  testFunction(2)
  testFunction(3)
  val memoTestingFunction = testFunction.memo() // 3
  println("Running memoTestingFunction 4 times")
  memoTestingFunction(2) // 4
  memoTestingFunction(2)
  memoTestingFunction(2)
```

```
    memoTestingFunction(3)
}
```

In this code, you:

1. Define a simple `testFunction` that returns double the input `Int`, printing a message to give evidence of the actual invocation.

2. Invoke `testFunction` four times. The first three times, you use the input 2, passing 3 instead in the last invocation.

3. Use memo to get the memoized version of `testFunction` you save in `memoTestingFunction`.

4. Invoke `memoTestingFunction` four times using the same parameters you used earlier for `testFunction`.

Run the code, and you get:

```
Running testFunction 4 times
Evaluating... 2
Evaluating... 2
Evaluating... 2
Evaluating... 3
Running memoTestingFunction 4 times
Evaluating... 2
Evaluating... 3
```

As you see, you have an output message every time you invoke `testFunction`. When you invoke `memoTestingFunction`, you have a message only the first time you pass a specific input value. This is exactly what you expect from memo.

Create a lazy stream with Kotlin

You learned that a lambda expression allows you to run some code — or evaluate some expression — later. This makes lambda expressions perfect for generating some sequences of values. Suppose you want to create a function returning the first N even numbers. A first, eager solution is the following. Add this to **Stream.kt**:

```
fun eagerEvenSequence(n: Int): List<Int> = List(n) { i -> i *
2 }
```

In this simple function, you create a List<Int> using the constructor List provides. It requires the size of the List and a lambda expression invoked for each element, which returns the value given its index. So far, so good. This solution has some problems, though:

1. The eagerEvenSequence function returns a List with all the values you might need. Here, the "might" is important because you *might not* need all of them.

2. If you just need the last value, you have to get the complete List first anyway.

3. If you need more values, you must invoke eagerEvenSequence with a new input value.

You can see all this by running the following code:

```
fun main() {
  println(eagerEvenSequence(5))
}
```

The output is:

```
[0, 2, 4, 6, 8]
```

In this case, the example is very simple, but in other cases, it might be useful to get a value of the sequence only *if* you really need it and *when* you really need it.

Next, add the following code to the same **Stream.kt** file:

```
fun evenPositiveStream(): () -> Int { // 1
  var count = -2 // 2
  return { count += 2; count } // 3
}
```

In this code, you:

1. Define evenPositiveStream as a function returning another function of type () -> Int, which provides an even Int value every time you invoke it.

2. Initialize count to -2. This weird initial value allows you to make the following line shorter and still return 0 as the first value after you add 2.

3. You return a lambda expression that adds 2 to count and returns the new value.

You can test the previous code by adding this to the same file:

```
fun main() {
  val evenSequence = evenPositiveStream() // 1
  5.times { // 2
    println(evenSequence())
  }
}
```

In `main`, you:

1. Create `evenSequence`, invoking `evenPositiveStream`.

2. Use the `times` utility function you find in **Utils.kt** to invoke `evenSequence` five times.

The output you get is:

```
0
2
4
6
8
```

More importantly:

1. You can persist the values of the sequence only if you really need them.

2. If you need more values, just invoke `evenSequence` more times.

> **Note**: You might argue that in the case of `eagerEvenSequence`, you could just return double the input parameter. This is true, but, as the next exercise proves, you're not always so lucky. :]

This is a very simple example of how lazy evaluation with lambda expressions allows you to create sequences in an optimal way.

> **Exercise 4.6**: Can you create a function `fibo` returning the values of a Fibonacci sequence? Remember, every value in a Fibonacci sequence is the sum of the previous two elements. The first two elements are 0 and 1. The first values are, then:

```
0  1  1  2  3  5  8  13  21 ...
```

Try to answer without the support of IntelliJ, and check your solutions in
Appendix D or the challenge project.

Normal-order evaluation

Note: The following two sections are optional. They give you some
information about the **normal-order evaluation** used by languages like
Haskell, in case you're curious to know more. If you're not curious, you can
skip right to the challenges.

At the beginning of the chapter, you learned that Kotlin evaluates all expressions
using applicative-order evaluation. This means it evaluates the expressions you pass
as input parameters of a function before the function itself. After that, you also
learned that Kotlin allows you to implement lazy evaluation using lambda
expressions. Some other languages, like Haskell, use **normal-order evaluation**
instead. But what does that mean, and is it possible to simulate normal-order
evaluation with Kotlin?

Normal-order evaluation always reduces the leftmost, outermost reducible function
expression. This means you evaluate the function before the expression you pass as a
parameter to the same function. Kotlin doesn't have applicative-order evaluation
like Haskell, but with lazy evaluation, you can achieve something similar. Suppose
you want to reduce the same function you saw at the beginning of the chapter:

```
3 * avg(x, y)
```

You want to evaluate the function before the expression you pass as a parameter.
Open **NormalOrder.kt** and add the following:

```
fun addL(x: () -> Int, y: () -> Int): () -> Int {
  return { println("addL"); x() + y() }
}
```

addL has some interesting things to note:

- The input parameters are not executed expressions but lazily executable lambda expressions.

- You don't evaluate the expression you use as the input parameter before the evaluation of addL but as part of it.

- You use println to have evidence of addL.

- The function returns a lambda expression.

You can now apply the same logic to the following functions. Add these to the same **NormalOrder.kt** file:

```
fun tripleL(x: () -> Int): () -> Int {
  return { println("tripleL"); addL(addL(x, x), x)() }
}

fun divideL(x: () -> Int, y: () -> Int): () -> Int {
  return { println("divideL"); x() / y() }
}

fun averageL(x: () -> Int, y: () -> Int): () -> Int {
  return { println("averageL"); divideL(addL(x, y), { 2 })() }
}
```

For testing its behavior, add the following main:

```
fun main() {
  tripleL(averageL({ 2 }, { 4 }))()
}
```

When you run the previous code, you get:

```
tripleL
addL
addL
averageL
divideL
addL
averageL
divideL
addL
averageL
divideL
addL
```

Try to mimic this by applying the substitution model. In this case, you have a longer sequence than you did earlier in this chapter because you evaluate the external function on the left first.

```
tripleL(averageL({2},{4}))()
addL(addL(averageL({2},{4})),averageL({2},{4}))),averageL({2},
{4})))()
addL({averageL({2},{4})()+averageL({2},{4})()}(),averageL({2},
{4}))()
{{averageL({2},{4})()+averageL({2},{4})()}()+averageL({2},{4})
()}()
{{{divideL(addL({2},{4}),2)}()+averageL({2},{4})()}()
+averageL({2},{4})()}()
{{addL({2},{4})()/2}()+averageL({2},{4})()}()+averageL({2},{4})
()}()
{{addL({2},{4})()/2}()+averageL({2},{4})()}()+averageL({2},{4})
()}()
{{(2+4)/2}()+averageL({2},{4})()}()+averageL({2},{4})()}()
{{(2+4)/2}()+{{divideL(addL({2},{4}),2)}()+averageL({2},{4})()}
()
{{(2+4)/2}()+{addL({2},{4})()/2}()+averageL({2},{4})()}()
{{(2+4)/2}()+{(2+4)/2}()+averageL({2},{4})()}()
{{(2+4)/2}()+{(2+4)/2}()+{{divideL(addL({2},{4}),2)}()}()
{{(2+4)/2}()+{(2+4)/2}()+{addL({2},{4})()/2}() }()
{{(2+4)/2}()+{(2+4)/2}()+{(2+4)/2}()}()
{3+3+3}()
{9}()
```

As you can see, the leftmost function is the one you're evaluating in each step.

Applicative-order vs. normal-order evaluations

Looking at the previous examples and considering how Kotlin works, you understand how lazy evaluation is a balanced compromise between applicative-order and normal-order evaluation strategies. It allows you to control where to define your expression and when to evaluate it. If you use the Kotlin lazy function, you also get the benefit of memoization, which is very good in the case of expensive — and pure — functions.

In particular, using the Kotlin lazy function, you get three different **synchronization modes** for free through the LazyThreadSafetyMode enum class. With this, you can decide how a lazy instance synchronizes initialization among multiple threads.

Possible values are:

- **SYNCHRONIZED**: The initialization is safe because only a single thread at a time can access the lambda expression you pass as a parameter. This is the default mode.

- **PUBLICATION**: The lambda expression you pass as a parameter can be evaluated several times on concurrent access to an uninitialized lazy instance value. However, only the first returned value will be used as the actual value.

- **NONE**: The lambda expression can be evaluated multiple times from different threads, and its behavior is undefined.

In the last example, you might have the impression that normal-order evaluates the same expressions multiple times, which is a problem that lazy evaluation solves elegantly. On the other hand, applicative-order evaluation doesn't always work well with recursion. If the function you pass as a parameter is recursive, it might not end. Or the expression could never return, like in this example you can write in **EvalExamples.kt**:

```kotlin
fun neverEnding(): Int { // 1
  while (true){}
}

fun double(x: Int): Int = x + x // 2

fun main() {
  double(neverEnding()) // 3
}
```

In this code, you:

1. Define `neverEnding` using an infinite loop as a function that never returns.

2. Create `double` as a simple function returning the double of its input parameter.

3. Define `main`, which simply uses `neverEnding` invocation as an input parameter of `double`.

Run this code, and the program will never complete.

Challenges

In this chapter, you learned many important concepts about expression evaluation, lambda functions and lazy evaluation. You've already done some interesting exercises, but here you have some additional challenges. Have fun! :]

Challenge 1: Handling nullability

In Exercise 4.5, you created myLazy, which allowed you to implement memoization for a generic lambda expression of type () -> A. Can you now create myNullableLazy, supporting optional types with the following signature?

```
fun <A> myNullableLazy(fn: () -> A?): () -> A? // ...
```

Challenge 2: Functions and set again

You might be aware of **Euler's number e**. It's a mathematical constant of huge importance that you can calculate in very different ways. It's an irrational number like **pi** that can't be represented in the form n/m. Here, you're not required to know what it is, but you can use the following formula:

$$e = \sum_{n=0}^{\infty} \frac{1}{n!} = 1 + \frac{1}{1} + \frac{1}{1 \cdot 2} + \frac{1}{1 \cdot 2 \cdot 3} + \cdots$$

Figure 4.2: Euler's formula

Can you create a sequence that provides the sum of the n terms of the given formula?

Key points

- You define **evaluation strategy** as the relationship between the point in your code where you define your expression and the point when the expression is actually evaluated.

- With **applicative-order evaluation**, a function is executed only when all the expressions you pass as input parameters are evaluated, starting from the **leftmost** parameter.

- A **lambda expression** is an anonymous function you can use as a value.

- **Type inference** is the mechanism a compiler uses to understand the element types involved in an expression.

- The type of lambda expression is a **function type**.

- A lambda expression is **contravariant** for the input type and **covariant** for the output type.

- **Memoization** is the process that allows you to save the result of a function in memory to reuse it more efficiently.

- **Pure functions** can always be memoized.

- **Pure evaluation** allows you to easily implement infinite sequences of values in a very efficient way.

Where to go from here?

Congratulations! You've completed another challenging chapter about expression evaluation and lambda functions. You had the chance to solve some fun exercises, and you've already started implementing some higher-order functions — which is the topic of the next chapter. See you there. :]

Chapter 5: Higher-Order Functions

In the previous chapters, you learned that a lambda expression is basically a function that can be used as a value. This means you can define a lambda expression and assign it to a variable. More importantly, you can pass a lambda expression as an input parameter or return the value of another function. Passing lambdas as parameters describes **higher-order functions**, which are the main topic of this chapter.

Here, you'll learn:

- The difference between an **imperative** and **declarative** approach.

- What **higher-order functions** are.

- What a **functional interface** is and what **SAM** means.

- Why interfaces with a single operation are fundamental in functional programming.

- How **inline** works when using higher-order functions.

You'll learn all this while using the Kotlin language and solving some fun exercises. Open up the starter project for this chapter in IntelliJ and keep reading.

Imperative vs. declarative approach

Before diving into the study of higher-order functions in Kotlin, it's important to mention why they're fundamental and why you should use them. One of the main reasons is that higher-order functions allow you to write your code in a **declarative** way.

But what does that mean? An example will make things easier.

Consider the following list of email address candidates that you'll find in **Imperative.kt** in this chapter's material:

```
val emails = listOf(
  "email@emmmaail.com",
  "max@fgh.it",
  "hsajdkjshh",
  "mike@mcarli.it",
  "first.second@ggg.com",
  "test@test.co.uk",
  "12345@qqq.com",
  "123.45",
  "12345@a.b.c.d",
  "fp_is_great@funprog.com",
  "aaaaaaaaa.bbbbb@cccc.com",
  "aaaaaaacccc.com",
  "valid@jjjj.lll",
)
```

Now, suppose you want to write a function that:

1. Filters invalid email addresses.

2. Uses only email addresses with more than 10 characters.

3. Takes just the first five valid email addresses.

A first approach is the imperative one. In the same **Imperative.kt** file, write the following code:

```
fun imperative(emails: List<String>): List<String> = // 1
  mutableListOf<String>() // 2
    .apply {
      for (email in emails) { // 3
        if (EMAIL_REG_EX.matches(email) && email.length > 10)
{ // 4
          add(email)
          if (size >= 5) { // 5
            break
          }
```

```
        }
      }
    }
```

In this code, you:

1. Define `imperative` as a function that returns the first five valid email addresses longer than 10 characters.

2. Initialize the `List` you'll return as the result.

3. Iterate over all the email addresses in input.

4. Check if the email is valid using the available regular expression `EMAIL_REG_EX`. Here, you also check if the email has a minimum length of over 10.

5. Stop when it gets 5 email addresses.

Now, add and run this:

```
fun main() {
    println(imperative(emails))
}
```

And you get the following output:

```
[email@emmmaail.com, mike@mcarli.it, first.second@ggg.com,
test@test.co.uk, fp_is_great@funprog.com]
```

This is an example of an **imperative approach** or **algorithmic programming**. Here, you write the code specifying the steps the computer must take to accomplish the goal. In this case, you're telling the computer exactly what steps to execute in a language it understands. If you want to change the criteria for filtering the emails, you need to first digest the code, apply the changes and update the unit tests. In this case, the goal you want to achieve is simple, but in many other cases, this could be a problem.

> **Note**: For an even more imperative approach, you can replace the enhanced `for` loop:

```
for (email in emails){...}
```

With:

```
for (i in 0 until email.size){
  val email = emails[i]
  // ...
}
```

The declarative approach is closer to how humans think. Now, add the following code to **Declarative.kt**:

```
fun declarative(emails: List<String>): List<String> = // 1
  emails
    .filter { EMAIL_REG_EX.matches(it) } // 2
    .filter { it.length > 10 } // 3
    .take(5) // 4
```

In this case, you:

1. Define `declarative` with the same signature as `imperative`.

2. Use `filter` to remove the invalid email addresses.

3. Use `filter` again to remove email addresses shorter than or equal to 10 characters.

4. Take the first 5 email addresses using `take`.

Now, add and run the following code:

```
fun main() {
  println(declarative(emails))
}
```

And you get exactly the same output:

```
[email@emmmaail.com, mike@mcarli.it, first.second@ggg.com,
test@test.co.uk, fp_is_great@funprog.com]
```

When you look at the code, you realize it's just a description of the steps you want to do, which follows the initial requirements. You *take* five email addresses from the ones you *filtered* because they matched the email regular expression and were longer than 10 characters. You might already see some of the declarative approach's advantages, but you can do even better than this.

Code readability

The declarative approach improves code readability. In the same **Declarative.kt** file, add the following code:

```
fun isEmailValid(email: String) = // 1
  EMAIL_REG_EX.matches(email)

fun isEmailLongEnough(email: String) = // 2
  email.length > 10

fun moreDeclarative(emails: List<String>): List<String> =
  emails
    .filter(::isEmailValid) // 3
    .filter(::isEmailLongEnough) // 4
    .take(5)
```

In this case, you:

1. Define isEmailValid, which is a pure function that checks if the input email address is valid.

2. Create isEmailLongEnough to check the length of the email address.

3. Use the reference ::isEmailValid as the parameter of the first filter.

4. Use ::isEmailLongEnough as the parameter of the second filter.

This is so declarative that you can read the code as if it were in normal, spoken English. You basically:

```
filter the valid emails
filter the emails that are long enough
take 5 of them
```

filter is a perfect example of a higher-order function, because it's a function that accepts another function as an input parameter. Look at the source code for filter, and you'll find the following:

```
public inline fun <T> Iterable<T>.filter(
  predicate: (T) -> Boolean
): List<T> {
  return filterTo(ArrayList<T>(), predicate)
}
```

Besides the implementation details, it's important to see how:

1. It's an extension function for `Iterable<T>`.

2. The input parameter is a predicate of type `(T) -> Boolean`. As you learned in Chapter 2, "Function Fundamentals", a predicate is any function that returns a `Boolean`. In this case, the predicate is a lambda accepting an object of type `T` as input, which is the type parameter for `Iterable<T>`.

In the rest of the book, you'll see many examples of this, and you'll see how functional programming and the declarative approach get along. :]

Higher-order functions

By now you should know what a higher-order function is — you've already written some of them. The most important one you saw in Chapter 2, "Function Fundamentals" is:

```
inline infix fun <A, B, C> Fun<B, C>.after(
    crossinline f: Fun<A, B>
): Fun<A, C> = { a: A ->
    this(f(a)) // HERE
}
```

This is an extension function on `Fun<B, C>`, which receives as input another function of type `Fun<A, B>` and returns a function of type `Fun<A, C>`, which is the composition of the two.

In this next section, you'll see some more examples of higher-order functions, which:

• Accept a lambda expression as input.

• Return a lambda expression as an output value.

• Use lambda expressions as input and as output values.

You'll also make everything fun with some nice exercises.

Accepting a lambda expression as input

You've already met one example of a higher-order function accepting a lambda expression as input. Now to write more. Open **SimpleHoF.kt** in the material for this project, and write the following code:

```
fun Int.times(fn: (Int) -> Unit) = (1..this).forEach(fn)
```

This function executes the lambda the provided number of times. In this code, you define:

- `times` as an extension function for the `Int` type.

- `fn` as an input parameter of type `(Int) -> Unit`, which is invoked the number of times described by the receiver. Remember that, in this case, the receiver is the `Int` value you invoke `times` on. In the case of `10.times{}`, the receiver is `10`.

- The range as `1..this`, and you iterate over it using `forEach` to execute `fn` that number of times.

You can test how `times` works by adding and running this:

```
fun main() {
  10.times {
    print(" $it")
  }
}
```

The output you get is:

```
 1 2 3 4 5 6 7 8 9 10
```

You probably think that, with the previous code, you cheated a little bit. :] `forEach` is another higher-order function Kotlin provides as an extension function for `Iterable<T>`, like the `filter` you met earlier:

```
public inline fun <T> Iterable<T>.forEach(action: (T) -> Unit):
Unit {
    for (element in this) action(element)
}
```

OK, assuming you don't want to use an existing higher-order function, you can replace the previous implementation with the following imperative-ish code:

```
fun Int.times(fn: (Int) -> Unit) {
  var i = 1
  while (i <= this) {
    fn(i++)
  }
}
```

When you run `main`, you get the same output:

```
1 2 3 4 5 6 7 8 9 10
```

Exercise 5.1: Kotlin provides you with `first`, which returns the first element of `Iterable<T>` for which a predicate you provide in input evaluates to `true`. Remember that `Iterable<T>` is the abstraction of all the collections providing `Iterator<T>` implementation.

```
public interface Iterable<out T> {
  public operator fun iterator(): Iterator<T>
}
```

`Iterator<T>` allows you to iterate over all the elements of a collection in a way that doesn't depend on the collection implementation itself:

```
public interface Iterator<out T> {

  public operator fun next(): T

  public operator fun hasNext(): Boolean
}
```

The current `first` signature is:

```
public inline fun <T> Iterable<T>.first(predicate: (T) ->
Boolean): T
```

Kotlin doesn't allow you to override the current extension function on
Iterable<T>. So, how would you implement first on Array<T>?

The current implementation of first throws an exception if the collection is
empty, so there's no first T. How would you implement the function
firstOrNull on Array<T> returning null in such a case?

Give it a try and check the challenge project or Appendix E to see how you did.

Implementing the strategy pattern in a functional way

Hey, isn't this a book about functional programming? What does the **strategy
pattern** (https://en.wikipedia.org/wiki/Strategy_pattern) have to do with this? As
you know, design patterns describe a general and reusable solution to a commonly
occurring problem within a given context. In particular, the strategy pattern is a
behavioral pattern that defines a family of algorithms, encapsulates each one and
makes them interchangeable. Sorting is a typical example. Open **Strategy.kt** and
write the following code:

```
fun bubbleSort(values: IntArray) {
  for (i in values.size - 1 downTo 0) {
    for (j in 0 until i) {
      if (values[j] > values[j + 1]) {
        swap(values, j, j + 1)
      }
    }
  }
}
```

This function sorts an input IntArray using the bubble sort. Understanding how it's
sorting is less important here than knowing that it's sorting Ints. Note, the swap
function is already available in **Util.kt**.

You can test how it works by executing the following:

```
fun main() {
  val array = intArrayOf(10, 5, 2, 7, 8, 3)
  bubbleSort(array)
  array.printAll()
}
```

printAll is a function in **Util.kt**. Run this code, and you get what you expect:

```
2 3 5 7 8 10
```

It's important to note that you can use the bubble sort to sort anything, not just Int. What you need is just a way to understand when a value is greater than another value of the same type. How, then, can you abstract bubbleSort so you can use it with any array of values of type T?

> **Note**: The bubble sort definitely isn't the most performant sorting algorithm. It's used here because it does not need a lot of code.

> **Note**: If you want to learn more about algorithm and data structures in Kotlin, Data Structures & Algorithms in Kotlin (https://www.raywenderlich.com/books/data-structures-algorithms-in-kotlin) is the best choice.

To solve this problem, you need to:

• Make bubbleSort generic.

• Provide bubbleSort what it's missing: a way to understand if one T is greater than another T.

In the same file, replace the previous code with the following:

```kotlin
fun <T> bubbleSort(
  values: Array<T>, // 1
  isLarger: (T, T) -> Boolean // 2
) {
  for (i in values.size - 1 downTo 0) {
    for (j in 0 until i) {
      if (isLarger(values[j], values[j + 1])) { // 3
        swap(values, j, j + 1) // 4
      }
    }
  }
}
```

In this code, you:

1. Define bubbleSort as a generic function with the type variable T.

2. Pass the strategy as a lambda function of type (T, T) -> Boolean, which returns true if the first value is greater than the second.

3. Use the isLarger lambda expression to compare each pair of values in the array.

4. Swap the values, if needed, using the swap overload you find in **Util.kt**.

To test the previous code, write:

```
fun main() {
  val array = arrayOf(10, 5, 2, 7, 8, 3)
  bubbleSort(array) { first, second ->
    first > second
  }
  array.printAll()
}
```

Run this code, and you again get:

```
 2 3 5 7 8 10
```

Exercise 5.2: The command pattern (https://en.wikipedia.org/wiki/Command_pattern) is another important design pattern that defines abstractions like Command and CommandExecutor. Command abstracts every possible operation that CommandExecutor can run. In other words, a Command represents a task and you can pass a Command to a CommandExecutor to run it. How would you represent them in a functional way?

Optionally, can you also provide a way to "redo" the most recent Command?

Functional interfaces

In the previous chapters, you learned the concept of **function type**. If you consider the previous strategy pattern example, you could've defined the type for the predicate parameter using `typealias`, like this:

```
typealias IsLarger<T> = (T, T) -> Boolean
```

With this, the bubble sort example would become:

```
fun <T> bubbleSort(
  values: Array<T>,
  isLarger: IsLarger<T> // HERE
) {
  for (i in values.size - 1 downTo 0) {
    for (j in 0 until i) {
      if (isLarger(values[j], values[j + 1])) {
        swap(values, j, j + 1)
      }
    }
  }
}
```

As you learned in Chapter 2, "Function Fundamentals", a function type is basically a way to represent a function in terms of:

• Input parameters and their type

• Return type

With `(T, T) -> Boolean`, you're basically representing the type of all the functions with two parameters of type T returning a Boolean. With the `typealias` keyword, you just gave that type the name `IsLarger<T>`.

Kotlin allows you to do something similar with **functional interfaces**. You find the same concept with the acronym **SAM**, which stands for **single abstract method**. For instance, open **FunctionalInterface.kt** and write the following definition:

```
fun interface IsLarger<T> { // 1
  fun isLarger(a: T, b: T): Boolean // 2
}
```

In this case, you:

1. Use the `fun` keyword as a qualifier for the `IsLarger<T>` interface.

2. Define `isLarger` as the only abstract function for the functional interface.

Using the previous definition, you can add the following code to the same file:

```
fun <T> bubbleSortFI( // 1
  values: Array<T>,
  largerStrategy: IsLarger<T> // 2
) {
  for (i in values.size - 1 downTo 0) {
    for (j in 0 until i) {
      if (largerStrategy.isLarger(values[j], values[j + 1]))
{ // 3
        swap(values, j, j + 1)
      }
    }
  }
}
```

In this case, you:

1. Create `bubbleSortFI` as a new version of the previous `bubbleSort`.

2. Define the strategy as a parameter of type `IsLarger<T>`.

3. Invoke `isLarger`, which is the operation you defined in `IsLarger<T>`.

Now, you can test `bubbleSortFI` in two different ways:

- Using `IsLarger<T>` as a normal lambda expression.

- Creating an `IsLarger<T>` implementation instance.

It's useful to look at both.

Functional interface as a lambda expression

Because you defined `IsLarger<T>` as a functional interface, you can use the same syntax you'd use with lambda expressions. Add the following code to the same **FunctionalInterface.kt** file:

```
fun main() {
  val array = arrayOf(10, 5, 2, 7, 8, 3)
  bubbleSortFI(array) { first, second -> // HERE
    first > second
  }
  array.printAll()
}
```

Here, you pass the parameter of type `IsLarger<T>` as a normal lambda expression the same way you did when using `typealias`.

Functional interface instances

Again, because you defined `IsLarger<T>` as a functional interface, Kotlin provides a very handy syntax in case you want to create an implementation instance of the fly. Replace the previous code in **FunctionalInterface.kt** with:

```
fun main() {
  val array = arrayOf(10, 5, 2, 7, 8, 3)
  val largerStrategy = IsLarger<Int> { first, second -> // HERE
    first > second
  }
  bubbleSortFI(array, largerStrategy)
  array.printAll()
}
```

Like in the previous example, although `IsLarger<T>` is an interface, you can quickly create an implementation instance using a syntax like:

```
FunctionInterfaceType { /* Lambda expression for the SAM */}
```

So, what's the difference between the definition of a function type using `typealias` and a functional interface?

Functional interface vs. typealias

It's crucial to note how `typealias` doesn't introduce a new type at all. It just allows you to give a different name to an existing type. On the other hand, when you define a **functional interface**, you're creating a *new type*.

> **Note**: Remember that `typealias` definitions aren't visible from Java.

The difference between a simple interface and a functional interface is the presence of a **single abstract method (SAM)**, which you provide using the same syntax you use for lambda expressions.

To better understand their differences, open **FunctionalVsLambda.kt** and add the following code:

```
typealias SinglePredicate<T> = (T) -> Boolean // 1

fun <T> SinglePredicate<T>.whoAmI() = println("I'm a typealias")
// 2
```

```
fun main() {
  val isEven = { number: Int -> number % 2 == 0 } // 3
  isEven.whoAmI() // 4
}
```

Here, you just:

1. Give the name `SinglePredicate<T>` to any function receiving a single parameter of type `T` and returning a `Boolean`.

2. Define `whoAmI` as an extension function for `SinglePredicate<T>`, which just prints a message saying that the receiver type is `typealias`.

3. Define the `isEven` lambda, which returns `true` if an `Int` value you pass as a parameter is even. Note how you're just creating a lambda with no relation to the name `SinglePredicate<T>` you defined earlier. It's just a lambda receiving an `Int` and returning a `Boolean`.

4. Invoke `whoAmI` on the previous lambda.

Compile and run the previous code, getting:

```
I'm a typealias
```

This is because the definition of `whoAmI` above would be exactly the same as:

```
fun <T> ((T) -> Boolean).whoAmI() =
  println("I'm a typealias")
```

Now, add the following code to the same file, replacing the existing `main` function:

```
fun interface ISinglePredicate<T> { // 1

  fun accept(value: T): Boolean // 2

  fun other() { // 3
    println("I can have other methods")
  }
}

fun <T> ISinglePredicate<T>.whoAmI() = // 4
  println("I'm a functional interface")

fun main() {
  val isEvenFI = ISinglePredicate<Int> { number -> number % 2 ==
0 } // 5
  isEvenFI.whoAmI() // 6
  isEvenFI.other() // 7
}
```

In this case, you:

1. Create ISinglePredicate<T> as a functional interface.

2. Define accept as the single abstract method for ISinglePredicate<T>.

3. Also define other, proving that a functional interface must have one and only one abstract method, but it can also have other methods. A small note about these methods later.

4. Create the same extension method, whoAmI, which prints the fact that this is about a functional interface.

5. Create isEvenFI as an ISinglePredicate<Int> implementation using the handy syntax mentioned earlier, recalling the lambda expressions.

6. Invoke whoAmI on isEvenFI.

7. Also invoke other on the same isEvenFI.

When you run this code, you get:

```
I'm a functional interface
I can have other methods
```

This proves that a functional interface is conceptually very similar to a function type you define using typealias, but it:

1. Allows you to define a new type.

2. Is more type-safe because, like in the previous example, it allows you to define extension methods for a very specific type of function. The whoAmI on the type alias works for *any* function with one parameter returning Boolean. The whoAmI on ISinglePredicate<Int> works just on instances of the same explicit type.

3. Allows you to define one and only one operation. The others can be methods working as default method implementations for an interface.

4. Invokes the abstract method of the functional interface. To achieve this, you need to state its name explicitly. With the function you define using typealias, you just use ( ) or invoke. With ISinglePredicate<T>, you need to call accept.

Note: In theory, an interface doesn't define any **methods** but just **operations**, which are public and abstract by definition. When you read the method of the interface, it means methods adding something more to the one the interface defines through its operations. An example of this is:

```
interface Reader {
  fun readChar(): Char?
  fun readString(): String {
    TODO("Call readChar() until it returns null")
  }
}
```

Here, `readChar` is the operation and `readString` is the method.

Exercise 5.3: Can you implement `Reader` in the previous note using a function interface? How would you test it?

Interfaces with multiple operations or methods

Exercise 5.3 should make you think about the relationship between functional programming and the concept of interfaces with multiple operations. Why do you think interfaces with a single operation (SAM) are so important?

The answer is very simple, and it can be summarized with the concepts you find in the **SOLID principles**. You won't revisit all of them here because it's not the main topic, but just think about the meaning of the I there, which stands for the interface segregation principle (https://en.wikipedia.org/wiki/Interface_segregation_principle).

This basically states that *no clients should be forced to depend on methods they don't use*. Functional interfaces, or lambda expressions, define a single operation and make it impossible for clients to depend on the lambda expressions if they don't use those functions.

At this point, you might argue that using just SAM would make it difficult to implement interfaces like Reader. That's not the case at all — and you'll prove it. :] Open **Solid.kt** and add the following code to define CharReader as the interface with the sole responsibility of providing a single Char at a time.

```
fun interface CharReader {
  fun readChar(): Char?
}
```

If you need to read a String, you can use the most fundamental principle of functional programming: **composition**. In the same file, add the following code:

```
fun interface StringReader {
  fun readString(charReader: CharReader): String
}
```

With this, you can implement StringReader by adding some code that's basically the same as what you probably implemented in Exercise 5.3:

```
val stringReader = StringReader { charReader ->
  val result = StringBuilder()
  do {
    val nextChar = charReader.readChar()
    if (nextChar != null) {
      result.append(nextChar)
    }
  } while (nextChar != null)
  result.toString()
}
```

To make everything more functional, add:

```
fun String.toCharReader(): CharReader {
  var pos = 0
  return CharReader {
    if (pos < this.length) this[pos++] else null
  }
}
```

This is an extension function on String returning a CharReader you can use like this:

```
fun main() {
  println(stringReader.readString("This is
String!".toCharReader()))
}
```

Run this code, and you get:

```
This is String!
```

In this single line of code, you:

1. Create `CharReader` from `String`.

2. Use `stringReader` to read `String` back from `CharReader`.

3. Print `String`.

Thinking functionally, you managed to apply the interface segregation principle, splitting `Reader` into two different functional interfaces, `CharReader` and `StringReader`, reducing the dependency drastically.

> **Note**: In Chapter 8, "Composition", you'll also learn to improve that code further. It has too many parentheses `()` and can be made more readable.

Returning a lambda expression as an output value

The return value of a higher-order function can also be a function. Open **ReturnFunction.kt** and write the following code:

```
fun countFrom(start: Int): () -> Int { // 1
  var count = start // 2
  return { // 3
    count++
  }
}
```

This function:

1. Has an input parameter of type `Int` and returns a function of type `() -> Int`.

2. Initializes `count` to the value of the `start` parameter.

3. Returns a function that returns `count` and then increments its value.

You can test `countFrom` with the following code:

```
fun main() {
  val countFromFive = countFrom(5)
```

```
    println(countFromFive())
    println(countFromFive())
    println(countFromFive())
}
```

Run it, and you get:

```
5
6
7
```

As you see, `countFrom` initializes `count`, which is then captured by the lambda it returns. All the variables outside the scope of a lambda function that the lambda can access represent its **closure**.

As in the previous example where `count` is incremented, the lambda can access its closure and, if not constant, can also modify it.

Exercise 5.4: Implement an extension function `isEqualsPredicate` on the generic type T that returns a predicate that tests if a given value is equal to the same T. The signature should be the following:

```
fun <T> T.isEqualsPredicate(): (T) -> Boolean
```

How would the same function be different if you use the following functional interface?

```
fun interface SinglePredicate<T> {
  fun accept(other: T): Boolean
}
```

Using lambda expressions as input and output

Functions with a lambda both as a return value and as an input parameter are the most interesting and *fun* (pun intended :]). You've actually seen many of these, and you'll find many more ahead in the book.

As a simple example here, you can keep playing with `Predicate`. Open **Predicates.kt** and write the following code:

```
fun interface Predicate1<T> {
    fun accept(value: T): Boolean
}
```

> **Note**: In this chapter, to make different examples coexist in the same project, sometimes you need to use a different name for the same concept. That's why you append 1 to `Predicate` here. Of course, you wouldn't do the same in your project.

This is a single functional interface for a predicate with a single parameter you've already met many times, such as during Exercise 5.4. Imagine, now, that you want to create a function and that accepts as input two `Predicate1<T>`s and returns another one, which is the **logical and** of the two. To be true, *both* predicates must be true.

You already know how to do this. In the same **Predicates.kt** file, add the following code:

```
infix fun <T> Predicate1<T>.and(
    other: Predicate1<T>
): Predicate1<T> = // 1
    Predicate1 { value ->
        this.accept(value) && other.accept(value) // 2
    }
```

In this code, you simply:

1. Create an infix extension function and on `Predicate1<T>`.

2. Return another `Predicate1<T>`, which evaluates the first one and, if true, `other`.

In the same way, define or like this:

```
infix fun <T> Predicate1<T>.or(
  other: Predicate1<T>
): Predicate1<T> =
  Predicate1 { value ->
    this.accept(value) || other.accept(value)
  }
```

You can use the same approach used in Exercise 5.4 with the following code:

```
fun <T> T.isEqualsPredicate1(): Predicate1<T> = // 1
  Predicate1 { value -> this == value }

fun <T> Iterable<T>.filterWithPredicate(predicate:
Predicate1<T>) = // 2
  filter(predicate::accept)

fun main() {
  val predicate = 4.isEqualsPredicate1() or
5.isEqualsPredicate1()   // 3
  listOf(1, 2, 3, 4, 4, 5, 6, 7, 8, 8)
    .filterWithPredicate(predicate) // 4
    .forEach(::println)
}
```

In this code, you:

1. Define isEqualsPredicate1 using Predicate1<T>.

2. Create filterWithPredicate on Iterable<T> for filtering values using Predicate1<T> instead of (T) -> Boolean.

3. Use the or you created earlier to create Predicate1<T> for filtering values 4 and 5.

4. Use filterWithPredicate with predicate.

Run this code, and you get:

```
4
4
5
```

This is really fun!

Exercise 5.5: Can you implement the same logic for implementing the example in the **Imperative vs. declarative approach** section using the definitions of Predicate1<T> and filterWithPredicate? Given a list of email addresses, you need to:

· Filter the valid email addresses.

· Filter the email addresses that are long enough.

· Take the first five of them.

Give it a try and check the solution in Appendix E.

Higher-order functions and the inline keyword

In Chapter 3, "Functional Programming Concepts", you learned about the convenience of using an **inline** keyword for lambda expressions or pure functions in general. When you just inline a pure function, IntelliJ warns you about the *insignificant* performance benefits. The same message also mentions that this isn't the same if the lambda was passed as an input parameter to a higher-order function. What does the compiler mean by this?

Open **Inline.kt** and add the following code:

```
fun executor(fn: () -> Unit) {
    fn()
}

fun main() {
    executor { println("Hello World!") }
}
```

In this very simple code, you:

1. Define executor, which just executes the lambda you pass as an input parameter.

2. Invoke executor in main.

In this case, you don't need to run this code, but repeat the same process you followed in Chapter 3, "Functional Programming Concepts" for the Kotlin decompiled code.

When you do so, you end up with something like this:

```
public final class InlineKt {
   public static final void executor(@NotNull Function0 fn) { //
1
      Intrinsics.checkNotNullParameter(fn, "fn");
      fn.invoke();
   }

   public static final void main() {
      executor((Function0)null.INSTANCE); // 2
   }

   // $FF: synthetic method
   public static void main(String[] var0) {
      main();
   }
}
```

As you see:

1. `executor` becomes a Java static method with `Function0` as an input parameter.

2. `main` contains the simple invocation of `executor`.

This is what you'd normally expect. Now, just add the `inline` keyword to `executor` like this:

```
inline fun executor(fn: () -> Unit) { // HERE
   fn()
}
```

The first thing to note is that the IntelliJ warning you got in Chapter 3 doesn't show up.

```
33       inline fun executor(fn: () -> Unit) {
34           fn()
35       }
```

Figure 5.1: No warnings from IntelliJ

Check the decompiled code, and you see that `main` becomes:

```
public static final void main() {
    int $i$f$executor = false;
    int var1 = false;
    String var2 = "Hello World!";
    boolean var3 = false;
    System.out.println(var2); // HERE
}
```

You can see how `main` no longer has an `executor` invocation. There's not even the invocation of the `fn` you pass as a parameter. The Kotlin compiler has copied the content of `fn` exactly where the previous `executor` invocation was.

The inlined `executor` is very simple, but if it contained more code, the resultant bytecode would also need much more space. On the other hand, you could return to the warning situation using the `noinline` keyword like this:

```
inline fun executor(noinline fn: () -> Unit) { // HERE
    fn()
}
```

In this case, the Kotlin compiler would complain again, like this:

```
33    inline fun executor(noinline fn: () -> Unit) {
34        fn(  Expected performance impact from inlining is insignificant. Inlining works best for functions
35    }        with parameters of functional types
36
```

Figure 5.2: Using the noinline keyword

This is because the decompiled code would be like the initial one.

Non-local returns

Inlining can be useful for another reason, though. Update the code in **Inline.kt** like the following:

```
fun executor(fn: () -> Unit) {
    fn()
}

fun main() {
    executor {
        var count = 0
        while (true) {
            count++
            if (count > 5) {
```

```
        return // ERROR
      }
    }
  }
  println("The End!")
}
```

If you don't inline `executor`, the Kotlin compiler will complain because it doesn't know from what context it should actually `return`.

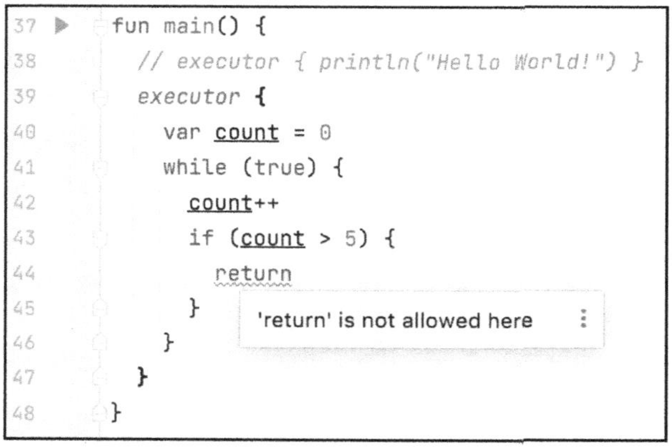

```
37 ▶    fun main() {
38          // executor { println("Hello World!") }
39          executor {
40            var count = 0
41            while (true) {
42              count++
43              if (count > 5) {
44                return
45              }        'return' is not allowed here    ⋮
46            }
47          }
48        }
```

Figure 5.3: Undefined return

Here, you have two options:

1. Use the label `return@executor` specifying that you want to exit from `executor`.

2. Inline `executor`.

In the first case, you can write:

```
fun main() {
  executor {
    var count = 0
    while (true) {
      count++
      if (count > 5) {
        return@executor
      }
    }
  }
  println("The End!")
}
```

In the second case, you can just *inline* executor like this:

```
inline fun executor(fn: () -> Unit) {
    fn()
}
```

You must be very careful, though, because the behavior of your program differs in the two cases.

When you use `return@executor`, you're saying that when you reach `return`, you're exiting from the body of `executor`. Run `main`, and you get:

```
The End!
```

If you *inline* executor, you're copying `return` in `main`, and reaching it means exiting from `main`. If you run the code, you get nothing because the `println` statement won't be reached.

The crossinline keyword

For completeness' sake, it's useful to look at the following code:

```
fun executor(fn: () -> Unit) { // 1
    fn()
}

inline fun executorExecutor(fn: () -> Unit) { // 2
    executor {
        fn() // ERROR
    }
}
```

Here, you note that:

1. executor isn't inlined.

2. executorExecutor is inlined and invokes the fn it receives as an input parameter using executor.

As you can see, the Kotlin compiler is complaining:

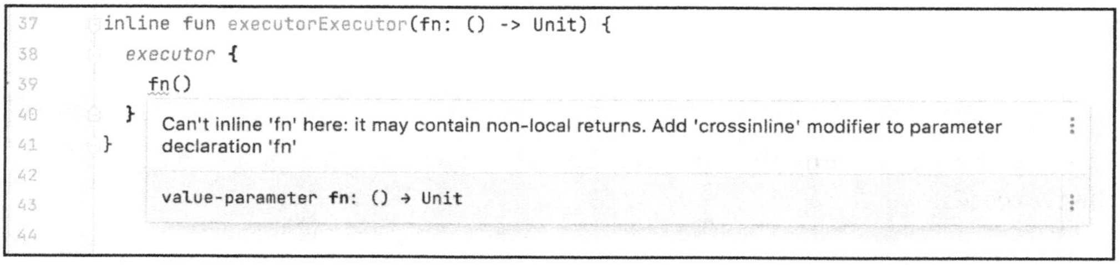

```
37    inline fun executorExecutor(fn: () -> Unit) {
38        executor {
39            fn()
40        }
             Can't inline 'fn' here: it may contain non-local returns. Add 'crossinline' modifier to parameter   ⋮
41    }       declaration 'fn'
42
43           value-parameter fn: () → Unit                                                                        ⋮
44
```

Figure 5.4: Can't inline 'fn' here; it may contain non-local returns

The message in Figure 5.4 explains everything.

The reason is that the compiler doesn't know how to handle `fn` non-local returns and suggests a solution of introducing the `crossinline` keyword to the parameter like this:

```kotlin
inline fun executorExecutor(crossinline fn: () -> Unit) {
    executor {
        fn()
    }
}
```

This informs the Kotlin compiler that the lambda you pass as an input parameter of `executorExecutor` can't contain any non-local return. If it does, you get an error:

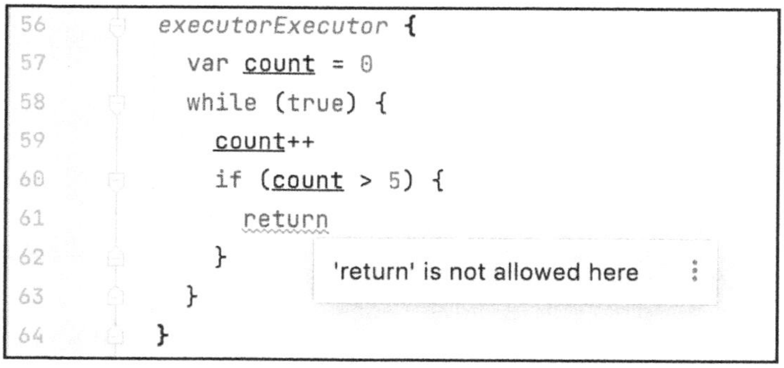

```
56    executorExecutor {
57        var count = 0
58        while (true) {
59            count++
60            if (count > 5) {
61                return
62            }           'return' is not allowed here   ⋮
63        }
64    }
```

Figure 5.5: 'return' is not allowed here

If you really want to allow `return` in `fn`, you can simply use `inline` for both executor and executorExecutor:

```
inline fun executor(fn: () -> Unit) { // HERE
  fn()
}

inline fun executorExecutor(fn: () -> Unit) { // HERE
  executor {
    fn()
  }
}
```

Challenges

In this chapter, you learned a lot about higher-order functions that are basically *functions of functions*. You've already done some interesting exercises, but now it's time for a few more challenges.

Challenge 5.1: Mapping is important

In this chapter, you learned how to implement different types of higher-order functions, and in the next chapter, you'll see many more. A very important one is called `map`. This is a function that applies a given function `fn` of type `(A) -> B` to all the elements of a collection of items of type `A`, getting a collection of items of type `B`.

Can you implement the function `map` for the `Array<A>` type with the following signature?

```
fun <A, B> Array<A>.map(fn: (A) -> B): Array<B>
```

When you run this code:

```
fun main() {
  val square = { a: Int -> a * a }
  val toString = { a: Int -> "This is $a" }
  arrayOf(1, 2, 3)
    .map(square)
    .forEach(::println)
  arrayOf(1, 2, 3)
    .map(toString)
    .forEach(::println)
}
```

You should get:

```
1
4
9
This is 1
This is 2
This is 3
```

Challenge 5.2: Prime number filtering

Write a higher-order function `all` returning a new array containing all the values in an `Array<T>` for which a given `Predicate1<T>` is true. You can find `Predicate1<T>`'s definition in **Predicates.kt**.

```
fun <T> Array<T>.all(predicate: Predicate1<T>) : Array<T>
```

Then, use it to return all the positive prime values in `Array<Int>`. A number is prime if it's not evenly divisible with any number other than 1 and itself.

Key points

- A **lambda expression** is a function you can use as a value.

- A **higher-order function** accepts other functions as input parameters or provides other functions as return values.

- The **declarative** approach makes code more readable.

- Kotlin allows you to define **functional interfaces**, which are a handy way to define interfaces with a single abstract method that can be used as lambda expressions.

- Functional interfaces are also called **SAM**, which stands for **single abstract method**.

- A **closure** of a function is the set of all the variables the function can access, which have been defined outside its own body.

- A lambda function can modify its non-constant closures.

- Always consider using the `inline` keyword for higher-order functions, but double-check that the behavior is what you expect, especially in the context of non-local returns.

- The `noinline` and `crossinline` keywords are two additional options you have to control the flow of your program when using higher-order functions.

Where to go from here?

Congratulations! In this chapter, you learned a lot about what higher-order functions are and how they can help you write your code in a more declarative way. Composition and higher-order functions are the essentials of functional programming. Right now, you're just at the beginning. In the next chapter, you'll be introduced to immutability and recursion: two important topics when using higher-order functions.

Chapter 6: Immutability & Recursion

In Chapter 5, "Higher-Order Functions", you learned everything about one of the pillars of functional programming. **Higher-order functions** don't just allow you to adopt a declarative approach for more readable code; they favor the use of pure functions with all the benefits and advantages you learned in Chapter 3, "Functional Programming Concepts".

Immutability is another fundamental principle very common in functional programming. Using **immutable objects** allows you to implement robust code, reducing errors in different situations. For instance, think of what happens when you run your code in concurrent environments, where race conditions and deadlocks are the enemies. Immutability helps reduce that risk! You'll see that creating immutable objects is relatively easy, but it comes at a cost you need to mitigate.

In this chapter, you'll learn:

- What immutability means in the context of the Kotlin language.

- What **read-only collections** are and how Kotlin uses them to simulate immutability.

- Why you'd want to pursue immutability.

- What the cost of immutability is when running code in a Java Virtual Machine (JVM).

- How immutability relates to functional programming.

- What **recursion** is and how it helps in the use of immutable objects.

- What **tail recursion** is and how it can optimize your code.

You'll learn all this by writing code in Kotlin and having some fun with interesting exercises and challenges. Open up the chapter project to get started.

Immutability

Immutability is a relatively simple concept to understand: It basically describes the process of writing your code using immutable objects. An immutable object is an object whose state can't be modified after it's created. You describe immutable objects using **immutable classes**.

In Chapter 2, "Function Fundamentals", you learned that the state of an object is the set of values of all its properties. Because of this, immutable classes describing immutable object instances don't define **mutators** or expose any mutable internal state.

Before diving into the study and implementation of functional data structures in Chapter 7, it's crucial to describe what immutability is and why it's important.

Kotlin and immutability

In *Effective Java*, a popular book written by Joshua Bloch, "Item 15" states: "Classes should be immutable unless there's a very good reason to make them mutable". This is a rule of thumb, but most programming languages leave immutable class implementation to the developers, and each language has its own patterns. Kotlin is no different.

A simple immutable Kotlin class

For instance, Kotlin data classes can be mutable or immutable depending on if you define properties using var or val. In any case, Kotlin forces you to make this choice **explicit**.

Open **Immutable.kt** in this chapter's material, and write the following code:

```
data class User(
    val id: Int,
    val username: String
)
```

User is an immutable class because you define each property using val and, as you'll see later, because String and Int are also immutable.

Looking at the decompiled code, you get something like the following:

```
public final class User {
   private final int id; // 1
   @NotNull
   private final String username; // 1

   public final int getId() { // 2
      return this.id;
   }

   @NotNull
   public final String getUsername() { // 2
      return this.username;
   }

   public User(int id, @NotNull String username) {
      Intrinsics.checkNotNullParameter(username, "username");
      super();
      this.id = id;
      this.username = username;
   }
   // ...
}
```

> **Note:** You learned how to get the decompiled code in IntelliJ in Chapter 3, "Functional Programming Concepts" in the section "Referentially transparent expressions and Kotlin inline functions".

Here, you see what's related to immutability:

1. Each property has a `private` and `final` instance variable. `private` allows them to be visible only in the same class and `final` forces them to be initialized in the constructor without any chance of changing later.

2. You have **getters** for each property exposing the related local `private` instance variable. In this case, you see how the getters are also `final` to prevent overriding them in a `User` subclass. This last point is redundant because Kotlin classes can't be extended by default, as you see in `final class User`. It's also worth noting that there are no **setters** for the two properties.

> **Note:** If you want to remove `final` from `User` in the generated code, you need to declare `User` as a normal open or abstract class in Kotlin. Remember that data classes can't be open or abstract.

Using defensive copy

In Kotlin, using `val` for all the properties is necessary but not sufficient to make a data class immutable. With `User`, this works because `id` is an `Int` and `username` is a `String`, which are immutable classes. To prove that this isn't enough to make the class fully immutable, add the following code to **Immutable.kt**:

```
data class WrongImmutableUser(
  val id: Int,
  val username: String,
  val dob: java.util.Date = Date() // HERE
)
```

Here, you define all the properties using `val`, and the decompiled code translates them in `private` and `final` instance variables with only getters. However, `WrongImmutableUser` isn't immutable because of the `Date` type. Just run the following code to prove it:

```
fun main() {
  val w = WrongImmutableUser(1, "maxcarli") // 1
  println(w) // 2
  w.dob.time = 1000L // 3
  println(w) // 4
}
```

Here, you:

1. Create an instance of `WrongImmutableUser`.

2. Print its initial value.

3. Access dob and change its state.

4. Print the state of `WrongImmutableUser` again.

Running the previous code, you'll see how the state has actually changed:

```
WrongImmutableUser(id=1, username=maxcarli, dob=Tue Aug 31
00:11:33 BST 2021)
WrongImmutableUser(id=1, username=maxcarli, dob=Thu Jan 01
01:00:01 GMT 1970)
```

> **Note**: The actual date you see in your output may differ. The `Date` default constructor uses the current time.

An option to avoid this modification is by using a **defensive copy**, which introduces complexity because it returns a copy of the mutable property using some verbose code like this:

```
data class WrongImmutableUser(
  val id: Int,
  val username: String,
  val _dob: java.util.Date = Date() // 1
) {
  val dob: Date // 2
    get() = Date().apply { // 3
      time = _dob.time
    }
}
```

In this case, you:

1. Define _dob as a parameter for the actual *date of birth* property.

2. Declare dob as a *read-only* property of the same type Date.

3. Create a copy of _dob's value every time the same property is accessed.

If you now run the same main you added earlier, you get the following output:

```
WrongImmutableUser(id=1, username=maxcarli, _dob=Tue Aug 31
00:24:44 BST 2021)
WrongImmutableUser(id=1, username=maxcarli, _dob=Tue Aug 31
00:24:44 BST 2021)
```

You tried to change the value of dob, but the state of WrongImmutableUser didn't change. This is because you acted on a copy of Date. This makes the original WrongImmutableUser immutable, but the code isn't the best, and you also need to document this behavior somewhere.

A simple mutable Kotlin class

To implement a mutable version of User, write the following code in the same **Immutable.kt** file:

```
data class MutableUser( // 1
  val id: Int, // 2
  var username: String // 3
)
```

This simple class has some important things to note:

1. The class MutableUser has a name giving information about the mutability. As you'll see later, the same happens with Kotlin collections where MutableList<T> is the mutable version of List<T>.

2. You declare the id using val.

3. You need just one var property to make the whole class mutable.

Look at the decompiled code, and you now get something like this:

```
public final class MutableUser {
    private final int id;
    @NotNull
    private String username; // 1

    public final int getId() {
        return this.id;
    }

    @NotNull
    public final String getUsername() {
        return this.username;
    }

    public final void setUsername(@NotNull String var1) { // 2
        Intrinsics.checkNotNullParameter(var1, "<set-?>");
        this.username = var1;
    }

    public MutableUser(int id, @NotNull String username) {
        Intrinsics.checkNotNullParameter(username, "username");
        super();
        this.id = id;
        this.username = username;
    }
    // ...
}
```

In this case, the properties you define using var:

1. Are translated into instance variables that aren't final.

2. Have setter or **mutator** methods.

Now, you can run the following code without any compilation errors:

```
fun main() {
    val mutableUser = MutableUser(8, "maxcarli")
    println(mutableUser)
```

```
    mutableUser.username = "massimo"
    println(mutableUser)
}
```

Getting this as output:

```
MutableUser(id=8, username=maxcarli)
MutableUser(id=8, username=massimo)
```

Immutable function parameters

Sometimes, people confuse the concept of **immutability** with the concept of **constant**. Of course, a way to make a class immutable is to have all its properties as constants, but:

- Immutability refers to **objects** whose state can't change after they're created.

- Constant refers to **references** or **variables** that can't change their values once initialized.

Open **Constants.kt** and add the following code:

```
fun main() {
    val constantUser = MutableUser(1, "Max") // 1
    constantUser = MutableUser(2, "Alice") // 2 ERROR
    constantUser.username = "Alice"// 3
}
```

In this case, you:

1. Define `constantUser` using `val`.

2. Can't change the value of `constantUser`, assigning the reference to a new `MutableUser`.

3. Can change the state of the object referenced by `constantUser` because of type `MutableUser`, which is mutable.

The same happens when you use a parameter of a function, like in the following code:

```
fun changeUsername(user: MutableUser) { // 1
    user = MutableUser(2, "Alice") // ERROR // 2
    user.username = "Alice"   // 3
}
```

In this case, you:

1. Define changeUsername with a user parameter of type MutableUser.

2. Try to assign a different value to user. This doesn't compile because function parameters are implicitly constant. If it were possible, you wouldn't see the effect of the assignment outside the function. Kotlin, like Java, doesn't have references like C++ does.

3. Can use user to change MutableUser's state because it's mutable.

It's interesting to look at the decompiled code:

```
public static final void changeUsername(@NotNull MutableUser
user) {
    Intrinsics.checkNotNullParameter(user, "user");
    user.setUsername("Alice");
}
```

In this code, nothing's preventing the reassignment of user, which is something happening at the Kotlin compiler level. Thank you, Kotlin!

Immutability and Kotlin collections

In the previous paragraphs, you created User as an example of an immutable class and MutableUser as its mutable companion. Kotlin uses the same naming convention for collections. When you refer to List<E>, you implicitly mean the immutable version of a list. If you need to modify the list, you need to refer to MutableList<E>.

It's fundamental to understand how List<E> differs from MutableList<E>. Look at the source code, and you'll find that List<E> is an interface in the **kotlin.collections** package containing some read-only operations, while MutableList<E> extends List<E>, adding **mutator** functions like add or remove.

Some of those are represented in the UML diagram in Figure 6.1:

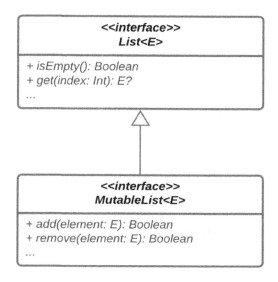

Figure 6.1: List<E> and MutableList<E> relationship

To explore this more, open **Collections.kt** and write:

```
fun main() {
  val immutableList = listOf(1, 2, 3, 4, 5) // 1
  val asMutableList = immutableList as MutableList<Int> // 2
  asMutableList.add(10) // 3
  // immutableList.add(10) // DOESN'T COMPILE
}
```

In this code, you:

1. Create immutableList as an immutable List<Int> you get from listOf.

2. Define asMutableList, casting immutableList to MutableList<Int>. This doesn't give any compilation errors. That's because a List<T> can possibly be a MutableList<T>, so the Kotlin compiler can't exclude that at compile time.

3. Invoke add on asMutableList.

Run the code, and you get:

```
Exception in thread "main"
java.lang.UnsupportedOperationException
  at java.util.AbstractList.add(AbstractList.java:148)
```

This doesn't mean add doesn't exist in the objects referenced by immutableList. It means the List<Int> implementation you get from listOf implements add in a way that it throws an UnsupportedOperationException when invoked. This isn't the same as having a List<Int> implementation with no add function at all.

You get the immutability of the object provided by listOf by hiding add behind the List<E> interface and making the object safe by throwing an exception in the add implementation. The same is true for other mutators like remove. For this reason, collections like List<T> are called **read-only collections**.

> **Note:** At the time of writing, there's a proposal (https://github.com/Kotlin/kotlinx.collections.immutable) for a different implementation of mutable, immutable and persistence collections.

In Chapter 7, "Functional Data Structures", you'll learn what an immutable collection is through the implementation of FList and FTree.

Immutability advantages

So far, you've learned how to implement immutability in Kotlin, but you haven't actually seen why you should pursue immutability. The main reasons are:

- Simplicity

- Consistency

- Avoiding duplication

- Thread safety

It's useful to give some examples for each of those:

Simplicity

Immutable classes are usually easier to implement and, for sure, easier to think about. The reason for this is in the definition itself of an immutable object. If an object can't change its state after it's been created, it means you don't have to implement mutators and logic to accept only values that are valid for the specific domain.

Consistency

Immutable objects are very good keys in a `Map` when mutable ones are dangerous. To prove that, add the following code to **Consistency.kt**:

```kotlin
data class MutableKey( // 1
  var id: Int
)

fun main() {
  val key1 = MutableKey(1) // 2
  val key2 = MutableKey(2) // 2
  val myMap = mutableMapOf( // 3
    key1 to "First",
    key2 to "Second"
  )
  println("Value for $key1 is ${myMap[key1]}") // 4
  key1.id = 2 // 5
  println("Value for $key1 is ${myMap[key1]} after key1 update")
// 6
  println("Value for $key2 is ${myMap[key2]}") // 6
  println("The Map is $myMap") // 7
  myMap.remove(key1).also { println("Removed $key1 from
myMap") } // 8
  myMap.remove(key2).also { println("Removed $key2 from
myMap") } // 8
  println("The Map after remove is $myMap") // 8
  println("Value for $key1 is ${myMap[key1]} after key1 remove")
// 9
  println("Value for $key2 is ${myMap[key2]} after key2 remove")
// 9
}
```

When you run `main`, you get the following output:

```
Value for Key(id=1) is First
Value for Key(id=2) is Second after key1 update
Value for Key(id=2) is Second
The Map is {Key(id=2)=First, Key(id=2)=Second}
Removed Key(id=2) from myMap
Removed Key(id=2) from myMap
The Map after remove is {Key(id=2)=First}
Value for Key(id=2) is null after key1 remove
Value for Key(id=2) is null after key2 remove
```

Following the points in the previous code, note how you:

1. Create `MutableKey` as a mutable data class with a simple `Int` property, id.

2. Initialize `key1` and `key2` using 1 and 2 as `id`, respectively.

3. Create `myMap` using `key1` and `key2` as the keys, and `"First"` and `"Second"` as the values, respectively.

4. Print the value for `key1`. As expected, you get the value `First`.

5. Mutate `key1`, assigning the value 2 to its `id` property. This is quite dangerous because you should already have a key for that `id`.

6. Print the values for `key1` and `key2`, getting `Second` in both cases. This isn't obvious because when changing the value of `id` for `key1`, you might expect that the related value `First` has overridden the existing value `Second`. This isn't the case, but the situation is actually even worse.

7. Print `myMap`'s current state, which contains two equal keys with two different values. How can that be possible?

8. Try to remove the values for both `key1` and `key2`, and then print `myMap`'s state again. You might expect an empty `Map`, but this isn't the case. The value for `key1` is still there. Or, at least, that's what you see in the output.

9. Access the values in the map for `key1` and `key2`, getting `null` for both.

There's definitely something wrong because of the mutability of `Key`. To prevent these things from happening, you should make `Key` immutable, which you can do by adding this to **Consistency.kt**:

```
data class Key(
    val id: Int // HERE
)
```

> **Note**: Key is immutable because `Int` is immutable and `id` cannot be reassigned.

Replace `MutableKey` with `Key` everywhere you're using it. Using `val` for `id` means the following line doesn't compile:

```
// ...
key1.id = 2
// ...
```

Comment out `key1.id = 2` so your code compiles. Run the previous code using your new immutable keys, and you get the following output:

```
Value for Key(id=1) is First
Value for Key(id=1) is First after key1 update
Value for Key(id=2) is Second
The Map is {Key(id=1)=First, Key(id=2)=Second}
Removed Key(id=1) from myMap
Removed Key(id=2) from myMap
The Map after remove is {}
Value for Key(id=1) is null after key1 remove
Value for Key(id=2) is null after key2 remove
```

In this case, `myMap`:

1. Contains both the keys for different `id` values and you can't change that by mutating the keys.

2. Is empty after removing the values for both `key1` and `key2`.

This is actually the proof that every class should be immutable unless there's a good reason to make it mutable. In this case, there isn't a good reason to make Key mutable.

Avoid duplication

In the previous example, you created two different instances of Key with two different values for id. It's interesting to see what happens if you create two different instances of the immutable version of Key for the same id. Run the following code after writing it in **Reuse.kt**:

```
fun main() {
  val key1 = Key(1) // 1
  val key2 = Key(1) // 1
  val myMap = mutableMapOf<Key, String>()
```

```
    myMap[key1] = "First" // 2
    println("Value for $key1 is ${myMap[key1]}") // 3
    println("The Map is $myMap") // 3
    myMap[key2] = "Second" // 4
    println("Value for $key2 is ${myMap[key2]}") // 5
    println("The Map is $myMap") // 5
}
```

In this case, the output is:

```
Value for Key(id=1) is First
The Map is {Key(id=1)=First}
Value for Key(id=1) is Second
The Map is {Key(id=1)=Second}
```

Here, you:

1. Create two Key instances using the same value for id.

2. Insert a value, "First", in myMap using key1.

3. Print the value for key1 and the whole map, getting what you expect.

4. Insert a new value, "Second", in myMap using key2.

5. Print the value for key2, checking that the new value has overridden the old one.

The previous code proves key1 and key2 are effectively the same key, and creating new instances of them is redundant. Because Key is immutable, there's no reason to create more instances for the same value of id. Reusing the same object also simplifies the job of the compilers that can implement and apply some low-level optimizations similar to the ones they apply to constants.

> **Note:** Later, you'll see some curious consequences of immutable instance reusability in the JVM when dealing with Java wrapper types like Integer, Long, etc.

Exercise 6.1: In this section, you learned it's useful to avoid creating multiple instances of immutable classes because they represent the same value. Given the following immutable class `Id`:

```
class Id(val id: Int)
```

How would you change it to prevent any client from creating multiple instances of `Id` for the same `id`?

When you run this code:

```
fun main() {
  val id1 = // Create Id for id = 1
  val id2 = // Create Id for id = 1
  val id3 = // Create Id for id = 2
  val id4 = // Create Id for id = 2
  println("${id1 === id2}")
  println("${id1 === id2}")
  println("${id1 === id3}")
  println("${id3 === id4}")
}
```

You get:

```
true
true
false
true
```

Exercise 6.2: What happens if the `Id` class in Exercise 6.1 is a data class?

Thread safety

Immutable objects can be used safely by different threads without falling into an inconsistent state. Concurrent programming is difficult, and you always need to adopt synchronization strategies to avoid classic problems like race conditions or deadlock. Using immutable objects helps, but it's not always enough.

A **race condition** happens when multiple threads access shared data, and the result depends on the order the operations happen. For instance, write this code in **Safety.kt**:

```kotlin
data class MutableCounter( // 1
  var count: Int = 0
)

val counter = MutableCounter() // 2

val task = {  // 3
  randomDelay() // 4
  counter.count++ // 3
  randomDelay() // 4
  if (counter.count == 2) { // 3
    println("Completed")
  }
}

fun main() { // 5
  thread(block = task)
  thread(block = task)
}
```

In this code, you:

1. Define `MutableCounter` as a simple mutable class, wrapping `Int` to use as a counter.

2. Initialize `counter` with an instance of `MutableCounter`.

3. Define a lambda that increments the value of `count` and prints a message if the counter value is 2.

4. Use `randomDelay`, found in **Util.kt**, which waits a random interval of time up to 100 milliseconds (ms).

5. Finally, create `main`, where you start two different threads running the same `task` on the same object `counter`.

Run `main` multiple times, and see how, sometimes, you get a single output like:

```
Completed
```

Other times, you get:

```
Completed
Completed
```

This is a typical example of a **race condition**, explained in Figure 6.2:

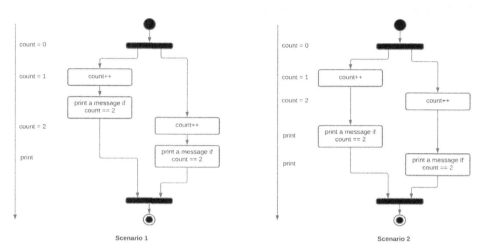

Figure 6.2: Race condition scenarios

- **Scenario 1**: One thread accesses count and increments its value to 1. The same thread checks if the value is 2, printing nothing. Now, the other thread accesses count, increments it to 2 and executes the same test. The test is now successful and prints the Completed message.

- **Scenario 2**: One thread accesses count and increments its value to 1. Before this thread reaches the test, the other one accesses count, incrementing the value to 2. Now, both threads execute the test, which is successful in both cases. It prints Completed and produces the double output.

You might argue that this happens because of randomDelay. This is true, but randomDelay simply simulates the scheduler's behavior, which is the component responsible for assigning each thread in the **runnable state** the right to proceed. To be considered thread-safe, your code should work whatever the scheduler algorithm is and hence, whatever order of instructions the different threads run.

But how can immutability solve this specific problem? Well, immutability helps you *avoid the race condition* because it prevents you from updating the state of a shared object. To solve the counter problem, you need to approach it differently. Here, you're basically assuming that you want to:

- Run the task to increment the counter and check its value in a concurrent way.

- Print the Completed message only once if the value of counter is 2.

In Chapter 17, "Sequence & Flow", you'll learn more about composition of suspendable functions. But a possible naive solution could be the following, which you can add in **Safety.kt**, making sure to comment out the existing `main`:

```kotlin
data class Counter( // 1
  val count: Int = 0
)

fun incAndCheck(counter: Counter): Counter {
  randomDelay()
  val newCounter = Counter(counter.count + 1) // 2
  randomDelay()
  if (newCounter.count == 2) {
    println("Completed")
  }
  return newCounter
}

fun main() {
  val counter = Counter()
  lateinit var counter1: Counter
  val th1 = thread { // 3
    counter1 = incAndCheck(counter)
  }
  th1.join() // 4
  thread {
    incAndCheck(counter1)
  }
}
```

Concurrent programming isn't easy because you need to use synchronization mechanisms to make your code work correctly with different scheduling algorithms. But don't worry, the steps are outlined below.

> **Note**: In Chapter 8, "Composition", you'll see how to solve this problem using the **Kleisli category** you learned in Chapter 3, "Functional Programming Concepts".

In the previous code, you:

1. Create `Counter` as an immutable class.

2. Implement `incAndCheck` as a function receiving one `Counter` as input and returning another `Counter` as output. Here, it's crucial to see how the `Counter` object you return is a new instance you create using `counter.count + 1`. Because of `println`, this isn't a pure function.

3. Create `th1` as a thread in `main`, where you start to execute `incAndCheck`.

4. Use `join` as the **synchronization mechanism** mentioned earlier. This allows you to make your code correct. With this, you're asking the main thread to wait for the completion of `th1`. When it completes, you have the right value of `counter1` to use for the run of the second thread.

You introduced synchronization to make the code correct at the cost of a lower throughput, which is the number of operations you can do in a period of time.

> **Note**: In the case of more than two threads, the solution would be different, much more complex, and is outside the scope of this book.

> **Note**: MapReduce (https://en.wikipedia.org/wiki/MapReduce) is a possible alternative to manage the counter problem, but it would have the challenge of executing the `println` message when the counter reaches the value 2. As a possible trade-off, you might choose to display the message in the end, checking if the counter is greater than or equal to 2.

In conclusion, immutability helps you make your code more robust, but you still need a way to use it properly in different situations.

The price of immutability

As you've seen so far, immutability has some advantages, but nothing comes for free. Sometimes, using mutable objects instead makes the code easier to write. For instance, write the following code in **ImmutabilityCost.kt**:

```kotlin
fun mutableIncAndCheck(counter: MutableCounter) { // 1
  randomDelay()
  counter.count++ // 1
  randomDelay()
  if (counter.count == 2) {
    println("Completed")
  }
}

fun main() {
  val counter = MutableCounter() // 2
  val th1 = thread { // 3
```

```
      mutableIncAndCheck(counter)
    }
    th1.join() // 4
    thread { // 5
      mutableIncAndCheck(counter)
    }
  }
```

In this case, you:

1. Define mutableIncAndCheck as a function that adds 1 to count of the
   MutableCounter you pass as a parameter and checks if the new value is 2.

2. Create a single instance of MutableCounter and assign it to counter.

3. Start a new thread, th1, invoking mutableIncAndCheck with counter.

4. Use join to wait for the completion of th1.

5. Start the second thread again, invoking mutableIncAndCheck with counter.

Run the previous code multiple times, and you'll always get Completed once.

This code is simpler because you don't have to do all the copies and pass them
around.

Another option is creating a **critical section**, which is a block of code that only one
thread can access at a time. Open **CriticalSection.kt** and write the following code:

```
@Synchronized // 1
fun syncedMutableIncAndCheck(counter: MutableCounter) {
  randomDelay()
  counter.count++
  randomDelay()
  if (counter.count == 2) {
    println("Completed")
  }
}

fun main() {
  val counter = MutableCounter()
  thread { // 2
    syncedMutableIncAndCheck(counter)
  }
  thread { // 2
    syncedMutableIncAndCheck(counter)
  }
}
```

In this code, you:

1. Use @Synchronized to make the body of syncedMutableIncAndCheck a critical section. This means that only one thread at a time can access it.

2. Start two different threads executing syncedMutableIncAndCheck on the same MutableCounter object.

Because only one thread can execute syncedMutableIncAndCheck at a time, there's no race condition on counter.

Immutability in JVM

At this point, a weird question might come to your mind. How can you change immutable objects? The example in the previous section gives you an answer. If you want to increment the count property of an immutable Counter object, you just create a new instance, like this:

```
val counter0 = Counter()
val counter1 = Counter(counter0.count + 1)
```

Is creating too many objects expensive? Of course, it is. Creating many objects forces the **garbage collector (GC)** to start minor and major collections, impacting the application's performance. Fortunately, there are also ways to reduce the impact:

1. Reuse the same value.

2. Use a **mutable companion**.

You'll learn more about these options below.

> **Note**: Garbage collection is a process responsible for reclaiming the memory used by objects that are no longer active or used. Depending on the GC algorithm, this process might have some impact on CPU usage, removing the application's resources with some visible effects. Minor and major collections are two different steps that a generational algorithm runs on young or old objects, respectively. GC is a very interesting topic, but outside the scope of this book.

Reuse the same value

Open **BasicTypes.kt** and write the following code:

```
fun main() {
  val a: Int? = 1
  val b: Int? = 1
  println("Equals ${a == b}")
  println("Same ${a === b}")
}
```

> **Note:** In this code, you're using `Int?`, which Kotlin, on JVM, maps to `Integer`. Compare this to `Int`, which Kotlin maps to the `int` primitive type and doesn't have the concept of reference. This is because `Integer` can be `null` and `int` can't. Because of this and the approaching introduction of **value classes**, the `===` operator for referential equality on basic types has been deprecated.

When you run it, you get:

```
Equals true
Same true
```

Because a and b are of type `Int?`, the compiler maps them to an instance of `Integer`. The instances should be different, and the referential equality should return `false`, but this isn't happening. The reason for this outcome isn't completely obvious. Replace the previous code with the following:

```
fun main() {
  val a: Int? = 200
  val b: Int? = 200
  println("Equals ${a == b}")
  println("Same ${a === b}")
}
```

Run the code, and you get:

```
Equals true
Same false
```

Hey, why is `1 === 1` `true` while `200 === 200` is `false`? This is a design choice done for performance reasons. When you assign the literal `200` to a and b, the compiler automatically boxes the primitive value into an `Integer`.

If the value's between –128 and 127, the JVM is smart enough to recycle the same values. If the literal is outside that interval, the JVM creates a new instance every time. This is because of the assumption that small values are more likely to be used multiple times in a program.

Use a mutable companion

Another option to have less impact on the GC is the creation of a mutable companion. A classic and very important example is the `StringBuffer` class as a mutable companion class for `String`. The `String` class is immutable, and `StringBuffer` is a classic thread-safe class encapsulating its state in a private instance variable kept safe using synchronized methods.

> **Note**: `StringBuilder` exposes the same `StringBuffer` interface, removing the synchronization on the methods. This makes `StringBuilder` more efficient than `StringBuffer`, and it's a good choice when thread safety is guaranteed in another way or not required.

Now you know all about immutability. You learned how to implement it in Kotlin and what the trade-offs are in terms of thread safety and performance. But what's the relationship between immutability and functional programming? Is immutability somehow related to the declarative approach you use when writing higher-order functions? Is it actually possible to create applications using only immutable objects? Is the immutability real, or is it just an illusion?

Immutability and functional programming

So far, you've learned that two of the main concepts in functional programming are:

- Pure functions

- Higher-order functions

In Chapter 3, "Functional Programming Concepts", you learned that a pure function doesn't have any side effects. This means the function doesn't mutate the state of any object external to the function itself. In Chapter 5, "Higher-Order Functions", you learned how to write your code using a declarative approach and pure functions.

Open **FPImmutability.kt**, and add the following code:

```kotlin
fun main() {
  var total = 0 // 1
  val list = listOf(1, 5, 10, 12, 34, 55, 80, 23, 35, 12, 80)
  for (i in 0 until list.size) {
    if (list[i] % 5 == 0) {
      total += list[i] // 2
    }
  }
  println("Total: $total")
}
```

This is **imperative code** that allows you to calculate the sum of the values in a list that are multiples of 5. It is not only imperative, but it contains a lot of mutable variables in particular:

1. total for the result.

2. i as the index of the for to iterate over all the values in the list.

Run main, and you get:

```
Total: 265
```

Now, replace the previous code with the following:

```kotlin
fun main() {
  val multipleOf5 = { value: Int -> value % 5 == 0 }
  val total = listOf(1, 5, 10, 12, 34, 55, 80, 23, 35, 12, 80)
    .filter(multipleOf5)
    .sum()
  println("Total: $total")
}
```

When you run this code, you get the same result:

```
Total: 265
```

In this case, you don't have anything mutable. You don't see any index to update for iterating over the list and no total to update with the elements that are multiples of 5 in the list. It's crucial to understand that this is what you *see*, but it doesn't mean it's actually what's *happening*. **Control-Click** on sum, and IntelliJ gets you to the following code:

```kotlin
@kotlin.jvm.JvmName("sumOfInt")
public fun Iterable<Int>.sum(): Int {
    var sum: Int = 0
```

```
        for (element in this) {
            sum += element
        }
        return sum
    }
```

This is how Kotlin implements `sum` on `Iterable<T>`. If you do the same on `filter`, you get this:

```
public inline fun <T> Iterable<T>.filter(predicate: (T) ->
Boolean): List<T> {
    return filterTo(ArrayList<T>(), predicate)
}
```

Selecting `filterTo`, you get here:

```
public inline fun <T, C : MutableCollection<in T>>
Iterable<T>.filterTo(destination: C, predicate: (T) -> Boolean):
C {
    for (element in this) if (predicate(element))
destination.add(element)
    return destination
}
```

This means that when you run the declarative code on `List<T>` with `filter` and `sum`, you're actually running code with all the mutations you had in your first imperative implementation. The difference is that *mutation is hidden* in a well-tested and safe place, which is perfectly fine.

The declarative approach you have with functional programming favors the use of immutable objects, but it doesn't completely prevent you from using mutable objects instead.

In fact, nothing prevents you from writing the following ugly implementation of the `sum` use case:

```
// DON'T DO THIS!!!
var total = 0
listOf(1, 5, 10, 12, 34, 55, 80, 23, 35, 12, 80)
  .forEach {
    if (it % 5 == 0) {
      total += it
    }
  }
println("Total: $total")
```

Although the output is correct, here, you're using the declarative function `forEach` to change the state of the external variable `total`. Please, don't do that!

Immutability and recursion

Recursion happens when a function calls itself to accomplish a specific task. Usually, this happens until a specific condition, the **terminal condition**, is achieved. Recursion is a very useful technique to use when dealing with immutable objects. Suppose you want to calculate, again, the sum of all the multiples of 5 in a list. Open **Recursion.kt** and write the following code:

```kotlin
fun recAddMulti5(list: List<Int>): Int { // 1
  fun loop(i: Int, sum: Int): Int = when { // 2
    i == list.size -> sum // 3
    list[i] % 5 == 0 -> loop(i + 1, sum + list[i]) // 4
    else -> loop(i + 1, sum)
  }
  return loop(0, 0) // 5
}

fun main() {
  val list = listOf(1, 5, 10, 12, 34, 55, 80, 23, 35, 12, 80)
  println(recAddMulti5(list))
}
```

Run the code, and you get the same value you got in the previous examples:

```
265
```

In the previous code, you:

1. Define `recAddMulti5` as the function that calculates the sum of the multiples of 5 in a list.

2. Implement `loop` as a recursive local function that receives, as input parameters, the index `i` of the current element and the partial `sum`. In the body, you evaluate different cases using a `when` expression.

3. Test the value of `i`. If the list is completed, the total `sum` is the value you get as input.

4. Check if the value at index `i` is a multiple of 5. If it is, you invoke `loop` again for the next index, adding the element at position `i` to the `sum`.

5. Invoke `loop` again for the next index with the same `sum` in all the other cases.

As you can see, there's no apparent mutation here. This is because, during the execution, no variables are changing their values, but you implement a similar behavior, passing parameters to a recursive function. This might look expensive and prone to **stack-overflow errors**, but not all recursive functions are equal. Some recursive functions can be implemented using a loop with an evident performance improvement. It's the case of **tail-recursive functions**.

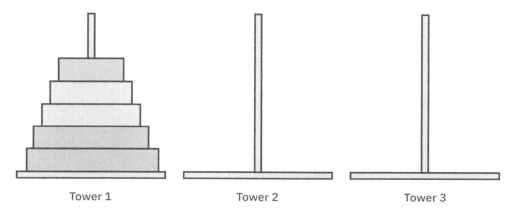

Figure 6a.2: Hanoi Towers

Exercise 6.3: The Tower of Hanoi (https://en.wikipedia.org/wiki/Tower_of_Hanoi) is a classic example of a recursive function. It is a famous game consisting of three rods and a set of n disks of different radii. At the beginning, all the disks are stacked on the first rod. You need to move all the disks from the first rod to the third, following some rules:

• Only one disk may be moved at a time.

• Each move consists of taking the top disk from one of the stacks and placing it on top of another stack or on an empty rod.

• No disk may be placed on top of a disk that's smaller than it.

Can you implement this in Kotlin?

Tailrec functions

In the previous paragraph, you learned how recursion helps you accomplish some tasks without any sort of mutation. Instead of changing the value of a variable in a cycle, you invoke a function, passing the new value as parameter.

To better explain this concept, add the following code to **TailRec.kt**:

```
fun imperativeFactorial(n: Int): Int {
  var result = 1 // 1
  for (value in 2..n) { // 2
    result *= value // 3
  }
  return result // 4
}


fun main() {
  println(imperativeFactorial(10))
}
```

This is the imperative implementation of the factorial of a number n. In this code, you:

1. Initialize result to 1.

2. Iterate over all the values from 2 to n.

3. Update current by multiplying it by value.

4. Return current.

Run this code, and you get:

```
3628800
```

> **Note**: You represent the factorial of a positive integer value, n, with **n!**, which is the result of multiplying all the integer values between 1 and n. For instance, 3! = 3 * 2 * 1 = 6.

So far, so good. In the previous paragraph, you learned that you can remove mutation with recursion. Now, add the following code to the same file:

```
fun recursiveFactorial(n: Int): Int = when (n) { // 1
  1 -> 1 // 2
  else -> n * recursiveFactorial(n - 1) // 3
}
```

In this case, you:

1. Define `recursiveFactorial` and use the when expression, checking the different values of the input parameter n.

2. Return 1 as the result of 1!.

3. Return the multiplication of n with the `recursiveFactorial(n-1)` otherwise.

Run this code, and the output is, of course, the same:

```
fun main() {
    println(recursiveFactorial(10))
}
```

```
3628800
```

The code is now shorter and more intuitive because it's closer to the definition of factorial. Take a closer look, and note how you always get the result by multiplying the value of n by `recursiveFactorial(n - 1)`. The following is a representation of what's actually happening when you invoke `recursiveFactorial(5)`:

```
recursiveFactorial(5)
5 * recursiveFactorial(4)
5 * 4 * recursiveFactorial(3)
5 * 4 * 3 * recursiveFactorial(2)
5 * 4 * 3 * 2 * recursiveFactorial(1)
5 * 4 * 3 * 2 * 1
5 * 4 * 3 * 2
5 * 4 * 6
5 * 24
120
```

In this case, note how the recursion is needed because, to return `recursiveFactorial(n)`, the function needs to calculate `recursiveFactorial(n - 1)` first until it reaches the terminal condition, which is the result of `recursiveFactorial(1)`.

Can you do better? In this case, yes! Add the following code to the same file:

```
fun tailRecFactorial(n: Int, fact: Int = 1): Int = when (n) { //
1
    1 -> fact // 2
    else -> tailRecFactorial(n - 1, n * fact) // 3
}
```

This looks similar to `recursiveFactorial`, but it's actually very different. In this case, you:

1. Define `tailRecFactorial` with two input parameters. The first is the value n that you want to calculate the factorial of. The second is the current result, `fact`.

2. Return `fact` when you reach the value 1 for n.

3. Return the result of `tailRecFactorial` for n − 1, adding the factor of n in the second parameter if n isn't 1.

Run this code, and the output is, of course, the same:

```
fun main() {
    println(tailRecFactorial(10))
}
```

```
3628800
```

This time, repeat the previous exercise for `recursiveFactorial(5)`, and you get the following sequence:

```
recursiveFactorial(5, 1) // 1
recursiveFactorial(4, 5) // 1 * 5
recursiveFactorial(3, 20) // 1 * 5 * 4
recursiveFactorial(2, 60) // 1 * 5 * 4 * 3
recursiveFactorial(1, 120) // 1 * 5 * 4 * 3 * 2
120
```

Note how you don't actually need an invocation of `recursiveFactorial(n − 1)` to complete for it to return the value of `recursiveFactorial(n)`. This is very important because it means that you could convert the recursion in a simple loop. This is an example of **tail recursion**. Tail recursion is a particular case of recursion, where the return value of a function is calculated as *a call to itself* and nothing else.

Look at the decompiled code, and you'll see something like the following:

```
public static final int tailRecFactorial(int n, int fact) {
    int var10000;
    switch(n) {
    case 1:
        var10000 = fact;
        break;
    default:
        var10000 = tailRecFactorial(n - 1, n * fact); // HERE
    }
    return var10000;
}
```

Kotlin isn't smart enough to understand that a function is tail recursive, so you have to give it an hint. Just add the `tailrec` keyword like this:

```
tailrec fun tailRecFactorial(n: Int, fact: Int = 1): Int = when
(n) { // HERE
  1 -> fact
  else -> tailRecFactorial(n - 1, n * fact)
}
```

The decompiled code now becomes:

```
public static final int tailRecFactorial(int n, int fact) {
    while(true) { // HERE
        switch(n) {
        case 1:
            return fact;
        default:
            int var10000 = n - 1;
            fact = n * fact;
            n = var10000;
        }
    }
}
```

The Kotlin compiler has replaced the recursion with a simple `while` loop, which has an important impact on performance.

Mastering recursion is an important skill when you deal with functional data structures, as you'll see next in Chapter 7, "Functional Data Structures".

Exercise 6.4: Tail-recursive functions usually provide better performance. Can you prove this using the `chrono` function in **Util.kt**?

```
/** Utility that measures the time for executing a lambda N
times */
fun chrono(times: Int = 1, fn: () -> Unit): Long {
  val start = System.nanoTime()
  (1..times).forEach({ fn() })
  return System.nanoTime() - start
}
```

Challenges

In this chapter, you learned a lot about immutability and recursion. You've already done some interesting exercises, but now it's time for a couple more challenges.

Challenge 6.1: Immutability and recursion

In "Immutability and recursion", you implemented `recAddMulti5` as a recursive function. Is the `loop` internal function tail recursive?

Challenge 6.2: Tail-recursive Fibonacci

Fibonacci is one of the most famous sequences you can implement using recursion. Remember, the nth Fibonacci number is the sum of the two previous Fibonacci numbers, starting with `0, 1, 1...`. Can you implement it as a tail-recursive function? Can you prove the tail-recursive function has better performance than the non-tail-recursive companion?

Key points

- **Immutable objects** are objects whose state can't be modified after they're created.

- **Immutable classes** describe immutable objects. They're usually simpler because they don't provide **mutators**.

- Classes should be immutable unless there's a very good reason to make them mutable.

- Immutable objects can be used safely by different threads without putting them into an inconsistent state.

- You can use immutable objects to make your code more robust, but they don't solve all your problems.

- **Recursion** is an important technique that allows you to handle mutation in a safe way.

- **Tail recursion** is a particular case of recursion where the return value of a function is calculated as a call to itself and nothing else.

Where to go from here?

Congratulations! In this chapter, you learned a lot about immutability and recursion. These are very important concepts that you need to master to really understand functional data structures — the next chapter's topic.

Chapter 7: Functional Data Structures

In Chapter 6, "Immutability & Recursion", you learned all about immutability and how to use it in Kotlin. You learned:

- How using immutable objects helps solve concurrency problems.

- The cost you have to pay in terms of code simplicity.

- How to implement recursive functions and use the `tailrec` keyword to improve performance.

Immutability and recursion are fundamental skills you need to understand and implement **immutable data structures** and, in particular, **persistence collections**. In this chapter, you'll learn:

- What an immutable data structure is.

- What it means for a data structure to be **persistent**.

- How to implement an **immutable and persistent list** as a classic example of *immutable* and *persistent* data structures.

- What **pattern matching** is and what you can actually achieve in Kotlin.

- What the main functions for a collection are and how to implement them in Kotlin.

As always, you'll learn all this by solving some interesting exercises and challenges.

Immutable data structure

In the "Immutability and Kotlin collections" section in Chapter 6, "Immutability & Recursion", you saw that the List<T> implementation you usually get in Kotlin isn't an actual immutable collection, but something called a **read-only collection**. This means builder functions like listOf<T>() return objects you see through the List<T> interface, but they aren't actually immutable. They still have mutators, but they just implement them by throwing exceptions when invoked.

As the name says, an **immutable** data structure is a data structure that *can't change after it's created*. However, you can still add or remove values in a sense. What you get from an immutable data structure after adding or removing an element is another data structure with the element added or removed. This might look like a waste of memory on the Java Virtual Machine with performance consequences because of the garbage collector. This isn't always true.

Persistent singly linked list

The **persistent singly linked list** is a classic example of a **functional data structure**. You'll find it often in functional programming tutorials because of its simplicity and because its implementation is a very good exercise of the typical functions a collection provides. Before diving into the code, it's useful to have a visual representation that explains how to handle immutable data structures.

Imagine you have to build a singly linked list which is, of course, initially empty like in Figure 7.1:

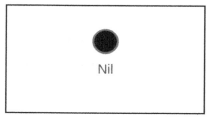

Figure 7.1: Empty functional list

You usually represent an empty list with the Nil value, but you could call it Zero, Empty or even Null. It's important to note how the empty list Nil doesn't depend on the type of values the list should contain. All the empty lists are the same.

You can then try to add an element, for instance, an `Int`, getting what's shown in Figure 7.2:

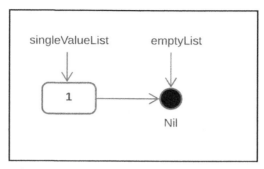

Figure 7.2: Functional list with one element

This new representation of a list is very interesting because it's somehow different from what you would've normally implemented using a classic object-oriented approach.

To prove this, add the following code in **ObjectOrientedList.kt** in the material for this chapter:

```
data class Node<T>( // 1
  val value: T,
  val next: Node<T>? = null
)

fun main() {
  val emptyList: Node<*>? = null // 2
  val singleValueList = Node(1) // 3
}
```

In this code, you define:

1. `Node<T>` as an immutable class with a property for `value` and one for the optional `next` element in the list of type `Node<T>?`.

2. `emptyList` as a constant of type `Node<*>` initialized with `null`.

3. `singleValueList` as a simple `Node<Int>`.

This is different from what you have in Figure 7.2 because there's no explicit relation between what you have in `singleValueList` and `emptyList`. Also, `emptyList` is just a `null` value that doesn't give meaning to the empty list object.

Of course, you can make the relation with `emptyList` explicit, modifying the previous code like this:

```kotlin
fun main() {
    val emptyList: Node<*>? = null
    val singleValueList = Node(1, emptyList as Node<Int>) // HERE
}
```

Here, you pass `emptyList` as a second parameter of the `Node<T>` primary constructor, and this requires you to do an explicit cast with `as`. IntelliJ isn't super happy, as you see in Figure 7.3:

```
40  ▶   fun main() {
41         val emptyList: Node<*>? = null
42         val singleValueList : Node<Int>   =
43            Node( value: 1, emptyList as Node<Int>)
44      }
                                    ┌─────────────────────────────────────────────┐
                                    │ Unchecked cast: Node<*>? to Node<Int>      ⋮ │
                                    │                                              │
                                    │ kotlin kotlin.kotlin_builtins                │
                                    │ public final class Int : Number, Comparable<Int> │
                                    └─────────────────────────────────────────────┘
```

Figure 7.3: Unsafe cast for the empty list

The following change would fix this warning, but again, it would just be another way of creating a simple `Node<T>`, and you'd lose the relation with `emptyList`:

```kotlin
fun main() {
    val singleValueList = Node(1, null)
}
```

To better understand how to implement the persistent singly linked list, look at Figure 7.4, illustrating the list you get by adding a second element:

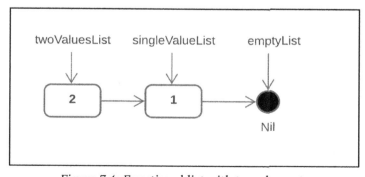

Figure 7.4: Functional list with two elements

Again, you might still have the references to the previous emptyList and
singleValueList, but now you can find a pattern in how you build the list. In this
case, the object-oriented code gives you a hint. Just add the following definition to
the bottom of main:

```
val twoValuesList = Node(2, Node(1, null))
```

This is quite normal code, but it gives you an idea; it helps you see every list as a
collection with the following characteristics:

1. It can be **empty**.

2. It can contain a value in the **head** with an optional list as the **tail**. These are
    represented as value and next respectively within Node.

3. In the last case, the tail can be empty.

This leads you to the following definition of FList<T>. Write it in **FList.kt**:

```
sealed class FList<out T> // 1
object Nil : FList<Nothing>() // 2
internal data class FCons<T>(
  val head: T,
  val tail: FList<T> = Nil
) : FList<T>() // 3
```

With this code, you define:

1. The **sealed class** FList<T>, which allows you to define a limited set of
    implementations that Kotlin forces you to define in the same file or package.

2. Nil as an object that represents the empty list. Because the empty list is the
    same for every type T, you can represent it as FList<Nothing>. This works
    because Nothing is a subtype of every other type and because FList<T> is
    covariant. You define the covariance of FList<T> using the **out** keyword. If you
    need a reminder on covariance, take a peek at Chapter 4, "Expression Evaluation,
    Laziness & More About Functions".

3. FCons<T> as the second way to represent FList<T>: a head with another
    FList<T> as tail. Note how Nil is the default tail.

> **Note**: The name Cons comes from the word "**Cons**tructor". For this reason,
> one of the names for FList<T> is ConsList<T>.

FList<T> builders

In Kotlin, you can create different collection implementations using some **builder methods**. For instance, you create a read-only list of Int with:

```
val readOnlyList = listOf(1,2,3)
```

You create a mutable map with:

```
val mutableMap = mutableMapOf(1 to "One", 2 to "Two")
```

What builder function would you create for FList<T>? Open **Builders.kt** and write the following code:

```
fun <T> fListOf(vararg items: T): FList<T> { // 1
  val tail = items.sliceArray(1 until items.size) // 2
  return if (items.isEmpty()) Nil else FCons(items[0],
fListOf(*tail)) // 3
}
```

This code allows you to create FList<T> using the following syntax:

```
fun main() {
  // ...
  val flist = fListOf(1, 2, 3)
}
```

In the previous code:

1. You define fListOf as a builder function using a vararg parameter for values of type T. It's important to note how the return type is FList<T>.

2. The type for the vararg parameter is actually an Array, so in this case, items has the type Array<T>. You then use sliceArray for getting another array containing everything but the first element. If the initial array is empty or contains just one element, tail will also be the empty Array<T>.

3. If items is empty, you return Nil. Otherwise, you return FCons<T> where head is the first element, and tail is the FList<T> you get, invoking fListOf recursively on the sliced array.

> **Note:** Note the use of the **spread operator** *, which allows you to use the values in an array as if they were a list of multiple vararg input parameters.

Safer FList<T> builders

Now, add the following code to `main` in the same **FList.kt** file:

```
fun main() {
  // ...
  val emptyList = fListOf() // ERROR
}
```

In this case, you have an error because you're not providing the specific value for the type parameter T. An easy fix would be to provide what's missing, like this:

```
fun main() {
  // ...
  val emptyList = fListOf<Int>()
}
```

But you know the empty list `Nil` is the same for every type, so the `Int` information should be obsolete. In this case, you have two different options:

1. Use `Nil` directly.

2. Use `fListOf()` as a parameter of another function, taking advantage of the type inference the Kotlin compiler provides.

Add this code to `main` as an example:

```
fun main() {
  val emptyList = Nil // 1
  val singleElementFList = FCons(2, fListOf()) // 2
}
```

In this code:

1. You use `Nil` directly.

2. You use `fListOf` when Kotlin is already expecting `FList<Int>` because of the `FCons<T>` you use for `singleElementFList`.

In the second point, there's a problem, though. `singleElementFList`'s type is `FCons<T>` and not `FList<T>`. How can you prevent the direct use of `Nil` and `FCons<T>`, forcing all the clients to use them through a reference of type `FList<T>`?

You already solved a similar problem in Exercise 6.1 in Chapter 6, "Immutability & Recursion". Comment out all the code in **Builders.kt**, open **FList.kt** and replace the FList<T> definition with the following:

```
sealed class FList<out T> {

  companion object { // 1
    @JvmStatic
    fun <T> of(vararg items: T): FList<T> { // 2
      val tail = items.sliceArray(1 until items.size)
      return if (items.isEmpty()) {
        empty()
      } else {
        FCons(items[0], of(*tail))
      }
    }

    @JvmStatic
    fun <T> empty(): FList<T> = Nil // 3
  }
}

internal object Nil : FList<Nothing>() // 4
internal data class FCons<T>(
  val head: T,
  val tail: FList<T> = Nil
) : FList<T>() // 5
```

In this code, you:

1. Use a **companion object** to define of and empty.

2. Implement of as the replacement for the previous fListOf. This allows you to use FList.of() syntax. The body is very similar to the fListOf you saw earlier. You replaced fListOf with of and Nil with the invocation of empty.

3. Define empty as a builder for the empty list Nil. It's important to see how the return type is FList<T>. This simplifies the use of empty() in the following examples.

4. Create Nil as an internal object.

5. Define FCons<T> as an internal data class.

To try this code, open **Main.kt** and add:

```
fun main() {
  val emptyList = FList.empty<Int>() // 1
  val singleElementList = FList.of(1) // 2
```

```
  val singleElementList2 = FCons(1, emptyList) // 3
  val twoElementsList = FList.of(1, 2) // 4
}
```

In this code, you:

1. Create `emptyList` using `FList.empty<Int>()`, which still needs a type to help the compiler with type inference.

2. Use `FList.of` to create `singleElementList` with one element.

3. Create another `FList<Int>` with a single element using `FCons<T>` passing `emptyList` as a second parameter.

4. Use `FList.of` with two `Int` values to properly create an `FList<Int>` with two elements.

Declaring `Nil` and `FCons<T>` as internal has the advantage of hiding the actual implementations in code in different modules and, as you'll see very soon, this might cause some problems. To understand what, it's very useful to introduce the concept of pattern matching.

Pattern matching

A simple exercise can help you understand what pattern matching is and how it can be helpful. Suppose you want to implement `size` as a function that returns the number of elements in a given `FList<T>`. Open **Accessor.kt** and write the following code:

```
// DOESN'T COMPILE IN ANOTHER MODULE
fun <T> FList<T>.size(): Int = when (this) { // 1
  is Nil -> 0 // 2
  is FCons<T> -> 1 + tail.size() // 3
}
```

Because `Nil` and `FCons<T>` are `internal`, the previous code wouldn't compile if implemented in a different module. However, you should note a few interesting things. Here, you:

1. Define the `size` extension function, which should return the number of elements in `FList<T>`. The result value is the evaluation of a `when` expression on `this`.

2. Return `0` if the current `FList<T>` is `Nil`, which is the empty `FList<T>`.

3. If the current `FList<T>` isn't `Nil`, it means it has a `head` and `tail`. `size` is then the `size` of the `tail` + 1.

As said, this code wouldn't compile if written in a different module because `Nil` and `FCons<T>` are `internal` classes. This doesn't allow the use of the **is** keyword to test if a reference of type `FList<T>` is actually `Nil` or `FCons<T>`. In the latter case, you'd also need a way to get the reference to `head` and `tail`. You need something very similar to what, in languages like Swift or Scala, is called pattern matching. Something that would make this pseudo-code compile is:

```
when(list){
  Nil -> {}
  (head, tail) -> {}
}
```

Unfortunately, that syntax doesn't work yet with Kotlin, and it probably never will.

> **Note**: Kotlin provides very limited pattern matching. For instance, if you release the constraint to have `Nil` and `FCons<T>` `internal`, you can make the previous code for `size` compile and, for `FCons<T>`, the `tail` property would be available as a consequence of the smart casting.

However, you can still do something to achieve a similar result. Open **FList.kt** and add the following code:

```
fun <T, S> FList<T>.match( // 1
  whenNil: () -> S, // 2
  whenCons: (head: T, tail: FList<T>) -> S // 3
) = when (this) {
  is Nil -> whenNil() // 4
  is FCons<T> -> whenCons(head, tail) // 5
}
```

In this code, you:

1. Define the `match` higher-order function as an extension of `FList<T>`. This function has two type parameters: T and S. T is the type for `FList<T>`. S is the type of result of the expression you want to evaluate if `Flist<T>` is `Nil` or `FCons<T>`.

2. Declare the first parameter `whenNil` as the lambda you want to evaluate if the `FList<T>` receiver is `Nil`. The lambda `whenNil` evaluates in a value of type S.

3. Define the second parameter, whenCons, as the lambda you want to evaluate if the FList<T> receiver is FCons<T>. Again, the lambda whenCons evaluates to a value of type S. Here, it's important to note how whenCons accepts head and tail as input parameters.

4. Check if the receiver FList<T> is Nil, retuning the evaluation of whenNil.

5. Use the smart casting Kotlin provides to extract head and tail if the receiver value is FCons<T> and use them as input parameters for whenCons.

Because you define match in **FList.kt**, is Nil and is FCons<T> are available. Now, return to **Accessor.kt**, and replace the previous implementation of size with the following:

```
fun <T> FList<T>.size(): Int = match(
  whenNil = { 0 }, // 1
  whenCons = { head, tail -> 1 + tail.size() } // 2
)
```

Here, you implement size, returning the result of the match function evaluating:

1. { 0 } if FList<T> is Nil.

2. {1 + tail.size()} if the receiver is FCons<T>.

To test the size function, just add the following code to the same file and run:

```
fun main() {
  println(FList.empty<Int>().size())
  println(FList.of(1).size())
  println(FList.of(1, 2, 3).size())
}
```

You'll get the following output:

```
0
1
3
```

Exercise 7.1: Implement the extension function isEmpty(), which returns true if FList<T> is empty and false otherwise.

Try to answer these questions without the support of IntelliJ and check your solutions in Appendix G or the challenge project.

> **Note**: The match function allows you to make the selection of the different states more explicit. FList<T> can be Nil or FCons<T>. You'll use it many times in the rest of the chapter, but you could do the same directly using Nil and FCons<T> and leveraging Kotlin's smart cast. Remember, you can use Nil and FCons<T> only in this module because of their internal visibility.

Other FList<T> accessors

You can use the match function you created earlier in the implementation of most of the functions you'll see in the following paragraphs. Another simple function is the one returning Flist<T>'s head. Open **Accessor.kt** and add the following code:

```
fun <T> FList<T>.head(): T? = match(
  whenNil = { null },   // 1
  whenCons = { head, _ -> head } // 2
)
```

In this case, you use match, returning:

1. null if the receiver is Nil.

2. head if the receiver is FCons<T>.

Again, you can easily test this by adding the following code to main in the same file:

```
fun main() {
  // ...
  println(FList.empty<Int>().head())
  println(FList.of(1).head())
  println(FList.of(1, 2, 3).head())
}
```

Run it, and check that you get the following output:

```
null
1
1
```

> **Exercise 7.2**: Implement the extension function tail(), which returns the tail of a given FList<T>.

Iteration

Iterating over a collection is one of the most important features a data structure provides. How would you allow clients to iterate over the elements in FList<T>? The List<T> interface provides the forEach higher-order function. Open **Iteration.kt** and add the following code:

```
fun main() {
  listOf(1, 2, 3).forEach {
    println(it)
  }
}
```

Of course, running this code, you'll get:

```
1
2
3
```

To implement the same forEach for your FList<T>, add the following code to the same file:

```
fun <T> FList<T>.forEach(fn: (T) -> Unit): Unit = match( // 1
    whenNil = {}, // 2
    whenCons = { head, tail -> // 3
      fn(head)
      tail.forEach(fn)
    }
)
```

Here, you define forEach:

1. With the lambda function fn as an input parameter. The lambda fn receives the current element of type T as input.

2. If the receiver is Nil, you do nothing.

3. If the receiver isn't Nil, you invoke fn(head) and then recursively invoke forEach on the tail.

Run the following code:

```
fun main() {
  // ...
  FList.of(1, 2, 3).forEach {
    println(it)
  }
}
```

And you'll get:

```
1
2
3
```

Exercise 7.3: Kotlin provides forEachIndexed for the Iterable<T> interface, which accepts as input a lambda of type (Int, T) -> Unit. The first Int parameter is the index of the item T in the collection. To test forEachIndexed, run the code:

```
listOf("a", "b", "c").forEachIndexed { index, item ->
  println("$index $item")
}
```

Getting the following output:

```
0 a
1 b
2 c
```

Can you implement the same for FList<T>?

Exercise 7.4: Another option to implement forEachIndexed is to make FList<T> an Iterable<T>. How would you do that? To make all the code coexist in the same codebase, call the Iterable<T> version IFList<T> with INil and ICons<T>.

Mutators

You just implemented some interesting functions to access elements in FList<T> or iterate over them. Now, it's time to do something even more interesting that will allow you to actually add or remove elements and update the **immutable singly linked list**.

Inserting

In this chapter's introduction, you saw, with some illustrations, how to add elements at the head of FList<T>. Later, in Exercise 7.5, you'll implement addHead. Implementing append to add an element at the end of FList<T> is a little more challenging because it implies copying the initial list to a new one. Open **Mutator.kt** and add the following code:

```
fun <T> FList<T>.append(newItem: T): FList<T> = match( // 1
    whenNil = { FList.of(newItem) }, // 2
    whenCons = { head, tail ->
        FCons(head, tail.append(newItem)) // 3
    }
)
```

In this code, you:

1. Define append as an extension function of FList<T> with a single input parameter newItem of type T. You still use match.

2. Create a new FList<T> if the current value is Nil, with the value to append as the only element. This will be the tail of the new FList<T> you're building.

3. Create a new FCons<T> when the current reference is FCons<T>, using head as the initial value and the list you get by appending newItem to tail.

To test the previous code, run:

```
fun main() {
  val initialList = FList.of(1, 2)
  val addedList = initialList.append(3)
  initialList.forEach {
    print("$it ")
  }
  println()
  addedList.forEach {
    print("$it ")
  }
}
```

You'll get:

```
1 2
1 2 3
```

To help visualize what's happening, think of it like this:

```
(1, (2, ())).append(3) // 1
(1, (2, ()).append(3)) // 2
(1, (2, ().append(3))) // 3
(1, (2, (3, ())))) // 4
```

Here:

1. You start invoking append(3) on an FList<Int> of 2 elements. Note how the last tail is Nil, represented by () above.

2. The first element is still 1, and the tail is the one you get, invoking append(3) on the previous tail.

3. Again, you invoke append(3) on the tail, which is Nil. This creates an FList<Int> with the only element 3.

4. The result is a new FList<Int> of 3 elements.

> **Exercise 7.5**: Implement addHead, which adds a new element at the head of an existing FList<T>.

Filtering

In the previous chapters, you met the filter function that lets you select elements using some predicate. How would you implement the filter function for FList<T>? In **Filter.kt**, add the following code:

```
typealias Predicate<T> = (T) -> Boolean // 1

fun <T> FList<T>.filter(predicate: Predicate<T>): FList<T> =
match(
  whenNil = { FList.empty() }, // 2
  whenCons = { head, tail ->
    if (predicate(head)) {
      FCons(head, tail.filter(predicate)) // 3
    } else {
      tail.filter(predicate) // 4
    }
```

```
        }
    )
```

Here, you:

1. Define `Predicate<T>`, which you met in previous chapters.

2. Implement `filter` using the `match` function. When the receiver is `Nil`, you return the empty list using `FList.empty()`. You could also return `Nil` directly here.

3. Evaluate the predicate on head when the receiver isn't empty. If it evaluates to `true`, you return `FList<T>` using the same head and what you get invoking `filter` on the `tail`.

4. Return what you get invoking `filter` on the `tail` if the predicate doesn't evaluate to `true` on the head.

To test the previous code, run:

```
fun main() {
  FList.of(1, 2, 3, 4, 5, 6, 7, 8, 9)
    .filter { it % 3 == 0 }
    .forEach { println(it) }
}
```

This filters the values that are multiples of 3 in `FList<Int>`. In this case, the output is:

```
3
6
9
```

Exercise 7.6: Kotlin defines the `take` function on `Iterable<T>` that allows you to keep a given number of elements. For instance, running the following code:

```
fun main() {
  listOf(1, 2, 3, 4, 5, 6, 7, 8, 9, 10)
    .take(3)
    .forEach { print("$it ") }
```

You'd get:

```
1 2 3
```

Can you implement the same take function for FList<T>?

Exercise 7.7: Kotlin defines the takeLast function on Iterable<T> that allows you to keep a given number of elements at the end of the collection. For instance, running the following code:

```
fun main() {
  listOf(1, 2, 3, 4, 5, 6, 7, 8, 9, 10)
    .takeLast(3)
    .forEach { print("$it ") }
}
```

You'd get:

```
8 9 10
```

Can you implement the same takeLast function for FList<T>?

Why FList<T> is a persistent data structure

So far, you've met the descriptors **immutable**, **functional** and **persistent** for data structures, and it's important to quickly emphasize what they are:

- **Immutable data structure**: This data structure can't change after it's been created. This means you can't replace a value in a specific position with another or remove another element. When performing this kind of operation, you need to get another immutable data structure, as you've seen for other immutable objects in Chapter 6, "Immutability & Recursion".

- **Functional data structure**: This is a data structure you can interact with using only pure functions. For instance, you get a new FList<T> filtering the data of another one using a predicate you represent using a pure function. As you learned in Chapter 3, "Functional Programming Concepts", a pure function doesn't have any side effects and is represented using a referentially transparent expression. In the following chapters, you'll see many other functions like map, flatMap and others.

- **Persistent data structure**: This data structure always preserves the previous version of itself when it's modified. They can be considered *immutable*, as updates aren't in place. The FList<T> you implemented in this chapter is persistent. You see this when you add a new value. The existing object is still there, and it just becomes the tail of the new one.

Challenges

In this chapter, you had a lot of fun implementing some of the classic functions you find in collections for the singly linked list FList<T>. You also had the chance to use the recursion skills you learned in Chapter 6, "Immutability & Recursion". Why not implement some more functions?

Challenge 7.1: First and last

Kotlin provides the functions first and last as extension functions of List<T>, providing, if available, the first and last elements. Can you implement the same for FList<T>?

Challenge 7.2: First and last with predicate

Kotlin provides an overload of first for Iterable<T> that provides the first element that evaluates a given Predicate<T> as true. It also provides an overload of last for List<T> that provides the last element that evaluates a given Predicate<T> as true. Can you implement firstWhen and lastWhen for FList<T> with the same behavior?

Challenge 7.3: Get at index

Implement the function get that returns the element at a given position i in FList<T>. For instance, with this code:

```
fun main() {
    println(FList.of(1,2,3,4,5).get(2))
}
```

You'd get:

```
3
```

Because 3 is the element at index 2. Consider 0 the index of the first element in FList<T>.

Key points

- An **immutable data structure** is a data structure that can't change after it's been created.

- A **functional data structure** is a data structure you can interact with using only pure functions.

- A **persistent data structure** is a data structure that always preserves the previous version of itself when it's modified.

- Kotlin doesn't have **pattern matching**, but you can achieve something similar using the **smart cast** feature.

- FList<T> is the implementation of a **singly linked list** and is a very common example of a functional, immutable and persistent data structure.

Where to go from here?

Congratulations! In this chapter, you had a lot of fun implementing the FList<T> functional data structure. You had the chance to apply what you learned in Chapter 6, "Immutability & Recursion", for implementation of the most common higher-order functions like filter, forEach, take and many others. It's crucial to say that these are just the first, and many others will come in the following chapters. In Chapter 9, "Data Types", you'll get to add more functions for FList<T>. For now, it's time to dive deep into the concept of composition. See you there!

Chapter 8: Composition

In Chapter 2, "Function Fundamentals", you learned that **category theory** is the theory of **composition**, which is probably the most important concept in functional programming. In this chapter, you'll learn *why* composition is crucial. In particular, you'll learn how to:

- Implement function composition in Kotlin.
- Use **curry** and **uncurry** to achieve composition with multi-input parameter functions.
- Implement **partial application** and learn why it's useful.
- Compose functions with side effects.
- Handle mutation as a special case of side effects.

As usual, you'll do this by writing Kotlin code with some interesting exercises and challenges.

Composition in Kotlin

In Chapter 2, "Function Fundamentals", you implemented the function in
Composition.kt:

```
inline infix fun <B, C, A> Fun<B, C>.after(
  crossinline f: Fun<A, B>
): Fun<A, C> = { a: A ->
  this(f(a))
}
```

`after` uses the `Fun<A, B>` typealias you defined like:

```
typealias Fun<A, B> = (A) -> B
```

Another way to see this is:

```
inline infix fun <A, B, C> Fun<A, B>.compose(
  crossinline g: Fun<B, C>
): Fun<A, C> = { a: A ->
  g(this(a))
}
```

To revise how they work, write and run the following code **Composition.kt**:

```
fun main() {
  val double = { a: Int -> a * 2 } // 1
  val square = { a: Int -> a * a } // 2
  val stringify = Int::toString // 3
  val stringifyDoubleSquareAfter =
    stringify after square after double // 4
  val stringifyDoubleSquareCompose =
    double compose square compose stringify // 5
  println(stringifyDoubleSquareAfter(2)) // 6
  println(stringifyDoubleSquareCompose(2)) // 6
}
```

Here, you:

1. Define `double` as a function that doubles the `Int` passed in. This is a **pure
   function**.

2. Define `square` as another pure function returning the square of the `Int` passed as
   input.

3. Assign the reference of the `toString` function of `Int` to `stringify`.

4. Use `after` to create `stringifyDoubleSquareAfter` as a composition of `double`, `square` and `toString`.

5. Use `compose` to create `stringifyDoubleSquareCompose` as another composition of `double`, `square` and `toString`.

6. Invoke `stringifyDoubleSquareAfter` and `stringifyDoubleSquareCompose`, passing the value 2 in input and printing the result.

When you run the code, you get:

```
16
16
```

The two functions return the same value, which isn't as obvious of an outcome as it seems. This works because, as you learned in Chapter 2, "Function Fundamentals", **types** and pure functions create a category and **associativity** is one of the three properties.

Compose multi-parameter functions

So far, so good. But in the previous example, you had very simple functions with one input parameter and one output parameter. How would you compose, for instance, the following functions? Copy these into **Curry.kt** to explore:

```kotlin
fun main() {
  val double = { a: Int -> a * 2 } // 1
  val square = { a: Int -> a * a } // 1
  val sum = { a: Int, b: Int -> a + b } // 2
  val stringify = Int::toString // 3
}
```

In this case:

1. `double` and `square` are the same two pure functions for calculating the double and the square of an `Int` value you saw earlier. The output type is `Int`.

2. `sum` is a pure function with two input parameters of type `Int`. The return value is of type `Int` as well, and it's the sum of the input values.

3. `stringify` is the same function you met earlier that returns the `String` representation of the `Int` input value.

So, how would you compose `double` and `square` with `sum` to return a function that makes the sum of the `double` and the `square` of a couple of `Int` values, as you see in Figure 8.1?

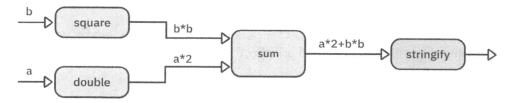

Figure 8.1: Composition of functions with multiple input parameters

You want to create a function equivalent to the following expression:

```
stringify(sum(double(10), square(2)))
```

To do this, you need to use a magic function: the **curry** function. You'll prove the curry function from a mathematical point of view in Chapter 10, "Algebraic Data Types". In this case, you'll use it to understand why, so far, you've only considered functions with a single input parameter. The truth is that *single input* parameter functions are *all you need*. Every function with multiple parameters can be represented as a higher-order function of a single parameter.

> **Note:** The term "curry" comes from **Haskell Curry**, a renowned American mathematician and logician. His first name, **Haskell**, is also the name of one of the most important functional programming languages.

Before writing the generic curry function, how would you represent `sum` as a function of a single parameter? In the same **Curry.kt** file, write the following code:

```
fun sum(a: Int): (Int) -> Int = { b: Int ->
    a + b
}
```

Here, you define `sum` as a higher-order function with a single input parameter that returns, as a result, another function of type `(Int) -> Int`. To understand how this works, add the following code to `main` in **Curry.kt** and run it:

```
val addThree = sum(3) // 1
val result = addThree(4) // 2
println(result) // 3
```

Here, you:

1. Use sum as a function with a single input parameter of type Int, which returns another function you save in addThree. In this case, addThree is a function that adds 3 to the value you pass in.

2. Invoke addThree, passing 4 as an input parameter, getting 7 as the result.

3. Print the result.

You get:

```
7
```

You may not know, but you just practiced currying!

Now, you need to answer the following two questions:

1. How do you write curry as a generic function?

2. How do you use curry to solve the problem in Figure 8.1?

It's time to have some more fun with higher-order functions.

A generic curry function

In the previous section, you implemented a version of sum that receives an Int as input and returns a function of type (Int) -> Int that adds the new parameter value to the initial value. Now it's time to implement curry as a generic function.

In the same **Curry.kt** file, add the following code:

```
typealias Fun2<A, B, C> = (A, B) -> C
```

Here, you define Fun2<A, B, C> as an alias of a function of two input parameters of types A and B, returning a value of type C. In the same file, add the following code:

```
fun <A, B, C> Fun2<A, B, C>.curry(): (A) -> (B) -> C = { a: A ->
// 1
  { b: B -> // 2
    this(a, b) // 3
  }
}
```

Here:

1. You define `curry` as an extension function of `Fun2<A, B, C>`. The return value is a function with a single input parameter a of type A.

2. The return value of the function in **1** is another function that, this time, has an input parameter b of type B.

3. Finally, the internal function has a body with the invocation of `this`, using the parameters a and b.

To understand how this works, write the following code in **Curry.kt**:

```
fun main() {
    // ...
    val curriedSum = sum.curry() // 1 (Int) -> (Int) -> Int
    val addThree = curriedSum(3) // 2 (Int) -> Int
    val result = addThree(4) // 3 Int
    println(result) // 4
}
```

> **Note**: You should use the two-parameter version of `sum` you used earlier:

```
val sum = { a: Int, b: Int -> a + b }
```

This code is very similar to what you implemented earlier. Here, you:

1. Use `curry` to get the curried version of `sum`. The type of `curriedSum` is `(Int) -> (Int) -> Int`.

2. Invoke `curriedSum`, passing 3 as input and getting a function of type `(Int) -> Int`, which you save in `addThree`. This is the function that adds 3 to the value you pass in.

3. Invoke `addThree`, passing 4 as input.

4. Print the result, 7.

Run the previous code, and you get:

```
7
```

The `sum` example is pretty simple. But how can you solve the problem in Figure 8.1?

A practical example

As a more complex problem, you want to compose double, square, sum and stringify to achieve what's in Figure 8.1 and represent the following expression:

```
stringify(sum(double(10), square(2)))
```

In the same **Curry.kt** file, add the following code:

```
fun main() {
  // ...
  fun comp(a: Int, b: Int): String { // 1
    val currySum: (Int) -> (Int) -> Int = sum.curry() // 2
    val doubleComposeSum: (Int) -> (Int) -> Int =
      double compose currySum // 3
    val right: (Int) -> Int = doubleComposeSum(a) // 4
    return (square compose right compose stringify)(b) // 5
  }


  fun comp(a: Int, b: Int): String { // 1
    val right = (double compose sum.curry())(a) // 2
    return (square compose right compose stringify)(b) // 3
  }
}
```

In this code, you:

1. Define an internal function, comp, which is a function of two Int parameters, a and b, to implement what's in Figure 8.1: double a, square b, add the results and convert to a String.

2. Curry sum to create a single input parameter version.

3. Compose double with the curried version of sum. Remember, double has type (Int) -> Int and sum.curry has type (Int) -> (Int) -> Int. This means the composition has type (Int) -> (Int) -> Int.

4. Invoke the composition with input a. As a result, you get a function of type (Int) -> Int in right. This function allows you to add an Int to a defined value that, in this case, is the result of double(a).

5. Invoke the result with the value of the input parameter b. Because now right has type (Int) -> Int, you can easily compose it with square and stringify.

To test the previous function, just add and run the following code in `main`:

```
println(comp(10, 2))
```

Which gives you:

```
24
```

This is the correct result of `10*2 + 2*2`!

In the `comp` implementation, you might complain that it has too many parentheses. Can you remove some of them? Of course, you can! In the same **Curry.kt** file add the following code:

```
infix fun <A, B> A.pipe(f: Fun<A, B>): B = f(this)
```

> **Note**: Some developers don't like using `infix` operators like `pipe` and prefer using parentheses. It's also sometimes difficult to find a name everybody agrees on. Languages that allow you to create custom operators usually represent the `pipe` with `|>`.

This is a Kotlin `infix` extension function of a type `A` accepting a function `f` of type `Fun<A, B>` as an input parameter. The implementation is simple and just invokes the function `f` to the receiver itself, getting a value of type `B`.

This simple function allows you to replace the previous `comp` implementation with the following:

```
fun comp(a: Int, b: Int): String = b pipe
    (square compose (a pipe
        (double compose sum.curry())) compose stringify)
```

Kotlin doesn't let you decide the precedence between `compose` and `pipe`, so you still need some parentheses. But here, you can represent all of `comp` with an expression on a single line.

That's quite a loaded expression! Take a moment to break it down piece by piece to help you understand it.

For more practice, try out the following exercises and use Appendix H to check your solutions.

Exercise 8.1: Earlier, you implemented the generic `curry` function that basically maps a function of type `(A, B) -> C` in a function of type `(A) -> (B) -> C`. Can you now implement the `uncurry` function, which does the inverse? It's a function that maps a function of type `(A) -> (B) -> C` into a function of type `(A, B) -> C`.

Exercise 8.2: Implement a higher-order function `flip` that maps a function of type `(A, B) -> C` into the function `(B, A) -> C`, flipping the order of the input parameters.

Exercise 8.3: The `curry` function maps a function of type `Fun2<A, B, C>` into a function of type `(A) -> (B) -> C`. How would you define an overload of `curry` for functions of three, four, five or, in general, n parameters?

Partial application

In the previous section, you learned how to use `curry` to compose functions with multiple input parameters. This is very useful, but, as you saw in Exercise 8.3, it can also be cumbersome in the case of many parameters. Additionally, most of the time, you don't need to use just a single parameter at a time. To understand this concept, write this code in **Partial.kt**:

```kotlin
fun interface Logger { // 1
  fun log(msg: String)
}

fun interface Calculator { // 2
  fun multiply(a: Double, b: Double): Double
}

fun interface DB { // 3
  fun save(result: Double)
}

fun interface CalculatorFactory { // 4
  fun create(db: DB, logger: Logger): Calculator
}

val calculatorFactoryImpl =
```

```
CalculatorFactory { db, logger -> // 5
  object : Calculator {
    override fun multiply(a: Double, b: Double): Double {
      val result = a * b
      db.save(result)
      logger.log("$a * $b = $result")
      return result
    }
  }
}
```

This is object-oriented code, and in particular, you define:

1. The `Logger` interface with the `log` operation.

2. `Calculator` as an interface for the `multiply` operation.

3. `DB`, simulating a database for persisting a value.

4. `CalculatorFactory` as a factory method implementation for the `Calculator` given a `DB` and `Logger`.

5. `calculatorFactoryImpl` as an implementation of `CalculatorFactory`, returning a `Calculator` implementation that uses `Logger` to log the operations and `DB` to persist the result.

The diagram in Figure 8.2 gives you an idea of the dependencies:

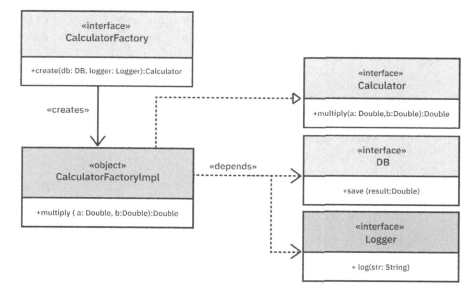

Figure 8.2: CalculatorFactory implementation

Add the following code to the same file as an example of the use of
`calculatorFactoryImpl`:

```
fun main() {
  val db = DB { // 1
    println("Saving value: $it")
  }
  val simpleLogger = Logger { // 2
    println("Logging: $it")
  }
  val fileLogger = Logger { // 3
    println("Logging on File: $it")
  }
  val calculator1 =
    calculatorFactoryImpl.create(db, simpleLogger) // 4
  val calculator2 =
    calculatorFactoryImpl.create(db, fileLogger) // 4
  println(calculator1.multiply(2.0, 3.0)) // 5
  println(calculator2.multiply(2.0, 3.0)) // 5
}
```

Here, you:

1. Create a simple `DB` implementation that just prints a message.

2. Do the same for `Logger`.

3. Create a different implementation for `Logger`. This one, you put in `fileLogger`.

4. Create two different `Calculator` implementations. `calculator1` uses the same
   `DB` as `calculator2` but a different `Logger` implementation. To create the
   `Calculator`s, you use the same `calculatorFactoryImpl` object.

5. Use `calculator1` and `calculator2`, printing the result.

Running `main`, you get:

```
Saving value: 6.0
Logging: 2.0 * 3.0 = 6.0 // HERE
6.0
Saving value: 6.0
Logging on File: 2.0 * 3.0 = 6.0 // HERE
6.0
```

As you see, the log differs in the output for the `Logger` implementation.

Is there a better way to create two different `Calculator` implementations that differ
only in the `Logger` used? Yes, with **partial application**. `CalculatorFactory` defines
the `create` function, which accepts two different parameters.

In the previous example, the value for the first parameter is the same for both
`Calculator` implementations. The second is different. The idea of partial
application is mapping the `create` function in `CalculatorFactory` in a different
function with a single input parameter that returns a function of the second
parameter, as you've seen in `curry`.

To understand how this works, replace the second part of `main` with the following:

```
fun main() {
  // ...
  val partialFactory = calculatorFactoryImpl::create.curry() //
1
  val partialFactoryWithDb = db pipe partialFactory // 2
  val calculator1 = partialFactoryWithDb(simpleLogger) // 3
  val calculator2 = partialFactoryWithDb(fileLogger) // 3
  println(calculator1.multiply(2.0, 3.0)) // 4
  println(calculator2.multiply(2.0, 3.0)) // 4
}
```

Here, you:

1. Define `partialFactory` as the function you get by applying `curry` to the `create`
    function of `calculatorFactoryImpl`.

2. Partially apply some of the parameters in common between all the `Calculator`
    implementations you want to create. You create this by invoking
    `partialFactory` with `db` as a unique parameter and saving the resulting
    function in `partialFactoryWithDb`.

3. Use `partialFactoryWithDb` to create `calculator1` and `calculator2`. Note how
    you get them by invoking `partialFactoryWithDb` and passing only the
    parameters that are different, which is the `Logger` implementation.

4. Use `calculator1` and `calculator2` and print their results.

Running the previous code, you get the same output.

The previous example is very simple and starts from a function with just two input
parameters. Partial application is more powerful when the number of input
parameters is high. You noticed how the order of the parameters is significant. You
could play with `flip` and the overloads of `curry`, but this would make the code very
complicated. That's why it's important to keep partial application in mind when you
design your functions.

> **Note**: You might have noticed some similarities between the previous example and what happens with dependency injection. What you've seen is an example of how to handle dependency injection in a functional way. In this case, object-orientated and functional programming aren't so different. Partial application is basically what Dagger calls "assisted injection". Dependency injection is outside the scope of this book, but if you want to learn all about it, Dagger by Tutorials (https://www.raywenderlich.com/books/dagger-by-tutorials) is the right place for you.

Designing for partial application

As mentioned earlier, partial application is more powerful when the function has many input parameters. You understand how the order of the parameters is important. Just imagine you have a function of six parameters, and you'd like to partially apply just the first, third and last parameters. Using `curry` and `flip` is possible, but it would make the code unreadable. On the other hand, it's very difficult to know how the function will eventually be partially applied, so what you can do is put the parameters:

1. Less likely to change first.

2. More likely to change last.

Often, existing functions already follow this pattern, which is handy for you.

As a final tip on this topic, you should also consider that having functions with too many parameters is generally bad practice.

Compose functions with side effects

What you've seen so far about composition involves pure functions, which are functions without any side effects and whose bodies are referentially transparent expressions. But what happens if the function isn't pure because of some side effects? To understand what happens, start with a simple pure function and add some side effects later.

> **Note**: If you need a reminder about pure functions or referential transparency, skip back to Chapter 3, "Functional Programming Concepts".

Open **SideEffects.kt** and add the following code:

```kotlin
fun pureFunction(x: Int) = x * x - 1
```

This is a basic function that removes 1 from the square of the input. It doesn't really matter what this function does, but you know that:

1. x * x - 1 is a referentially transparent expression.

2. It has no side effects because you can invoke pureFunction(5) infinite times, and you'll always get the same result as output, as you can see when you run the following code:

```kotlin
fun main() {
    pureFunction(5) pipe ::println
    pureFunction(5) pipe ::println
    pureFunction(5) pipe ::println
}
```

Getting:

```
24
24
24
```

So far, so good. Now, it's time to add a side effect with the following code you write in the same file:

```kotlin
fun functionWithEffect(x: Int): Int { // 1
    val result = x * x - 1 // 2
    println("Result: $result") // 3
    return result // 4
}
```

In this code, you:

1. Define functionWithEffect, which returns the same result as pureFunction but has a side effect.

2. Calculate and store the result in result.

3. Use println to print a log message, which is a side effect.

4. Return the result.

Now, test `functionWithEffect` by running the following code:

```
fun main() {
  // ...
  functionWithEffect(5) pipe ::println
  functionWithEffect(5) pipe ::println
  functionWithEffect(5) pipe ::println
}
```

The output is:

```
Result: 24
24
Result: 24
24
Result: 24
24
```

As you see, with the same input value, `pureFunction` and `functionWithEffect` return the same value as output. However, they're different because `functionWithEffect` also logs some messages in the standard output. As you learned in Chapter 3, "Functional Programming Concepts", running `functionWithEffect` changes the world because of a side effect. Because of this, `functionWithEffect` isn't pure.

It's important to note, again, how the result value doesn't tell you anything about the side effect, which you can see only because of the console. You might also think that it's not so bad because it's *just a message in the standard output.*

The problem is that this is just an example, and a side effect could be something more important, like writing to a database or file or sending a request to a server. Reading the function signature, you don't have any information about what the side effect is. More importantly, how would you test the `functionWithEffect` function? This isn't the only problem.

Side effects break composition

In Chapter 11, "Functors", you'll learn all about the map function. But to whet your appetite a little, `map` is a function that allows you to apply a function to all the elements in a container. To understand how it works, run the following code in the same **SideEffect.kt** file.

```
fun main() {
  // ...
  listOf(1, 2, 3) // 1
```

```
      .map(::pureFunction) pipe ::println // 2, 3
}
```

Here, you:

1. Use `listOf` to create a `List<Int>` of three elements.

2. Invoke `map`, passing the reference to `pureFunction`.

3. Print the result.

Running the previous code, you get:

```
[0, 3, 8]
```

This is the `List<Int>` you get when invoking `pureFunction` on each element of the initial input. The `map` function has a very important property that says:

```
map(f).map(g) === map(f compose g)
```

This says that invoking `map` with the function `f` first and then with the function `g` is equivalent of invoking `map` on the composition of `f` and `g`. This means you can prove this by running the following code:

```
fun main() {
  listOf(1, 2, 3)
    .map(::pureFunction).map(::pureFunction) pipe ::println
  listOf(1, 2, 3)
    .map(::pureFunction compose ::pureFunction) pipe ::println
}
```

And getting:

```
[-1, 8, 63]
[-1, 8, 63]
```

It's interesting to test if the same is true for `functionWithEffect`. To see, you just need to run the following code:

```
fun main() {
  //...
  listOf(1, 2,
3).map(::functionWithEffect).map(::functionWithEffect)
pipe ::println
  listOf(1, 2, 3).map(::functionWithEffect
compose ::functionWithEffect) pipe ::println
}
```

This time, the output is:

```
Result: 0     // 1
Result: 3     // 2
Result: 8     // 3
Result: -1    // 4
Result: 8     // 5
Result: 63    // 6
[-1, 8, 63]   // 7
Result: 0     // 1
Result: -1    // 2
Result: 3     // 3
Result: 8     // 4
Result: 8     // 5
Result: 63    // 6
[-1, 8, 63]   // 7
```

This time, you can see how the output for rows 2, 3 and 4 are different. They're different because in the first example, all of the contents of the list are transformed using the first invocation of `functionWithEffect` before working through the second.

Where, in the second example, the first element is transformed by the composed `functionWithEffects` before moving to the second element.

This means that the side effect you get from the composition isn't the composition of the side effect. This is proof that functions with side effects *don't compose*. How can you solve this problem, then?

> **Note**: Using map with the composition is also an improvement in performance because it allows you to iterate over the elements in List<T> just once.

A composable effect

In the previous example, you proved that functions with side effects don't compose well. One of the reasons is that composition means using the result of a first function as the input of the second. If the side effect isn't part of the output, this makes composition difficult. What about removing the side effect from the body of the function and passing the same information as part of the value as output?

In the same **SideEffects.kt** file, add the following code you already met in part in Chapter 3, "Functional Programming Concepts":

```
fun functionWithWriter(x: Int): Pair<Int, String> { // 1
  val result = x * x - 1 // 2
  return result to "Result: $result" // 3
}
```

1. Now, you define `functionWithWriter` as a function that returns `Pair<Int, String>`.

2. The first `Int` property of the resulting `Pair<Int, String>` is the same result as `functionWithEffect`.

3. The second `String` property is the message you used to print in `functionWithEffect`.

Now, `functionWithWriter` doesn't have any side effects, but the `String` you want to print is part of the output. This makes `functionWithWriter` a pure function. `functionWithWriter` doesn't print anything, but it delegates the responsibility of handling the side effect to the caller. But now you have a bigger problem: `functionWithWriter` doesn't compose with itself, and the following code doesn't compile:

```
// DOESN'T COMPILE
val compFunWithWriter =
  ::functionWithWriter compose ::functionWithWriter
```

This is because the `compose` function you created doesn't match the signature of `functionWithWriter`, which has an `Int` as input type and a `Pair<Int, String>` as output. You know how to fix this, remembering that `compFunWithWriter` is basically a `Writer<Int>` where:

```
typealias Writer<A, B> = (A) -> Pair<B, String>
```

In Chapter 3, "Functional Programming Concepts", you also learned how to implement the `compose` function for `Writer`. In the same **SideEffects.kt** file, along with the previous `typealias`, write the following code:

```
infix fun <A, B, C> Writer<A, B>.compose( // 1
  g: Writer<B, C>
): Writer<A, C> = { a: A -> // 2
  val (b, str) = this(a) // 3
  val (c, str2) = g(b) // 4
  c to "$str\n$str2\n" // 5
}
```

Here, you:

1. Define `compose` as an extension function of `Writer<A, B>` that accepts another `Writer<B, C>` as an input parameter.

2. Return a function with a parameter of type `A`.

3. Invoke the receiver with a and, using de-structuring, get the two parts of the resulting `Pair<Int, String>` respectively in `Int` b and `String` str.

4. Invoke g, passing the value of b you got at the previous instruction, de-structuring the result in c and `String` str2 again.

5. Return `Pair<Int, String>` using the result c and the concatenations of `str` and `str2`.

Now, this code will compile:

```
// NOW COMPILES!
val compFunWithWriter =
  ::functionWithWriter compose ::functionWithWriter
```

Of course, you can compose multiple functions of type `Writer<T>`, as you can see by running the following code:

```
fun main() {
  val square = { a: Int -> a * a } // 1
  val double = { a: Int -> a * 2 } // 1
  val squareFunAndWrite = square compose ::functionWithWriter //
2
  val doubleFunAndWrite = double compose ::functionWithWriter //
3
  val compFunWithWriter = squareFunAndWrite compose
doubleFunAndWrite // 4
  compFunWithWriter(5).second pipe ::println // 5
}
```

Here, you:

1. Define `square` and `double` as simple lambda expressions.

2. Define `squareFunAndWrite` as composition of `square` and `functionWithWriter`.

3. Define `doubleFunAndWrite` as composition of `double` and `functionWithWriter`.

4. Define `compFunWithWriter` as a composition of `squareFunAndWrite` and `compFunWithWriter`.

5. Finally, invoke `compFunWithWriter`, printing the result of the second property.

You'll get:

```
Result: 624
Result: 1557503
```

As you learned in Chapter 3, "Functional Programming Concepts", this is something related to the **Kleisli category**, but it's also a very important pattern in the world of functional programming.

A common composition pattern

What you saw in the previous example is a common pattern in functional programming, and it works with different types of functions. Instead of handling composition for the type:

```
typealias Writer<A, B> = (A) -> Pair<B, String>
```

How would you implement composition of the following type you define by adding this to **GeneralComposition.kt**:

```
typealias Opt<A, B> = (A) -> B?
```

In Chapter 9, "Data Types", you'll learn much more about the optional type along with many other fundamental data types. In this case, it's interesting to see how you'd compose functions of type Opt<A, B>.

You might think you can use the existing compose function because Opt<A, B> is somehow included in the following, considering the B of Fun<A, B> as the B? of Opt<A, B>:

```
typealias Fun<A, B> = (A) -> B
```

But the following code doesn't compile:

```
data class User(val id: Int, val username: String)

fun main() {
  val strToInt = { str: String ->
    try {
      str.toInt()
    } catch (nfe: NumberFormatException) {
      null
    }
  }
  val findUser = { id: Int ->
    if (id == 3) User(3, "Max") else null
```

```
    }
    val strToUser = strToInt compose findUser // DOESN'T COMPILE
  }
```

The reason is that `strToInt` returns an optional `Int?` but `findUser` accepts an `Int`. You can repeat the same pattern you learned for `Writer<T>` by adding the following `compose` function:

```
infix fun <A, B, C> Opt<A, B>.compose( // 1
  g: Opt<B, C> // 2
): Opt<A, C> = { a: A -> // 3
  val b = this(a) // 4
  if (b != null) { // 5
    g(b) // 6
  } else {
    null // 7
  }
}
```

In this function, you:

1. Define `compose` as an infix extension function of `Opt<A, B>`.

2. Declare g as the input parameter of type `Opt<B, C>`.

3. Return a function with the input parameter a of type A and `Opt<A, C>` as the output type.

4. Invoke the receiver function with the value of a. What you get is an optional B?.

5. Check if b is null.

6. Invoke g with b and return the result of type C? if b isn't null.

7. Return `null` if b is `null`.

In the previous code, you understand how the logic in the body of the function might be different, but it follows a common pattern you'll see many more times in the following chapters.

> **Note:** Notice how similar this pattern is to using the Kotlin **safe-call operator** (https://kotlinlang.org/docs/null-safety.html#safe-calls). The difference is that your above `compose` is composing functions rather than simply calling a function on an object.

Now, update `main` like this:

```kotlin
fun main() {
  val strToInt = { str: String ->
    try {
      str.toInt()
    } catch (nfe: NumberFormatException) {
      null
    }
  }
  val findUser = { id: Int ->
    if (id == 3) User(3, "Max") else null
  }
  val strToUser = strToInt compose findUser // 1
  strToUser("a") pipe ::println // 2
  strToUser("2") pipe ::println // 3
  strToUser("3") pipe ::println // 4
}
```

Here, you:

1. Create `strToUser` as a composition of `strToInt` and `findUser`. Now, `strToUser` returns `null` if either `strToInt` or `findUser` returns `null`.

2. Use `strToUser` for an invalid user ID.

3. Use `strToUser` for a missing user ID.

4. Use `strToUser` for an existing user ID.

Run the code, and you get:

```
null
null
User(id=3, username=Max)
```

Where only the third case returns something that isn't `null`.

Exercise 8.4: How would you apply the previous pattern for `Array<T>`? Basically, you need a way to compose functions of type:

```
typealias ToArray<A, B> = (A) -> Array<B>
```

In other words, if you have two functions:

```
val fun1: (A) -> Array<B>
val fun2: (C) -> Array<C>
```

Can you implement compose so that the following will compile and `fun2` is applied to all elements resulting from `fun1`?

```
fun1 compose fun2
```

Give it a try, and check your solution with the one in Appendix H.

Currying again

Implementing `compose` for a specific type of function is a pattern you'll see many times in this book, and in general, when you use functional programming. In the previous example, you learned how to compose a function with a particular side effect. The overloaded `println` function you used for printing `Int` values is a function of type `(Int) -> Unit`. You also used the overload of type `(String) -> Unit`. In any case, it's a function with a `String` input and `Unit` as output. Open **CurryAgain.kt** and write the following code:

```kotlin
fun functionWithAnotherEffect(x: Int): String {
  val result = x * x - 1
  return "Result: $result calculated on $
{System.currentTimeMillis()}"
}
```

This function isn't pure because the expression it represents isn't referentially transparent. It depends on some external state that, in this case, you access through the `currentTimeMillis` method of `System`. To prove that, just add and run the following code:

```kotlin
fun main() {
  functionWithAnotherEffect(5) pipe ::println
  functionWithAnotherEffect(5) pipe ::println
}
```

And you get something similar to:

```
Result: 24 calculated on 1632737433997
Result: 24 calculated on 1632737434014
```

Every time you invoke `functionWithAnotherEffect` with the same input, you get different values as output. So, how would you make `functionWithAnotherEffect` pure, and how would you handle composition?

In the `println` example, you had a function of type `(Int) -> Unit` and you just moved the input for the effect to the output. Now, the function `System::currentTimeMillis` has type `() -> Long`. A possible solution is moving the value you get from `System::currentTimeMillis` to an input parameter like this:

```
fun functionWithAnotherEffect(time: Long, x: Int): String {
  val result = x * x - 1
  return "Result: $result calculated on $time"
}
```

Now, `functionWithAnotherEffect` is pure because the output depends only on the input parameters. This allows you to test the function very easily. Just replace the previous `main` with the following:

```
fun main() {
   functionWithAnotherEffect(123L, 5) pipe ::println
   functionWithAnotherEffect(123L, 5) pipe ::println
}
```

Run it, and you'll get what you expect:

```
Result: 24 calculated on 123
Result: 24 calculated on 123
```

At this point, you need to solve two problems:

1. You don't always want to pass a first parameter value to `functionWithAnotherEffect`. You only need it when you're testing the function. When you just want to use it, you don't always want to pass the value you get from `System.currentTimeMillis()`.

2. You broke composition.

The first problem is easy to solve using Kotlin's optional parameter. Just update `functionWithAnotherEffect` like this:

```
fun functionWithAnotherEffect(
  time: Long = System.currentTimeMillis(), x: Int
): String {
  val result = x * x - 1
  return "Result: $result calculated on $time"
}
```

Now, you can run this code where you used the explicit value as input for the `time` parameter just when you want to test `functionWithAnotherEffect`.

```
fun main() {
    functionWithAnotherEffect(x = 8) pipe ::println
    functionWithAnotherEffect(123L, 5) pipe ::println
    functionWithAnotherEffect(123L, 5) pipe ::println
}
```

Here, you'll get:

```
Result: 63 calculated on 1632738736781 // FOR NORMAL USE
Result: 24 calculated on 123 // FOR TEST
Result: 24 calculated on 123 // FOR TEST
```

What about composition, then? Well, that problem is solved with just a little bit of *curry*!

Just note how `::functionWithAnotherEffect` has type:

```
(Long, Int) -> String
```

This means that `::functionWithAnotherEffect.curry()` has type:

```
(Long) -> (Int) -> String
```

To get the function to use during tests, you just need to use the following code:

```
fun main() {
    // ...
    val forTesting = 123L pipe ::functionWithAnotherEffect.curry()
    // 1
    forTesting(5) pipe ::println // FOR TEST // 2
    forTesting(5) pipe ::println // FOR TEST // 2
}
```

Here, you:

1. Invoke `curry` on `::functionWithAnotherEffect` and then invoke the resulting function with an input value of type `Long`, which is the time value you use during tests.

2. Verify that the output is always the same for the same input.

Running the previous code, you get what you'd expect:

```
Result: 24 calculated on 123
Result: 24 calculated on 123
```

For `::functionWithAnotherEffect`, you can reuse all the things you learned in the section "Compose multi-parameter functions".

Compose mutation

In this final case of handling composition, it's time to have some fun. The goal is to handle composition when the side effect of a function implies mutation. To understand how this works, open **Mutation.kt** and add the following code:

```
data class MutableCounter( // 1
  var count: Int = 1
)

val counter = MutableCounter() // 2

fun squareWithMutationEffect(x: Int): Int { // 3
  val result = x * x
  counter.count *= 10
  return result
}

fun doubleWithMutationEffect(x: Int): Int { // 4
  val result = x * 2
  counter.count /= 2
  return result
}
```

The code is quite easy to understand. Here:

1. `MutableCounter` is a mutable data class wrapping a simple count variable of type `Int`, initialized to 1.

2. You create `counter` as a `MutableCounter` instance.

3. `squareWithMutationEffect` is a simple function that returns the square of the input `Int`. It also has a side effect that multiplies the current value in the `MutableCounter` by 10.

4. `doubleWithMutationEffect` is another simple function that doubles the input `Int` and divides the current value of the counter by 2 as a side effect.

You have the same problem you solved in the section "A common composition pattern", but now the effect is a mutation of a shared state you represent with an instance of `MutableCounter`.

How can you now make `squareWithMutationEffect` and `doubleWithMutationEffect` pure and somehow compose the effects? What if you also handle mutation using immutable objects instead? It looks quite challenging, but you can actually do this with what you've learned so far.

First, comment out `squareWithMutationEffect` and `doubleWithMutationEffect` and add the following code:

```
typealias Updater<T> = (T) -> T // 1

fun squareWithEffect(x: Int): Pair<Int, Updater<MutableCounter>>
{ // 2
  val result = x * x // 3
  return result to { counter -> counter.count *= 10;
counter } // 4
}

fun doubleWithEffect(x: Int): Pair<Int, Updater<MutableCounter>>
{ // 2
  val result = x * 2 // 3
  return result to { counter -> counter.count /= 2; counter } //
4
}
```

Things are getting more interesting. In this code, you:

1. Define `Updater<T>` as the abstraction of any function that maps objects in another object of the same type. Of course, identity would be a special case of `Updater<T>` because it wouldn't do anything.

2. Replace `squareWithMutationEffect` and `doubleWithMutationEffect` with `squareWithEffect` and `doubleWithEffect`, respectively, which differ for the return type that's now `Pair<Int, Updater<MutableCounter>>`. `first` is the result of the function and `second` is the function you need to run on `MutableCounter` to update its state.

3. Calculate the result.

4. Return `Pair<Int, Updater<MutableCounter>>` using a lambda expression as `Updater<MutableCounter>`.

Now, here's the interesting part. How would you compose functions like this? The types `squareWithEffect` and `doubleWithEffect` are similar to `Writer<A, B>`, but in that case, it was defined as:

```
typealias Writer<A, B> = (A) -> Pair<B, String>
```

Now, the second element of the `Pair<A, B>` isn't `String`, but `Updater<S>`. This doesn't change so much because you can apply what you learned in the section "A common composition pattern".

In the same **Mutation.kt** file, add the following code:

```
typealias WithMutation<A, B, S> = (A) -> Pair<B, Updater<S>>
```

This defines `WithMutation<A, B, S>` as the counterpart of `Writer<A, B>` for this use case:

- A and B are respectively the input and output of a function.

- S is the type of object for the function to mutate.

Using this, you can finally write the `compose` overload like this:

```
inline infix fun <A, B, C, S> WithMutation<A, B, S>.compose(
    crossinline g: WithMutation<B, C, S> // 1
): WithMutation<A, C, S> = { a: A -> // 2
    val (b, op) = this(a) // 3
    val (c, op2) = g(b) // 4
    c to (op compose op2) // 5
}
```

In this code, you:

1. Define `compose` as an infix extension function of `WithMutation<A, B, S>` in the usual way.

2. Return a function with the input parameter a of type A.

3. Invoke the receiver, passing a and de-structuring the result in a variable b of type B and a function op of type `Updater<S>`.

4. Invoke g, passing b as an input parameter. Using de-structuring, you get the result you save in c of type C along with the `Updater<S>` you save in op2.

5. Return `Pair<C, Updater<S>>` where the second property is the composition of op and op2.

Functional Programming in Kotlin by Tutorials

Remember, the definition of Updater<S> is basically a Fun<S, S> for which you already have a compose overload.

As a quick test, add and run the following code:

```
fun main() {
    val composed = ::squareWithEffect compose
        ::doubleWithEffect compose ::squareWithEffect // 1
    val counter = MutableCounter() // 2
    val (result, compUpdate) = composed(3) // 3
    result pipe ::println // 4
    counter pipe compUpdate pipe ::println // 5
}
```

Here, you:

1. Use compose to compose ::squareWithEffect with ::doubleWithEffect and then ::squareWithEffect again.

2. Save the shared mutable state in counter. Its type is MutableCounter.

3. Use de-structuring to get the result in result and the composed mutation in compUpdate.

4. Print the value of result.

5. Apply compUpdate to counter and print the current state.

Run the code, and you get:

```
324 // 1
MutableCounter(count=50) // 2
```

This is because:

1. The result of ((3 * 3) * 2) * ((3 * 3) * 2) is 18 * 18.

2. The counter starts at 1. Then, you multiply by 10, getting 10. Next, you divide by 2, getting 5. Finally, you multiply by 10 again, getting 50.

Of course, the client is responsible for the execution of the effect. But, can you do something better? Of course, you can. Do you really need a MutableCounter?

Composition with immutable objects

In the previous example, you used `MutableCounter`, but the good news is that you don't have to change much if you want to use an immutable `Counter`. Open **ImmutableComposition.kt**, and add the following code:

```
data class Counter(  // 1
  val count: Int = 1
)

fun squareWithImmutableEffect(x: Int): Pair<Int,
Updater<Counter>> {
  val result = x * x
  return result to { counter -> Counter(counter.count * 10) } //
2
}

fun doubleWithImmutableEffect(x: Int): Pair<Int,
Updater<Counter>> {
  val result = x * 2
  return result to { counter -> Counter(counter.count / 2) } //
3
}

fun main() {
  val composed = ::squareWithImmutableEffect compose
    ::doubleWithImmutableEffect compose
    ::squareWithImmutableEffect
  val counter = Counter() // 4
  val (result, compUpdate) = composed(3)
  result pipe ::println
  counter pipe compUpdate pipe ::println
}
```

This code has a few significant differences from the one in the previous section:

1. You define `Counter` as an immutable class.

2. `squareWithImmutableEffect` doesn't change the current shared and mutable state. However, it creates a new `Counter` using the data of the one in input.

3. `doubleWithImmutableEffect` does the same, creating a new `Counter`.

4. You print the result in the same way as the previous example.

Run this code, and you get:

```
324
Counter(count=50)
```

This is the same result you got using `MutableCounter`, but this time you used `Counter`, which is immutable.

Challenges

This is one of the most important chapters of the book because composition is the essence of functional programming. You already did some interesting exercises, so now it's time for a couple challenges.

Challenge 8.1: Callable stuff

In this chapter, you learned how to implement the `compose` function in different scenarios following a common pattern. Consider, now, the following function type:

```
typealias WithCallable<A, B> = Fun<A, Callable<B>>
```

How would you implement `compose` for `WithCallable<A, B>`? This is using `java.util.concurrent.Callable` (https://docs.oracle.com/javase/8/docs/api/java/util/concurrent/Callable.html) defined as:

```
interface Callable<V> {
  @Throws(Exception::class)
  fun call(): V
}
```

Challenge 8.2: Parameters or not parameters?

Suppose you have the following functions:

```
val three = { 3 } // 1

val unitToThree = { a: Unit -> 3 } // 2
```

In this code:

1. `three` is a function of type `() -> Int`, returning 3.

2. `unitToThree` is a function of type `(Unit) -> Int`, also returning 3.

They look like the same function, but they're actually not. This is because you need a `Unit` to invoke `unitToThree`. This also has consequences when you compose. Consider the following code:

```
fun main() {
  val double = { a: Int -> a * 2 } // 1
  val comp2 = unitToThree compose double // 2   COMPILE
  val comp1 = three compose double // 3   DOESN'T COMPILE
}
```

Here, you:

1. Define a simple `double` function.

2. Compose `unitToThree` with `double`. This compiles.

3. Try to compose `three` with `double`. This doesn't compile.

The reason is that you don't have any `compose` overload with the type `() -> T` as a receiver. The type `(Unit) -> T` instead falls into `Fun<A, B>`.

Can you implement a higher-order function, `addUnit`, that converts a function of type `() -> T` in the equivalent `(Unit) -> T` and `removeUnit` that does the opposite? Using these functions, how would you fix the code in the previous `main`?

Key points

- **Composition** is the most important concept of functional programming.

- **Category theory** is the theory of composition.

- Functions with a single input parameter are all you need. Using **curry**, each function with multiple parameters can be mapped into higher-order functions of a single parameter.

- The name curry comes from **Haskell Curry**, an American mathematician and logician.

- **Partial application** is a generalized version of currying. It allows you to decide what parameters to provide initially and what to provide later.

- You can think of partial application as a way to implement **dependency injection** in a functional way.

- The **Kleisli category** helps you understand how to implement composition of functions with side effects. The idea is to bring the effect as part of the return type, but this usually breaks composition.

- `Writer<T>` leads you to a general pattern in the implementation of composition.

- You can use the same pattern to manage composition of functions that contain mutation logic.

Where to go from here?

Wow! In this chapter, you've done a great job! Congratulations. Composition is probably the most fascinating part of functional programming and gives you a lot of gratification when you see your code compile and work.

This chapter completes the first section of the book. In the following section, you'll enter the core of functional programming, starting with the concept of data types. See you there!

Section II: Data Types & Typeclasses

In this section, you'll learn some of the types you see when using functional programming. You'll see concepts you likely already know, like "List" and "Optional", while discovering some of their very important properties as they relate to functional programming.

Chapter 9: Data Types

In the first section of the book, you learned about the concept of **type**. In particular, you learned that a type for a variable is a way to represent the set of possible values you can assign to it. For instance, saying that a is an Int means you can assign only integer values to a. The same is true for more complex types like String or custom types like User and so on.

In this chapter, you'll meet **data types**, another crucial concept that's somewhat orthogonal to the concept of type. For instance, the Optional<T> data type is a classic example. It represents the concept of either having an object of type T or not, and doesn't depend on what T actually is.

In particular, you'll learn:

- What a data type is.

- How to define the Optional<T> data type.

- The Optional<T> type in the context of data types.

- What lift , map and flatMap functions are.

- The common and important data types List<T> and Either<A, B>.

- What the fold and foldRight functions are and why they're useful.

As always, you'll learn all this using the Kotlin language and some fun exercises and challenges.

What is a data type?

In the first section of the book, you learned the crucial definition of a type. You saw that a type is basically a way to represent a set of values you can assign to a variable or, in general, use in your program. Consider, for instance, the following code:

```
var a: Int = 10
var s: String = "Hello World!"
var b = true
```

Here, you can say that:

1. a is a variable of type Int. This means you can assign only integer values to a.

2. s is of type String, and you can assign any possible String you can create in Kotlin.

3. You can assign to the Boolean variable b only a value of either true or false.

A type doesn't just tell you what value you can assign but also what you can't. In the previous code, you can't assign true to a, for instance.

You also learned that types and functions together make a category, which is the pillar of composition.

A data type is a different concept that uses the previous types as type parameters. In general, you represent them as M<T> in the case of a single type parameter. Other data types have multiple parameters. For example, you represent a data type with two type parameters as M<A, B>.

As you'll see, you can think of a data type as a **container** that provides some common functions so you can interact with its content. The best way to understand data types is by providing some examples, starting with a classic: Optional<T>.

The Optional<T> data type

As mentioned earlier, you can often think of a data type as a container that provides some context. Optional<T> is a classic example because it represents a container that can either:

- Contain a single element of type T.

- Be empty.

Open **Optional.kt** and write this code:

```
sealed class Optional<out T> { // 1

  companion object {
    @JvmStatic
    fun <T> lift(value: T): Optional<T> = Some(value) // 4

    @JvmStatic
    fun <T> empty(): Optional<T> = None // 5
  }
}

object None : Optional<Nothing>() // 2
data class Some<T>(val value: T) : Optional<T>() // 3
```

In this code, you:

1. Define Optional<T> as a sealed class. Note that it has a type parameter T, and it's *covariant*.

2. Define None as an object representing the case when the container is empty. All empty containers are the same, and you need the type parameter to be covariant, so you inherit from Optional<Nothing>.

3. Define Some<T> as a data class with a single property of type T.

4. Use some factory methods to get an object of type Some<T> as an Optional<T>. The first method is lift, which allows you to get Optional<T> from a given value of type T.

5. Do the same for None with empty().

> **Note**: If you need a reminder about covariance, look back at Chapter 4, "Expression Evaluation, Laziness & More About Functions".

But how can you use the Optional<T> data type? A simple test can help.

Using Optional<T>

In **OptionalTest.kt**, add the following code:

```
fun strToInt(value: String): Optional<Int> = // 1
  try {
    Optional.lift(value.toInt()) // 2
```

```
    } catch (nfe: NumberFormatException) {
      Optional.empty() // 3
    }

  fun double(value: Int): Int = value * 2 // 4
```

In this code, you:

1. Create `strToInt` as a function that accepts a `String` and wants to return the `Int` value in it. This operation can fail, so the return type is an `Optional<Int>`.

2. Return `Some<Int>` with the `Int` value in case of success.

3. Return `None` in case of error.

4. Define `double` as a simple function from `Int` to `Int`.

Now, how would you implement code that doubles the value you get from `strToInt`? A first solution is the following:

```
fun main() {
  val res = strToInt("10") // 1
  when (res) {
    is Some<Int> -> { // 2
      val res2 = double(res.value)
      println("Result is $res2")
    }
    is None -> println("Error!") // 3
  }
}
```

In this code, you:

1. Invoke `strToInt`, passing a valid `String`, getting an `Optional<Int>` returned, which you store in `res`.

2. Check the result and, if it's a `Some<Int>`, you pass the value to `double` and print the result.

3. Print an error message in case of error.

Run the code, and you get:

```
Result is 20
```

To test the error, just pass a value to strToInt that isn't a valid Int, like:

```
val res = strToInt("10aaa")
```

Running this code, you get:

```
Error!
```

The previous code isn't the best, though. You invoke strToInt and then use a verbose when expression to understand what to do next. Of course, you can do better.

Using lift, map and flatMap

In the previous example, you have strToInt, which is a function of type (String) -> Optional<T>. You want to compose this with double of type (Int) -> Int. Of course, you can't, because double accepts an Int and strToInt provides an Optional<Int>. To solve this problem, you have two main options. The first is:

1. Use strToInt to get an Optional<Int>.

2. Check if it's a Some<Int> and get the Int in it.

3. Pass the Int to double.

The second — and better — option is:

1. **Lift** String to an Optional<String>.

2. Apply a transformation to the Optional<String>, getting an Optional<Int>.

3. Apply the double transformation to Optional<Int>, getting another Optional<Int>.

4. Extract the contents of Optional<Int>, or a default value if it's missing.

The first option is the one you already implemented in the previous paragraph. It's time to implement the second, then. You call the first step lift because you're basically taking a value of type T and "lifting" it to an object of type M<T>. In this case, M represents the Optional data type, but you'll also find the lift function in other data types.

Figure 9.1 describes what you'll implement:

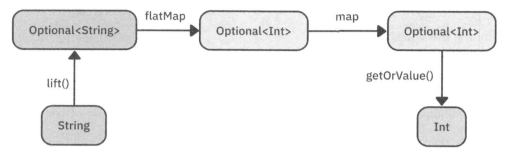

Figure 9.1 - Lift with Optional<T>

In the same **OptionalTest.kt** file, replace the previous `main` with the following. A keen eye might note that it won't compile yet:

```
fun main() {
    // ...
    Optional
        .lift("10")
        .flatMap(::strToInt) // 1
        .map(::double) // 2
        .getOrDefault(-1) // 3
        .pipe(::println)
}
```

Note: You'll find the `pipe` definition you learned in Chapter 8, "Composition" in **Definitions.kt** in the material for this project.

At the moment, this code doesn't compile because you need to implement:

1. `flatMap`
2. `map`
3. `getOrDefault`

You'll learn all about `map` and `flatMap` in Chapter 11, "Functors" and Chapter 13, "Understanding Monads", respectively. At the moment, it's important to have an idea of how they work to make the previous code compile.

Implementing map

Starting with the map function, you see that it receives a function of type Fun<A, B> as input and returns an Optional<B>. Remember that:

```
typealias Fun<A, B> = (A) -> B
```

To better understand how it works, add the following code in **Optional.kt**:

```
fun <A, B> Optional<A>.map(fn: Fun<A, B>): Optional<B> = // 1
  when (this) {
    is None -> Optional.empty() // 2
    is Some<A> -> Optional.lift(fn(value)) // 3
  }
```

In this code, you:

1. Define map as an extension function for Optional<A>. Note how it accepts a function of type Fun<A, B> and returns an Optional<B>.

2. Check if the receiver is None. If it is, the result is also None. Note how you use Optional.empty(), which allows you to return an Optional<B> by type inference.

3. Use lift to return Some<B>, passing the result of the invocation of the function fn.

One function down. Next is flatMap.

Implementing flatMap

While double is a Fun<Int, Int>, strToInt has type Fun<Int, Optional<Int>>, making it incompatible with map. You need something more. Add this code to **Optional.kt**:

```
fun <A, B> Optional<A>.flatMap(
  fn: Fun<A, Optional<B>>
): Optional<B> = when (this) { // 1
  is None -> Optional.empty() // 2
  is Some<A> -> {
    val res = fn(value) // 3
    when (res) {
      is None -> Optional.empty() // 4
      is Some<B> -> Optional.lift(res.value) // 5
    }
  }
}
```

This code is a little more complex. Here:

1. You define flatMap as an extension function of Optional<A>. Note how it accepts a parameter of type Fun<A, Optional<B>> and returns an Optional<B>.

2. You check if the receiver is None. In this case, you just return Optional.empty().

3. Otherwise, invoke fn on the value in Some<B> and check its result.

4. If it's None, you return Optional.empty().

5. If it's Some<B>, you return a new Optional<B>, using the same result and the lift function.

Note how even though fn already returns Optional<B>, you're still wrapping the result in a new Optional<B> instance. This is because every function should return a new immutable object.

Great! One more function to go before you can compile your code.

Implementing getOrDefault

To ensure the previous code compiles, you also need to add getOrDefault to **Optional.kt**:

```
fun <A> Optional<A>.getOrDefault(defaultValue: A): A =
  when (this) { // 1
    is None -> defaultValue // 2
    is Some<A> -> value // 3
  }
```

In this code, you:

1. Define getOrDefault as an extension function for the Optional<A> type. Note how it accepts a value of type A.

2. Check the current receiver and return defaultValue if it's None.

3. Return value if the receiver is Some<A>.

Now, the previous code in **OptionalTest.kt** compiles. Run it, and you get:

```
20
```

To check the case with the default value, replace the previous `main` with the following:

```
Optional
  .lift("10aa")
  .flatMap(::strToInt)
  .map(::double)
  .getOrDefault(-1)
  .pipe(::println)
```

Run it, and you get:

```
-1
```

A quick review

In the previous section, you met three of the most critical concepts in functional programming. You'll learn more about them in the following chapters. In particular, you learned:

- What a **data type** is and in what sense it behaves as a **container**.

- How to interact with the *content* of the container the data type represents using map. You'll learn all about **functors** in Chapter 11, "Functors". For now, it's important to understand that invoking map on a data type M<A> passing a function of type Fun<A, B> as a parameter, you'll get M<B>.

- How to interact with the content of a data type M<A> using a function of type Fun<A, M<B>>. In this case, map doesn't work. Instead, you need a function called flatMap. You'll learn all about flatMap in Chapter 13, "Understanding Monads". So far, you just need to understand that invoking flatMap on a data type M<A> passing a function of type Fun<A, M<B>> as a parameter, you'll get M<B>.

Now, it's time to learn the most common and important data types while implementing for them lift, map, flatMap and the equivalent of getOrDefault.

But first, here are some exercises to test your new knowledge! You can find solutions in Appendix I and the challenge matterials for this chapter.

> **Exercise 9.1:** In this chapter, you learned what the Optional<T> data type is, and you implemented some important functions for it, like lift, empty, map and flatMap. Kotlin defines its own optional type represented by ?. How would you implement the lift, empty and getOrDefault functions for it?

Exercise 9.2: In this chapter, you learned what the Optional<T> data type is, and you implemented some important functions for it, like lift, empty, map and flatMap. Kotlin defines its own optional type represented by ?. How would you implement the map and flatMap functions for it?

Exercise 9.3: How would you replicate the example you implemented in **OptionalTest.kt** using T? instead of Optional<T>? Use the solutions of Exercise 9.1 and Exercise 9.2 to implement this example.

The List<T> data type

So far, you've learned that you can think of a data type as a container with a specific context. The context of an Optional<T> is about something that can be there or not. Another fundamental data type is List<T>. In this case, the context is the ability to contain an ordered list of items. It's important to say that Kotlin already provides the functions you implemented for Optional<T> and T?.

Open **ListTest.kt** and add the following code:

```
fun countUpTo(value: Int) = List(value) { it } // 1

fun main() {
  val emptyList = emptyList<Int>() // 2
  val intList = listOf(1, 2, 3) // 3
  intList.map(::double).forEach(::println) // 4
  println("---")
  intList.flatMap(::countUpTo).forEach(::println) // 5
}
```

In this code, you have examples of:

1. Defining countUpTo, which is a function of type Fun<Int, List<Int>>. countUpTo just generates a List<Int> with values from 0 to the value you pass in input. It doesn't really matter what this function does; the type of countUpTo is what matters.

2. Creating an empty List<Int> using the emptyList builder function.

3. Using listOf to create a List<Int>.

4. Using `map` to apply the `double` function to all the elements of a `List<Int>`. Note that you invoke the `map` function on `List<Int>`, and you get another `List<Int>`.

5. Using `flatMap`, passing the reference to `countUpTo`.

When you run that code, you get:

```
2 // 1
4
6
---
0 // 2
0
1
0
1
2
```

As you can see:

1. `map` returns a new `List<Int>` that contains values that are the `double` of the values of the original list.

2. `flatMap` returns a `List<Int>` of the `List<Int>` you get applying `countUpTo` to each element. The *flat* in the name also gives the idea that you don't get a `List<List<Int>>`, but the values of the list you get from `countUpTo` are *flattened* in a single `List<Int>`.

Folding

`List<T>` has a couple of magic functions that are very important and useful in the implementation of other functions. To see why, open **Folding.kt** and add the following code:

```kotlin
fun List<Int>.imperativeSum(): Int {
    var sum = 0
    for (i in 0 until size) {
        sum += this[i]
    }
    return sum
}
```

Note: In Chapter 12, "Monoids & Semigroups", you'll learn even more about the fold functions.

At this point, you're probably disappointed because this function calculates the sum of all the values in a `List<Int>` using an imperative approach. In Chapter 5, "Higher-Order Functions", you learned how to use a declarative approach, and in Chapter 6, "Immutability & Recursion", you learned how to use recursion to achieve immutability. In any case, the previous code teaches you that you basically accumulate the different values of the list in a `sum` variable. You can also use that in your tests to check if other implementations are correct. Run this code:

```kotlin
fun main() {
  val list = listOf(1, 2, 3, 4, 5, 6, 7, 8, 9, 10)
  list.imperativeSum() pipe ::println
}
```

And you get the following output, which is the sum of the first ten positive integers.

```
55
```

> **Note**: If you want to have some fun, you can use the following expression as an alternative way of printing the result of `imperativeSum`.

```kotlin
List<Int>::imperativeSum compose ::println epip list
```

> You already have `pipe`, `epip` and `compose` in the **Composition.kt** and **Definitions.kt** files in the material for this chapter.

With all this in mind, add the following code:

```kotlin
fun List<Int>.declarativeSum(): Int {
  tailrec fun helper(pos: Int, acc: Int): Int {
    if (pos == size) {
      return acc
    }
    return helper(pos + 1, this[pos] + acc)
  }
  return helper(0, 0)
}
```

You're basically doing the same as the imperative approach but using `helper` as a `tailrec` function receiving as input the index `pos` of the current value in the list and `acc` as the current sum. In this case, there's no mutation, and the approach is declarative. Test `declarativeSum` by running this code:

```
val list = listOf(1, 2, 3, 4, 5, 6, 7, 8, 9, 10)
list.declarativeSum() pipe ::println
```

And getting the same result:

```
55
```

So far, so good. But this code works only for `Int`s. You can do much better. To understand how, add the following code for a function that calculates the product of the values in a `List<Int>`:

```
fun List<Int>.declarativeProduct(): Int {
  tailrec fun helper(pos: Int, acc: Int): Int {
    if (pos == size) {
      return acc
    }
    return helper(pos + 1, this[pos] * acc)
  }
  return helper(0, 1)
}
```

Run:

```
val list = listOf(1, 2, 3, 4, 5, 6, 7, 8, 9, 10)
list.declarativeProduct() pipe ::println
```

And you get:

```
3628800
```

Note that `declarativeProduct` follows the same pattern as `declarativeSum` with some crucial differences:

1. Of course, `declarativeSum` calculates the sum and `declarativeProduct` the product. More importantly, they differ in the way you accumulate all the elements into a sort of… accumulator, `acc`. In `declarativeSum`, you add the current value to `acc`. In `declarativeProduct`, you multiply the current value by `acc`.

2. In `declarativeSum`, the initial value for the accumulator is `0`. In `declarativeProduct`, the initial value is `1`.

From the previous observations, you entail that you can represent `declarativeProduct` and `declarativeSum` using a common abstraction accepting as input something that tells where one differs from the other. In this case:

1. The initial value for the accumulator.

2. How you *combine* each element with the current value you've accumulated.

In the same **Folding.kt** file, add the following code:

```
fun <T, S> List<T>.declarativeFold(
  start: S,
  combineFunc: (S, T) -> S
): S { // 1
  tailrec fun helper(pos: Int, acc: S): S { // 2
    if (pos == size) {
      return acc
    }
    return helper(pos + 1, combineFunc(acc, this[pos])) // 3
  }
  return helper(0, start) // 4
}
```

In this code, you:

1. Define `declarativeFold` as an extension function of `List<T>`, which accepts as an input parameter an initial value of type `S` for the accumulator and a function of type `(S, T) -> S` that tells how you combine an element with the accumulator itself. Note how the return type is `S`, which is the type of the accumulator.

2. Implement a `helper` function with two input parameters. The first is the position `pos` of the current element you're evaluating. The second is the current value `acc` for the accumulator. If you reach the end of the list, you return the current value for the accumulator, `acc`. Note how `helper` is a `tailrec` function.

3. Call `helper` recursively for the next position, `pos + 1`, if you're not at the end of `List<T>`. Note how the value for the accumulator is what you get by invoking `combineFunc` with the current `acc` value and the current element.

4. Invoke `helper` from the first position, `0`, and the initial value, `start`.

With this function, you can run the following code:

```
list.declarativeFold(0) { acc, item ->
  acc + item
} pipe ::println
list.declarativeFold(1) { acc, item ->
```

```
    acc * item
} pipe ::println
```

Getting the output you'd expect:

```
55
3628800
```

In this case, you invoke the same `declarativeFold` function, passing:

1. `0` as initial value { `acc, item -> acc + item`} as a combine function for the sum.

2. `1` as initial value { `acc, item -> acc * item`} as a combine function for the product.

As mentioned at the beginning of this section, you'll see how powerful this function is. Before proceeding, it's also important to say that `List<T>` already has a `fold` function with the same signature as `declarativeFold`, which you created with a different name to avoid conflicts.

This means you can use the existing `fold` like in this code:

```
val list = listOf(1, 2, 3, 4, 5, 6, 7, 8, 9, 10)
list.fold(0) { acc, item -> acc + item } pipe ::println
list.fold(1) { acc, item -> acc * item } pipe ::println
```

Getting exactly the same result:

```
55
3628800
```

The Kotlin `List<T>` also provides a `foldRight` method, which differs in how the combination happens. It's very important to look at this function as well.

Folding right

Imagine you have a list of objects, and you want to group them together. To do this, you have two different options. You can:

- Start from the first element and accumulate the other objects as soon as you iterate over them.

- Start from the first element and, because you have others, put that object aside and go to the next one. You repeat this operation until you get the last object.

Then, you start to take the most recent object you put aside and combine it with the one you have in your hands. You repeat this operation until you combine the object you put aside first.

Some code can probably help. Consider the following code you wrote earlier, using a shorter list to save some space.

```
val list = listOf(1, 2, 3, 4, 5)
list.declarativeFold(0) { acc, item -> acc + item }
pipe ::println
```

In this code, you use declarativeFold to calculate the sum of the first 5 integers you previously put into a List<Int>. It's useful to see what happens when you run this code:

```
(1,2,3,4,5).declarativeFold(0)
helper(0, 0) // 1
  helper(1, combineFunc(0, 1))   // 2
    helper(2, combineFunc(1, 2))   // 2
      helper(3, combineFunc(3, 3)) // 2
        helper(4, combineFunc(6, 4)) // 2
          helper(5, combineFunc(10, 5)) // 2
            15  // 3
          15
        15
      15
    15
  15
15
```

You can see that:

1. Initially, you invoke helper(0, 0) because you start from the index, 0, and the initial value is 0.

2. When you're not at the end of the List<Int>, you invoke helper again, passing the new position, pos + 1, as the next to evaluate and the new value for the sum you're accumulating. To get this, you need to invoke combineFunc, passing the current value of acc and the current element in the List<Int>. You do this until you reach the end of the List<Int>. Because you're returning the result of the same helper, this is a tailrec function.

3. At the end of the list, you return the value of acc.

It's also useful to see how the values in the list are actually aggregated:

```
combineFunc(combineFunc(combineFunc(combineFunc(combineFunc(0,
1), 2), 3), 4), 5)
```

Replacing the `combineFunc` invocation with +, as an example, you get:

```
((((0 + 1) + 2) + 3) + 4) + 5)
```

Note how you're accumulating values on the left, taking one new item at a time from the right. This is why the `declarativeFold` you implemented is also called `foldLeft`.

However, that's not the only way to implement this. In the same **Folding.kt** file, add this code:

```
fun <T, S> List<T>.declarativeFoldRight(
  start: S,
  combineFunc: (T, S) -> S
): S { // 1
  fun helper(pos: Int): S { // 2
    if (pos == size) { // 3
      return start
    }
    return combineFunc(this[pos], helper(pos + 1)) // 4
  }
  return helper(0)
}
```

In this case:

1. You define `declarativeFoldRight` as an extension function of `List<T>`. Note how the first parameter is the same initial value for the accumulator as for `declarativeFold`. However, the second parameter, `combineFunc`, differs because now the type S is the second parameter. This helps you to visualize the folding by keeping what you accumulate on the right.

2. The `helper` function now has a single parameter: the position, `pos`, of the current item.

3. When the recursion reaches the end of the list, you return the initial value, `start`.

4. If you're not at the end of the list, you return the result of the invocation of `combineFunc`, passing the current item as the first parameter and the result of the recursive invocation of `helper` for the following item.

Here's also a visual representation of what's happening in this case:

> **Note**: Here, combineFunc is replaced with comb to save some space!

```
(1,2,3,4,5).declarativeFoldRight(0)
  helper(0)
    comb(1, helper(2))
      comb(1, comb(2, helper(3)))
        comb(1, comb(2, comb(3, helper(4))))
          comb(1, comb(2, comb(3, comb(4, helper(5)))))
            comb(1, comb(2, comb(3, comb(4, comb(5,
helper(6))))))
              comb(1, comb(2, comb(3, comb(4, comb(5, 0))))))
            comb(1, comb(2, comb(3, comb(4, 5))))
          comb(1, comb(2, comb(3, 9)))
        comb(1, comb(2, 12))
      comb(1, 14)
    15
15
```

Using + again in place of the combineFunc invocation, you have:

```
(1 + (2 + (3 + (4 + (5 + 0)))))
```

Here, note two main things:

1. The recursive nature of the invocations isn't tailrec because the invocation of helper isn't the last operation.

2. You start combining from the last element and keep adding while returning from the invocation stack.

Run this code:

```
val list = listOf(1, 2, 3, 4, 5, 6, 7, 8, 9, 10)
list.foldRight(0) { item, acc -> acc + item } pipe ::println
list.foldRight(1) { item, acc -> acc * item } pipe ::println
```

And you get the same result you got previously:

```
55
3628800
```

> **Note**: Notice that acc is the second param in the lambda you use as
> combineFunc. This is for consistency with the Kotlin foldRight function.

This is true because addition and multiplication are *symmetrical*, so a + b = b + a
and a * b = b * a. To see the difference, you just need to use a non-symmetric
function like String concatenation. Run this code:

```
val list = listOf(1, 2, 3, 4, 5, 6, 7, 8, 9, 10)
list.map(Int::toString).declarativeFold("") { acc, item ->
  acc + item
} pipe ::println
list.map(Int::toString).fold("") { acc, item ->
  acc + item
} pipe ::println
list.map(Int::toString).declarativeFoldRight("") { item, acc ->
  acc + item
} pipe ::println
list.map(Int::toString).foldRight("") { item, acc ->
  acc + item
} pipe ::println
```

And see that the results are different when using declarativeFold and
declarativeFoldRight or the existing Kotlin implementations:

```
12345678910
12345678910
10987654321
10987654321
```

Here, you can see that using declarativeFold or fold produces a different result
than declarativeFoldRight or foldRight.

> **Exercise 9.4**: Implement a function that reverses a String using one of the
> folding functions you've implemented in this chapter.

> **Exercise 9.5**: In this chapter, you implemented declarativeFold and
> declarativeFoldRight as extension functions for List<T>. How would you
> implement them for Iterable<T>?

What about FList<T>?

In Chapter 7, "Functional Data Structures", you implemented FList<T> — whose code is available in **FList.kt** in this chapter's material — as an example of a functional data structure. The existing of is equivalent to the lift function you learned here. It basically "lifts" the values you pass as a vararg to an FList<T>. Also, empty already provides the empty FList<T>. But what about fold, foldRight, map and flatMap?

> **Note**: Implementing all these functions for FList<T> is a great exercise. Feel free to try it out on your own, skip this section or come back to it later if you want and go straight to learning about the Either<A, B> data type. In any case, see you there!

Implementing fold and foldRight

In the previous section, you learned what fold and foldRight are, but you didn't have any proof of how important these functions are. As a first step, you'll implement fold and foldRight for FList<T>. Open **FListExt.kt** and add the following code:

```
tailrec fun <T, S> FList<T>.fold(
  start: S,
  combineFunc: (S, T) -> S
): S = when (this) { // 1
  is Nil -> start // 2
  is FCons<T> -> {
    tail.fold(combineFunc(start, head), combineFunc) // 3
  }
}
```

In this code:

1. You define fold as an extension function of FList<T>. It accepts an initial value of type S and a combineFunc of type (S, T) -> S.

2. You use the same pattern you learned in Chapter 7, "Functional Data Structures". Here, you test if the current receiver is Nil. If it is, you just return the initial value, start.

3. Otherwise, you're combining head with the start value. It's important to see that you're using this combined value as the new starting value when invoking fold again on the tail. The fold invocation on tail makes this function tailrec.

Test the previous implementation by running the following code:

```
fun main() {
    val numbers = FList.of(1, 2, 3, 4, 5, 6, 7, 8, 9, 10)
    numbers.fold(0) { acc, item -> acc + item } pipe ::println
    numbers.fold(1) { acc, item -> acc * item } pipe ::println
}
```

You get exactly what you got previously with a List<Int>.

```
55
3628800
```

In the same **FListExt.kt** file, now add this code:

```
fun <T, S> FList<T>.foldRight(
    start: S,
    combineFunc: (T, S) -> S
): S = when (this) {
    is Nil -> start
    is FCons<T> -> {
        combineFunc(head, tail.foldRight(start, combineFunc))
    }
}
```

In this code, note that foldRight isn't tailrec anymore, similar to its List<T> counterpart. This is because you return the result of combineFunc.

Test it again by adding this code to main and running it:

```
FList.of(
    *("supercalifragilisticexpialidocious"
        .toCharArray().toTypedArray())
)
    .foldRight(StringBuilder()) { item, acc ->
        acc.append(item)
        acc
    } pipe ::println
```

Besides the magic of converting a `String` into an `Array<Char>`, you're using `foldRight` on the `String` itself. The output is:

```
suoicodilaipxecitsiligarfilacrepus
```

Implementing map

`map` is one of the most crucial functions, and you'll meet it many times when implementing your code. Its implementation is very simple. In **FListExt.kt**, add the following code:

```
fun <T, S> FList<T>.map(fn: Fun<T, S>): FList<S> = // 1
  when (this) {
    is Nil -> FList.empty() // 2
    is FCons<T> -> FCons(fn(head), tail.map(fn)) // 3
  }
```

This code follows most of the patterns you've seen in the previous examples. Here:

1. You define `map` as an extension function of `FList<T>`. It accepts a function of type `Fun<T, S>` and returns an `FList<S>`.

2. You return `Nil` if the current receiver is `Nil`.

3. If the current receiver isn't `Nil`, it means it has a head of type T. In this case, you return a new `FList<S>` where the head is the value of type S you get from `fn(head)` and the tail is what you get by invoking `map` on it.

To test `map`, run the following code:

```
FList.of(1, 2, 3, 4, 5)
  .map(::double)
  .forEach(::println)
```

And the output is:

```
2
4
6
8
10
```

Implementing flatMap

flatMap is probably the most challenging function to implement. It's also part of the proof that fold and foldRight should be fundamental elements of your functional programming skills.

To implement the actual flatMap, you need another function. In **FListExt.kt**, add the following code:

```
fun <T> FList<T>.append(rhs: FList<T>): FList<T> =
  foldRight(rhs, { item, acc -> FCons(item, acc) })
```

As the name says, this appends an FList<T> to another you have as the receiver. This is another example of the use of the magic foldRight. Here, you:

- Start with the FList<T> you want to append as the initial value.

- Then, iterate over the elements in the receiver FList<T>, adding it as head every time.

Run this code in main to test how append works:

```
val first = FList.of(1, 2, 3)
val second = FList.of(4, 5, 6)
first
  .append(second)
  .forEach(::println)
```

You get:

```
1
2
3
4
5
6
```

Finally, in the same file, add the following code:

```
fun <T, S> FList<T>.flatMap(
  fn: Fun<T, FList<S>>
): FList<S> = foldRight(
  FList.empty() // 1
) { item, acc ->
  fn(item).append(acc) // 2
}
```

Here's another use of `foldRight`. In this code, you:

1. Start with the empty `FList<S>`.

2. Invoke `fn` on each item in the receiver, `FList<T>`, getting an `FList<S>`. The value you return is the `FList<S>` you get by appending the previous accumulator.

To test this code, run the equivalent example you met earlier with `List<T>`. First, add this function:

```
fun countUpToFList(value: Int) = FList.of(*Array(value) { it })
```

Here, you define `countUpToFList` as a simple function that, given a value, returns an `FList<Int>` from 1 to the value itself. Note that you're using the spread (∗) operator to pass in an `Array` for varargs.

Then, use `countUpToFList` to test your `flatMap` in `main`:

```
val intList = FList.of(1, 2, 3)
intList.flatMap(::countUpToFList).forEach(::println)
```

This is similar to what you've done in previous chapters.

When you run this code, you get:

```
0
0
1
0
1
2
```

The Either<A, B> data type

`Optional<T>`, `List<T>` and `FList<T>` are examples of data types with a single type parameter. Life isn't always so simple, however, and sometimes you need something more.

While `Optional<T>` represents a kind of container that can either be empty or contain an object of type T, there might be a case when the container is *never* empty and contains a value of type A *or* a value of type B. For instance, black or white, true or false, 1 or 0 or, more philosophically, right or wrong. This data type is `Either<A, B>`.

Open **Either.kt**, and add the following code:

```
sealed class Either<out A, out B> { // 1

  companion object {
    @JvmStatic
    fun <A> left(left: A): Either<A, Nothing> = Left(left) // 4

    @JvmStatic
    fun <B> right(right: B): Either<Nothing, B> =
Right(right) // 4
  }
}

data class Left<A>(val left: A) : Either<A, Nothing>() // 2
data class Right<B>(val right: B) : Either<Nothing, B>() // 3
```

In this code, you define:

1. Either<A, B> as a sealed class in the type parameters A and B. Note how Either<A, B> is covariant for both A and B.

2. Left<A> as a data class containing a value of type A.

3. Right<B> as a data class containing a value of type B.

4. The builders left and right, which return a Left<B> and a Right<A>, respectively, as objects of the abstract type Either<A, B>.

The use of a sealed class guarantees that an Either<A, B> can only be an object Left<A> or Right<B>. But when would this be useful? As mentioned earlier, a classic example deals with error handling. In this scenario, the name of the possible values gives a hint. Right<A> is successful, and Left<B> represents something wrong.

Open **EitherTest.kt**, and add the following code:

```
fun strToIntEither(
  str: String
): Either<NumberFormatException, Int> = try {
  Either.right(str.toInt())
} catch (nfe: NumberFormatException) {
  Either.left(nfe)
}
```

This is another version of the strToInt function that converts a String to the Int it contains. As you know, this can fail and throw a NumberFormatException. This would make the function impure because an exception is a side effect.

In the previous chapters, you learned that you can make a function pure by moving the side effect as part of the return value. This is what's happening here. The only difference now is that the return value is an `Either<NumberFormatException, Int>`. In the case of success, `strToIntEither` returns `Right<Int>`. In the case of failure, it returns `Left<NumberFormatException>`.

The question now is: How do you interact with this value? The good news is that you already know the answer. `Either<A, B>` is a container with an object of type A or B in it. Every container should provide functions that allow you to interact with the content. The most important functions are still `map` and `flatMap`. Of course, their meaning is slightly different in the context of `Either<A, B>`. You can start simple, with `map`.

Implementing map

The most important and — fortunately — the easiest functionality to implement is `map`. But how can you provide a function of type `Fun<A, B>` if you don't even know if `Either<A, B>` is `Left<A>`or `Right<B>`? The answer is very simple: You provide two. Add the following code to **Either.kt**:

```
fun <A, B, C, D> Either<A, B>.bimap(
  fl: (A) -> C,
  fr: (B) -> D
): Either<C, D> = when (this) {
  is Left<A> -> Either.left(fl(left))
  is Right<B> -> Either.right(fr(right))
}
```

As you see, `bimap` accepts two functions as input parameters. The first, `fl`, is the function of type `Fun<A, C>` — you apply this to the value of type A if `Either<A, B>` is `Left<A>`. `fr`, however, is a function of type `Fun<B, C>` — you apply this if `Either<A, B>` is `Right<B>`.

> **Note**: In Chapter 11, "Functors", you'll learn that a data type providing a function like `bimap` is a **bifunctor**.

Sometimes, you don't want to provide two functions. For this reason, `Either<A, B>` should also provide two different map functions.

To see how, just add the following code in the same **Either.kt** file:

```
fun <A, B, C> Either<A, B>.leftMap(
  fl: (A) -> C
): Either<C, B> = when (this) {
  is Left<A> -> Either.left(fl(left)) // 1
  is Right<B> -> this // 2
}

fun <A, B, D> Either<A, B>.rightMap(
  fr: (B) -> D
): Either<A, D> = when (this) {
  is Right<B> -> Either.right(fr(right)) // 3
  is Left<A> -> this // 4
}
```

In this case:

1. `leftMap` applies the function of type `Fun<A, C>` to the value in `Left<A>`.

2. You return the receiver itself if the receiver is `Right<B>`.

3. `rightMap` applies the function of type `Fun<B, D>` to the value in `Right<A>`.

4. You return the receiver itself if the receiver is `Left<A>`.

Before showing an example using these, it's helpful to see some accessor methods.

Implementing accessors

If you think of every data type as a container, it's often useful to define a function to get their content, like the `getOrDefault` function you met earlier. In this case, you can use different approaches. In Scala, for instance, the `Either<A, B>` type provides a `getOrDefault` only for the `Right<B>` value.

If you decide to do the same, you can add the following code to the same **Either.kt** file:

```
fun <A, B> Either<A, B>.getOrDefault(
  defaultValue: B
): B = when (this) {
  is Left<A> -> defaultValue
  is Right<B> -> right
}
```

This function returns defaultValue if it's Left<A> and the right value if it's Right<B>.

Nothing prevents you from implementing a specific function for Left<A> and Right<B>, like these you can add to the same file:

```
fun <A, B> Either<A, B>.getRightOrDefault(
  defaultValue: B
): B = when (this) {
  is Left<A> -> defaultValue
  is Right<B> -> right
}

fun <A, B> Either<A, B>.getLeftOrDefault(
  defaultValue: A
): A = when (this) {
  is Left<A> -> left
  is Right<B> -> defaultValue
}
```

Defining a flip function that swaps the two types, like this, is also interesting:

```
fun <A, B> Either<A, B>.flip(): Either<B, A> = when (this) {
  is Left<A> -> Either.right(left)
  is Right<B> -> Either.left(right)
}
```

This allows you to use getOrDefault after flip to access the value for Left<A>. A lot of fun!

These functions allow you to run an example of the use for bimap, mapLeft and mapRight. Open **EitherTest.kt** and add the following code:

```
fun main() {
  val squareValue = { a: Int -> a * a }
  val formatError = { ex: Exception ->
    "Error ${ex.localizedMessage}"
  }
  strToIntEither("10").bimap(formatError, squareValue) // 1
```

```
    .getOrDefault(-1).pipe(::println)
  strToIntEither("10").bimap(formatError, squareValue) // 2
    .flip().getOrDefault("No Error!")
    .pipe(::println)
  strToIntEither("10").rightMap(squareValue) // 3
    .getOrDefault(-1).pipe(::println)
  strToIntEither("10aaa").leftMap(formatError) // 4
    .getOrDefault("Generic Error").pipe(::println)
}
```

You can try different combinations, but here you have examples of using:

1. bimap passing formatError to format the error message in the case of the Left<A> value, and squareValue to square the value in the case of Right<B>.

2. bimap with the same formatError and squareValue functions, but using flip to get the value in the case of Left<A>.

3. rightMap to square the value only in the case of Right<B>.

4. leftMap to format the error message only in the case of Left<A>.

Implementing flatMap

As mentioned earlier, Either<A, B> is usually **right-biased**. This means you usually find functions like map and flatMap applicable to the Right<B> side of it, which usually represents success. Left<A> usually represents failure, and there's not normally too much to do in this case. For this reason, you'll implement flatMap for the Right<B> side. In **Either.kt**, add the following code:

```
fun <A, B, D> Either<A, B>.flatMap(
  fn: (B) -> Either<A, D>
): Either<A, D> = when (this) { // 1
  is Left<A> -> Either.left(left) // 2
  is Right<B> -> {
    val result = fn(right) // 3
    when (result) {
      is Left<A> -> Either.left(result.left) // 4
      is Right<D> -> Either.right(result.right) // 5
    }
  }
}
```

In this case, you:

1. Define `flatMap` as an extension function for `Either<A, B>`. Note how the function `fn` you pass in as a parameter has type `(B) -> Either<A, D>`, which means the type for `Left<A>` doesn't change. In Chapter 12, "Monoids & Semigroups", you'll see much more about this. Finally, the return type is `Either<A, D>`.

2. Return a `Left<A>` if the receiver is already of that type.

3. Invoke `fn` in the `right` value if the receiver is a `Right<B>`, getting an `Either<A, D>`.

4. Return a `Left<A>` if you get a `Left<A>` as a result of `fn`.

5. Finally, return a new `Right<D>`, using the value of the same type you get from `fn`.

As a simple example, add the following code to **EitherTest.kt**:

```
fun main() {
  val squareValue = { a: Int -> a * a }

  strToIntEither("10")
    .rightMap(squareValue)
    .rightMap(Int::toString)
    .flatMap(::strToIntEither) // HERE
    .getOrDefault(-1)
    .pipe(::println)
}
```

Running the previous code, you get:

```
100
```

Using `Either<A, B>` in a failure/success scenario is very common, and for this reason, Kotlin provides the `Result<T>` data type, which you'll learn about in Chapter 14, "Error Handling With Functional Programming".

Challenges

You've already done some interesting exercises dealing with data types. But here's an opportunity to have some more fun with a few challenges.

Challenge 9.1: Filtering

How would you implement a `filter` function on a List<T> using `fold` or `foldRight`? You can name it `filterFold`. Remember that given:

```
typealias Predicate<T> = (T) -> Boolean
```

The `filterFold` function for a List<T> should have this signature:

```
fun <T> List<T>.filterFold(predicate: Predicate<T>): List<T> {
  // Implementation
}
```

Challenge 9.2: Length

How would you implement the `length` function for a List<T> that returns its size using `fold` or `foldRight`?

Challenge 9.3: Average

How would you implement the `avg` function for a List<Double> that returns the average of all the elements using `fold` or `foldRight`?

Challenge 9.4: Last

How would you implement the `lastFold` function for a List<T> that returns the last element using `fold` or `foldRight`? What about `firstFold`?

Key points

- A **type** is basically a way to represent a *set of values* you can assign to a variable or, in general, use in your program.

- A **data type** is a way to represent a value in a specific context. You can usually think of a data type as a container for one or more values.

- Optional<T> is a data type that represents a container that can be empty or contain a value of type T.

- lift is the function you use to "elevate" a value of type T into a data type of M<T>.

- map allows you to interact with a value in a data type applying a function. You'll learn all about map in Chapter 11, "Functors".

- flatMap allows you to interact with a value in a data type M<T> using a function that also returns an M<T>. You'll learn all about flatMap in Chapter 13, "Understanding Monads".

- List<T> is a data type that contains an ordered collection of values of type T.

- fold and foldRight are magical functions you can use to implement many other functions.

- The Either<A, B> data type allows you to represent a container that can only contain a value of type A or a value of type B.

- You usually use Either<A, B> in the context of success or failure in the execution of a specific operation.

- Either<A, B> has two type parameters. For this reason, it defines functions like bimap, leftMap and rightMap that you apply explicitly on one of the values.

- Some data types with multiple parameters, like Either<A, B>, have functions that are biased on one of them. For instance, Either<A, B> is right-biased and provides functions that implicitly apply to its Right<B> side.

Where to go from here?

In this chapter, you had a lot of fun and implemented many important functions for the most important data type. In the following chapters, you'll see even more data types and learn about functors and monads in more detail. In the next chapter, you'll have some fun with math. Up next, it's time to learn all about **algebraic data types**.

Chapter 10: Algebraic Data Types

In Chapter 2, "Function Fundamentals", you saw that math and functional programming have a strong relationship. You learned that category theory is the theory of composition, which is one of the main concepts of functions. In Chapter 9, "Data Types", you also learned the concept of data types by studying examples like Optional<T>, List<T>, Either<A, B> and others. In this chapter, you'll learn about the strong relationship between a data type and math. In particular, you'll learn:

- What **algebra** is and how it translates to the class construct and the Either<E, T> data type in Kotlin.

- How and when **algebraic data types** are useful, including a practical example.

- After addition and multiplication, you'll see what the implications of exponents are.

- How to mathematically prove the **currying** operation.

- What a simple List<T> has in common with algebra.

Understanding algebraic data types and their use will help you master functional programming, as they're especially useful for encoding business logic in applications.

Time to do some coding magic with Kotlin and some interesting exercises!

> **Note**: This is a very theoretical chapter that gives you some mathematical proofs of the concepts you've met so far in the book. Feel free to skip it or read it later if you want.

What is algebra?

Algebra is a category of arithmetic that lets you combine numbers with letters representing numbers by using specific rules. Here's an example of a simple algebraic expression:

```
a * X ^ 2 - b * X + c
```

In this example, you have:

- Numbers, like the 2.

- Letters, like a, b and c.

- Operations, like multiplication $*$, addition + and exponentiation $\wedge$.

Algebra is the set of rules that allow you to *combine* all those different symbols. But what does this have to do with Kotlin and functional programming?

Algebra and functional programming have a lot in common. Because of this, programmers can use algebra to understand exactly how functional programming constructs work, starting with product types.

Data types and multiplication

The Kotlin APIs define many classes, including Pair<A, B>, which has the following simple code:

```
public data class Pair<out A, out B>(
    public val first: A,
    public val second: B
) : Serializable {
    // ...
}
```

This class consists of a simple pair of values, the first of type A and the second of type B.

In Chapter 2, "Function Fundamentals", you saw that a type is a way to represent all the possible values a variable of that type can assume. For instance, a Boolean type can contain a value of true or false.

What about the `Pair<A, B>` type? How many values are available for a variable of type `Pair<A, B>`? To understand this, consider the type you're defining by copying the following code into **Struct.kt**, which you'll find in this chapter's material:

```
typealias BoolPair = Pair<Boolean, Boolean>
```

To count all the possible values for a variable of type `BoolPair`, simply add the following code:

```
val bool1 = true to true
val bool2 = true to false
val bool3 = false to true
val bool4 = false to false
```

From a pair of `Boolean` variables, which you can consider a value of 2, you get 4 values in total. But do you get those four values by adding 2 + 2 or multiplying 2 * 2?

Answer this question by adding the following definition to the same file:

```
enum class Triage {
   RED, YELLOW, GREEN
}
```

This defines the `Triage` type, which is an `enum` with three different values: `RED`, `YELLOW` and `GREEN`. Next, add the following code:

```
typealias BoolTriage = Pair<Boolean, Triage>
```

This defines a `Pair` consisting of a `Boolean` and a `Triage`. Now, repeat the same question: How many values does this type have?

To find out, simply use the following code:

```
val triple1 = true to Triage.RED
val triple2 = true to Triage.YELLOW
val triple3 = true to Triage.GREEN
val triple4 = false to Triage.RED
val triple5 = false to Triage.YELLOW
val triple6 = false to Triage.GREEN
```

Which proves the possible values are:

```
Boolean * Triage = 2 * 3 = 6
```

This illustrates that a `Pair<A, B>` has as many values as the product of multiplying A's values by B's values. This is called the **Cartesian product of A and B**, which you can represent as **A × B**. This concept becomes much easier if you use the analogy of a type with a set of values you learned in Chapter 2, "Function Fundamentals". If **A** represents all the values of type A and **B** all the values of type B, the set **A × B** represents the product of the types A and B. **A × B** is the set of all pairs (`a, b`) where a is an element of **A** and b an element of **B**.

Now, look at what happens when incorporating the `Unit` type into the multiplication.

Exercise 10.1: What's the cardinality of the following type?

```
typealias Triplet = Triple<UByte, Boolean, Unit>
```

Note: The cardinality of a set is the number of elements that set can represent. For example, the cardinality of a Boolean would be 2, and the cardinality of the Triage class above is 3.

Product with the unit type

You already know the `Unit` type has a single instance with the same name, `Unit`. In **Struct.kt**, add the following definition:

```
typealias UnitTriage = Pair<Unit, Triage>
```

Now, note that the number of possible values is the value you get by adding the following code to the same file:

```
val unit11 = Unit to Triage.RED
val unit21 = Unit to Triage.YELLOW
val unit31 = Unit to Triage.GREEN
```

You then have:

```
Unit * Triage = 1 * 3 = 3
```

This proves the Unit is equivalent to the value 1 when you multiply by it. It's also important to note that:

```
Unit * Triage = 1 * 3 = 3 = 3 * 1 = Triage * Unit
```

This leads you to:

```
val unit12 = Triage.RED to Unit
val unit22 = Triage.YELLOW to Unit
val unit32 = Triage.GREEN to Unit
```

Which you can think of as values of type:

```
typealias TriageUnit = Pair<Triage, Unit>
```

In the case of Unit and multiplication, consider the following declaration:

```
Unit * Triage = 1 * 3 = 3 * 1 = Triage * Unit
```

It looks like TriageUnit and UnitTriage are the same. They aren't, but, in terms of functions, they're not so different. You can implement a function that maps every element of TriageUnit to *one and only one* element of UnitTriage and vice versa. This function is then **isomorphic**. This means a function of type Fun<A, UnitTriage> isn't so different from Fun<A, TriageUnit>. This is because you can think of the latter as the composition of the former with an isomorphic function.

> **Note**: Isomorphism was introduced in Chapter 2, "Function Fundamentals". You'll continue learning more in Chapter 11: "Functors", and Chapter 12: "Monoids & Semigroups".

For a more practical example, consider a function like the following:

```
fun isEven(a: Int): Boolean = a % 2 == 0
```

This function has type Fun<Int, Boolean> and returns true if the Int value in input is even. Consider, now, the following function:

```
fun booleanToInt(even: Boolean): Int = if (even) 1 else 0
```

This is an isomorphic function of type Fun<Boolean, Int> that maps true to 1 and false to 0. You also could've mapped true to 0 and false to 1. The important part is the meaning of the following function:

```
val isEvenInt = ::isEven compose ::booleanToInt
```

In this case, you just use different values to represent the same information about the Int passed as input. isEvenInt has type Fun<Int, Int> instead of the type Fun<Int, Boolean> of isEven. The Int value's information you get from isEvenInt is actually the same as the Boolean you get from isEven. From a mathematical point of view, you can think of them as the same thing and say that TriageUnit and UnitTriage are isomorphic types. From a category theory point of view, you can say that isomorphic types have the same structures.

Exercise 10.2: What's the cardinality of the following type?

```
typealias Unique = Pair<Unit, Unit>
```

Is this isomorphic with Unit?

Multiplying the Nothing type

In Chapter 2, "Function Fundamentals", you learned about the Nothing type. It's helpful to know what Nothing means in terms of algebraic data types. In **Struct.kt**, add the following definition:

```
typealias NothingTriage = Pair<Nothing, Triage>
```

When you try to add the following code, you get an error. This is because you can't have a value of type Nothing, so you can't create an instance of the NothingTriage type.

```
val nothing1 : NothingTriage = Pair(???, Triage.RED)
```

This means the type Nothing corresponds to the value 0 for multiplication purposes. In this case, you can say that:

```
Nothing * Triage = 0 * 3 = 0 = 3 * 0 = Triage * Nothing
```

Using the set analogy, Nothing represents the empty set. You might wonder if an empty Set<A> is different from an empty Set<B>. They're definitely isomorphic. You can then say that NothingTriage and Nothing are isomorphic types, as it would be the type you define like:

```
typealias TriageNothing = Pair<Triage, Nothing>
```

Multiplying classes

In the previous examples, you used `Pair<A, B>`, but what happens if you define a class like so:

```
data class Struct(
    val enabled: Boolean,
    val triage: Triage,
    val value: Byte
)
```

Based on what you've already learned, you can say that:

```
Struct = Boolean * Triage * Byte = 2 * 3 * 256 = 1536
```

The number of possible values is the product of multiplying all the values of the aggregated types. In this example, `Byte` has **256** values, so the total number of values is **1,536**.

But what happens when you do something like this instead:

```
data class AnotherStruct(
    val enabled: Boolean,
    val triage: Triage,
    val name: String
)
```

`String` has many possible values, so you can't determine an exact result — but having an exact result isn't important. As you'll see later, the important thing is to understand that you can represent the relationship between types as a multiplication operation.

Data types and addition

The next question is about addition, which is another fundamental algebraic operation. Open **Either.kt** and copy the following code, which you might remember from Chapter 9, "Data Types":

```
sealed class Either<out A, out B>
data class Left<A>(val left: A) : Either<A, Nothing>()
data class Right<B>(val right: B) : Either<Nothing, B>()
```

This is the `Either<E, A>` data type, representing a value of type A *or* a value of type B. For your next step, you'll repeat the same exercise. But this time, you'll try to understand how many values the `Either<A, B>` type has in relation to the number of values of A and B.

Start by adding the following definition to **Either.kt**:

```
typealias EitherBooleanOrBoolean = Either<Boolean, Boolean>
```

Then, add the following code:

```
val either1 = Left(true)
val either2 = Left(false)
val either3 = Right(true)
val either4 = Right(false)
```

This is the list of all possible values of the `EitherBooleanOrBoolean` type, which you can think of as:

```
Boolean + Boolean = 2 + 2 = 4
```

This, perhaps, isn't the best example because, as you saw earlier, 4 is 2 + 2 but also 2 * 2. However, you've already learned how to solve this problem.

In this case, just add the following definition to **Either.kt**:

```
typealias EitherBooleanOrTriage = Either<Boolean, Triage>
```

Now, add the following values:

```
val eitherTriage1: Either<Boolean, Triage> = Left(true)
val eitherTriage2: Either<Boolean, Triage> = Left(false)
val eitherTriage3: Either<Boolean, Triage> = Right(Triage.RED)
val eitherTriage4: Either<Boolean, Triage> =
Right(Triage.YELLOW)
val eitherTriage5: Either<Boolean, Triage> = Right(Triage.GREEN)
```

This proves that:

```
Boolean + Triage = 2 + 3 = 5
```

The `Boolean` type has **2** values and the `Triage` type has **3** values, so the `EitherBooleanOrTriage` type has **2 + 3 = 5** values in total.

Exercise 10.3: What's the cardinality of the following type?

```
typealias MultiEither = Either<UByte, Either<Boolean, Triage>>
```

Is `MultiEither` isomorphic with `MultiEither2`, which you define in the following way?

```
typealias MultiEither2 = Either<Either<UByte, Boolean>, Triage>
```

Addition with Unit and Nothing types

Now it's easy to see the role of the `Unit` and `Nothing` types in the case of `Either<A, B>`. You already know how to understand this. Enter the following code in **Either.kt**:

```
typealias EitherBooleanOrNothing = Either<Boolean, Nothing>

val boolNothing1: Either<Boolean, Nothing> = Left(true)
val boolNothing2: Either<Boolean, Nothing> = Left(false)
```

Now, it's simple to understand that:

```
Boolean + Nothing = 2 + 0 = 2
```

The `Nothing` type, as you saw earlier, translates to **0**.

And now for the `Unit` case, enter:

```
typealias EitherBooleanOrUnit = Either<Boolean, Unit>

val boolUnit1: Either<Boolean, Unit> = Left(true)
val boolUnit2: Either<Boolean, Unit> = Left(false)
val boolUnit3: Either<Boolean, Unit> = Right(Unit)
```

Which translates to:

```
Boolean + Unit = 2 + 1 = 3
```

Like when you multiplied it earlier, the `Unit` type counts as **1**.

Putting algebra to work

After some simple calculations, you now understand that a class can represent values that are, in number, the product of multiplying the possible values of the aggregated types. You also learned that Either<A, B> has as many values as the sum of the values of types A and B.

But how is this knowledge useful?

As a simple example, open **TypeSafeCallback.kt**, and enter the following definition:

```
typealias Callback<Data, Result, Error> =
    (Data, Result?, Error?) -> Unit
```

This is the definition of a Callback<Data, Result, Error> type. It could, for example, represent the operation you invoke to notify something of the result of an asynchronous task.

It's important to note that you define the Result and Error types as optional.

With this type, you want to consider that:

• You always receive some data back from the asynchronous function.

• If the result is successful, you receive the content in a Result object, which is null otherwise.

• If there are any errors, you receive a value of type Error, which is also null otherwise.

To simulate a typical use case of the previous type, enter the following code into **TypeSafeCallback.kt**:

```
// 1
class Response
class Info
class ErrorInfo

// 2
fun runAsync(callback: Callback<Response, Info, ErrorInfo>) {
    // TODO
}
```

In this code, you:

1. Define some types to use as placeholders. You don't really care about what's inside those classes here.

2. Create `runAsync` with a parameter of `Callback<Data, Result, Error>`.

An example of when to implement `runAsync` is when you're performing an asynchronous operation, and you invoke the callback function then pass the corresponding parameter. For instance, in the case of success, `runAsync` might result in the following, where you return some `Response` and the `Info` into it:

```
fun runAsync(callback: Callback<Response, Info, ErrorInfo>) {
    // In case of success
    callback(Response(), Info(), null)
}
```

If there's an error, you could use the following code to return the `Response` along with `ErrorInfo`, which encapsulates information about the problem.

```
fun runAsync(callback: Callback<Response, Info, ErrorInfo>) {
    // In case of error
    callback(Response(), null, ErrorInfo())
}
```

But there's a problem with this: The type you define using the `Callback<Data, Result, Error>` typealias isn't type-safe. It describes values that make no sense in `runAsync`'s case. That type doesn't prevent you from having code like the following:

```
fun runAsync(callback: Callback<Response, Info, ErrorInfo>) {
    // 1
    callback(Response(), null, null)
    // 2
    callback(Response(), Info(), ErrorInfo())
}
```

Here, you might:

*   Have a `Response` without any `Info` or `ErrorInfo`.

*   Return both `Info` and `ErrorInfo`.

This is because the return type allows those values. You need a way to implement type safety.

Using algebra for type safety

Algebraic data types can help with type safety. You need to translate the semantic of `Callback<Data, Result, Error>` into an algebraic expression. Then, apply some mathematic rules.

What you're expecting from the callback is:

```
A Result AND an Info OR a Result AND an ErrorInfo
```

You can represent the previous sentence as:

```
Result * Info + Result * ErrorInfo
```

Now, apply the associative property (https://en.wikipedia.org/wiki/Associative_property) and get:

```
Result * (Info + ErrorInfo)
```

This is similar to what you saw earlier.

Next, translate this to the following and add it to **TypeSafeCallback.kt**:

```
typealias SafeCallback<Data, Result, Error> =
    (Pair<Data, Either<Error, Result>>) -> Unit
```

The safe version of `runAsync` now looks like the following code, which you can also add to **TypeSafeCallback.kt**:

```
fun runAsyncSafe(callback: SafeCallback<Response, Info,
ErrorInfo>) {
    // 1
    callback(Response() to Right(Info()))
    // 2
    callback(Response() to Left(ErrorInfo()))
}
```

The only values you can return using the safe callback are:

1. A `Response` and an `Info` object, in the case of success.

2. In the case of an error, the same `Response` but with an `ErrorInfo`.

More important than what you *can* do is what you *can't* do. You can't return *both* `Info` and `ErrorInfo`, but you must return *at least one* of them.

Other algebraic properties

The analogy between types and algebra is fun because it reveals some interesting facts. For instance, you know that:

```
A * 1 = A = 1 * A
```

Which translates into:

```
A * Unit = A = Unit * A
```

This tells you that `Pair<A, Unit>` is the same as `Pair<Unit, A>`, which is the same as A, as you saw earlier in this chapter about **isomorphism**.

Another way to say this is that adding a property of type `Unit` to an existing type doesn't add any useful information.

You also know that:

```
A + 0 = A = 0 + A
```

Becomes:

```
A + Nothing = A = Nothing + A
```

This represents a type you can write as:

```
typealias NothingType<A> = Either<Nothing, A>
```

Finally, write:

```
A * 0 = 0 = 0 * A
```

Which becomes:

```
A * Nothing = 0 = Nothing * A
```

You can write this as:

```
typealias NothingPair<A> = Pair<A, Nothing>
```

You can't create a `Pair` using a value of type A and `Nothing`, so this is basically the `Nothing` type.

Algebra with the Optional type

Another curious thing is that:

```
A + 1 = A + Unit = Either<A, Unit>
1 + A = Unit + A = Either<Unit, A>
```

This means the `Either<A, Unit>` type has all the possible values of A plus a single value that is `Unit`. This is something you could represent like this:

```
sealed class Opt<out A>
object None : Opt<Unit>()
class Some<A>(value: A) : Opt<A>()
```

Do you recognize it? This is basically the `Optional<T>` type you learned about in Chapter 9, "Data Types". You have a value of type A, or you have another single and unique value, which is `None` here, but could also be `Unit`.

Fun with exponents

So far, you've seen what multiplication and addition mean in the context of types. Next, you'll see what you can express using exponents.

Start by writing the following expression:

```
// 1
A ^ 2 = A * A = Pair<A, A>
// 2
A ^ 3 = A * A * A = Pair<A, Pair<A, A>> = Pair<Pair<A, A>, A>
// ...
```

Starting from a given type A, you can see that:

1. You can represent the value **A ^ 2** as **A * A**, which is equivalent to `Pair<A, A>`.

2. For the same reason, you can think of **A ^ 3** as **A * A * A**, which is equivalent to `Pair<A, Pair<A, A>>` or `Pair<Pair<A, A>, A>`.

The same is true for each value of the exponent.

But what about the meaning of the expression **A ^ B**, where A and B are types? How many possible values can you represent with a type that corresponds with the expression, like `Boolean ^ Triage`?

This is less intuitive and needs some more work.

If the analogy between types and algebra is true, the number of values for the type Boolean ^ Triage should be **8** because:

```
Boolean ^ Triage = 2 ^ 3 = 8
```

But what does the number **8** represent? It represents how you can take the number of values of Boolean to the power of the number of values of Triage. This can happen in multiple ways — which are the number of ways to associate a Boolean value with a value of the Triage type.

This perfectly describes the (Triage) -> Boolean function type. Prove this by adding the following code to **Exponents.kt**:

```kotlin
fun func0(triage: Triage): Boolean = when (triage) {
    Triage.RED -> false
    Triage.YELLOW -> false
    Triage.GREEN -> false
}

fun func1(triage: Triage): Boolean = when (triage) {
    Triage.RED -> false
    Triage.YELLOW -> false
    Triage.GREEN -> true
}

fun func2(triage: Triage): Boolean = when (triage) {
    Triage.RED -> false
    Triage.YELLOW -> true
    Triage.GREEN -> false
}

fun func3(triage: Triage): Boolean = when (triage) {
    Triage.RED -> false
    Triage.YELLOW -> true
    Triage.GREEN -> true
}

fun func4(triage: Triage): Boolean = when (triage) {
    Triage.RED -> true
    Triage.YELLOW -> false
    Triage.GREEN -> false
}

fun func5(triage: Triage): Boolean = when (triage) {
    Triage.RED -> true
    Triage.YELLOW -> false
    Triage.GREEN -> true
}

fun func6(triage: Triage): Boolean = when (triage) {
```

```
        Triage.RED -> true
        Triage.YELLOW -> true
        Triage.GREEN -> false
    }

    fun func7(triage: Triage): Boolean = when (triage) {
        Triage.RED -> true
        Triage.YELLOW -> true
        Triage.GREEN -> true
    }
```

There are exactly **8** different ways of mapping a `Triage` value into a `Boolean` value. Think of **A ^ B** as equivalent to a function from B to A. You can then assert that:

```
A ^ B = (B) -> A
```

The consequences of this are surprising.

Proving currying

In Chapter 8, "Composition", you learned about the `curry` function. It basically allows you to define the equivalence between a function of type `(A, B) -> C` with a function of type `(A) -> (B) -> C`. But where does `curry` come from? Is it something that always works, or is it a fluke? It's time to prove it.

In the previous section, you learned that exponential A `^` B can be translated in a function from B to A of type `(B) -> A` or `Fun<B, A>`. One of the most important properties of exponents is the following:

```
(A ^ B) ^ C = A ^ (B * C)
```

The equality, =, is *symmetric*, so you can also write:

```
A ^ (B * C) = (A ^ B) ^ C
```

Now, recall what you've already learned about multiplication and exponentiation, and translate that to:

```
(Pair<B, C>) -> A = (C) -> (B) -> A
```

Using some Kotlin notation, you can write this as:

```
(B, C) -> A = (C) -> (B) -> A
```

Sorting the types' variables in an easier way, you can read that equation by saying that a function of two input parameters, A and B with output C — (A, B) -> C — is equivalent to a function with an input parameter of A and an output parameter of function type (B) -> C. This is exactly what you'd call currying. Here's what you'll find in **Curry.kt** in the material for this chapter:

```
fun <A, B, C> Fun2<A, B, C>.curry(): (A) -> (B) -> C = { a: A ->
  { b: B ->
    this(a, b)
  }
}
```

This proves the equivalence between the two function types.

Nothing and exponents

As you may know, in math:

```
A ^ 0 = 1
```

Using the type analogy, now write:

```
A ^ Nothing = Unit
```

Which means:

```
(Nothing) -> A = Unit
```

In this case, the tricky thing is that = means isomorphism. So how can you read the previous definition? In Chapter 2, "Function Fundamentals", you saw a function of type Fun<Nothing, A>, which you called the "absurd function" because you can't invoke it. To invoke that function, you need a value of type Nothing, which doesn't exist. Because you can never invoke that function, all the functions of that type are the same. They all have the same meaning, and they all produce — or better, *never* produce — the same result.

Another way to say that all those functions are the same is: If you take one of those, all the others are equivalent. You can represent all of them with just one, and a way to represent a singleton is with Unit.

Powers and 1

Keep having fun with the following equivalence:

```
1 ^ A = 1
```

Whatever the exponent is for 1, you always get 1. Using equivalence with types, you can say that:

```
(A) -> Unit = Unit
```

This means there's only one function from a type A to `Unit`. It's a way to reinforce the definition of a terminal object that states there's a unique morphism from any object to it.

Now, consider this:

```
A ^ 1 = A
```

Which translates to:

```
(Unit) -> A = A
```

This is another way to define the `unit` function you also learned about in Chapter 2, "Function Fundamentals".

Exponentials and addition

Another important property for exponents is:

```
A ^ (B + C) = A ^ B * A ^ C
```

Which translates to:

```
(Either<B, C>) -> A = Pair<(B) -> A, (C) -> A>
```

This basically means that a function accepting a value of type B or C to produce a value of type A is isomorphic with a couple of functions — the first from B to A and the second from C to A.

Using algebra with the List type

As a last bit of fun with algebra and types, enter the following definition into **List.kt**:

```kotlin
sealed class NaturalNumber
// 1
object Zero : NaturalNumber()
// 2
data class Successor(val prev: NaturalNumber) : NaturalNumber()
```

This is a simple **sealed class**, which represents all natural numbers as:

1. The Zero value.

2. A set of all the possible Successors.

As an example, add the following to the same file:

```kotlin
// 1
val ZERO = Zero
// 2
val ONE = Successor(Zero)
// 3
val TWO = Successor(Successor(Zero)) // Successor(ONE)
// 4
val THREE = Successor(Successor(Successor(Zero))) //
Successor(TWO)
// 5
// ...
```

Here, you define:

1. The first value as ZERO.

2. ONE as the successor of ZERO.

3. TWO as the successor of ONE.

4. THREE as the successor of TWO.

5. And so on...

What's more interesting is comparing the previous definition with the one of Either<A, B>:

```
NaturalNumber = 1 + NaturalNumber
```

This is because you translate Either into an addition operation.

But the previous addition becomes:

```
NaturalNumber = 1 + NaturalNumber
NaturalNumber = 1 + (1 + NaturalNumber)
NaturalNumber = 1 + (1 + (1 + NaturalNumber))
NaturalNumber = 1 + (1 + (1 + (1 + NaturalNumber)))
...
```

This suggests that the set of NaturalNumber can be seen as a sequence of ones, one for each natural number. Now, consider the List<A> data type. Using the same reasoning, think of it as something you can define by entering the following code into **List.kt**:

```
sealed interface FList<out A>
object Nil : FList<Nothing>
data class FCons<A>(
  val head: A,
  val tail: FList<A> = Nil
) : FList<A>
```

Does it ring a bell? You used this in Chapter 7, "Functional Data Structures". This means that a FList<A> can be empty, or you can think of it as a head and tail, which may or may not be empty. You can then create a list of five values in the following way and add it to **List.kt**:

```
val countList =
  FCons(1, FCons(2, FCons(3, FCons(4, FCons(5, Nil)))))
```

An immutable characteristic of math is that it *always* makes all the pieces work together.

Functional lists and algebra

Now, what if you want to calculate the sum of the elements in FList<Int>? You do it by implementing a recursive function, like this:

```
fun FList<Int>.sum(): Int = when (this) {
  is Nil -> 0
  is FCons<Int> -> head + tail.sum()
}
```

Now, test it by copying and running the following code in **List.kt**:

```
fun main() {
    println(countList.sum())
}
```

And you get:

```
15
```

So far, so good. But from an algebraic point of view, you write the previous FList<A> type like this:

```
FList<A> = 1 + A * FList<A>
```

This is because it can be the Nil (and so the 1) or a Pair of an object of type A and another FList<A>.

Now, repeat what you did in the case of the NaturalNumber and get:

```
FList<A>  = 1 + A * FList<A>
          = 1 + A * (1 + A * FList<A>) = 1 + A + A ^ 2 + A *
FList<A>
          = 1 + A + A ^ 2 + A ^ 3 + A ^ 4 * FList<A>
...
```

This allows you to see FList<A> as a possible combination of all the possible FList<A>s of length 0, 1, 2, 3 and so on.

The + here has the meaning of a logical **OR**, so an FList<A> is an empty FList OR a single element of type A OR a pair of elements of type A OR a triplet of elements of type A and so on.

Write this as:

```
FList<A> = 1 + A * FList<A>      =>
FList<A> - A * FList<A> = 1      =>

FList<A> * (1 - A) = 1           =>

               1
FList<A> =  -------
            (1 - A)
```

This is the geometric series (https://en.wikipedia.org/wiki/Geometric_series), which is equivalent to:

```
               1
FList<A> =  -------  = 1 + A + A^2 + A^3 + A^4 + .... + A^N + ...
            (1 - A)
```

It's curious how a complex data type like List<A> has an algebraic relationship.

Key points

- **Algebra** is a category of arithmetic that lets you combine numbers with letters representing numbers by using specific rules.

- You can think of a type as the **Cartesian product** of the types of its properties. For instance, Pair<A, B> is the Cartesian product of A and B.

- A Cartesian product of a type A and a type B is a new type, represented as A × B. Its values are all the pairs (a, b) that you can create using a value a from A and a value b from B.

- The term **isomorphic** means "having the same form or structure". Two types, A and B, are isomorphic if a function of type Fun<A, B> maps each value of A to one and only one value in B and vice versa.

- Two isomorphic types are equivalent in the sense that you can use one or the other without adding or removing any type of information.

- Exponents like A ^ B are equivalent to the function type Fun<B, A>.

- Exponents' properties allow you to have evidence of some important functional programming concepts. For instance, the fact that (A ^ B) ^ C = A ^ (B * C) proves **currying**.

Where to go from here?

Wow! In this chapter, you had a lot of fun using math to prove some important functional programming tools like currying. As mentioned in the chapter's introduction, these concepts give you some helpful information for thinking more functionally. In the next chapter, you'll start learning all about the concept of **functors** and the map function.

Chapter 11: Functors

In Chapter 9, "Data Types", you met the map function for the first time. You learned that it's one of the most important functions many data types provide and that it's related to the concept of a **functor**. But what is a functor, and why is map so important? In this chapter, you'll learn:

- What a **functor** is and how it's related to category theory.

- How to apply the concept of a functor to the category of types and functions.

- What **functor laws** are and how to use **equational reasoning** to verify them.

- How to use the FList<T> and List<T> functors.

- What a **bifunctor** is in relation to category theory.

- How to implement bimap for algebraic data types.

This is a very theoretical chapter without exercises or challenges. However, it's helpful for getting you into a more functional mindset.

What is a functor?

The definition of **functor** is quite simple. A functor is basically a way to **map** one category in another while *preserving the structure*. But what does *structure of a category* mean? The first step to understanding is a quick revision of the concept of *category*.

In Chapter 2, "Function Fundamentals", you learned that a category is a bunch of *objects* and some arrows between them, which are called **morphisms**. A category has three fundamental properties:

- Composition
- Associativity
- Identity

In Figure 11.1, you see an example of a category with two objects and one morphism between them in addition to the identity morphisms that, by definition, must be present for all objects.

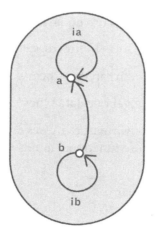

Figure 11.1: Category structure

Note: Remember that in a category, every object must have a morphism, called identity. You represent this as an arrow from the object back to itself. This is always true, even though, for simplicity, you won't see them in all the following pictures.

Categories tend to have structures because objects and morphisms give them a sort of pattern. For instance, you might have another category, like in Figure 11.2, that also has two objects and a morphism between them. Although they're two distinct categories, you can recognize that they have the same structure or recall the same pattern.

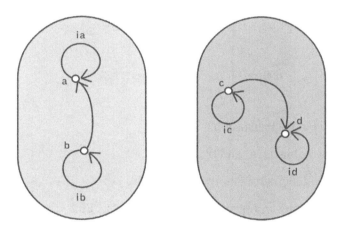

Figure 11.2: Category patterns

This offers the chance to map a category into another one, keeping the same structure, which recalls the same pattern. In the previous example, the pattern has two objects and one morphism between them.

A functor, then, is something more than just mapping between two categories. It must also preserve the structure. This means a functor has to map objects into objects and morphisms into morphisms, following some rules.

Consider, then, two categories, **C** and **D**, as in Figure 11.3:

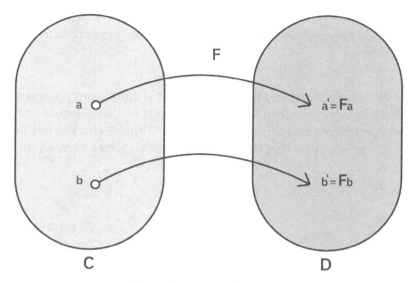

Figure 11.3: Mapping objects

There you have:

- A category **C** with two objects, **a** and **b**.

- A category **D** with two objects, **a'** and **b'**.

- A functor **F** mapping object **a** to **a'** and object **b** to **b'**.

As you see in the image, you can represent **a'** as **Fa** and **b'** as **Fb**.

Now, category **C** might have some structure you can represent with a morphism **f** from **a** to **b**. The structure depends on the category, but in this example, you can think of **f** as a single morphism from **a** to **b**. If this is the case, a functor also has to map **f** into another morphism in the category **D**. This is where the concept of *preserving the structure* becomes fundamental. If category **C** has a morphism **f** from **a** to **b**, a functor must map it to another morphism, which you represent as **Ff**, between **a'** and **b'**.

You can also say that the functor must map the morphism **f** to a morphism **Ff** from **Fa** to **Fb**.

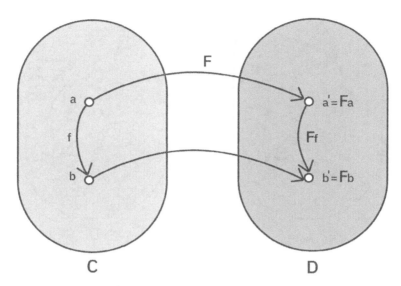

Figure 11.4: Mapping morphisms

Note: It's important to say that you might map **f** into another morphism between two objects different from **a'** and **b'**. That's perfectly legal, but you wouldn't define a functor in that case.

Of course, you might have many different morphisms between **a** and **b**. In category theory, the set of all the morphisms between two objects has a name: the **hom-set**.

With **C(a, b)**, you can represent the hom-set of all the morphisms between **a** and **b** in the category **C**. At the same time, **D(Fa, Fb)** can represent the hom-set of all the morphisms between **Fa** and **Fb**. A functor, then, is a way to map each morphism in **C(a, b)** to a morphism in **D(Fa, Fb)**. Because the hom-sets are sets, and you're mapping elements of a set into elements of another set, a *functor is a function*.

A functor is an exceptional function, though, because mapping all the morphisms of the hom-set **C(a, b)** to morphisms in the hom-set **D(Fa, Fb)** isn't enough. A functor must also preserve — guess what — *composition*! Consider, then, Figure 11.5:

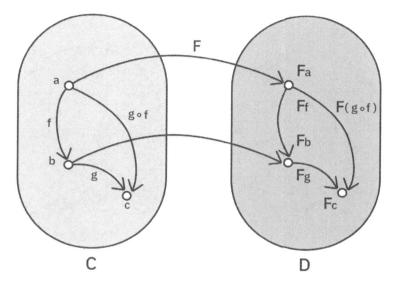

Figure 11.5: Functor composition

This figure has several important things to note:

- The category **C** has three different objects: **a**, **b** and **c**, with a morphism **f** from **a** to **b** and a morphism **g** from **b** to **c**.

- If **C** is a category, because of the *composition* property, another morphism must exist from **a** to **c**: the composition of the morphisms **f** and **g**. You represent it as **g** ∘ **f** and read it as "g after f".

- From the definition of a functor, you know that it maps **a** to **a'** = **Fa**, **b** to **b'** = **Fb** and **c** to **c'** = **Fc** in the category **D**.

- The functor also maps the morphism **f** to **Ff** and the morphism **g** to **Fg**.

- Because **D** is a category, there must be a morphism from **Fa** to **Fc** that's the composition of the morphisms **Ff** and **Fg**. You represent this as **Fg** ∘ **Ff** and read it as "Fg after Ff".

What makes **F** a functor is that **F (g ∘ f) = Fg ∘ Ff**. In other words, the *functor of the composition* is the *composition of a functor*. This is the formal definition of the *preservation of structure* concept.

It's crucial to note that:

- Not all mappings between objects and morphisms work like this. On the contrary, most don't.

- What's true for a morphism **f** from **a** to **b** must be true for the entire hom-set of all the morphisms from **a** to **b**.

- In the case of identity, it must be true that **F ia = i Fa**. This means that a functor must map identity morphisms **ia** for every object **a** to the identity for the object **Fa**, which you can represent as **i Fa**.

The points above are the rules a functor must follow, usually referred to as the **functor laws**. In short, a functor *must preserve*:

- **Composition**, which means that **F (g ∘ f) = Fg ∘ Ff**.

- **Identity**, which means that **F ia = i Fa**.

This is true for all the categories. But you, as an engineer, are interested in one particular category: the category of types and functions.

> **Note**: To better understand these concepts, take your time reviewing this section as many times as you need. Try to imagine categories with different structures and how the functor would change in each case.

Functors in programming

In the previous section, you learned what a functor is in terms of category theory. But, as a programmer, you're particularly interested in one category: the one where objects are types and morphisms are functions. In this case, you're working with **endo-functors**. The "endo" prefix means "internal" and emphasizes that the functor maps types in types and functions in functions.

> **Note**: Even if the functors in programming are endo-functors, you usually ignore the prefix and just call them functors.

> **Note**: In this chapter, you'll use different letters as type parameters. Sometimes you'll use T and other types A and B. The name you use isn't important, but in general, you'll use T when referring to the generic data type and A and B when dealing with functions of type Fun<A, B>.

In your context, then, a functor maps *types to types*. It's crucial to note that this must work for any type in the category. To represent a functor, you need a way to declare the type as a parameter and replace that parameter with the specific type you need. The good news is that you already know how to do this using generic types and type parameters. If **F** is your functor, you'll represent it as **F<A>** where **A** is the type parameter. You often call **F<A>** a **type constructor** because you create a type, **F<A>**, starting from the type **A**.

But a functor doesn't map just objects — it also must map functions. How can it do that? The best way to understand this is with an example. Open **Optional.kt** in this chapter's material, and look at the code you implemented in Chapter 9, "Data Types":

```kotlin
sealed class Optional<out T> {

  companion object {
    @JvmStatic
    fun <T> lift(value: T): Optional<T> = Some(value)

    @JvmStatic
    fun <T> empty(): Optional<T> = None
  }
}

object None : Optional<Nothing>()
data class Some<T>(val value: T) : Optional<T>()
```

The Optional<T> data type provides the context of some object that can be present or not. To make things clearer, the **Optional** here is the **F** you've used so far to represent a functor, and Optional<T> is its type constructor, **F<T>**. When you replace the type parameter, you can have Optional<Int>, Optional<Boolean>, Optional<User>, etc. What you'll define for Optional<T> will be valid whatever T's specific type is.

Note: As you learned in Chapter 9, "Data Types", you can use functions like lift to create an Optional<T> from an object of type T or, in general, an F<T> from a T.

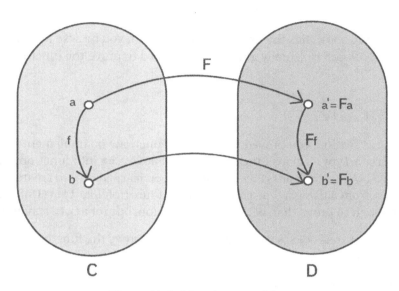

Figure 11.4: Mapping morphisms

Now, look at Figure 11.4 and assign a specific meaning to every object and morphism. In the source category, you have two types, A and B, and a function f from A to B of type Fun<A, B>. You know how to map the type A to Optional<A> and the type B to Optional<B>. To make Optional<T> a function, you need a way to map the function f of type Fun<A, B> to a function from Optional<A> to Optional<B> of type Fun<Optional<A>, Optional<B>>. This is precisely the map function you implemented in Chapter 9, "Data Types", like this:

```
fun <A, B> Optional<A>.map(fn: Fun<A, B>): Optional<B> =
    when (this) {
        is None -> Optional.empty()
        is Some<A> -> Optional.lift(fn(value))
    }
```

Note how the type of map is Fun<Fun<A, B> -> Fun<Optional<A>, Optional<B>>> because it:

- Receives as input a function of type Fun<A, B>.

- Returns an output of a function of type Fun<Optional<A>, Optional<B>>.

Another way to represent the type of map is:

```
((A) -> B)) -> ((Optional<A>) -> Optional<B>)
```

The function map above has the right type, but how can you be sure the Optional<T> with the previous map is actually a functor? You need to prove the functor laws.

Functor laws

In the previous section, you proved that the map function you implemented in Chapter 9, "Data Types", maps functions of type Fun<A, B> into functions of type Fun<Optional<A>, Optional<B>>. Previously, you learned how to create an Optional<A> from A using a type constructor or a function like lift. Unfortunately, this isn't enough to prove that, with the map function, Optional<T> is now a functor.

To prove that Optional<T> is a functor, you need to prove the functor laws, and specifically, that it preserves *composition* and *identity*.

To prove that your Optional<T> with the map you implemented is a functor, you need to prove that:

- **F ia = i Fa**

- **F (g ∘ f) = Fg ∘ Ff**

Proving these for the Optional<T> data type is a useful exercise. To do so, you use a technique called **equational reasoning**. Equational reasoning works here because Kotlin allows you to define pure functions as equalities. The left side is equal to the right side, and you can use the substitution model — as you learned in Chapter 3, "Functional Programming Concepts" — to replace the invocation of the function with the expression itself. Replacing the function invocation with the expression it represents is a technique called **inlining**. Of course, equality is symmetric, so you can also replace an expression with the invocation to the related function. In this case, you use a technique called **refactoring**.

> **Note:** Not all programming languages provide tools to easily prove the functor laws. Sometimes, other programming languages provide unit tests to prove the same properties more empirically.

Preserving identity for Optional<T>

To prove that the Optional<T> data type and map function you implemented above are a functor, you need to prove some laws. The first is about identity. You basically need to prove the following equation:

```
F ia = i Fa
```

In other terms, given the identity function:

```
fun <A> id(a: A): A = a
```

You need to prove that by invoking map on an Optional<T> passing the id function, you get the identity for Optional<T>. Suppose, then, you have an Optional<T> you defined in this way, shown here again for convenience:

```
sealed class Optional<out T> {

  companion object {
    @JvmStatic
    fun <T> lift(value: T): Optional<T> = Some(value)

    @JvmStatic
    fun <T> empty(): Optional<T> = None
  }
}

object None : Optional<Nothing>()
data class Some<T>(val value: T) : Optional<T>()
```

This definition says that an Optional<A> can be None or a Some<T>. You also defined map like this:

```
fun <A, B> Optional<A>.map(fn: Fun<A, B>): Optional<B> =
  when (this) {
    is None -> Optional.empty()
    is Some<A> -> Optional.lift(fn(value))
  }
```

What you need to do is replace the function `fn` with an identity and see if you get the identity for `Optional<T>`. That would then be a function that returns exactly the same `Optional<T>` you pass as an input parameter.

If the `Optional<T>` is `None`, and the function `fn` is `id`, the map function becomes:

```
fun <A, B> Optional<A>.map(): Optional<A> = Optional.empty()
```

If the `Optional<T>` is `Some<T>`, and the function is `id`, you get:

```
fun <A, A> Optional<A>.map(): Optional<A> =
Optional.lift(id(value))
```

Note that because `id` is the identity function, you can replace the type `B` with `A`. Given that `id(value) = value`, you get:

```
fun <A, A> Optional<A>.map(): Optional<A> = Optional.lift(value)
```

Or:

```
fun <A, A> Optional<A>.map(): Optional<A> = Some(value)
```

To summarize what you've just done, you'll get:

• None if the `Optional<T>` is `None`.

• Some<T> if the `Optional<T>` is `Some<T>`.

This is the identity function for `Optional<T>`!

Preserving composition for Optional<T>

To prove that `Optional<T>` with the map function you implemented is a functor, you also need to prove that it preserves composition, which means that:

```
F (g ∘ f) = Fg ∘ Ff
```

In this case, you also have two possible cases. If your `Optional<T>` is `None`, the map function becomes:

```
fun <A, B> Optional<A>.map(): Optional<B> = Optional.empty()
```

This means that if you have `None`, whatever function you apply, you always get `None`. This is true if you apply just `f`, `g` or the composition of the two. In the case of `None`, the left and right members are then the same.

In case of Some<T>, the map function becomes:

```
fun <A, B> Some<A>.map(fn: Fun<A, B>): Some<B> = Some(fn(value))
```

This means that you basically lose the option for the case when the value isn't present. You remove the effect of the context, which consists in removing the F from the equation, getting:

```
g ∘ f = g ∘ f
```

This is true by definition, so you can conclude that the Optional<T> and map function you created defines a functor.

The FList<T> and List<T> functors

In Chapter 9, "Data Types", you implemented map for the FList<T> data type and used the map implementation Kotlin provides for the List<T> type. In this chapter, you won't prove that FList<T> and List<T> are functors, but you'll see an interesting property of the fact that they are. This is a consequence of the functor laws you previously proved for Optional<T>.

As you know, if you have two functions, f and g, and any functor F, the following equivalence is true:

```
F ( g ∘ f ) = Fg ∘ Ff
```

In the case of FList<T> and List<T>, you can write this as:

```
val list = FList.of(1, 2, 3, 4, 5, 6, 7, 8, 9, 10) // 1
val left = list.map(f).map(g) // 2
val right = list.map(g after f) // 3
```

In this code, you:

1. Create an FList<Int>, but it could also be a List<Int>.

2. Invoke map a first time, passing the function f as a parameter and then a second time passing g as a parameter. This is the code version of the left side of the previous equation.

3. Invoke map, passing the composition of f and g as a parameter.

The functor laws say that the two sides of the equation are the same. The good news is in terms of performance. If N is the length of the list, the left side has complexity O(2N) while the right side has complexity O(N). In terms of complexity, a constant doesn't matter: The composition g ∘ f takes approximately the same time as invoking f first and then g. In this case, you still have a single iteration, and the equivalent provides you the opportunity to write more readable code.

Bifunctors

In the previous sections, you learned what a functor is in terms of category theory, and you proved the functor laws for the Optional<T> data type. You also saw that knowing FList<T> and List<T> are functors helps you structure your code in an easier — and, probably more performant — way. Optional<T>, FList<T> and List<T> all have a single type parameter. In Chapter 9, "Data Types", you also implemented Either<A, B> as an example of a data type with multiple type parameters. So, what's the relationship between the concept of a functor and Either<A, B>?

To understand this, start from the two categories in Figure 11.6:

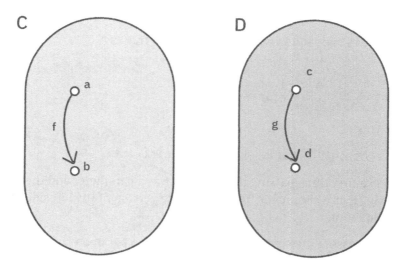

Figure 11.6: Couple of categories

Here, you have the categories:

- **C**, with the objects **a** and **b** and a morphism **f** between them.

- **D**, with the objects **c** and **d** and a morphism **g** between them.

So far, so good. Now, consider what's in Figure 11.7:

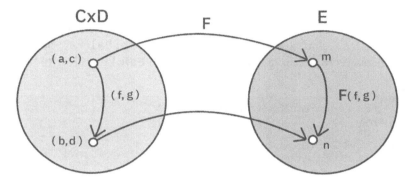

Figure 11.7: The product category

In this figure, you have:

- The category **C×D**, which is the **Cartesian product** of the category **C** and **D**. This means each object in the category **C×D** is a couple of objects, **(c, d)**, where **c** is an object of **C**, and **d** is an object of **D**.

- The morphism **f** from **a** to **b** in **C** and the morphism **g** from **c** to **d** in **D** becomes the morphism **(f, g)**. Note how you go from the object **(a, b)** to **(c, d)** using both the functions, **(f, g)**.

- Of course, **C×D** is a category, and you can create a functor **F** to another category **E** in the same way you did previously.

The main difference is that now the type constructor contains *two* different type parameters, not just one, which is why it's called a **bifunctor**.

The relationship between bifunctors and algebraic data types you learned in Chapter 10, "Algebraic Data Types", is intriguing. As you know, the type Pair<A, B> is an example of the product of types, while Either<A, B> is an example of the sum. In both cases, you can define a function, bimap, like the following one you already implemented in **Either.kt** in this chapter's material:

```
fun <A, B, C, D> Either<A, B>.bimap(
  fl: Fun<A, C>,
  fr: Fun<B, D>
): Either<C, D> = when (this) {
  is Left<A> -> Either.left(fl(left))
  is Right<B> -> Either.right(fr(right))
}
```

Depending on if Either<A, B> is a Left<A> or a Right<B>, you apply the function fl or fr, respectively. You never apply both. In the case of Pair<A, B>, you'd implement the same function in a similar way. Open **Pair.kt**, and write the following code:

```
fun <A, B, C, D> Pair<A, B>.bimap(
  fl: Fun<A, C>,
  fr: Fun<B, D>
): Pair<C, D> = fl(first) to fr(second)
```

As you see, you define:

- bimap as an extension function of the Pair<A, B> type, receiving two functions as input parameters.

- fl as the first input parameter of type Fun<A, C> and fr as the second input parameter of type Fun<B, D>.

- Pair<C, D> as the return type for bimap.

It's essential that you always invoke both fl and fr on the first and second properties, respectively, getting the object of type Pair<C, D> in return.

You won't prove it in this book, but the good news is that you can define a functor or bifunctor for any algebraic data type.

Typeclasses

In the last three chapters, you learned how to implement some of the most important data types and saw how to make them work as functors. When you say that List<T> is a functor, you know that you can use a map function accepting another function as a parameter, and the functor laws will be valid. If you have multiple type parameters, you can say the same things about bifunctors and the bimap function.

It also means that many data types have some common behavior. You usually refer to this common behavior with the concept of a **typeclass**. A *functor* is then a *typeclass*. In the following chapters, you'll learn about other typeclasses like monoids, semigroups, monads and so on.

Key points

- A **functor** is a way to map one category to another while preserving their structures.

- You define the structure of a category using objects and morphisms.

- A functor maps *objects to objects* and *morphisms to morphisms*.

- A **type constructor** is the mechanism a language provides to define a new data type using generics.

- Preserving structure means to preserve *identity* and *composition*.

- The **functor laws** are a formal definition of what it means to preserve identity and composition.

- You can define the category **C×D** as a **Cartesian product** of existing categories **C** and **D**. **C×D** has as objects all the pairs **(c, d)** you can create using all the **c** from **C** and **d** from **D**.

- You define morphisms in **C×D** depending on the specific type constructor.

- A functor mapping objects and morphisms from the category **C×D** is called a **bifunctor**.

- Bifunctors define the `bimap` function.

- A **typeclass** is the concept you use to represent common behaviors across different data types.

Where to go from here?

Congratulations! In this chapter, you learned more about functors, providing a solid base to the code you implemented in Chapter 9, "Data Types". At the end of the chapter, you also met the concept of a typeclass. A functor is a typeclass. In the next chapter, you'll see a couple of very important typeclasses: **monoids** and **semigroups**.

Chapter 12: Monoids & Semigroups

In this chapter, you'll learn everything you need to know about a couple of very important typeclasses. You may be surprised that you've used these typeclasses all the time without knowing it:

- **Monoids**

- **Semigroups**

You'll understand their meaning in the context of category theory, and more importantly, you'll learn their implications in your favorite category: types and functions. In particular, you'll see:

- A first, *familiar* definition of **monoid**.

- A possible monoid typeclass definition in Kotlin.

- What **property-based testing** is.

- How to use property-based testing to verify the monoid laws.

- How monoids are handy when used with `Foldable` data types.

- The meaning of a monoid in category theory.

- What a semigroup is and how it differs from a monoid.

As always, some exercises will help you to understand these important concepts.

What is a monoid?

A monoid is a simple concept, but it has significant consequences and applications. To define a monoid, you need:

- A **set** of objects.

- A **binary operation**.

The operation *must*:

- Be **associative**.

- Have a **unit** value.

Being *associative* means that, given the elements **a**, **b** and **c** and the operation **op**, the following property must always be true:

```
a op (b op c) = (a op b) op c
```

The *unit* for the operation **op** is a particular element of the set that, whatever the element **a** is, makes the following equivalences always true:

```
a op unit = a
unit op a = a
```

Monoids are everywhere, and providing a familiar example is simple. A very important monoid is:

- The set of integer numbers.

- Addition.

Addition is associative because:

```
a + (b + c) = (a + b) + c
```

The particular integer value that's the *unit* for the addition is, of course, **0**. This is because:

```
a + 0 = a
0 + a = a
```

Addition is a good example but can also be misleading. For instance, addition is *commutative*, which means that:

```
a + b = b + a
```

Instead, *a monoid doesn't need to be commutative.*

> **Exercise 12.1**: Can you find an example of a monoid whose operation isn't commutative? Remember, you can find the solutions for all exercises and challenges in Appendix K.

> **Exercise 12.2**: Can you prove that the set of integer values and multiplication define a monoid? In this case, what would the *unit* element be?

From the previous definition, you understand that you can have many different types of monoids using the same set but a different operation or vice versa. But then, how would you define the typeclass Monoid in code?

The Monoid<T> typeclass

If you use the set analogy for types, you can think of a monoid for a type T as:

- A commutative combine operation of type (T, T) -> T.

- A unit element of type T.

> **Note**: It's important to understand that you could do this in multiple ways. The method you'll implement here is just one possibility.

Open **Monoid.kt** in this chapter's material, and add the following code:

```
interface Monoid<T> { // 1
  val unit: T // 2
  val combine: (T, T) -> T // 3
}
```

In this code, you define:

1. `Monoid<T>` as an interface with a generic type parameter T.

2. `unit` as the *unit* value of type T.

3. `combine` as a function of type `(T, T) -> T`.

The previous definition has a few significant things to note that have consequences on some implementation details. You might have the following questions in particular:

- `combine` has two input parameters of type T and returns another value of the same type T. You learned that composition is easier with functions with a single parameter. How, then, can you improve the `Monoid<T>` definition?

- `Monoid<T>` is an interface that a type might implement to provide `unit` and `combine` implementations. But you also know that you might have two monoids for the same set of values. For instance, multiplication and addition are both monoids on `Int`. How could you then provide a different monoid implementation for the same type T?

- At compile time, there's no way to force the validity of the property about *associativity* and *unit*. This depends on the `combine` implementation. What can you do, then, to have confidence your implementation will work properly?

In Chapter 8, "Composition", you implemented the `curry` function in the way you find in **Definitions.kt**:

```
typealias Fun2<A, B, C> = (A, B) -> C

fun <A, B, C> Fun2<A, B, C>.curry(): (A) -> (B) -> C = { a: A ->
  { b: B ->
    this(a, b)
  }
}
```

curry allows you to represent a function of two input parameters of type `(A, B) -> C` as a higher-order function of a single parameter that returns another function of type `(A) -> (B) -> C`. This suggests that you can replace the previous `Monoid<T>` definition with the following in the same **Monoid.kt**:

```
interface Monoid<T> {
  val unit: T
  val combine: (T) -> (T) -> T // HERE
}
```

As you can see, now `combine` has a single input parameter of type `T` and returns a function of type `(T) -> T`. But you can do even better by replacing the previous definition with the following:

```
public interface Monoid<T> {
  val unit: T
  val combine: T.(T) -> T // HERE
}
```

Creating a single `Monoid<T>` implementation is relatively easy. Before implementing some, it's important to emphasize that it's not correct to say that some type A is a monoid. A monoid needs a type, which is essentially a set of values. It also needs an associative operation with *unit*. This means you can't just make your class A to implement `Monoid<A>` because you need something more.

Previously, you used the `Int` type. Depending on if you're using addition or multiplication, you can define two different monoids. Open **Monoid.kt** and add the following code:

```
object MonoidIntAdd : Monoid<Int> { // 1
  override val unit: Int
    get() = 0 // 2
  override val combine: Int.(Int) -> Int // 3
    get() = Int::plus // 4
}
```

In this code, you define:

1. `MonoidIntAdd` as an object implementing the `Monoid<Int>` interface. It represents a monoid for `Int` and *addition*. You use an `object` because you don't have to handle any states. `unit` is just a value, and `combine` is a pure function.

2. `0`, which is the *unit* value for *addition*.

3. `combine` as a function of type `Int.(Int) -> Int` which, as you'll see very soon, might have some advantages in Kotlin. If it's more familiar, you might also use the previous definition of `Monoid<T>` with `combine` of type `(T) -> (T) -> T`.

4. `combine` using the `Int::plus` definition, which is of type `Int.(Int) -> Int`. This is actually the main reason for defining `combine` as a function of type `T.(T) -> T`.

Exercise 12.3: How would you implement the monoid `MonoidIntMult` for `Int` and *multiplication*? Then, check out the solution in Appendix K.

344 Functional Programming in Kotlin by Tutorials

> **Exercise 12.4**: How would you implement the monoid `MonoidStringConcat` for `String` and String *concatenation*?

As you see, implementing a monoid is relatively simple, and you'll implement others very soon. But how can you be sure that your implementation is *actually a monoid*?

Property-based testing

In the first part of this chapter, you learned that typeclasses are defined using particular rules often called *laws*. You already met them in Chapter 11, "Functors". You also created some very simple `Monoid<T>` implementations that you're confident follow the monoid rules, but how can you be sure of that? Answering this question is an ideal opportunity to introduce a technique called **property-based testing**.

As you know, testing is one of the most challenging parts of the development process of any piece of software. To understand why, just look at the code in **PropertyTest.kt**:

```
fun sum(a: Int, b: Int): Int = a + b
```

The question now is: How can you test this code? `sum` is a basic function that adds two values you pass as input. The first approach is to implement some unit tests. You can implement some tests like the following. Add this code to **PropertyTestTest.kt**:

```
class PropertyTestTest {

  @Test
  fun `sum test using predefined values`() {
    Truth.assertThat(sum(2, 3)).isEqualTo(5)
    Truth.assertThat(sum(2, 5)).isEqualTo(7)
    Truth.assertThat(sum(-2, 5)).isEqualTo(3)
  }
}
```

Here, you're testing that 2 + 3 = 5, 2 + 5 = 7 and −2 + 5 = 3.

Run the tests by clicking the icon in Figure 12.1, and you'll get what's in Figure 12.2, proving that all the tests pass.

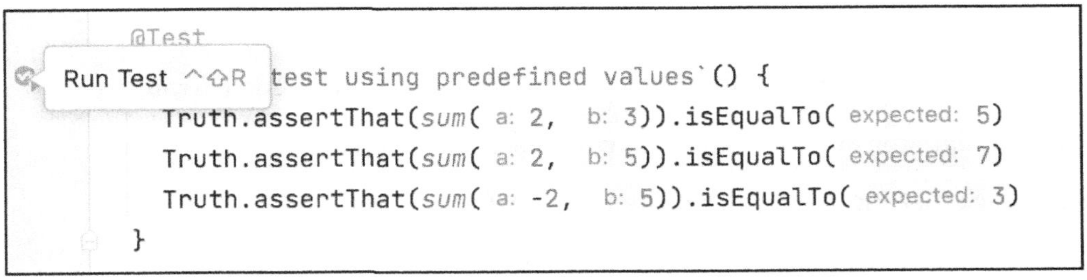

Figure 12.1: Run your tests

Figure 12.2: All tests pass!

But you're only testing *some* of the possible values! What about *all* the other possible inputs? You could add more cases, but how many tests do you actually need to implement to be sure your function is correct?

In this specific case, sum accepts two parameters of type Int. This means the possible combinations in input are the number of elements in the **Cartesian product** Int × Int, which has 4,294,967,295 × 4,294,967,295 elements! Of course, you can't implement *all* those tests, so you need a smarter solution. What about generating some random values and checking whether sum works correctly?

In the same **PropertyTestTest.kt**, add the following code:

```
@Test
fun `sum test using random values`() {
  val firstValue = Random.nextInt() // 1
  val secondValue = Random.nextInt() // 2
  val expectedValue = firstValue + secondValue // 3
  Truth.assertThat(sum(firstValue, secondValue)) // 4
    .isEqualTo(expectedValue)
}
```

In this code, you:

1. Use Random.nextInt to get a random Int for the first parameter you store in firstValue.

2. Do the same for the second parameter, which you put in secondValue.

3. Calculate the expected value using +, which you store in expectedValue.

4. Check that the value you get from sum is what you expected.

Run the test as in Figure 12.3, and make it pass again.

```
        @Test
  C  Run Test ^⇧R  test using random values`() {
            val firstValue : Int   = Random.nextInt()
            val secondValue : Int  = Random.nextInt()
            val expectedValue : Int  = firstValue + secondValue
            Truth.assertThat(sum(firstValue, secondValue))
               .isEqualTo(expectedValue)
        }
```

Figure 12.3: Random input tests

If you run it once, you might've just been lucky. A possible option is to run the test more times. Add the following code in **PropertyTestTest.kt**, and run it again:

```
@Test
fun `sum test using random values 100 times`() {
  100.times {
    val firstValue = Random.nextInt()
    val secondValue = Random.nextInt()
    val expectedValue = firstValue + secondValue
    Truth.assertThat(sum(firstValue, secondValue))
      .isEqualTo(expectedValue) o
  }
}
```

In this case, everything also seems fine, like in Figure 12.4:

Figure 12.4: Multiple random tests pass

This *seems* fine, but it's not quite so simple. Can you see why?

The answer is highlighted in the following code:

```
@Test
fun `sum test using random values`() {
  val firstValue = Random.nextInt()
  val secondValue = Random.nextInt()
  val expectedValue = firstValue + secondValue // HERE
  Truth.assertThat(sum(firstValue, secondValue))
    .isEqualTo(expectedValue)
}
```

To test sum, you're re-implementing the same feature! How can you test that sum is correct if you compare its result with a value you get by doing exactly the same thing? Of course, it passes — but they might both be wrong.

So the big problem now is: How would you test sum *without*:

- Re-implementing the same operation in tests?

- Using specific examples?

The answer is property-based testing.

An example of property-based testing

In the previous section, you saw that implementing good testing isn't obvious, even for a basic function like sum. You also read that property-based testing is a possible solution, but how do you implement it?

The first step is to think about how sum is different from other operations. For instance, you previously learned that addition is commutative, meaning that for any **a** and **b**:

```
a + b = b + a
```

You know that this isn't true for all operations. Subtraction, for example, is *not* commutative. You can then add the following test to **PropertyTestTest.kt**:

```
@Test
fun `test sum is commutative`() {
  100.times {
    val firstValue = Random.nextInt() // 1
    val secondValue = Random.nextInt() // 1
    val result1 = sum(firstValue, secondValue) // 2
    val result2 = sum(secondValue, firstValue) // 3
```

```
        Truth.assertThat(result1).isEqualTo(result2) // 4
      }
    }
```

In this code, you:

1. Get two random values for `firstValue` and `secondValue`.

2. Invoke `sum` using `firstValue` and `secondValue` as first and second parameters.

3. Invoke `sum` with the same parameter values but in a different order.

4. Check that the results you got in the two cases are the same.

If you run this test, you'll see it passes. This is an improvement over the previous solutions, but unfortunately, it's not enough. You can easily test this by replacing the + with * in **PropertyTest.kt**:

```
fun sum(a: Int, b: Int): Int = a * b
```

The previous test still passes because, like addition, multiplication is also commutative. You don't just give up, then, wondering what the difference is between addition and multiplication.

There are many, but a possible solution is that adding 1 twice to any value **a** is the equivalent of adding 2 to the same **a**. This isn't true with multiplication. Multiplying by 1 twice isn't equivalent to multiplying by 2 once. To spot the multiplication you introduced earlier, add the following test to **PropertyTestTest.kt**:

```
@Test
fun `test addition is not multiplication`() {
  100.times {
    val randomValue = Random.nextInt() // 1
    val result1 = sum(sum(randomValue, 1), 1) // 2
    val result2 = sum(randomValue, 2) // 3
    Truth.assertThat(result1).isEqualTo(result2) // 4
  }
}
```

In this case, you:

1. Get a random `Int` value you put in `randomValue`.

2. Invoke `sum`, adding 1 to `randomValue` and then again to add 1 to the previous result.

3. Use sum, adding 2 to randomValue.

4. Check if the values you got are the same.

Run this test using the bugged sum implementation, and you'll get what's in Figure 12.5:

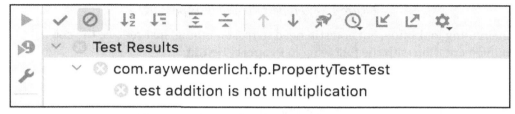

Figure 12.5: Spotting the multiplication bug

You can fix the problem in the sum implementation and restore this in **PropertyTest.kt**:

```
fun sum(a: Int, b: Int): Int = a + b
```

Now, comment out all the tests, keeping just the following, which you implemented as property-based tests:

```
class PropertyTestTest {
  // ...
  @Test
  fun `test sum is symmetric`() {
    100.times {
      val firstValue = Random.nextInt()
      val secondValue = Random.nextInt()
      val result1 = sum(firstValue, secondValue)
      val result2 = sum(secondValue, firstValue)
      Truth.assertThat(result1).isEqualTo(result2)
    }
  }

  @Test
  fun `test addition is not multiplication`() {
    100.times {
      val randomValue = Random.nextInt()
      val result1 = sum(sum(randomValue, 1), 1)
      val result2 = sum(randomValue, 2)
      Truth.assertThat(result1).isEqualTo(result2)
    }
  }
}
```

Run them, and you'll see them all passing, like in Figure 12.6:

Figure 12.6: Property-based tests passing.

Everything looks fine, but you still need to fix something. Just replace the sum implementation with the following in **PropertyTest.kt**:

```
fun sum(a: Int, b: Int): Int = 0
```

Because sum always returns the same value, all the previous tests pass! Of course, this isn't good. The output must be a function of the input. You don't want to fail in the very first tests you wrote when you knew exactly what values to pass as input, and you had to re-implement the same sum in the tests.

A possible solution to this is the use of a special value that allows you to somehow predict the result without knowing all the input values. To understand what this value is, add the following test to **PropertyTestTest.kt**:

```
@Test
fun `test using unit value for addition`() {
  100.times {
    val randomValue = Random.nextInt() // 1
    val result1 = sum(randomValue, 0) // 2
    val expected = randomValue // 3
    Truth.assertThat(result1).isEqualTo(expected) // 4
  }
}
```

In this test, you:

1. Store a random Int value in randomValue.

2. Invoke sum, passing randomValue as the first parameter and 0 as the second.

3. Use the same randomValue as the expected result when adding 0.

4. Check if the result is what you're expecting.

When you run the previous test with the last bugged sum implementation, you'll see the test fails, like in Figure 12.7:

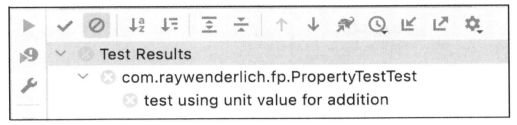

Figure 12.7: Using unit to spot wrong sum implementation.

Resume the correct sum implementation in **PropertyTest.kt** like this:

```
fun sum(a: Int, b: Int): Int = a + b
```

All the tests now pass!

It's crucial now to understand what you actually did. Instead of implementing unit tests using specific input values, you focused on the main properties of addition and proved that they're valid regardless of the input values. This is the idea behind the concept of property-based testing.

You might wonder if this idea can somehow be abstracted and generalized. The answer is yes!

Generalizing property-based testing

In the previous section, you used the property-based technique to test, with acceptable confidence, the implementation of a simple sum function. Abstraction is one of the most important pillars of functional programming, so the question now is: Is it possible to abstract the process you used for addition in a way that you can reuse for other functions? Of course you can!

> **Note:** Some frameworks, like Kotest (https://kotest.io/), allow you to use property-based testing in your code in a more robust and complete way. In this case, you'll just implement some of the main abstractions as an example of the technique. It's up to you to decide if you want to use Kotest, another framework or implement your own.

As you learned above, property-based testing uses some randomly generated values you can represent using the Generator<T> abstraction. In **PropertyTest.kt**, add the following code:

```
fun interface Generator<T> { // 1
  fun generate(n: Int): List<T> // 2
}
```

Here, you define:

1. The Generator<T> abstraction as a generic functional interface. Generator<T> is supposed to generate random values of type T.

2. generate as a function accepting an Int input parameter that defines the number of random elements you need to generate. The result value is List<T>, and it's supposed to be a list of length n. This allows you to handle any number of random values.

In the same file, add the following implementation for Int values:

```
object IntGenerator : Generator<Int> {
  override fun generate(n: Int): List<Int> = List(n) {
    Random.nextInt()
  }
}
```

This is self-explanatory and simply returns a List<Int> containing n random Int values.

Now, you need a way to represent properties like *commutativity, associativity* and so on. A simple way to do this is adding the following definition in **PropertyTest.kt**:

```
interface Property<T> { // 1
  operator fun invoke( // 2
    gen: Generator<T>, // 3
    fn: (List<T>) -> T // 4
  ): Boolean // 5
}
```

In this code, you:

1. Define Property<T> as a generic interface in the type parameter T.

2. Declare invoke as the operator to define in every Property<T> implementation. This allows you to check the property directly using ().

3. Pass the Generator<T> as invoke's first parameter. Each Property<T> is responsible for using the generator to get all the values it needs.

4. Need a function of the generated input values List<T> that returns another value of type T. The return type could be different in case you'd need to test more complex properties.

5. Require Boolean as the return type for invoke. This tells you whether the property is verified. Again, you're keeping things simple, but in Chapter 14, "Error Handling With Functional Programming", you'll see how to get more information from a failing property verification using Either<A, B> or Kotlin's built-in Result<T>.

As a first example of using Property<T>, it's useful to define the implementation for the *commutativity property*. In **PropertyTest.kt**, add the following code:

```
class CommutativeProperty<T> : Property<T> { // 1
  override fun invoke(
    gen: Generator<T>,
    fn: (List<T>) -> T
  ): Boolean {
    val values = gen.generate(2)  // 2
    val res1 = fn(listOf(values[0], values[1])) // 3
    val res2 = fn(listOf(values[1], values[0])) // 4
    return res1 == res2 // 5
  }
}
```

This is some very interesting code, where you:

1. Create CommutativeProperty<T> as a Property<T> implementation. Note how CommutativeProperty<T> is still generic in the type T.

2. Invoke generate on the Generator<T> you get as invoke's input parameter to get 2 values you need to prove commutativity.

3. Invoke the function fn you get as invoke's input parameter, passing the random values in the same order you got from Generator<T>.

4. Do the same, but using the random values you got from Generator<T> in a *different order*.

5. Check if the two results are the same. This is required to prove the *commutative property*.

Now, in a very similar way, you can implement `Property<T>` for associativity. In
PropertyTest.kt, add the following code:

```kotlin
class AssociativeProperty<T> : Property<T> {
  override fun invoke(
    gen: Generator<T>,
    fn: (List<T>) -> T
  ): Boolean {
    val values = gen.generate(3) // 1
    val res1 = fn(
      listOf(fn(listOf(values[0], values[1])), values[2])) // 2
    val res2 = fn(
      listOf(values[0], fn(listOf(values[1], values[2])))) // 3
    return res1 == res2 // 4
  }
}
```

In this case, you:

1. Need 3 values of type `T`.

2. Invoke the function `fn` you get as `invoke`'s input parameter like `op(op(a, b),
    c)`, assuming a, b and c are the 3 random values, and op is the operation you're
    testing.

3. Do the same, but like `op(a, op(b, c))`.

4. Verify that the results in the two cases are the same.

Finally, you can implement `Property<T>` for the identity property by adding the
following code in **PropertyTest.kt**:

```kotlin
class IdentityProperty<T>(
  private val unit: T // 1
) : Property<T> {
  override fun invoke(
    gen: Generator<T>,
    fn: (List<T>) -> T
  ): Boolean {
    val randomValue = gen.generate(1)[0] // 2
    val res1 = fn(listOf(randomValue unit)) // 3
    val res2 = fn(listOf(unit, randomValue)) // 4
    return res1 == randomValue && res2 == randomValue // 5
  }
}
```

In this case, the implementation is slightly different. Here, you:

1. Need the `unit` element, which depends on the specific type T and operation.

2. Generate a single `randomValue` of type T.

3. Invoke `fn` in the form `op(randomValue, unit)`.

4. Do the same by invoking `fn` in the form `op(unit, randomValue)`.

5. Verify that `unit` is actually the unit for the given operation you invoke through `fn`.

It's finally time to use these properties in a property-based test. But first, add the following utility function to **PropertyTest.kt**:

```
infix fun <T> Property<T>.and(
  rightProp: Property<T>
): Property<T> = object : Property<T> { // 1
  override fun invoke( // 2
    gen: Generator<T>,
    fn: (List<T>) -> T
  ): Boolean =
    this@and(gen, fn) && rightProp(gen, fn) // 3
}
```

This utility function simplifies the verification of multiple properties, putting them all in and. Here, you:

1. Define and as an infix extension function of `Property<T>`, accepting another `Property<T>` in input. The return type is still a `Property<T>`, which is the logical AND with the receiver.

2. Create the `Property<T>` implementation to return using the receiver and the `Property<T>` you get as input.

3. Simply invoke the receiver `Property<T>` and the `rightProp` you get as an input parameter. This means that the returning `Property<T>` will evaluate to `true` if and only if both the receiver property and the one you pass as `rightProp` evaluate to `true`.

Now, open **PropertyTestTest.kt**, and add the following test:

```
@Test
fun `Property-based test for sum`() {
  100.times {
    val additionProp =
      CommutativeProperty<Int>() and // 1
```

```
            AssociativeProperty() and
            IdentityProperty(0)
    val evaluation = additionProp(IntGenerator) { // 2
      sum(it[0], it[1])
    }
    Truth.assertThat(evaluation).isTrue() // 3
  }
}
```

In this test, you:

1. Create instances of CommutativeProperty<Int>, AssociativeProperty<Int>
    and IdentityProperty. Using the and utility function, you compose them into a
    single Property<Int> implementation you store in additionProp.

2. Evaluate additionProp, passing a reference to the IntGenerator and a lambda
    containing the actual invocation of sum, passing the values you get from the
    Generator<Int> in a List<Int>. You store the result in evaluation.

3. Confirm that all the properties are verified by testing the value of evaluation,
    which must be true.

Run the previous test, and you'll see that all the tests pass! You can also verify that
the test fails if you change the sum implementation like you did above.

> **Exercise 12.5**: In the previous section, you proved that *addition* is different
> from *multiplication* using op(op(a), 1) and op(a, 2). The two expressions
> are equal for any Int a if op is addition, but the same isn't true if op is
> multiplication. Can you implement a Property<Int> implementation for this
> rule and use it to create a new test?
>
> You can find the solution in Appendix K and the challenge project for this
> chapter.

A crucial aspect of what you just did is that the properties you've defined for sum
aren't just properties you use for testing. They're actually the *specification* for sum or
addition in general. Every operation that satisfies CommutativeProperty,
AssociativeProperty and IdentityProperty *is* addition.

Property-based testing and monoids

Property-based testing comprises much more than what you've learned here. Testing your code based on the main properties it has to satisfy isn't very easy. Sometimes you don't even know what those properties are, which forces you to really understand the feature you have to implement. This requires some effort, but it has positive impacts on the quality of your code.

In this chapter, you've learned what property-based testing is. You also implemented a very small framework with the goal of having a way to verify if your monoid implementations work. Property-based testing is useful with monoid laws but is also one of the main techniques for verifying any typeclass law.

To prove this, you'll now implement a Monoid<String> implementation for the String type and the String *concatenation* operation. Then, you'll prove it's actually a monoid.

> **Note**: Spoiler alert! You should've already implemented a Monoid<String> for the String type and String concatenation operation as an exercise. If you haven't, please review Exercise 12.4 before proceeding.

You know that a Monoid<T> consists of a type T, which represents a set of values and a binary operation that's *associative* and has a *unit*. A possible implementation for String with String concatenation, then, is the following. Add this to **Monoid.kt** if not already present in your exercise solution:

```
object MonoidStringConcat : Monoid<String> {
  override val unit: String
    get() = ""
  override val combine: String.(String) -> String
    get() = String::plus
}
```

To implement a property-based test for this implementation, you need a Generator<String>. A possible implementation is the following, which you can add to **PropertyTest.kt**:

```
class StringGenerator(
  private val minLength: Int = 0,
  private val maxLength: Int = 10
) : Generator<String> {
  val chars = "abcdefghijklmnopqrstuvwxyz" +
    "ABCDEFGHIJKLMNOPQRSTUVWXYZ" +
```

```
    "1234567890!±§!@£$%^&*()_+-="
override fun generate(n: Int): List<String> = List(n) {
  val length = Random.nextInt(minLength, maxLength)
  val currentString = StringBuilder()
  (1..length).forEach {
    currentString.append(
      chars[Random.nextInt(0, chars.length)])
  }
  currentString.toString()
  }
}
```

The next step is providing `Property<T>` implementation for:

- **Associativity**

- **Identity**

Hey, you already have them! In the **test** build type, create a new file named **StringMonoidTest.kt**, like in Figure 12.8:

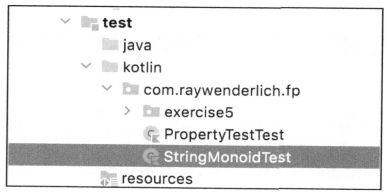

Figure 12.8: Create a StringMonoidTest file.

Now, add the following code:

```
class StringMonoidTest {

  @Test
  fun `test string concat using generators`() {
    100.times {
      val stringConcatProp =
        AssociativeProperty<String>() and // 1
          IdentityProperty("") // 2
      val evaluation = stringConcatProp(StringGenerator()) { //
3
        MonoidStringConcat.combine(it[0], it[1]) // 4
      }
```

```
    Truth.assertThat(evaluation).isTrue() // 5
      }
    }
  }
```

In this code, you:

1. Use an `AssociativeProperty<String>` instance.

2. Create an instance of `IdentityProperty<String>` using the empty `String` as a *unit*.

3. Combine the two properties in `stringConcatProp` and invoke it, passing an instance of `StringGenerator`.

4. Use `MonoidStringConcat.combine` as the operation to test.

5. Verify that `evaluation` always evaluates to `true`.

Run the test, and you'll get what's in Figure 12.9:

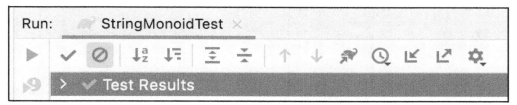

Figure 12.9: MonoidStringConcat is a monoid!

Great! You managed to implement a monoid *and* test its properties using property-based testing.

But why are monoids so important? Where do you actually use them?

Monoids and foldable types

In Chapter 9, "Data Types", you implemented two of the most important functions a data type usually provides: `fold` and `foldRight`. These are very helpful functions you can use, for instance, to calculate the sum of the values in a `List<Int>`, like the following in **Foldable.kt**:

```
fun List<Int>.sumList() = fold(0) { a, b -> a + b }
```

As an example of `foldRight`, you implemented the function `reverseString` like this:

```
fun String.reverseString() = foldRight("") { char, str -> str + char }
```

> **Note**: You called these functions `sumList` and `reverseString` so they wouldn't conflict with the existing `sum` and `reverse`.

To test these functions, just run the following code:

```
fun main() {
    listOf(1, 2, 3, 4, 5, 6, 7, 8, 9, 10).sumList() pipe ::println
    "supercalifragilisticexpialidocious".reverseString()
    pipe ::println
}
```

Getting the following output:

```
55
suoicodilaipxecitsiligarfilacrepus
```

As you see, `fold` and `foldRight` both need an initial value and a `combine` function that's reminiscent of the concept of `Monoid<T>`. It's crucial to note how a `Monoid<T>` has a single type parameter T, so the `combine` has type `(T, T) -> T`. This makes `fold` and `foldRight` basically the same.

For this reason, it's often useful to create an abstraction for any object with a `fold` function like this, which you should add in the same **Foldable.kt** file:

```
typealias Foldable<T> = Iterable<T>
```

Kotlin defines `fold` as an extension function for `Iterable<T>`, so you can create a `Foldable<T>` typealias of it and then define the following function:

```
fun <T> Foldable<T>.fold(monoid: Monoid<T>): T =
    fold(monoid.unit, monoid.combine)
```

Once your data type implements `Iterable<T>`, it also has the `fold` function accepting a `Monoid<T>` as an input parameter.

For example, you can implement the previous `sumList` function like this:

```
fun List<Int>.sumList() = fold(MonoidIntAdd)
```

How can you implement the `reverseString` using a `Monoid<String>` instead? You learned that `combine` in a monoid doesn't need to be commutative. It'd be useful, then, to implement a function that `commutates` a `Monoid<T>` like the following you can write in **Foldable.kt**:

```
fun <A, B, C> (A.(B) -> C).swap(): (B.(A) -> C) = { a: A -> // 1
  a.this@swap(this)
}

fun <T> Monoid<T>.commutate(): Monoid<T> = object : Monoid<T>
{ // 2
  override val unit: T
    get() = this@commutate.unit
  override val combine: T.(T) -> T
    get() = this@commutate.combine.swap()
}
```

This isn't obvious code. Here, you implement:

1. `swap` as a function that converts a function of type `A.(B)->C` in a function of type `B.(A)->C`, basically swapping the receivers of types A and B.

2. `commutate` as an extension function for `Monoid<T>` that swaps the input parameter for the `combine` function of the `Monoid<T>` you use as a receiver. The *unit* is the same, while the `combine` is the one you get invoking `swap` in the `combine` for the receiver.

A `String` doesn't implement `Iterable<T>`, so you need to provide a specific `fold` overload for `CharSequence` you implement like this:

```
fun CharSequence.fold(monoid: Monoid<String>): CharSequence = //
1
  this.fold(monoid.unit) { a, b ->
    monoid.combine(a, "$b") // 2
  }
```

The problem here is that you have to:

1. Use a `Monoid<String>`.

2. Convert the `Char` you get as an input parameter for the `fold` lambda in a `String`.

Now, you can implement `reverseString` like this:

```
fun String.reverseString() = fold(MonoidStringConcat)
```

When you run the following code:

```
fun main() {
    listOf(1, 2, 3, 4, 5, 6, 7, 8, 9, 10).sumList() pipe ::println
    "supercalifragilisticexpialidocious".reverseString()
pipe ::println
}
```

You get:

```
55
supercalifragilisticexpialidocious // WRONG
```

Here, you see that the `reverseString` doesn't do its job. But you can fix this easily with the following implementation that uses `commutate` to invert the `combine` function of the `MonoidStringConcat` you pass as an input parameter:

```
fun String.reverseString() =
    fold(MonoidStringConcat.commutate())
```

Run `main` again, and now you'll get what you expect:

```
55
suoicodilaipxecitsiligarfilacrepus // OK!
```

Monoids and category theory

Now that you've learned what a monoid is from a practical point of view, it's useful to see what it actually is in the context of category theory. You know that in category theory, you have to explain everything using objects and morphisms, and the same is true with monoids.

Look at Figure 12.10:

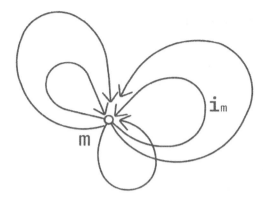

Figure 12.10: Monoid in a category

This is a category with a single object, **m**. Of course, because it's a category, you have an identity **im**, but you also have many other morphisms from **m** to itself. You also have composition, so you can compose all those morphisms, getting other morphisms. Compared to other categories, in this case, all the morphisms are composable because they all start and end at **m**.

The *uniqueness* of the object in this category is the characteristic that gives it the name **monoid**.

You already learned that a monoid needs a set of values and a binary associative operation along with a special value called a *unit*. How is this definition related to the one you saw in category theory?

Look at Figure 12.10, and you see that the category with one object, **m**, has only one hom-set, **M(m, m)**. Remember, the hom-set is the set of all morphisms between objects that, in this case, are equal to **m**, which is the only object of the category. Because that's a category, you say that for every couple of morphisms in **M(m, m)**, another morphism exists: the composition of the two that you can call, for instance, multiplication. The composition is also part of **M(m, m)**. This is equivalent to the combine you met in the first — and more familiar — definition of monoid.

In **M(m, m)**, you also have a special morphism, called *unit*, that you compose with any other morphisms **m**, getting **m** itself. This is true because every category must have the identity morphism.

Finally, composition is associative, as is the composition of any triplet of morphisms in the hom-set **M(m, m)**.

It's surprising how all the concepts you've seen in the previous examples can be explained using objects and morphisms in category theory.

The semigroup typeclass

Most of this chapter is dedicated to the monoid typeclass, which you know is defined as a set of values, or type, along with:

- A binary associative operation called combine.

- A special element called *unit*.

You represented a monoid using the following abstraction:

```
public interface Monoid<T> {
  val unit: T
  val combine: T.(T) -> T
}
```

Looking at Monoid<T>, you might ask if the unit is always necessary, and the answer is no. In the case of fold, you used the *unit* as a possible initial value. What if you don't need it?

An example is the implementation of a function that merges two List<T>s into one. In **Semigroup.kt**, add the following code:

```
fun <T> mergeAndCombine(
  listA: List<T>,
  listB: List<T>,
  combine: (T, T) -> T
): List<T> {
  var i = 0
  var j = 0
  val result = mutableListOf<T>()
  while (i < listA.size || j < listB.size) {
    val first = if (i < listA.size) listA[i] else null
    val second = if (j < listB.size) listB[i] else null
    if (first != null && second != null) {
      result.add(combine(first, second))
```

```
      } else if (first != null) {
        result.add(first)
      } else if (second != null) {
        result.add(second)
      }
      i++
      j++
    }
    return result
  }
```

The implementation for mergeAndCombine has some controlled mutability. It allows you to use a combine function when creating a List<T> from two other List<T>s, which might have different sizes. This is an example of a function that doesn't need a *unit*.

In this case, the typeclass that defines a set of values and an associative binary operation is a **semigroup** you can represent like this in **Semigroup.kt**:

```
public interface Semigroup<T> {
  val combine: T.(T) -> T
}
```

This allows you to update the definition of Monoid<T> in **Monoid.kt** like this:

```
public interface Monoid<T> : Semigroup<T> {
  val unit: T
}
```

A *monoid* is basically a *semigroup* with a *unit*. This allows you to implement mergeAndCombine like this:

```
fun <T> mergeAndCombine(
  listA: List<T>,
  listB: List<T>,
  semigroup: Semigroup<T>
): List<T> { // 1
  var i = 0
  var j = 0
  val result = mutableListOf<T>()
  while (i < listA.size || j < listB.size) {
    val first = if (i < listA.size) listA[i] else null
    val second = if (j < listB.size) listB[i] else null
    if (first != null && second != null) {
      result.add(semigroup.combine(first, second)) // 2
    } else if (first != null) {
      result.add(first)
    } else if (second != null) {
      result.add(second)
```

```
        }
        i++
        j++
    }
    return result
}
```

This code is very similar to the previous one where you:

1. Pass a Semigroup<T> as a parameter.

2. Use the semigroup to combine the values in the two List<T>s.

As a simple test, add and run the following code:

```
object SemigroupIntMult : Semigroup<Int> {
    override val combine: Int.(Int) -> Int
        get() = Int::times
}

fun main() {
    val listA = listOf(1, 2, 3, 4, 5, 6)
    val listB = listOf(3, 5, 6)
    mergeAndCombine(listA, listB, SemigroupIntMult) pipe ::println
}
```

Getting in output:

```
[3, 10, 18, 4, 5, 6]
```

Key points

- A **monoid** is a set of values with an *associative binary operation* and a *unit* element.

- A monoid doesn't need to be commutative.

- The existence of the *associative binary operation* and the *unit* element are the **monoid laws**.

- **Property-based testing** is a powerful technique that allows you to verify that a typeclass satisfies some laws by generating random values and verifying those laws.

- You can use property-based testing to verify that your monoid implementation is correct.

- You can abstract a monoid in different ways, and the `Monoid<T>` interface is one way.

- Monoids work very well with `Foldable` data types, which provide implementations for `fold` and `foldRight`.

- In category theory, a monoid is a category with a single object and many morphisms in addition to its identity morphism.

- A **semigroup** is a typeclass defining a *binary associative function* without the need for a *unit* element.

- A **monoid** is a semigroup *with a unit element*.

Where to go from here?

Congratulations! You've completed these very important and fun chapters about monoids. Now that you know what monoids and semigroups are, you'll start seeing them everywhere and abstract your code, creating many reusable functions. You're now ready for one of the most exciting concepts: **monads**!

Chapter 13: Understanding Monads

The **monad** is probably one of the most important concepts in functional programming, and it has the reputation of being very difficult to understand. This is probably true, but the amount of effort you need also depends on the approach you want to follow.

A possible approach is based on the formal definition: *A monad is a monoid in the category of endofunctors*. None of the concepts mentioned in this definition are new to you. In Chapter 2, "Function Fundamentals", you learned the concept of *categories*. In Chapter 11, "Functors", you learned everything you needed to know about *functors*. Finally, in Chapter 12, "Monoids & Semigroups", you learned the concept of *monoids*. Unfortunately, this approach also requires some mathematical knowledge that's outside of the scope of this book.

For this reason, in this book, you'll look at monads in a pragmatic way. Here, you'll start from the problem of the composition of functions in the Kleisli category and prove that monads are a beautiful way to do it.

In this chapter, you'll have the opportunity to:

- Revise the concept of a **category**.

- Meet the **Kleisli category** again.

- Meet the `fish` operator, >=>, and the `bind` operator, >>=.

- Revise the concept of **functor** using the functor laws in the implementation of `fish` and `bind`.

- Implement `fish` for the `List<T>` typeclass.

- Understand why monads are so important.

- See some practical examples of monads for `Optional<T>` and `List<T>`.

You'll learn all this by using some exercises.

The road to monads!

As mentioned in this chapter's introduction, you already have all the skills you need to understand the concept of monads. You just need some guidance. You basically need to revise some of the concepts you've met in the previous chapters and use them to learn something new. In this section, you'll follow a pragmatic approach to solving a simple problem. Given two functions:

- f of type `(A) -> M<B>`

- g of type `(B) -> M<C>`

You want to define a new function of type `(A) -> M<C>` that's the composition of the two. What you represent with `M<A>` is a generic typeclass you usually get from A using a **type constructor**. Examples of `M<A>` are `List<A>` or `Optional<A>`.

> **Note**: One way to abstract any possible typeclass `M<A>` is called **higher kind**. At the moment, Kotlin doesn't provide this feature. But some frameworks — like Arrow, which you'll learn in Chapter 19 — provide tools to generate something similar. Arrow, for instance, uses the `@higherkind` annotation to generate a class `Kind<ForM, T>` as an abstraction of `M<T>`. With this, `Optional<A>` would become `Kind<ForOptional, A>` where `ForOptional` is a placeholder representing the `Optional<A>` type. The `Optional` type also generated from this `Kind`. For right now, don't worry about it. You'll learn everything about this in Chapter 19, "Arrow". The only thing you need to understand is that what you'll create using `M<A>` or `Kind<ForM, A>` will be valid for any specific typeclass.

What you want to implement isn't a classic composition between two functions because the output type for f is `M<B>`, but the input type for g is B. Solving this problem is precisely what will allow you to understand what a monad is.

It's time to start from the concept of **category**.

> **Note**: In this chapter, you'll represent generic types like M<T>. Sometimes, you'll represent the same type with M<A>, M<B> or using any other letter for the type parameter like M<X>. When defining a function, which letter you use doesn't matter. As an example, this means you can define a lift like:

```
fun <T> lift(value: T): M<T> { ... }
```

> Or like:

```
fun <A> lift(value: A): M<A> { ... }
```

> The important thing is using different letters when it matters, like:

```
fun <A, B, C> Fun<A, B>.compose(g: Fun<B, C>): Fun<A, C> { ... }
```

> In short, don't be confused by the specific letter used.

What is a category?

As you've learned so far, a category is the model you use to study the *theory of composition*. A category is a bunch of **objects** and some arrows between them called **morphisms** that follow some fundamental properties:

1. Composition

2. Associativity

3. Identity

There are different types of categories, but the one that's most important for you is the category of **types and functions**. For this category, the previous properties become:

1. For every pair of functions f of type (A) -> B, and g of type (B) -> C, there *must be* a function of type (A) -> C that's the composition of f and g. You usually represent this function as g ∘ f, which you read as "g after f", or as f compose g, where compose is a function you defined as:

```
typealias Fun<A, B> = (A) -> B

inline infix fun <A, B, C> Fun<A, B>.compose(
    crossinline g: Fun<B, C>
): Fun<A, C> = { a: A ->
    g(this(a))
}
```

2. For all functions f of type (A) -> B, g of type (B) -> C, and h of type (C) -> D, you can say that:

```
h ∘ (g ∘ f) = (h ∘ g) ∘ f
```

Or, in another way, that:

```
(f compose g) compose h = f compose (g compose h)
```

3. For every type A, there's always a function of type (A) -> A. You call this **identity** and represent it as ia. It has the following property for every function f:

```
ia ∘ f = f ∘ ia = f
```

But why are functions and compositions so important? You already learned that it's easier to understand programs if you decompose them into many small pieces, as you can implement and test them more easily. All these pieces are *functions*. To build your program, you need to put all the functions together using *composition*.

The properties of a category are definitions you need to remember and digest to really understand how particular functions compose themselves. Some functions are special and allow you to define fundamental categories. One of these is the **Kleisli category**.

The Kleisli category

In the category of types and functions, your objects are types like A, and the morphisms are functions of type (A) -> B. So far, so good.

In the previous chapters, you learned that you can start from a type A and create a new type you represent as M<A> using a **type constructor**. For instance, given a type A, you can define the type Optional<A> or the type List<A>. In the first example, you replaced M with Optional, and in the second, M with List. To get an M<A> from A, you defined the lift function. M is also the way you define a *typeclass*.

> **Note**: From this point, you'll use M<A> to define any new type you create from A using a type constructor. As mentioned earlier, to do so, you'd need a generic way to represent any M<A>. To ensure the code you'll write compiles, use a simple workaround: You'll represent M<A> as a typealias of some existing typeclass.

You define a category in terms of objects and morphisms. In a Kleisli category, objects are types. Some of these types are in the form of A, and others are in the form of M<A>. For instance, Int is a possible type, and Optional<String> is another. It's the same for Int and List<String>. They all are types. In a Kleisli category, morphisms are functions of the type (A) -> M<B>. You're basically considering functions between a type A and a possible embellishment or decoration of the type B you represent with M<B>.

> **Note**: Spoiler alert: M<A> is also a functor, as you'll see later.

An example of these functions have type (A) -> Optional<B>, (A) -> List<B> or the (A) -> Pair<B, String> you defined as Writer<A, B> in Chapter 3, "Functional Programming Concepts".

```
typealias Writer<A, B> = (A) -> Pair<B, String>
```

The `Writer<A, B>` type is a perfect example because you implemented the composition using the following code:

```
infix fun <A, B, C> Writer<B, C>.after(
  w: Writer<A, B>
): Writer<A, C> = { a: A ->
  val (b, str) = w(a)
  val (c, str2) = this(b)
  c to "$str\n$str2\n"
}
```

Because `Writer<A, B>` is just a typealias of `(A) -> Pair<B, String>`, you might think of it as a special case of `(A) -> M<B>` where `M<B>` is `Pair<B, String>`.

> **Note**: Second spoiler alert: `Writer<A, B>` with the `after` function is a monad!

Of course, this is the implementation of composition for the typeclass `Writer<A, B>`. Can you implement the same for all the functions of the Kleisli category? The answer is yes! To understand how, imagine this is possible using a special operator you call `fish` and represent as `>=>`. How can you implement the `fish` operator, `>=>`, then?

> **Note**: Yes, you really call that operator "fish"! This is the name Bartosz Milewski gave it in his Category Theory course on YouTube. The reason is that it looks like a shark. You'll give it a more formal name later.

The fish operator >=>

Suppose you want to define a composition between two functions in the Kleisli category. Given a function f of type `(A) -> M<B>` and a function g of type `(B) -> M<C>`, you want to define an operator, called the **fish operator**, which you represent as `>=>`. It does the following:

```
((A) -> M<B>) >=> ((B) -> M<C>) -> ((A) -> M<C>)
```

Or

```
f >=> g
```

The result of f >=> g is a function of type (A) -> M<C>. To better understand how to implement this operator, it's crucial to note that the output type for f is M<B>, while the type for the input of g is B. There's some *type impedance* because B isn't M<B>. The goal is to define what you really need to create an implementation of the fish operator for all the typeclasses M.

What you need to get is a function of type (A) -> M<C>, which is a function from A to M<C>. Open **Monad.kt** in the material for this project and add the following code:

```
typealias M<T> = List<T> // 1

infix fun <A, B, C> Fun<A, M<B>>.fish( // 2
  g: Fun<B, M<C>> // 3
): (A) -> M<C> = // 4
  { a: A ->
    TODO("Add implementation")
  }
```

Here, you define:

1. M<T> as a typealias of List<T>, as mentioned earlier. This allows you to successfully compile all the code you'll write.

2. fish as an *infix* extension function for the type Fun<A, M<B>>.

3. g as the parameter for fish of type Fun<B, M<C>>.

4. Fun<A, M<C>> as the return type of fish.

At the moment, you just know that you need to return a function of A, so you define it as a *lambda* with a single parameter a of type A.Because you have f, the first — and probably the only — thing you can do now is apply it to the input a of type A like this:

```
infix fun <A, B, C> Fun<A, M<B>>.fish(
  g: Fun<B, M<C>>
): (A) -> M<C> =
  { a: A ->
    val mb : M<B> = this(a) // HERE
    TODO("Add implementation")
  }
```

Here, mb has type M<B>, which you defined explicitly to make the code clearer.

Now, you have g, which has type (B) -> M<C>. The question is: How can you use mb of type M<B> and g of type (B) -> M<C> to get a value of type M<C>?

At this point, you don't know it yet, but you can delegate this operation to another operator called bind, which you represent with >>=.

> **Note:** Kotlin doesn't allow you to define operators with the names >=> or >>=. This is why you'll use the names fish and bind.

Represent the type of >>= with the following code you add in **Monad.kt**:

```
infix fun <B, C> M<B>.bind(
  g: Fun<B, M<C>>
): M<C> {
  TODO("Add implementation")
}
```

Here, you define bind as an extension function of M<B>, accepting g of type (B) -> M<C> as an input parameter, and returning a value of type M<C>. Assuming you have the implementation of bind for your typeclass M, fish becomes:

```
infix fun <A, B, C> Fun<A, M<B>>.fish(
  g: Fun<B, M<C>>
): (A) -> M<C> =
  { a: A ->
    val mb = this(a)
    mb.bind(g) // HERE
  }
```

> **Note:** As you can easily verify, the previous code compiles as soon as you use M<A> as a typealias of List<A>. This is also true for any other type that — as you'll see later — provides a map function or, in other words, is a *functor*.

At this point, it's crucial to understand that:

- bind is somehow related to the typeclass M.

- If you define bind for M, you also define fish.

These two sentences are very powerful because they allow you to have a first pragmatic definition of monad.

A pragmatic definition of monad

A first pragmatic definition of **monad** comes from what you learned above. A monad is basically a typeclass M for which you define the following two functions:

- bind of type (M<A>, Fun<A, M<B>>) -> M<B>

- lift of type (A) -> M<A>

Given bind and lift, you can implement the fish operator and compose two functions in the related Kleisli category. This means that a possible way to define a monad is through a Monad<T> interface, like the following you add to **Monad.kt**:

```
interface Monad<T> {

    fun lift(value: T): Monad<T>

    fun <B> bind(g: Fun<T, M<B>>): Monad<B>
}
```

Implementing bind isn't so obvious, but you can make the implementation easier as soon as you realize that M<T> is a functor!

What is a functor?

In Chapter 11, "Functors", you learned that a functor is essentially a way to *map* objects and morphisms of a category **C** in objects and morphisms in a category **D** following some rules that you call *functor laws*.

You probably remember that a *functor preserves structure*, and you represent this with the following properties:

- **Composition**, which means that **F (g ∘ f) = F g ∘ F f**.

- **Identity**, which means that **F ia = i Fa**.

The first law says that a functor maps the morphism **g ∘ f** composition of **f** and **g** in the composition of the morphisms **Fg** and **Ff**.

The second law says that a functor maps the identity of the source category in the identity of the category you use as the destination.

The good news now is that the types you're representing with M<A> are exactly the functor you called **Fa** before. If you think of the objects for the source category types A and the objects of the destination category as M<B>, you understand that a function of type (A) -> M<B> is exactly the functor that maps an object of the source category to the object of the destination category.

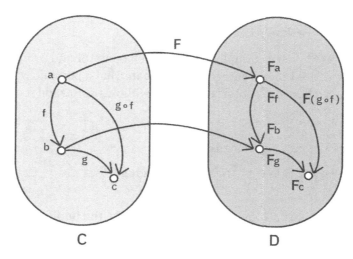

Figure 13.1: Mapping objects

As you see in Figure 13.1, the composition of **Ff** and **Fg** is equal to **F (g ∘ f)**. You can write this like:

```
Fg ∘ Ff = F (g ∘ f)
```

To make the concept more familiar, replace **F** with M and see that:

1. **F** is basically a way to map the object **a** of type A in **C** to the object of type **Fa** in **D**. If you replace **F** with M, you realize that this is exactly the function that allows you to map values of type A to values of type M<A>.

2. A function **f** of type (A) -> B in **C** is mapped to a function **Ff** of type (M<A>) -> M<B> in **D**.

3. Composing a function **f** of type (A) -> B with **g** of type (B) -> C in the category **C** is equivalent to composing the two functions of type (M<A>) -> M<B> and (M<B>) -> M<C> in **D**.

4. Finally, the functor laws say that composing **f** and **g** and then lifting to M is equivalent to lifting **f** and **g** using M and then composing.

In other words, given a value of type A, you can do the following:

1. Apply **f** to the value of type A and get a value of type B.

2. Apply **g** to the value of type B and get a value of type C.

3. Lift the result of type C into a value of type M<C>.

Another option is to:

1. Lift the value of type A into a value of type M<A>.

2. Invoke map on the value of type M<A>, passing the function **f** as a parameter and getting a value of type M<B>.

3. Invoke map on the value of type M<B>, passing **g** as a parameter and getting a value of type M<C>.

The functor laws say that the values of type M<C> you get in the two distinct ways are exactly the same.

Now, you'll use these properties to simplify the implementation of the bind operator, >>=.

Monads as functors

You want to find an easier way to implement bind for all the M<B>. What the bind operator does is apply g to a value of type M<B>. Because M<B> is a functor and g is of type (B) -> M<C>, you can apply g to M<B>, invoking the map function. This is because a functor rule says that lift and map is equivalent to map and lift.

In other words, given a type A, you can first lift it to M<A> and then apply a function f of type (A) -> B using M<A>.map(f). Or you can first apply the function f to the value of type A and get a value of type B and then lift it, getting an M<B>.

Given that, you can rewrite bind in **Monad.kt** like this:

```
infix fun <B, C> M<B>.bind(
    g: Fun<B, M<C>>
): M<C> {
    val tmp : M<M<C>> = map(g) // HERE
    TODO("Fix the return type")
}
```

As defined explicitly, the type of the temporal variable tmp is M<M<C>>. What you get from map is a *double embellishment*. As you did earlier, you can think of a function, called flatten, that does exactly what its name states. It flattens the type M<M<A>> to a single M<A>. Now, add the following function to **Monad.kt**:

```
fun <A> M<M<A>>.flatten(): M<A> {
  TODO("")
}
```

And change bind like this:

```
infix fun <B, C> M<B>.bind(
  g: Fun<B, M<C>>
): M<C> =
  map(g).flatten() // HERE
```

> **Note**: Here, you're assuming that M<A> has the map function following the functor laws. If you've used M<A> as a typealias of List<A>, this comes for free.

With this, you can also simplify the implementation for fish like this:

```
infix fun <A, B, C> Fun<A, M<B>>.fish(
  g: Fun<B, M<C>>
): (A) -> M<C> =
  { a: A ->
    this(a).bind(g) // HERE
  }
```

What you need now is an implementation of flatten for your typeclass M. A practical example can help you understand how to do that.

A practical example of a monad

As an example of what you've found so far, you'll now implement the fish operator for List<T>. All you have to do is define the implementation for listFlatten.

> **Note**: As you've done before, you change the name of flatten in listFlatten to avoid conflict with the code you wrote above. You'll do the same for other functions.

You basically need to define the following function in the **ListMonad.kt** file you find in the material for this chapter:

```
fun <T> List<List<T>>.listFlatten(): List<T> {
  TODO("")
}
```

This function starts from a List<List<T>> and must return a List<T>. One of the implementations to do that is the following, which you can add to the same **ListMonad.kt**:

```
fun <T> List<List<T>>.listFlatten(): List<T> =
  this.fold(mutableListOf()) { acc, item ->
    acc.apply {
      addAll(item)
    }
  }
```

You can also define listBind like this:

```
infix fun <B, C> List<B>.listBind(
  g: Fun<B, List<C>>
): List<C> =
  map(g).listFlatten()
```

Finally, the implementation for listFish is:

```
infix fun <A, B, C> Fun<A, List<B>>.listFish(
  g: Fun<B, List<C>>
): Fun<A, List<C>> = { a: A ->
  this(a).listBind(g)
}
```

As proof of this, you can add the following code to **ListMonad.kt**:

```
val countList: (Int) -> List<Int> =
  { n: Int -> List(n) { it + 1 } } // 1

val intToChars =
  { n: Int -> List(n) { 'a' + n } } // 2

fun main() {
  val fished = countList listFish intToChars // 3
  fished(3) pipe ::println
}
```

In this example, you define:

1. `countList` as a function of type `(Int) -> List<Int>` that returns a list containing values from 1 to an `Int` value you pass in as input. For instance, given 2, it returns the `List<Int>` with values 1 and 2.

2. `intToChars` as a function of type `(Int) -> List<Char>` that returns the `List<Char>` you get by adding the input value to a. For instance, passing 2, you get a `List<Char>` with two cs.

3. `fished` as a variable of type `(Int) -> List<Char>` containing the composition of `countList` and `intToChars`.

Run the previous code, and you get:

```
[b, c, c, d, d, d]
```

Of course, this is just an example, and it doesn't really matter what the two functions you're composing do. The important thing is that `listFish` works. But, what's the logic of `listFish`?

In the previous section:

1. You saw that a monad is a functor, and it has a `map`.

2. You implemented `flatten` as a way to map values of type `M<M<A>>` in values of type `M<A>`.

The `map` and `flatten` names should remind you of a function called `flatMap`, which you met in Chapter 7, "Functional Data Structure". This is the same function, and what you learned here is the reason for its name.

To prove it, just add the following code in `main` in **ListMonad.kt**:

```kotlin
fun main() {
  // ...
  countList(3).flatMap(intToChars) pipe ::println
}
```

Run the code now, and you get exactly the same result:

```
[b, c, c, d, d, d]
```

Exercise 13.1: How would you make the Optional<T> data type you created in Chapter 9, "Data Types", a monad? If you need help, you can check out the solution in Appendix L.

Exercise 13.2: What's the relation between the fish operator, >=>, and flatMap? Can you express the latter in terms of the former for Optional<T>? A solution is in Appendix L if you need it.

Why monads?

This is all fascinating, but why do you really need monads? The answer is in the problem monads solve and precisely in the composition of what you call **Kleisli arrows** and represent as a function of type (A) -> M<B>.

In Chapter 3, "Functional Programming Concepts", you learned the difference between a pure and impure function. A pure function:

• Has body that's *referentially transparent*.

• Doesn't have any *side effects*.

You also learned that you can transform a function with side effects into a pure function by just making the effect part of the returning type. The Writer<A, B> type is a great example of this. In Exercises 13.1 and 13.2, you implemented flatMap for the Optional<T> type. It's basically a method to compose functions of type (A) -> Optional<B>.

> **Note**: From here, you'll use a flatMap implementation for Optional<T> that's the solution to Exercise 13.1. Feel free to solve the exercise first or go directly to the solution in **Appendix L** and copy its code in **OptionalMonad.kt**. If you solved the exercise, just use that code directly.

A **partial function** is a function that isn't valid for all the values in its domain. A very simple example is the following, which you should write in **OptionalMonad.kt**:

```
fun strToInt(str: String): Int =
  str.toInt()
```

This is a very simple function that converts a String in an Int. Of course, not all the Strings contain a value that can be converted into Ints. Run:

```
fun main() {
  strToInt("123") pipe ::println
}
```

And you get:

```
123
```

Run the code:

```
fun main() {
  strToInt("onetwothree") pipe ::println
}
```

And you get:

```
Exception in thread "main" java.lang.NumberFormatException: For
input string: "onetwothree"
    at
java.lang.NumberFormatException.forInputString(NumberFormatExcep
tion.java:65)
```

This is because "onetwothree" can't be converted to Int. strToInt is an example of a *partial function* because it doesn't make sense for all the values in its domain. More importantly, strToInt is *not pure* because it has side effects, which is the exception that it throws when the input isn't valid. How can you make strToInt pure? You already know the answer. You make the effect part of the return type.

In Chapter 14, "Error Handling With Functional Programming", you'll see a better way to handle this case, but for now, you can just model the result using an Optional<Int> and replace the current strToInt implementation with the following:

```
fun strToInt(str: String): Optional<Int> = // 1
  try {
    Optional.lift(str.toInt()) // 2
  } catch (nfe: NumberFormatException) {
    None // 3
  }
```

In this code, you:

1. Replace the strToInt return type with Optional<Int>.

2. Convert the String value to Int and lift the result in the case of success.

3. Return None in the case of NumberFormatException.

Now, run the main again, and you get something like this:

```
com.raywenderlich.fp.exercise1.None@372f7a8d
```

Besides the fact that toString() isn't implemented for None, you see that you get None as the result. A test for this would now be as easy as writing in the **OptionalMonadKtTest.kt** file in the material for this project:

```
class OptionalMonadKtTest {

  @Test
  fun `When input is not valid returns None`() {
    assertThat(strToInt("onetwothree")).isEqualTo(None)
  }
}
```

Once you have a pure strToInt, you might need to compose it with another function that also returns an Optional<T>. A possible example of a function you might need to compose with the previous is the following, which you can add to **OptionalMonad.kt**:

```
fun root(number: Int): Optional<Double> =
  if (number < 0) None else
Optional.lift(sqrt(number.toDouble()))
```

This is another *partial function* that accepts only positive values.

> **Note**: In this case, you're ignoring imaginary numbers.

How can you then compose `strToInt` with `root`? The answer is simple now, and it's one you accomplish with the following code:

```
fun main() {
  val strToRoot = ::strToInt optionalFish ::root // 1
  strToRoot("onetwothree") pipe ::println // 2
  strToRoot("123") pipe ::println // 3
}
```

Here, you:

1. Use `optionalFish` to get the function `strToRoot`, which is the composition of `strToInt` and `root`.

2. Invoke `strToRoot` with a value *not* in the domain.

3. Invoke `strToRoot` again with a valid input.

Running the previous code, you get something like:

```
com.raywenderlich.fp.exercise1.None@1f32e575
Some(value=11.090536506409418)
```

If you want to use the `flatMap` you implemented in Exercise 13.2, run the following code:

```
fun main() {
  // ...
  strToInt("onetwothree").flatMap(::root) pipe ::println
  strToInt("123").flatMap(::root) pipe ::println
}
```

Getting the same output:

```
com.raywenderlich.fp.exercise1.None@1f32e575
Some(value=11.090536506409418)
```

Monads are important because they allow you to compose functions that handle side effects as part of the return type.

Key points

- A **monad** is a *monoid* in the *category* of *endofunctors*.

- Monads solve the problem of the composition of **Kleisli arrows**, which are functions of type (A) -> M<B>.

- Kleisli arrows are how you model functions from a type A to an embellished version of a type B you represent as M<B>.

- The embellishment of a type M<A> is a way to encapsulate effects in the return type of a function.

- Monads are functors and provide a map function following the functor laws.

- You implement the fish operator, >=>, to achieve composition between two Kleisli arrows. It composes a function of type (A) -> M<B> with a function of type (B) -> M<C> to get a function of type (A) -> M<C>.

- The bind operator, >>=, is a way to solve the type impedance between a function returning a value of type M<B> and a function accepting a value of type B in input.

- The flatten function allows you to simplify the way you implement bind in the case of functors. It has type (M<M<A>>) -> M<A>.

- You can implement flatMap using fish, bind and flatten.

- Monads are the way you compose functions encapsulating side effects in the result type.

Where to go from here?

Congratulations! This is probably the most challenging chapter of the book but also the most rewarding. You now understand what a monad is, and you'll see many different and important monads in the third section of the book. Now, it's time to write some code and apply all the concepts you learned in the first two sections of the book.

Section III: Functional Programming in Practice

Time to put all that knowledge to work. In this section, you'll use all the principles you've learned so far to see the functional programming way for handling errors and managing state changes. You'll also meet some libraries you can use in your projects to quickly introduce functional programming.

Chapter 14: Error Handling With Functional Programming

In the first two sections of this book, you learned everything you need to know about pure functions. You learned that a pure function has a body that's referentially transparent and, maybe more importantly, doesn't have side effects. A side effect is a "disturbance" of the world external to the function, making the function difficult to test. Exceptions are a very common example of a side effect. A function containing code that throws an exception isn't pure and must be fixed if you want to use all the concepts you've learned so far.

In this chapter, you'll learn how to handle exceptions — and errors in general — using a functional programming approach. You'll start with a very simple example before exploring the solution Kotlin provides using the Result<T> data type. In particular, you'll learn:

- What **exception handling** means.

- How to handle exceptions as side effects.

- How to "purify" functions that throw exceptions.

- How to use Optional<T> in functions with exceptions.

- How to use Either<E, T> to handle exceptions in a functional way.

- How to implement a ResultAp<E, T> monad.

- How to compose functions that can throw exceptions.

- What the Kotlin Result<T> data type is and how to use it in your application.

You'll learn all this with a practical example that allows you to fetch and parse some content from the internet. This is the same code you'll use in the **RayTV** app, which allows you to access data about your favorite TV shows.

> **Note**: You'll use the RayTV app in the following chapters as well.

You'll also have the chance for some fun with a few exercises.

Exception handling

> **Note**: Feel free to skip this section if you already have a clear understanding of what exceptions are and why they exist.

Every application is the implementation of a set of use cases in code. A use case is a way you describe how a specific user can interact with a system. Figure 14.1 is an example of a use case describing the scenario when a RayTV app user wants to search for their favorite TV show.

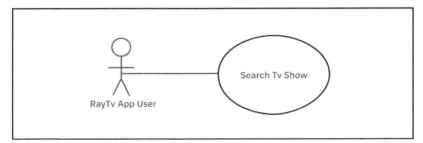

Figure 14.1: RayTV search use case

This **use case diagram** says two main things:

1. Who can access the specific feature of the app. In this case, it's the RayTV app user.

2. What the RayTV app can do. In this case, it allows the user to search for a TV show by name.

Usually, you also describe the use case in words by writing a document like this:

```
Use Case: Search TV shows
Actors: RayTV app
Prerequisites: The user starts the RayTV app.
Steps:
1. The user selects the search option.
2. The app shows the keyboard.
3. The user inputs some text.
4. The user taps the search button.
5. The app accesses the search service and fetches the results.
6. The app displays the results in a list.
Final state: The app displays the results of the search.
```

It describes what the user can do and how the system reacts. This use case is very specific, though. It describes when everything works fine. You call this the **happy path** or **principal use case**. Many things *can* go wrong. For instance, a network error can happen, or the search simply doesn't produce any results. In this case, you describe these situations using **alternative use cases**, like the one in Figure 14.2:

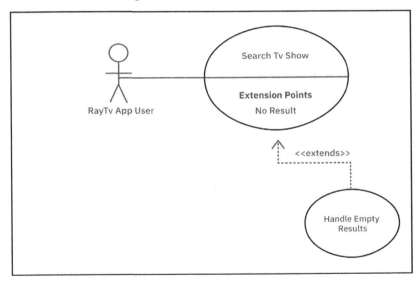

Figure 14.2: RayTV alternative use case

In this case, you describe the scenario as a use case that shows what happens when the happy path isn't followed. In this case, the search doesn't produce any result. Usually, you describe this scenario with a document like this:

```
Use Case: Handle empty results
Actors: RayTV app
Prerequisites: A TV show search produced no results.
```

```
Steps:
1. The app displays a message that says the search has produced
no results.
Final state: The app waits for action from the user.
```

This is all good, but what do use cases have to do with errors and exceptions? Well, exceptions aren't always bad things. They're just a way programming languages represent alternative scenarios. In general, you have three different types of situations:

- **Errors**: These represent cases when something *really* wrong happens. They aren't recoverable, and the developer should understand the cause and solve it. Typical examples are `VirtualMachineException`, `IOError` or `AssertionError`.

- **Checked exceptions**: This is the type of exception that describes alternative use cases. If you have a connection error, you should somehow handle it. A user entering an invalid credit card number is a common occurrence, so it's something your code should be prepared to handle. These are checked because in some programming languages, like Java, you have to explicitly declare them in the signature of the method that can throw them.

- **Unchecked exceptions**: `RuntimeException` is another way to describe this type of exception because it can happen at runtime. A typical one is `NullPointerException`, which is thrown when you access a member of an object through a null reference. Although you can recover from a `RuntimeException`, they usually describe bugs you should eventually fix.

Kotlin doesn't have checked exceptions, which means you don't need to declare them as part of the function throwing them. This doesn't mean you shouldn't handle the exception. Kotlin represents them with classes extending `Throwable` and still provides you the `try-catch-finally` expression. So what's the best way to handle exceptions controlling the flow of your program? Now that you have a solid functional programming background, you know that exceptions are side effects. How can you use what you've learned to handle exceptions elegantly and efficiently? Monads, of course! :]

> **Note**: It's interesting to remember how the type of the following expression is `Nothing`:

```
throw IOException("Something bad happens")
```

Remembering the analogy between types and sets, you know that Nothing is a subtype of any other type. This means the value you return when you throw an exception has a type compatible with the return type of the function itself.

Handling exception strategies

In Chapter 13, "Understanding Monads", you learned that functions throwing exceptions are impure. An exception changes the world outside the body of a function. In the same chapter, you also learned how to *purify* a function by changing the side effect to be part of the return type. The same works for exceptions, and you can achieve this using different data types depending on the strategy you want to adopt. Different strategies include:

1. **Fail fast**: Stopping the execution flow of your program and returning the first error that happens. You use this approach when you can't proceed because you need data that you failed to get in a previous step.

2. **Collection errors**: Proceeding in your program flow, collecting all the errors and making them part of the final result. Validation of some data is a classic example. An address, for instance, can be wrong for many different reasons, and you'd like to collect them all.

For each of these strategies, you can use functional programming:

1. Optional<T> or Either<E, T> for failing fast.

2. **Applicative functors** for collection errors.

It's now helpful to see both of them using some practical examples.

Some preparation

Before describing the different ways of handling exceptions, it's useful to look at some of the classes you find in the material for this chapter. These are the classes you initially find in the **fp_kotlin_cap14** project, and you'll see them again in the RayTV app in their final state. The RayTV app will allow you to search for a TV show and display some of the show's information on the screen. This is basically the use case in Figure 14.1.

Note: For the RayTV app, you'll use a simple API from TVmaze (https://www.tvmaze.com/), which doesn't require a key or registration.

In the **tools** sub-package, you already have the code for:

- **Fetching** the TV show data, given some query as input.

- **Parsing** the JSON to get the information you need encapsulated into a model you find in the **model** sub-package.

Note: All the sub-packages are related to the main package for the application, which is **com.raywenderlich.fp**.

In **TvShowFetcher.kt**, you have the code to send a request to the server, which returns a String.

```
object TvShowFetcher {
  fun fetch(query: String): String {
    val encodedUrl = java.net.URLEncoder.encode(query, "utf-8")
    val localUrl =
      URL("https://api.tvmaze.com/search/shows?q=$encodedUrl")
    with(localUrl.openConnection() as HttpURLConnection) {
      requestMethod = "GET"
      val reader = inputStream.bufferedReader()
      return reader.lines().toArray().asSequence()
        .fold(StringBuilder()) { builder, line ->
          builder.append(line)
        }.toString()
    }
  }
}
```

In **TvShowParser.kt**, you have the code that parses the JSON, returning a list of ScoredShow, which is the class you use to describe each result.

Note: TvShowParser uses the kotlinx.serialization library.

```
object TvShowParser {
  /** Parses the input json */
  fun parse(json: String): List<ScoredShow> = Json {
    ignoreUnknownKeys = true
  }.decodeFromString<List<ScoredShow>>(
```

```
    ListSerializer(ScoredShow.serializer()), json
  )
}
```

How `TvShowFetcher` and `TvShowParser` accomplish the fetching and parsing of the data from the server isn't relevant. However, it's crucial to note that neither `fetch` nor `parse` handles exceptions. If something goes wrong, you'll get an exception that the callers should handle.

To prove that, run some unit tests you find where shown in Figure 14.3:

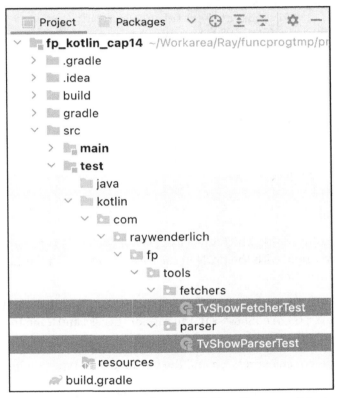

Figure 14.3: TvShowFetcher and TvShowParser unit tests

Of course, `TvShowFetcher` makes a network request, which can fail for many reasons, like a simple missing connection. The `TvShowParser` can fail simply by getting an incorrect JSON input. But how can you handle these exceptions?

Handling errors with Optional<T>

The RayTV app sends a request to the server, gets some JSON back, parses it and displays the result to the user. This is the happy path, but many things *can* go wrong. Both TvShowFetcher::fetch and TvShowParser::parse can fail.

Open **ShowSearchService.kt** in **optional** and add the following code:

```kotlin
fun fetchTvShowOptional(
  query: String
): Optional<String> = try { // 1
  Optional.lift(TvShowFetcher.fetch(query))
} catch (ioe: IOException) {
  Optional.empty()
}

/** Invokes the parser returning an Optional */
fun parseTvShowString(
  json: String
): Optional<List<ScoredShow>> =
  try { // 2
    Optional.lift(TvShowParser.parse(json)) // 2
  } catch (e: SerializationException) {
    Optional.empty()
  }
```

Here, you define:

1. fetchTvShowOptional, which invokes TvShowFetcher::fetch and returns an Optional<String> with the JSON in the case of success. In the case of an error, it simply returns None.

2. parseTvShowString, which invokes TvShowParser::parse and returns an Optional<List<ScoredShow>> in the case of success and None in the case of an error.

Both use the try-catch expression and the Optional<T> type you find in **lib**.

Now, fetchTvShowOptional has type (String) -> Optional<String> and parseTvShowString has type (String) -> Optional<List<ScoredShow>>. What if you want to fetch and then parse?

This is exactly what you learned in Chapter 13, "Understanding Monads", where you implemented flatten and bind to basically create flatMap.

In Chapter 9, "Data Types", you implemented flatMap like:

```
fun <A, B> Optional<A>.flatMap(
  fn: Fun<A, Optional<B>>
): Optional<B> = when (this) {
  is None -> Optional.empty()
  is Some<A> -> {
    val res = fn(value)
    when (res) {
      is None -> Optional.empty()
      is Some<B> -> Optional.lift(res.value)
    }
  }
}
```

In Chapter 13, "Understanding Monads", you implemented this too, providing an implementation for flatten. In any case, you compose fetchTvShowOptional and parseTvShowString, adding this code to **ShowSearchService.kt** in the **optional** package:

```
fun fetchAndParseTvShow(query: String) =
  fetchTvShowOptional(query)
    .flatMap(::parseTvShowString)
```

fetchAndParseTvShow is now the composition of fetchTvShowOptional and parseTvShowString, and it has type (String) -> Optional<List<ScoredShow>>.

To test how it works, just run this:

```
fun main() {
  fetchAndParseTvShow("Big Bang Theory") // 1
    .getOrDefault(emptyList<ScoredShow>()) pipe ::println // 2
}
```

Here, you:

1. Invoke fetchAndParseTvShow, getting an Optional<List<ScoredShow>>.

2. Use getOrDefault to provide a default value in the case of an error.

Getting something like:

```
[ScoredShow(score=1.2612172, show=Show(id=66, name=The Big Bang
Theory, genres=[Comedy], url=https://www.tvmaze.com/shows/66/
the-big-bang-theory, image=ShowImage(original=https://
static.tvmaze.com/uploads/images/original_untouched/
173/433868.jpg, medium=https://static.tvmaze.com/uploads/images/
medium_portrait/173/433868.jpg), summary=<p><b>The Big Bang
Theory</b> ... </p>, language=English))]
```

This is quite good because it allows you to test each function in isolation and then trust the composition between two functions in the Kleisli category, as you learned in Chapter 13, "Understanding Monads". However, you can do much better. Disconnect your computer and run the code again, and you'll get the following output:

```
[]
```

Is this an error, or is this the actual result coming from the server? With the previous code, you'd never know. You need a way to get more information about the error. Regardless, a good point about this solution is that you don't invoke parseTvShowString at all if the fetchAndParseTvShow fails.

Handling errors with Either<E, T>

The Optional<T> data type is very useful, but it just tells you *if* you have a response; it doesn't tell you *what the error is* if something goes wrong. In this case, a data type like Either<E, T> can help you. In **lib**, you'll find **Either.kt**, which contains all the code you implemented in Chapter 9, "Data Types". To see how to use it, just add the following code to **ShowSearchService.kt**, this time in the **either** sub-package:

```kotlin
fun fetchTvShowEither(
  query: String
): Either<IOException, String> = try {
  Either.right(TvShowFetcher.fetch(query)) // 1
} catch (ioe: IOException) {
  Either.left(ioe)
}

/** Invokes the parser returning an Optional */
fun parseTvShowEither(
  json: String
): Either<SerializationException, List<ScoredShow>> = try {
  Either.right(TvShowParser.parse(json)) // 2
} catch (e: SerializationException) {
  Either.left(e)
}
```

This case is somewhat similar to `Optional<T>`, but using `Either<E, T>`. Here, you define:

1. `fetchTvShowEither`, which invokes `TvShowFetcher::fetch` and returns the result as `Either.Right<String>` in the case of success and the exception in an `Either.Left<IOException>` in the case of an error. Note how the result type is `Either<IOException, String>`.

2. `parseTvShowEither`, which invokes `TvShowParser::parse` and returns the result as `Either.Right` in the case of success and the exception in an `Either.Left` in the case of an error. In this case, the return type is `Either<SerializationException, List<ScoredShow>>`.

As you did with `Optional<T>`, you use `flatMap` to create the following, which you add to the same file:

```
fun fetchAndParseTvShowEither(query: String) =
  fetchTvShowEither(query)
    .flatMap(::parseTvShowEither)
```

Here, you use `flatMap` to compose `fetchTvShowEither` and `parseTvShowEither` in a function of type `(String) -> Either<Exception, List<ScoredShow>>`. Note how the type parameter value for `Left<T>` is `Exception` and not `IOException` or `SerializationException`. This is because `Exception` is the common ancestor type of the two, and this depends on the specific implementation of `flatMap` you implemented in Chapter 9, "Data Types", and you find in **Either.kt** in **lib**:

```
fun <A, B, D> Either<A, B>.flatMap(
  fn: (B) -> Either<A, D>
): Either<A, D> = when (this) {
  is Left<A> -> Either.left(left)
  is Right<B> -> {
    val result = fn(right)
    when (result) {
      is Left<A> -> Either.left(result.left)
      is Right<D> -> Either.right(result.right)
    }
  }
}
```

To test `fetchAndParseTvShowEither`, simply add and run the following code:

```
fun main() {
  fetchAndParseTvShowEither("Big Bang Theory")
    .leftMap {
      println("Error: $it")
    }
    .rightMap {
      println("Result: $it")
    }
}
```

Getting:

```
Result: [ScoredShow(score=1.2627451, show=Show(id=66, name=The
Big Bang Theory, genres=[Comedy], url=https://www.tvmaze.com/
shows/66/the-big-bang-theory, image=ShowImage(original=https://
static.tvmaze.com/uploads/images/original_untouched/
173/433868.jpg, medium=https://static.tvmaze.com/uploads/images/
medium_portrait/173/433868.jpg), summary=<p><b>The Big Bang
Theory</b> is a comedy...</p>, language=English))]
```

The interesting part happens when you have some errors. Disconnect your computer from the network and run the code again. You'll get something like:

```
Error: java.net.UnknownHostException: api.tvmaze.com
```

If you restore the network and "sabotage" `parseTvShowEither` by adding some text to the `json` parameter like this:

```
fun parseTvShowEither(json: String):
Either<SerializationException, List<ScoredShow>> =
  try {
    Either.right(TvShowParser.parse(json+"sabotage")) // HERE
  } catch (e: SerializationException) {
    Either.left(e)
  }
```

You'll get:

```
Error:
kotlinx.serialization.json.internal.JsonDecodingException:
Unexpected JSON token at offset 1589: Expected EOF after
parsing, but had s instead
JSON input: .....ze.com/episodes/1646220}}}}]sabotage
```

As you see, the first exception that happens is the one you'll get as output. This is also true because you can't parse JSON you don't have in the case of a fetching error.

In some cases, you want to collect all the exceptions that happen, which is a classic use of the **applicative functor**.

Applicative functor

In the previous section, you learned how to handle exceptions using Optional<T> and Either<E, T> data types following a *fail fast* approach that stops the execution flow at the first exception. With Either<E, T>, you also get what's wrong. In Chapter 9, "Data Types", you learned that Either<A, B> is a **bifunctor**, which is an algebraic data type representing the addition of two types, A and B. In the previous use case, you used Left<E> to represent the error case and Right<T> for the success case.

In the context of error handling, you usually create a dedicated data type you call Result<E, T>.

> **Note**: As you'll learn later, Kotlin provides a built-in Result<T> data type, which is different from the one you'll create in this section. To avoid conflicts, you'll call yours ResultAp<E, T>, where the Ap suffix represents its applicative behavior.

As a first step, open **ResultAp.kt** in **applicative** and add the following code:

```kotlin
sealed class ResultAp<out E : Throwable, out T> { // 1

  companion object {
    @JvmStatic
    fun <E : Throwable> error(
      error: E
    ): ResultAp<E, Nothing> = Error(error) // 2

    @JvmStatic
    fun <T> success(
      value: T
    ): ResultAp<Nothing, T> = Success(value) // 2
  }
}
data class Error<E : Throwable>(
  val error: E
) : ResultAp<E, Nothing>() // 3
data class Success<T>(
  val value: T
```

```
) : ResultAp<Nothing, T>() // 3

fun <E1 : Throwable, E2 : Throwable, T> ResultAp<E1,
T>.errorMap(
  fl: (E1) -> E2
): ResultAp<E2, T> = when (this) { // 4
  is Error<E1> -> ResultAp.error(fl(error))
  is Success<T> -> this
}

fun <E : Throwable, T, R> ResultAp<E, T>.successMap(
  fr: (T) -> R
): ResultAp<E, R> = when (this) { // 5
  is Error<E> -> this
  is Success<T> -> ResultAp.success(fr(value))
}
```

ResultAp<E, T> is very similar to Either<E, T> and, besides the name, it differs in that:

1. Parameter type E has Throwable as its upper bound. This allows you to just use exceptions for the type E, but you can also remove that limitation if you prefer.

2. Factory methods are now called error and success to make their meaning explicit.

3. Error and Success types replace Left and Right.

4. mapLeft becomes errorMap.

5. mapRight becomes successMap.

Exercise 14.1: ResultAp<E, T> is very similar to Either<E, T>. Can you implement flatMap for it as well?

Exercise 14.2: In the previous paragraphs, you implemented a simple system to fetch and parse data using both Optional<T> and Either<E, T>. Can you do the same using ResultAp<E, T>?

Yeah, it's true. With ResultAp<E, T>, you haven't done much yet, but now comes the fun!

ResultAp<E, T> as an applicative functor

One of the most important things you've learned in this book is that *functions are values*, which is why you can implement *higher-order functions*. This also means that T in ResultAp<E, T> can be a function type like (T) -> T. So, what would the meaning be of a function ap with the following signature?

```
fun <E : Throwable, T, R> ResultAp<E, T>.ap( // 1
  fn: ResultAp<E, (T) -> R> // 2
): ResultAp<E, R> { // 3
  // ...
}
```

In this code, ap:

1. Is an extension function for the ResultAp<E, T> type.

2. Accepts a parameter of type ResultAp<E, (T) -> R> where the value in the case of success is a function (T) -> R.

3. Returns ResultAp<E, R>.

This is basically a way to apply a function to a value only in the case of success, as you see in the implementation you add in **ResultAp.kt** in **applicative**:

```
fun <E : Throwable, T, R> ResultAp<E, T>.ap(
  fn: ResultAp<E, (T) -> R>
): ResultAp<E, R> = when (fn) {
  is Success<(T) -> R> -> successMap(fn.value)
  is Error<E> -> when (this) {
    is Success<T> -> Error(fn.error)
    is Error<E> -> Error(this.error)
  }
}
```

Cool. Now you understand what it is, but how can ap be useful in the context of exception handling? A typical case involves validation.

Open **Validation.kt** in **validation** and add the following User data class.

```
data class User(
  val id: Int,
  val name: String,
  val email: String
)
```

Now, imagine you want to create a User starting with some values you enter from a UI, and those values require some sort of validation. To simulate that, add this code to the same file:

```
class ValidationException(msg: String) : Exception(msg) // 1

/** Name validation */
fun validateName(
  name: String
): ResultAp<ValidationException, String> =
  if (name.length > 4) {
    Success(name)
  } else {
    Error(ValidationException("Invalid name"))
  } // 2

/** Email validation */
fun validateEmail(
  email: String
): ResultAp<ValidationException, String> =
  if (email.contains("@")) {
    Success(email)
  } else {
    Error(ValidationException("Invalid email"))
  } // 3
```

> **Note**: Of course, you *can* make the ValidationException more informative, explaining what's wrong and how to fix it.

In this code, you define:

1. ValidationException as a simple Exception, representing validation errors.

2. validateName as a function that validates the name property.

3. validateEmail as doing the same for emails.

Now comes the magic! Just add this to the same file:

```
fun main() {
  val userBuilder = ::User.curry() // 1
  val userApplicative = ResultAp.success(userBuilder) // 2
  val idAp = ResultAp.success(1) // 3
  validateEmail("max@maxcarli.it") // 6
    .ap(
      validateName("") // 5
        .ap(
          idAp.ap(userApplicative) // 4
```

```
      )
    )
    .errorMap { // 7
      println("Error: $it"); it
    }
    .successMap { // 7
      println("Success $it")
    }
}
```

This code has numerous interesting points:

1. `::User` is how you represent a reference to a constructor in Kotlin. As mentioned, this is a function of type `(Int, String, String) -> User`. Using the curry implementations you find in **Curry.kt** in **lib**, you get a function of type `(Int) -> (String) -> (String) -> User`, which you save in `userBuilder`.

2. Using `ResultAp::success`, you save the reference of a function of type `ResultAp<ValidationException, (Int) -> (String) -> (String) -> User>` in `userApplicative`.

3. You don't validate the value for `id`, so you just create a `ResultAp.Success<Int>` from it.

4. Remember that `userApplicative` has type `ResultAp<ValidationException, (Int) -> (String) -> (String) -> User>`. Invoking ap on `idAp`, you basically get a `ResultAp<ValidationException, (String) -> (String) -> User>`. Note how this invocation has somehow swallowed the `Int` parameter.

5. You now pass the value you got from the previous point to ap of the `Result<ValidationException, String>` you get from `validateName`. This swallows another parameter, and you get a `ResultAp<ValidationException, (String) -> User>`.

6. Finally, you now pass the last value to the `ResultAp<ValidationException, String>` you get from `validateEmail` and get a `Result<ValidationException, User>`, which is the final result.

7. You can use `errorMap` to handle the `ValidationException` or `successMap` to handle instances of `User` that survived validation.

Run the previous code, and you'll get:

```
Error: com.raywenderlich.fp.validation.ValidationException:
Invalid Name
```

This is because the name you're passing is empty.

Just apply this change to add a name and run the code again:

```
fun main() {
  // ...
  validateEmail("max@maxcarli.it")
    .ap(
      validateName("Massimo") // HERE
        .ap(idAp.ap(userApplicative))
    )
    // ...
}
```

You'll get:

```
Success User(id=1, name=Massimo, email=max@maxcarli.it)
```

This looks good, but you still have two problems to solve:

1. As an expert functional programming engineer, you probably don't like all those parentheses. It would be nice to make the syntax simpler.

2. If you enter an invalid email *and* an invalid name, you only get the error about the former. It would be nice to know about both.

You can solve the first problem by adding the following code that creates `appl` as an infix version of ap:

```
infix fun <E : Throwable, A, B> ResultAp<E, (A) -> B>.appl(
  a: ResultAp<E, A>
) = a.ap(this)
```

Now, you can write the `main` like this:

```
fun main() {
  val userBuilder = ::User.curry()
  val userApplicative = ResultAp.success(userBuilder)
  val idAp = ResultAp.success(1)
  (userApplicative appl
      idAp appl
      validateName("Massimo") appl
      validateEmail("max@maxcarli.it"))
    .errorMap {
      println("Error: $it"); it
    }
    .successMap {
      println("Success $it")
    }
}
```

Now, `appl` allows you to follow the same order for validation of the parameters in `::User`. The only problem is a limitation of Kotlin that doesn't allow you to set the precedence between the operators, forcing you to use parentheses before `errorMap` and `successMap`.

Run the previous code, and you'll get:

```
Success User(id=1, name=Massimo, email=max@maxcarli.it)
```

The second problem gives you another opportunity to use a concept you learned about in previous chapters: **semigroups**.

Applicative functors and semigroups

As mentioned, the previous code doesn't allow you to get all the validation errors, only the first. Open **ValidationSemigroup.kt** and add the following code:

```
fun main() {
  val userBuilder = ::User.curry()
  val userApplicative = ResultAp.success(userBuilder)
  val idAp = ResultAp.success(1)
  (userApplicative appl
      idAp appl
      validateName("") appl // HERE
      validateEmail("")) // HERE
    .errorMap {
      println("Error: $it"); it
    }
    .successMap {
      println("Success $it")
    }
}
```

Run this code, and you get:

```
Error: com.raywenderlich.fp.validation.ValidationException:
Invalid email
```

This is correct, but you can do better. Both `name` and `email` are invalid, but the error message has no mention of the former. You need to find a way to somehow *accumulate* the errors into one. In Chapter 12, "Monoids & Semigroups", you learned that a **monoid** describes a way to *combine* two values into a single value of the same type. You can represent the properties of a monoid in different ways. For example, in **ValidationSemigroup.kt**, add the following definition:

```
interface Semigroup<T> {
```

```
    operator fun plus(rh: T): T
}
```

The Semigroup<T> interface here defines types with the plus operator. Now, you can create a different type of ValidationException, which is also a Semigroup, like this:

```
data class ValidationExceptionComposite( // 1
  private val errors: List<ValidationException> // 2
) : Exception(), Semigroup<ValidationExceptionComposite> {

  override fun plus(
    rh: ValidationExceptionComposite
  ): ValidationExceptionComposite =
    ValidationExceptionComposite(this.errors + rh.errors) // 3

  override fun getLocalizedMessage(): String {
    return errors.joinToString { it.localizedMessage } // 4
  }
}
```

In this code, you:

1. Create ValidationExceptionComposite as a data class extending Exception and implementing Semigroup<ValidationExceptionComposite>.

2. Define errors as a variable containing all the ValidationExceptions you want to combine.

3. Implement plus, creating a new ValidationExceptionComposite whose errors are the union of the errors of the two operands.

4. Override getLocalizedMessage, composing all the localizedMessages.

The next step now is to implement a version of ap, you call apsg, that handles Semigroups. In **ValidationSemigroup.kt** add the following code:

```
fun <E, T, R> ResultAp<E, T>.apsg(
  fn: ResultAp<E, (T) -> R>
): ResultAp<E, R> where E : Throwable, E : Semigroup<E> = // 1
  when (fn) {
    is Success<(T) -> R> -> successMap(fn.value)
    is Error<E> -> when (this) {
      is Success<T> -> Error(fn.error)
      is Error<E> -> Error(this.error + fn.error) // 2
    }
  }
```

The main things to note here are:

1. The type parameter E has two upper bounds. It must be a Throwable and a Semigroup<E>.

2. This is where the magic happens. Because E is a Semigroup<E>, you can use the + operator to combine them. Here, you have the case when you already have an error and you find a new one.

As you did previously for ap, you can provide an infix version by adding this code:

```
infix fun <E, T, R> ResultAp<E, (T) -> R>.applsg(
  a: ResultAp<E, T>
) where E : Throwable, E : Semigroup<E> = a.apsg(this)
```

To use the new ValidationExceptionComposite, you need to provide new validation functions. Add the following:

```
fun validateNameSg(
  name: String
): ResultAp<ValidationExceptionComposite, String> =
  if (name.length > 4) {
    Success(name)
  } else {
    Error(ValidationExceptionComposite(
      listOf(ValidationException("Invalid name"))
    ))
  }

fun validateEmailSg(
  email: String
): ResultAp<ValidationExceptionComposite, String> =
  if (email.contains("@")) {
    Success(email)
  } else {
    Error(ValidationExceptionComposite(
      listOf(ValidationException("Invalid email"))
    ))
  }
```

Note how you now use ValidationExceptionComposite, which contains a list of ValidationException.

Finally, you can replace the main and use the new operators like this:

```
fun main() {
  val userBuilder = ::User.curry()
  val userApplicative = ResultAp.success(userBuilder)
  val idAp = ResultAp.success(1)
```

```
(userApplicative applsg
    idAp applsg
    validateNameSg("") applsg
    validateEmailSg(""))
.errorMap {
    println(it.localizedMessage); it
}.successMap {
    println("Success $it")
}
}
```

Run this code, and you'll get:

```
Invalid email, Invalid name
```

Fix the email and run the code, getting:

```
Invalid name
```

Finally, fix the name and run the code, getting:

```
Success User(id=1, name=Massimo, email=max@maxcarli.it)
```

This is how, using ResultAp<E, T> as a specialized version of Either<E, T> and Semigroups, you implemented a **typeclass** called **applicative functor** to handle validation in a good, functional way.

The Kotlin Result<T> data type

As mentioned earlier, the Kotlin standard library has a Result<T> type that is similar to ResultAp<E, T>, which you implemented earlier.

> **Note**: If you want to learn all about the Result<T> API, the Kotlin Apprentice (https://www.raywenderlich.com/books/kotlin-apprentice) book is the right place to go.

Looking at the source code for Result<T>, you'll notice that it's not implemented as a **sealed class**. Result<T> has a single parameter type T, but the actual internal value has type Any?. This is because Result<T> handles the Failure case, assigning an instance of the internal class Result.Failure to value.

The goal here is to see if Result<T> is a *functor* first and then a *monad*.

Result<T> as a functor

To prove that Result<T> is a functor, you should verify the *functor laws*, and in particular, that:

1. `map id == id`

2. `map (f compose g) == (map f compose map g)`

First, you see that Result<T> APIs have map with the following implementation:

```
@InlineOnly
@SinceKotlin("1.3")
public inline fun <R, T> Result<T>.map(
  transform: (value: T) -> R
): Result<R> {
  contract {
    callsInPlace(transform, InvocationKind.AT_MOST_ONCE)
  }
  return when {
    isSuccess -> Result.success(transform(value as T))
    else -> Result(value)
  }
}
```

Removing the contract part and replacing transform with id, you get:

```
public inline fun <R, T> Result<T>.map(): Result<R> {
  return when {
    isSuccess -> Result.success(id(value))
    else -> Result(value)
  }
}
```

In the case of success, you get:

```
public inline fun <R, T> Result<T>.map(): Result<R> =
  Result.success(id(value))
```

Because id(value) = value, you have:

```
public inline fun <R, T> Result<T>.map(): Result<R> =
  Result.success(value)
```

In the case of failure, you get:

```
public inline fun <R, T> Result<T>.map(): Result<R> =
  Result(value)
```

Considering that the value in the case of failure is the `Result.Failure` instance itself, this completes the proof of the first functor law.

Proving the second law can be more verbose, but you can actually make it shorter by noting that the function `transform` you pass as a parameter is only used in the case of success. If you have a success, `Result<T>`, and map a function `f` first and then a function `g`, you'll get the same value you'd get mapping `f compose g`.

Another, more pragmatic and quick proof that `Result<T>` is a functor is the presence of the `map` in the APIs. Looking at the same APIs, you can't find a `flatMap` function, which makes you wonder if the `Result<T>` data type is a monad or not.

Result<T> as a monad

As mentioned at the end of the previous section, the Kotlin `Result<T>` data type doesn't have a `flatMap`. What happens, then, if you need to compose a function of type `(A) -> Result<B>` with a function of type `(B) -> Result<C>`? Well, in Chapter 13, "Understanding Monads", you learned how to handle this case with a generic data type `M<A>`. It's time to do the same for `Result<T>`.

Open **ResultMonad.kt** in **result** and add the following code:

```
infix fun <A, B, C> Fun<A, Result<B>>.fish( // 1
  g: Fun<B, Result<C>>
): (A) -> Result<C> =
  { a: A ->
    this(a).bind(g)
  }

infix fun <B, C> Result<B>.bind( // 2
  g: Fun<B, Result<C>>
): Result<C> =
  map(g).flatten()
```

In this code, you simply replaced `M<T>` with `Result<T>` in the definition of the operators:

1. `fish`

2. `bind`

To do this, you need to implement `flatten` like the following:

```
fun <A> Result<Result<A>>.flatten(): Result<A> = // 1
  if (isSuccess) {
    getOrNull()!! // 2
  } else {
```

```
      Result.failure(exceptionOrNull()!!) // 3
    }
```

Here, you:

1. Define `flatten` as an external function of `Result<Result<A>>` with `Result<A>` as the return type.

2. Return its value in the case of success. Note that the value of `Result<Result<A>>` has type `Result<A>`.

3. Return what you get from `Result::failure`, passing the exception in the case of failure.

Now, you can add the following code to the same file:

```
fun <A> Result<A>.lift(value: A): Result<A> = // 1
  Result.success(value)

fun <A, B> Result<A>.flatMap(fn: Fun<A, Result<B>>): Result<B> =
  map(::lift fish fn).flatten() // 2
```

Here, you define:

1. `lift`, which is basically `Result::success` with a different name.

2. `flatMap` using `fish`, `lift` and `flatten`.

Now, you have all you need to implement `ShowSearchService` with `Result<T>`, as you did with `Optional<T>`, `Either<E, T>` and `ResultAp<E, T>`.

Using Result<T> as a monad

Open **ShowSearchService.kt** in **result** and add the following code:

```
fun fetchTvShowResult(query: String): Result<String> = try {
  Result.success(TvShowFetcher.fetch(query)) // 1
} catch (ioe: IOException) {
  Result.failure(ioe) // 2
}

fun parseTvShowResult(json: String): Result<List<ScoredShow>> =
  try {
    Result.success(TvShowParser.parse(json /* +"sabotage"
*/)) // 1
  } catch (e: SerializationException) {
    Result.failure(e) // 2
  }
```

This code should be very familiar to you now. Here, you:

1. Use `Result::success` to create the `Result<T>` to return in the case of success, encapsulating the result. Note that in `fetchTvShowResult`, there is a commented "sabotage" `String` you can uncomment to simulate a failure in the parsing of the JSON in input.

2. Use `Result::failure` to create the `Result<T>` to return in the case of failure. In this case, you encapsulate the exception as a `Throwable`.

As the next step, add the following code:

```
fun fetchAndParseTvShowResult(query: String) =
  fetchTvShowResult(query)   // 1
    .flatMap(::parseTvShowResult) // 2
```

Here, you:

1. Invoke `fetchTvShowResult`, getting a `Result<String>` as a result.

2. Use `flatMap` passing `parseTvShowResult` as parameter.

Finally, add the following code:

```
fun main() {
  fetchAndParseTvShowResult("Big Bang Theory")
    .fold(onFailure = {
      println("Error: $it")
    }, onSuccess = {
      println("Result: $it")
    })
}
```

Run `main`, and you'll get something like the following:

```
Result: [ScoredShow(score=1.2637222, show=Show(id=66, name=The
Big Bang Theory, genres=[Comedy], url=https://www.tvmaze.com/
shows/66/the-big-bang-theory, image=ShowImage(original=https://
static.tvmaze.com/uploads/images/original_untouched/
173/433868.jpg, medium=https://static.tvmaze.com/uploads/images/
medium_portrait/173/433868.jpg), summary=<p><b>...</p>,
language=English))]
```

As you did before, run again with your computer disconnected from the network, getting:

```
Error: java.net.UnknownHostException: api.tvmaze.com
```

Now, reconnect your computer and uncomment the "sabotage" `String` in `parseTvShowResult` that's making the function fail. This time, you'll get:

```
Error:
kotlinx.serialization.json.internal.JsonDecodingException:
Unexpected JSON token at offset 1589: Expected EOF after
parsing, but had s instead
JSON input: .....ze.com/episodes/1646220}}}}]sabotage
```

Now, the Kotlin `Result<T>` data type is also a monad. :]

Meet the RayTV app

In the first part of the chapter, you learned how to handle exceptions in a functional way. You implemented two functions for fetching and parsing some data about TV shows using APIs provided by TVmaze (https://www.tvmaze.com/).

Using Android Studio, open the **RayTV** project in the material for this chapter. When you run the project, after the splash screen, you'll get what's in Figure 14.4:

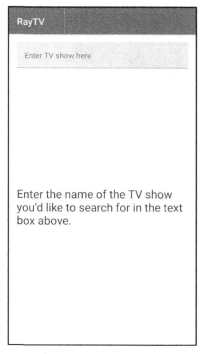

Figure 14.4: RayTV app

Enter some text in the TextField at the top of the screen, and you'll get some results like the following:

Figure 14.5: TV show search results

When you select a TV show from the list, you see its details, as in Figure 14.6:

Figure 14.6: TV show details

You'll play with the RayTV app more in the following chapters. In this case, it's interesting to look at how it handles errors.

Open **ShowSearchService.kt** in **tools.api** and look at the following code:

```kotlin
fun fetchTvShowResult(query: String): Result<String> =
  try {
    Result.success(TvShowFetcher.fetch(query))
  } catch (ioe: IOException) {
    Result.failure(ioe)
  }

fun parseTvShowResult(json: String): Result<List<ScoredShow>> =
  try {
    Result.success(TvShowParser.parse(json /* +"sabotage" */))
  } catch (e: SerializationException) {
    Result.failure(e)
  }

fun fetchAndParseTvShowResult(query: String) =
  fetchTvShowResult(query)
    .flatMap(::parseTvShowResult)
```

These are the same functions you implemented in the first part of the chapter. What's more interesting is how the app uses them.

Open **SearchViewModel.kt** in **ui.screen.search** and look at the following code:

```kotlin
@HiltViewModel
class SearchViewModel @Inject constructor() : ViewModel() {

  var searchState = mutableStateOf<SearchState>(NoSearchDone) //
1
    private set

  private var currentJob: Job? = null

  fun findShow(showName: String) {
    currentJob?.cancel()
    currentJob = viewModelScope.launch(Dispatchers.IO) {
      searchState.value = SearchRunning // 1
      fetchAndParseTvShowResult(showName) // 2
        .fold(onFailure = { // 3
          searchState.value = FailureSearchResult(it)
        }, onSuccess = { // 4
          if (!it.isEmpty()) {
            searchState.value = SuccessSearchResult(it)
          } else {
            searchState.value = NoSearchResult // 5
          }
        })
    }
  }
}
```

Besides some code related to the use of Jetpack Compose, Coroutines and Hilt, you can note the following:

1. The initial state is `NoSearchDone` and becomes `SearchRunning` every time you start a new search.

2. Every time you call `findShow`, you invoke `fetchAndParseTvShowResult`, passing the `String` to search.

3. You use `fold` and change the state to `FailureSearchResult` in the case of failure, encapsulating the `Throwable`.

4. In the case of success, you set the state to `SuccessSearchResult`, encapsulating the result.

5. Here, you also use a special case if the query is successful but you don't get any result.

In `SearchViewModel`, you basically bind every specific `Result` to a different UI state.

> **Note**: If you want to learn everything you need to know about coroutines, the Kotlin Coroutines by Tutorials (https://www.raywenderlich.com/books/kotlin-coroutines-by-tutorials) book is the right place to go. Jetpack Compose by Tutorials (https://www.raywenderlich.com/books/jetpack-compose-by-tutorials) is the best resource for learning how to create UI using Compose. With Dagger by Tutorials (https://www.raywenderlich.com/books/dagger-by-tutorials), you'll learn everything you need to know about Dagger and Hilt. Finally, Real World Android by Tutorials (https://www.raywenderlich.com/books/real-world-android-by-tutorials) will help you understand the best way to put all these technologies together.

Now, open **SearchComposable.kt** in **ui.screens.search** and find the following code:

```
// ...
  ErrorAlert(errorMessage = {
    stringResource(R.string.error_message)
  }) {
    result is FailureSearchResult
  }
// ...
```

ErrorAlert is a Composable function you find in **Util.kt** in **ui.screens**. It displays itself only if the current state is a FailureSearchResult.

To verify how it works, just enable the "sabotage" in parseTvShowResult in **ShowSearchService.kt** or disconnect your machine and run the app. When you try to search for a TV show, you'll get what's in Figure 14.7:

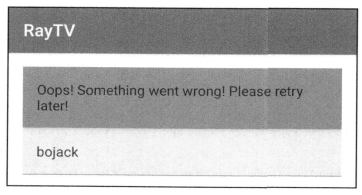

Figure 14.7: RayTV error message

Key points

- **Error handling** is a fundamental part of any software application.

- Many programming languages model errors using **exceptions**.

- Exceptions are a classic example of side effects.

- For exceptions, you can use the same process you used for other impure functions: Make the side effect a part of the result type.

- You can use Optional<T> and Either<E, T> to model functions throwing exceptions.

- **Applicative functors** and **semigroups** are useful in the case of multiple validations.

- The Kotlin standard library provides the Result<T> data type.

- Result<T> is a **functor** but not a **monad**.

- You can make Result<T> a monad by following the same process you used in Chapter 13, "Understanding Monads".

Where to go from here?

Congratulations! In this chapter, you had the chance to apply all the principles and concepts you learned in the first two parts of the book in a real example. In the next chapter, you'll learn everything you need to know about **state**.

Chapter 15: Managing State

In Section II, you learned about the concept of **data type** using the analogy of a **container** providing its content some **context**. For instance, Optional<A> represents a box that can either be empty or contain a value of type A. The context of a data type is important when you make it a **functor** or a **monad**. In the case of a functor, you can apply to Optional<A> a function Fun<A, B> and get an Optional<B>. If the initial Optional<A> is empty, you'll get an empty Optional<B>. If Optional<A> contains a value of type A, you apply the function Fun<A, B>, to get a value of type B wrapped in an Optional<B>. If the function you apply is of type Fun<A, Optional<B>>, you give Optional<A> the superpower of a monad and use flatMap to get an Optional<B> whose content depends on whether the value A is present. Different data types provide different contexts and behave differently as functors and monads.

> **Note**: An empty Optional<A> is different from an empty Optional<B> if A is different from B. In short, an empty box of pears is different from an empty box of apples. :]

You also learned that a **pure function** describes an expression that's **referentially transparent** and, more importantly, doesn't have any **side effects**. These two properties are connected because when an expression isn't referentially transparent, it uses some data that's outside the scope of the function, which is a side effect. A side effect changes the **state** of the universe outside the function body.

The question now is: Can you create a data type representing a box that encapsulates some data *and* the effect that happens when you apply functions with `map` or `flatMap` to the same data? With this data type, you wouldn't prevent the change of some state, but you'd be able to control it.

The solution is the `State<T>` data type, which is the topic of this chapter. Here, you'll learn:

- What `StateTranformation<S, T>` is.

- How to implement a `State<S, T>` data type.

- How the `State<S, T>` data type works as a functor.

- How to implement `State<T>` as an **applicative functor**.

- What the `State<S, T>` monad is.

- How to apply the `State<S, T>` monad in a practical example.

This is probably one of those chapters you'll need to read multiple times, but it'll definitely be worth it!

The problem

To describe how the `State<S, T>` data type works, it's helpful to start with a very simple example. You can follow along with it in the **Inventory.kt** file in the material for this project. Start by adding this code:

```
data class Product(val id: String, val name: String)
```

This is a simple `Product` data class representing — *ahem* — a *product*. :] During an inventory, you want to assign a **SKU** to it.

> **Note**: A stock keeping unit (SKU) is a scannable bar code that you usually find printed on product labels in retail stores. It's used to track inventory movement automatically.

In this case, suppose the SKU has the format `RAY-PROD-####`, where `####` represents a four-digit number that must be unique for each product.

> **Note**: Please ignore the fact that, with this format, you can only have 10,000 different SKUs. This just allows the code to remain simple so you can focus on the state. Of course, you *can* implement your SKU generator algorithm however you want.

You represent a product after the inventory as an instance of `SkuProduct`, which you add to the same file:

```
data class SkuProduct(val product: Product, val sku: String)
```

To assign a unique SKU to every product, use the following code:

```
var count = 0 // 1

fun createSku(): String = // 2
  "RAY-PROD-${String.format("%04d", count++)}" // 3
```

In this code, you:

1. Initialize the global variable `count` to `0`.

2. Define `createSku` as a function returning a unique SKU as a `String`.

3. Update `count`, allowing you to get a different SKU at each `createSku` invocation.

To test the previous function, add and run the following code:

```
fun main() {
  val prod1 = Product("1", "Cheese")
  val prod2 = Product("2", "Bread")
  val prod3 = Product("3", "Cake")

  SkuProduct(prod1, createSku()) pipe ::println
  SkuProduct(prod2, createSku()) pipe ::println
  SkuProduct(prod3, createSku()) pipe ::println
}
```

Getting in output:

```
SkuProduct(product=Product(id=1, name=Cheese), sku=RAY-
PROD-0000)
SkuProduct(product=Product(id=2, name=Bread), sku=RAY-PROD-0001)
SkuProduct(product=Product(id=3, name=Cake), sku=RAY-PROD-0002)
```

Everything looks fine, but it's actually not! Now that you know all about pure functions and side effects, you surely noted that createSku isn't pure — every time you invoke it, you change the state of the universe that, in this case, you represent with count.

At this point, you have two main goals:

• Make createSku pure.

• Simplify its usage in your inventory.

The first step is introducing the concept of **state transformation**.

State transformation

createSku is impure because of the side effect related to the count update, which happens every time you invoke createSku. This creates the SKU based on the current value of count, which is the current state. createSku also updates the state, preparing for the next invocation. You can generalize this behavior with the following definition, which you can add to **State.kt**:

```
typealias StateTransformer<S> = (S) -> S
```

StateTransformer<S> is a function that, given the current state of type S, returns the new value for the state which has, of course, the same type. In the case of the product inventory example, this function would be:

```
val skuStateTransformer: StateTransformer<Int> =
  { state -> state + 1 }
```

This is because you replaced S with Int, and the transformation consists of adding 1 to the current state.

In your example, you need to use the state to create a new SKU and use skuStateTransformer to update the state. A better abstraction to handle this behavior is the following:

```
typealias StateTransformer<S, T> = (S) -> Pair<T, S>
```

> **Note:** The different order for the type parameters S and T in the definition and the returning Pair<T, S> might introduce some confusion. The important thing is to be consistent in the code that follows.

This is the abstraction for all the functions receiving a state of type S as input, and returning both a value of type T and the new state of type S. The returned T might depend on the current state.

In this case, you rewrite `skuStateTransformation` like this:

```
val skuStateTransformer: StateTransformer<Int, String> = { state
->
   "RAY-PROD-${String.format("%04d", state)}" to state + 1
}
```

Now, `skuStateTransformer` has type `StateTransformer<Int, String>` and receives an `Int` as input, which is the current state, and returns the SKU based on that state and the new state.

To see how this works, replace `main` with the following:

```
fun main() {
   val prod1 = Product("1", "Cheese")
   val prod2 = Product("2", "Bread")
   val prod3 = Product("3", "Cake")

   val state0 = 0 // 1
   val (sku1, state1) = skuStateTransformer(state0) // 2
   SkuProduct(prod1, sku1) pipe ::println // 3
   val (sku2, state2) = skuStateTransformer(state1) // 4
   SkuProduct(prod2, sku2) pipe ::println // 5
   val (sku3, state3) = skuStateTransformer(state2) // 6
   SkuProduct(prod3, sku3) pipe ::println // 7
}
```

In this code, you:

1. Initialize the beginning state of `state0` at `0`.

2. Invoke `skuStateTransformer`, passing the current value for the state, `state0`, and getting the SKU and the new state you save in `sku1` and `state1`, respectively.

3. Use `sku1` to create the `SkuProduct` for `prod1`.

4. Invoke `skuStateTransformer`, passing the new state, `state1`, and getting a new SKU and the new state you save in `sku2` and `state2`, respectively.

5. Use `sku2` to create the `SkuProduct` for `prod2`.

6. Again, invoke `skuStateTransformer` with `state2`.

7. Use `sku3` to create the `SkuProduct` for `prod3`, and so on...

Run this code, and you'll get:

```
SkuProduct(product=Product(id=1, name=Cheese), sku=RAY-
PROD-0000)
SkuProduct(product=Product(id=2, name=Bread), sku=RAY-PROD-0001)
SkuProduct(product=Product(id=3, name=Cake), sku=RAY-PROD-0002)
```

Looking at this code, you can't say you made everything easier to use. This is because you have to:

1. Create an initial state.

2. Invoke the `StateTransformer<S, T>` to get a new state.

3. Pass the new state to another `StateTransformer<S, T>` to get the next state.

4. Keep going until you get all the type T values you need.

You should find a way to make all these "passing values" for the state automatic and somehow hidden under the hood. This is what you'll achieve in the following paragraphs, and *this* is what the state monad is for.

A state transformer visual intuition

Before proceeding, there's something you should fix. `skuStateTransformer` receives an `Int` as input and returns a `String` for the SKU and another `Int` for the new state. In the inventory problem, you need something else because you need to start from a `Product` and get a `SkuProduct`.

To do this, add the following definition to **Inventory.kt**:

```
val assignSku: (Product, Int) -> Pair<SkuProduct, Int> = // 1
  { product: Product, state ->
    val newSku = "RAY-PROD-${String.format("%04d", state)}" // 2
    SkuProduct(product, newSku) to state + 1 // 3
  }
```

In this code, you:

1. Define `assignSku` as a function of two input parameters of types `Product` and `Int`, respectively, and a `Pair<SkuProduct, Int>` as output.

2. Create the SKU using the current `state`.

3. Return the `SkuProduct` and the new state.

In the first section of the book, you learned a magic trick called **currying**. It allows you to convert any function with multiple input parameters into a chain of functions with a single input parameter. If you apply `curry` to `assignSku`, you get a function of type `(Product) -> (Int) -> Pair<SkuProduct, Int>`. Look at the second part of this function type, and you'll recognize the `(Int) -> Pair<SkuProduct, Int>` type, which is the same as `StateTransformer<Int, SkuProduct>`. To make everything explicit, you can say that `assignSku` has type `(Product) -> StateTransformer<Int, SkuProduct>`.

To prove this, add the following code in **Inventory.kt**, and see that it compiles:

```
val curriedAssignSku:
     (Product) -> StateTransformer<Int, SkuProduct> =
  assignSku.curry()
```

> **Note:** curry and other higher-order functions you implemented in the previous chapters are already available in the **lib** sub-package of the project in the material.

At this point, a visual representation of `assignSku` can be helpful. Look at Figure 15.1:

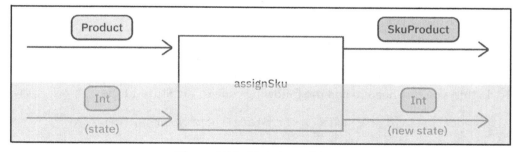

Figure 15.1: State transformer

You can see that `assignSku` has a visible part that maps a `Product` into a `SkuProduct` and an invisible one that's responsible for updating the state.

What you want to achieve is a way to implement `(Product) -> SkuProduct` while keeping the state transformation hidden.

Now, replace the `main` with the following:

```kotlin
fun main() {
    val prod1 = Product("1", "Cheese")
    val prod2 = Product("2", "Bread")
    val prod3 = Product("3", "Cake")

    val state0 = 0
    val (skuProd1, state1) = curriedAssignSku(prod1)(state0)
    skuProd1 pipe ::println
    val (skuProd2, state2) = curriedAssignSku(prod2)(state1)
    skuProd2 pipe ::println
    val (skuProd3, state3) = curriedAssignSku(prod3)(state2)
    skuProd3 pipe ::println
}
```

Run the code, and you'll get:

```
SkuProduct(product=Product(id=1, name=Cheese), sku=RAY-
PROD-0000)
SkuProduct(product=Product(id=2, name=Bread), sku=RAY-PROD-0001)
SkuProduct(product=Product(id=3, name=Cake), sku=RAY-PROD-0002)
```

You can already see some minor improvements, but you still want to remove the need to pass the current state.

Introducing the State<S, T> data type

The `StateTransformer<T, S>` type you defined earlier is a **function type**. What you need now is a **data type** so you can apply all the typeclasses; like functor, applicative and monad; you applied for `Optional<T>`, `Either<A, B>` or `Result<T>`. To do this, you just need to add the following code to the **State.kt** file:

```kotlin
data class State<S, T>(val st: StateTransformer<S, T>)
```

If you want to think of this in terms of containers again, you can look at the `State<S, T>` as a box whose context is about the encapsulation of a `StateTransformer<S, T>` that describes how the state changes at every action you do through the box itself.

To make things a little bit easier and remove the effort due to the definition of the `State<S, T>` data type, add the following code:

```kotlin
operator fun <S, T> State<S, T>.invoke(state: S) = st(state)
```

In this case, you can start from a State<S, T> and use the invoke function or the (), pass the current state, and apply to it the StateTransformer<S, T> it encapsulates. Just remember that the type for invoke is (State<S, T>) -> (S) -> Pair<T, S>.

Now that you have the State<S, T> data type, you need to add some magic starting from lift up to the **monadic** superpower. Now, the *real* fun starts. :]

Implementing lift

The first operation you need to implement is lift, also called return in other languages. This is the function you use to get a value of type T and put it into the box related to the specific data type, in this case, State<S, T>. In **State.kt**, change the State<S, T> definition like this:

```
data class State<S, T>(
  val st: StateTransformer<S, T>
) {

  companion object { // 1
    @JvmStatic
    fun <S, T> lift(
      value: T // 2
    ): State<S, T> = // 3
      State({ state -> value to state }) // 4
  }
}
```

In this code, you implement lift:

1. Using a companion object as a common pattern.

2. With an input parameter of type T.

3. Returning a State<S, T>.

4. Creating the State<S, T> using a StateTransformer<S, T> that simply keeps the state the same and returns the input value as a result.

With lift, you can start from a simple value and get a State<S, T> for it, like this:

```
fun main() {
  val initialState = State.lift<Int, Product>(Product("1",
"Cheese"))
}
```

Just note how you need to help the Kotlin type inference by providing the type for the input type parameters S and T. This is because Kotlin infers T's type from the value you pass, but it can't understand S's type on its own.

State<S, T> as a functor

After `lift`, it's time to make State<S, T> a functor. This means providing an implementation of the map function of type (State<S, A>) -> (Fun<A, B>) -> (State<S, B>).

Before writing the code, take some time to think about what it means for a State<S, A> to be a functor. You start with a value of type A and, using map, you apply a function of type Fun<A, B>, getting a value of type B. The State<S, A> needs to handle the state update. To understand how it works, add the following code to the **StateFunctor.kt** file:

```kotlin
fun <S, A, B> State<S, A>.map( // 1
  fn: Fun<A, B> // 2
): State<S, B> = // 3
  State { state ->   // 4
    val (a, newState) = this(state) // 5
    fn(a) to newState // 6
  }
```

In this code, you:

1. Define map as an extension function for the type State<S, A>.

2. Have a function of type Fun<A, B> as an input parameter.

3. Return a value of type State<S, B> according to the concept of functors.

4. Create an instance of State<S, B>, passing in a lambda with an input parameter state of type S. Note how you can omit the ( ) because the only parameter, and also the last, is a lambda expression.

5. To get the new state and the value of type A, you need to invoke the state transformer of type StateTransformer<S, A> encapsulated in the receiver. Remember that you can do this because you defined the invoke operator on the State<S, T> type above. Another option would be simply to invoke st(state).

6. Invoke the input parameter fn, passing the value of type A you got in the previous step, and get the value you return along with the new state.

In the previous code, it's essential to understand that the *new state* you get with
State<S, B> is the *same* as what you get with the initial State<S, A>. The
difference is that the value of type B in State<S, B> is the one you get applying
Fun<A, B> to the value of type A in State<S, A>.

As an example, add the following code to **StateFunctor.kt**:

```
val skuSerial = { sku: String -> sku.takeLast(4) } // 1

val skuState: State<Int, String> = State { state: Int -> // 2
  "RAY-PROD-${String.format("%04d", state)}" to state + 1
}

val skuSerialState = skuState.map(skuSerial) // 3

fun main() { // 4
  skuState(0) pipe ::println
  skuSerialState(0) pipe ::println
}
```

Here, you define:

1. skuSerial, which has the type Fun<String, String> and returns the last 4
   characters of the input String.

2. skuState as the State<Int, String> for the generation of the SKUs.

3. skuSerialState as the State<Int, String> you get from skuState passing
   skuSerial as an argument of map.

4. main that prints the result of skuState and skuSerialState passing the same
   value as the initial state.

When you run the code, you'll get:

```
(RAY-PROD-0000, 1)
(0000, 1)
```

As you see, the new state is the same, but skuSerial has been applied to the value of
type String.

State<S, T> as an applicative functor

Looking at the signature of map for the State<S, A>, notice that it accepts a
function of type Fun<A, B> as input. As you know, Fun<A, B> is the type of function
with a single input parameter of type A returning a value of type B.

It's interesting, now, to generalize map as accepting functions with multiple input parameters. For instance, in the **Curry.kt** file in **lib**, you find the following code:

```
typealias Fun2<T1, T2, R> = (T1, T2) -> R
typealias Fun3<T1, T2, T3, R> = (T1, T2, T3) -> R
typealias Fun4<T1, T2, T3, T4, R> = (T1, T2, T3, T4) -> R
```

Using curry, you know they're equivalent to the following types:

```
typealias Chain2<T1, T2, R> = (T1) -> (T2) -> R
typealias Chain3<T1, T2, T3, R> = (T1) -> (T2) -> (T3) -> R
typealias Chain4<T1, T2, T3, T4, R> =
  (T1) -> (T2) -> (T3) -> (T4) -> R
```

> **Note**: In the previous code, you considered up to four input parameters, but, of course, you *could* consider all the cases up to N.

If you want to generalize map for functions of different input parameters, you could just provide an implementation of map for each of those. For instance, in the case of Fun2<A, B, C>, you could define the following:

```
fun <S, A, B, C> State<S, Pair<A, B>>.map2(
  fn: Fun2<A, B, C>
): State<S, C> =
  State { state ->
    val (pair, newState) = this(state) // Or st(state)
    val value = fn(pair.first, pair.second)
    value to newState
  }
```

Replace Fun2<A, B, C> with Chain2<A, B, C>, and you get:

```
fun <S, A, B, C> State<S, Pair<A, B>>.map2(
  fn: Chain2<A, B, C> // 1
): State<S, C> =
  State { state ->
    val (pair, newState) = this(state) // Or st(state)
    val value = fn(pair.first)(pair.second)  // 2
    value to newState
  }
```

Here, you:

1. Use Chain2<A, B, C> in place of Fun2<A, B, C>.

2. Get the value to return with fn(pair.first)(pair.second) instead of passing the two parameters together, like fn(pair.first, pair.second).

With Fun2<A, B, C>, this isn't a problem, but imagine if you had to implement all these map versions for all the possible options. This would be *very* tedious. Fortunately, this is the case where the **applicative functor** typeclass comes into play. Similar to what you saw in Chapter 14, "Error Handling With Functional Programming", to define all possible maps for all the possible functions with multiple parameters, you just need two basic functions you've already met. The first is your lift that, in the context of an applicative functor, is called pure. The second is the ap function that, in the context of the State<S, T> data type, has the following signature:

```
fun <S, T, R> State<S, T>.ap(
    fn: State<S, (T) -> R>
): State<S, R> {
    // TODO
}
```

As you can see, ap is an extension function for the type State<S, T> and accepts in input a State<S, (T) -> R> where the value is actually a function from T to R. The result, then, is a State<S, R>.

Before implementing its body, it's interesting to see how you can use ap to handle functions of multiple parameters. You do this using the **applicative style**.

Suppose you want to apply a function with three parameters of type Fun3<A, B, C, R>, which is equivalent to a Chain<A, B, C, R> typealias of (A) -> (B) -> (C) -> R. As a simple example, add the following code to **StateApplicative.kt**:

```
fun replaceSuffix(
    input: String,
    lastToRemove: Int,
    postfix: String
) = input.dropLast(lastToRemove) + postfix
```

This is a basic function of three parameters that removes the lastToRemove characters from an input String, replacing them with postfix. It has the type Fun3<String, Int, String, String>.

You can make it of type Chain<String, Int, String, String> using curry, like this:

```
val cReplaceSuffix = ::replaceSuffix.curry()
```

To use the applicative style, add the following code:

```
infix fun <S, A, B> State<S, (A) -> B>.appl(a: State<S, A>) =
  a.ap(this) // 1

fun main() {
  val initialStateApp = State
    .lift<Int, Chain3<String, Int, String, String>>(
      cReplaceSuffix
    ) // 2
  val inputApp = State.lift<Int, String>("1234567890") // 3
  val lastToRemoveApp = State.lift<Int, Int>(4) // 3
  val postfixApp = State.lift<Int, String>("New") // 3
  val finalStateApp = initialStateApp appl
    inputApp appl lastToRemoveApp appl postfixApp // 4

  inputApp(0) pipe ::println // 5
  finalStateApp(0) pipe ::println // 5
}
```

In this code, you:

1. Define appl for State<S, A>, the same way you did in Chapter 14, "Error Handling With Functional Programming", to make the code more readable.

2. Use lift to create State<Int, Chain3<String, Int, String, String>>, passing cReplaceSuffix.

3. Do the same for all the input parameters. Note how inputApp and postfixApp have type State<Int, String>, and lastToRemoveApp has type State<Int, Int>.

4. Using the infix operator appl, you apply the applicative style, which remains associative. This means it works as if it were (((initialStateApp appl inputApp) appl lastToRemoveApp) appl postfixApp).

5. Print the initial and final values as output.

Of course, at the moment, you can't run this code because you still need to implement app.

Replace the previous skeleton with the following code:

```
fun <S, T, R> State<S, T>.ap( // 1
  fn: State<S, (T) -> R> // 2
): State<S, R> = // 3
  State { s0: S -> // 4
    val (t, s1) = this(s0) // 5
    val (fnValue, s2) = fn(s1) // 6
    fnValue(t) to s2 // 7
  }
```

In this code, you:

1. Define ap as an extension function for State<S, T>.

2. Accept a parameter of type State<S, (T) -> R> as input. Note how the value is a function of type (T) -> R.

3. Use State<S, R> as the return type.

4. Invoke the State<S, R> constructor, passing a lambda with the current state s0 as the initial state.

5. Get the value of type T and the new state s1, invoking the current receiver with the initial state.

6. Use the new state s1 as input for fn to get the value of type (T) -> R and the final state s2.

7. Get the final result, invoking fn on the value of type T you got in Step 5 and using the final state s2.

Note how you get the values from the current receiver first and then from the input State<S, (T) -> R>. Also, note how the state updates twice. The first update is based on the current receiver of type State<S, T>, and the second is because of the one of input State<S, (T) -> R>.

Now, you can finally run main, getting:

```
(1234567890, 0)
(123456New, 0)
```

As you can see, you applied replaceSuffix to the input String, but the value for the state of type Int remained the same. This is actually expected because this works exactly like the functor. It just gives you the chance to apply functions with multiple parameters to the value of type T in State<S, T>, leaving the state unchanged.

State<S, T> as a monad

Now, it's finally time to give State<S, T> the power of a monad by implementing flatMap. To do that, you could follow the same process you learned in Chapter 13, "Understanding Monads", providing implementation to fish, bind, flatten and finally flatMap. That was a general process valid for all monads, but now you can go straight to the solution, starting with the following code you write in **StateMonad.kt**:

```
fun <S, A, B> State<S, A>.flatMap( // 1
  fn: (A) -> State<S, B> // 2
): State<S, B> = TODO() // 3
```

Here, you:

1. Define flatMap as an extension function for the State<S, A> data type.

2. Provide fn as an input parameter of type (A) -> State<S, B>.

3. Return a State<S, B>.

So, if the State<S, A> data type is a way to encapsulate some state and the logic to update it, flatMap is the tool you use to compose a function of type (A) -> State<S, B> coming from the Kleisli category.

You'll probably be surprised at how simple the flatMap implementation is. Just replace the previous definition with the following code:

```
fun <S, A, B> State<S, A>.flatMap(
  fn: (A) -> State<S, B>
): State<S, B> =
  State { s0: S -> // 1
    val (a, s1) = this(s0) // 2
    fn(a)(s1) // 3
  }
```

Here, you:

1. Use the State<S, B> constructor, passing the state transformation as a body. Of course, the state transformation has the initial state s0 as an input parameter.

2. Invoke the receiver of type State<S, A>, passing the initial state. In this way, you get the value a of type A and the new state s1 of type S. Remember that the type for the state S never changes, but its value can.

3. Pass the value a as an input parameter of the function fn of type `(A)` -> `State<S, B>` you have as input, getting a value of type `State<S, B>`. To get the final `Pair<B, S>`, you need to invoke the `State<S, B>` with the state s1.

As a simple example of how to use `State<S, T>` as a monad, add the following code to the same **StateMonad.kt** file:

```
val assignSkuWithState: // 1
    (Product) -> State<Int, SkuProduct> =
  { prod: Product ->
    State(curriedAssignSku(prod)) // 2
  }

fun main() {
  val prod1 = Product("1", "First Product") // 3
  val initialState = State.lift<Int, Product>(prod1) // 4
  val finalState = initialState.flatMap(assignSkuWithState) // 5
  finalState(0) pipe ::println // 6
}
```

In this code, you define a main, where you:

1. Implement assignSkuWithState as a function of type `(Product)` -> `State<Int, SkuProduct>` responsible for assigning a new SKU to a Product into a SkuProduct and updating the current state.

2. Implement assignSkuWithState, simply encapsulating the `StateTransformer<Int, SkuProduct>` from the curriedAssignSku you defined in **Inventory.kt**, into a `State<Int, SkuProduct>`.

3. Define a simple Product you use as an input parameter.

4. Use lift to define the `State<Int, Product>` from the value prod1 of type Product. This is the initial state, initialState.

5. Invoke flatMap, passing the reference to assignSku. This is where the composition magic happens, and you get a `State<Int, SkuProduct>` that you save in finalState.

6. Invoke finalState, passing the initial state value 0, and send the result to the standard output.

Run the code, and you'll get:

```
(SkuProduct(product=Product(id=1, name=First Product), sku=RAY-
PROD-0000), 1)
```

The initial value for the state was 0, and this is the one `assignSku` used to generate the SKU RAY–PROD–0000. The new value for the state is 1. This is because `lift` doesn't apply the state transformation but returns a value for the state that's the same value you have in input.

A practical example

In the previous example, you didn't have the chance to appreciate the hidden state transformation that the `State<S, T>` monad does for you behind the scenes. As a more complicated example, suppose you have an `FList<Product>`, and you want to assign each one a unique value for the SKU, getting an `FList<SkuProduct>` as output.

Open **StateMonadInventory.kt**, and add the following code:

```
val products = FList.of(
  Product("1", "Eggs"),
  Product("2", "Flour"),
  Product("3", "Cake"),
  Product("4", "Pizza"),
  Product("5", "Water")
)
```

This is a simple `FList<Product>` with some dummy data, and you want to get an `FList<SkuProduct>`, assigning each one a unique SKU value.

A possible solution implies the use of the map function, like this:

```
var currentCount = 0
fun inventoryMap(products: FList<Product>): FList<SkuProduct> {
  return products.map {
    SkuProduct(it,
      "RAY–PROD–${String.format("%04d", currentCount++)}")
  }
}
```

To see how this works, run the following code:

```
fun main() {
  inventoryMap(products).forEach(::println)
}
```

Getting:

```
SkuProduct(product=Product(id=1, name=Eggs), sku=RAY-PROD-0000)
SkuProduct(product=Product(id=2, name=Flour), sku=RAY-PROD-0001)
SkuProduct(product=Product(id=3, name=Cake), sku=RAY-PROD-0002)
SkuProduct(product=Product(id=4, name=Pizza), sku=RAY-PROD-0003)
SkuProduct(product=Product(id=5, name=Water), sku=RAY-PROD-0004)
```

But, there's a *but*! inventoryMap isn't pure because it uses and changes currentCount, which is part of the external world. A possible solution could be to move currentCount inside inventoryMap, like this:

```
fun inventoryMapWithCount(
  products: FList<Product>
): FList<SkuProduct> {
  var internalCount = 0
  return products.map {
    SkuProduct(it,
      "RAY-PROD-${String.format("%04d", internalCount++)}")
  }
}
```

The output would be the same. internalCount now has the scope inventoryMapWithCount, and it's not considered as a side effect. The problem now is that internalCount starts from 0 every time you invoke inventoryMapWithCount, so it'll produce duplicated SKUs.

In this chapter, you learned that a possible solution is to add the current state as part of the input parameter and define a listInventoryHelper function, like the following:

```
fun listInventory(
  products: FList<Product>
): (Int) -> Pair<Int, FList<SkuProduct>> =
  when (products) { // 1
    is Nil -> { count: Int -> count to Nil } // 2
    is FCons<Product> -> { count: Int -> // 3
      val (newState, tailInventory) =
        listInventory(products.tail)(count)
      val sku = "RAY-PROD-${String.format("%04d", newState)}"
      newState + 1 to FCons(
        SkuProduct(products.head, sku), tailInventory)
    }
  }
```

In this code:

1. You check if the current product is empty or an `FCons<Product>`.

2. If it's empty, you get a `Nil`, and you just need to return it along with the current unchanged state.

3. If you have an `FCons<Product>`, you need to handle the head first, getting a SKU and creating the related `SkuProduct`. For the tail, you just need to invoke `listInventory` recursively.

To test the code, run:

```
fun main() {
    listInventory(products)(0).second.forEach(::println)
}
```

Getting:

```
SkuProduct(product=Product(id=1, name=Eggs), sku=RAY-PROD-0004)
SkuProduct(product=Product(id=2, name=Flour), sku=RAY-PROD-0003)
SkuProduct(product=Product(id=3, name=Cake), sku=RAY-PROD-0002)
SkuProduct(product=Product(id=4, name=Pizza), sku=RAY-PROD-0001)
SkuProduct(product=Product(id=5, name=Water), sku=RAY-PROD-0000)
```

This approach works, but you can improve it. The main issues are:

1. The SKUs are assigned in reverse order. This might not be a problem as long as they're unique.

2. You need to handle the internal state explicitly. This is error-prone and might lead to errors that are difficult to debug.

Fortunately, the `State<S,  T>` monad helps. To understand how, you need to create a utility function first. Add the following code to **State.kt**:

```
fun <S, A, B, C> State<S, A>.zip( // 1
  s2: State<S, B>, // 2
  combine: (A, B) -> C // 3
): State<S, C> = // 4
  State { s0 -> // 5
    val (v1, s1) = this(s0) // 6
    val (v2, s2) = s2(s1) // 7
    combine(v1, v2) to s2 // 8
  }
```

In this code, you:

1. Define `zip` as an extension function of `State<S, A>`.

2. Declare a first input parameter of type `State<S, B>,`.

3. Use the second input parameter, `combine` of type `(A, B) -> C`.

4. Return a `State<S, C>` whose value is the value of type `C` you get by invoking `combine` on the values of types `A` and `B`.

5. Create the result, invoking the `State<S, C>` constructor.

6. Invoke the receiver with the initial state, getting the value of type `A` and the new state.

7. Use the new state to get the value of type `B` and an updated version of the state.

8. Get the value of type `C`, invoking `combine`, and return the result along with the last version of the state.

Now, you can finally add the following code to **StateMonadInventory.kt**:

```kotlin
val addSku: (Product) -> State<Int, SkuProduct> = // 1
  { prod: Product ->
    State<Int, SkuProduct> { state: Int ->
      val newSku = "RAY-PROD-${String.format("%04d", state)}"
      SkuProduct(prod, newSku) to state + 1
    }
  }

fun inventory(
  list: FList<Product>
): State<Int, FList<SkuProduct>> = // 2
  when (list) { // 3
    is Nil -> State.lift(Nil) // 4
    is FCons<Product> -> {
      val head = State.lift<Int, Product>(list.head) // 5
        .flatMap(addSku)
      val tail = inventory(list.tail) // 6
      head.zip(tail) { a: SkuProduct, b: FList<SkuProduct> -> //
7
        FCons(a, b)
      }
    }
  }
```

Here, you:

1. First, define addSku, which returns a State<Int, SkuProduct> given a Product as input.

2. Define inventory as a function accepting an FList<Product> as input and returning a State<Int, FList<SkuProduct>> as output.

3. Check if the current FList<Product> is a Nil or FCons<Product>.

4. If it's a Nil, you just return the same encapsulated into a State<Int, FList<SkuProduct>> using lift.

5. If it's an FCons<Product>, you handle the head first. First, you use lift to get a State<Int, Product>, and then use flatMap with addSku to get a State<Int, SkuProduct>.

6. Invoke inventory recursively on the tail to get the related state of type State<Int, FList<SkuProduct>>.

7. Use zip to combine the State<Int, FList<SkuProduct>> for the head and the tail in a single FList you return as a result.

To test how this works, add and run the following code:

```
fun main() {
    inventory(products)(0).first.forEach(::println)
}
```

Getting as output:

```
SkuProduct(product=Product(id=1, name=Eggs), sku=RAY-PROD-0000)
SkuProduct(product=Product(id=2, name=Flour), sku=RAY-PROD-0001)
SkuProduct(product=Product(id=3, name=Cake), sku=RAY-PROD-0002)
SkuProduct(product=Product(id=4, name=Pizza), sku=RAY-PROD-0003)
SkuProduct(product=Product(id=5, name=Water), sku=RAY-PROD-0004)
```

As you can see, now the SKUs have the right order, but, more importantly, all the state management is handled entirely under the hood. In the last version of inventory, you don't pass over any state, and the code is completely functional.

Key points

- A **data type** is like a container that provides some context to its content.

- A **state** represents any value that can change.

- You can use the concept of state to model the side effect of an impure function.

- The context of a data type impacts how you interact with its content when applying some functions.

- The State<S, T> data type encapsulates the concept of state transition.

- StateTransformer<S, T> abstracts a value and a state update.

- State<S, T> is a data type that encapsulates a StateTransformer<S, T>.

- You can make State<S, T> a functor providing the implementation for map.

- map on a State<S, T> applies a function to the value of type T but leaves the state unchanged.

- Making State<S, T> an applicative functor allows you to apply functions with multiple parameters.

- You can make State<S, T> a monad, providing implementation for the flatMap.

- The State<S, T> allows you to define two different types of transactions. The first, on the value, is visible. The second, on the state transition, is hidden.

Where to go from here?

Congratulations! This is definitely one of the most challenging chapters of the book. Using most of the concepts from the first two sections of the book, you learned how to use the State<S, T> data type and how to implement lift, map, app, appl and flatMap. Finally, you applied the State<S, T> monad to a real example, showing how it's possible to keep the state transaction hidden. The concept of side effects is one of the most important in functional programming, and in the next chapter, you'll learn even more about it.

Chapter 16: Handling Side Effects

In Chapter 15, "Managing State", you implemented the State<S, T> **data type** and gave it the superpowers of a **functor**, **applicative** and **monad**. You learned that State<S, T> describes the context of some state of type S that changes based on some transformations you apply every time you interact with the value of type T in it. Making the State<S, T> a monad means you can compose different functions of type (A) -> State<S, B>. The State<S, B> data type is just a way to encapsulate a StateTransformer<S, T>. This means you can compose functions of type (A) -> StateTransformer<S, B> that's basically a function of type (A) -> (S) -> Pair<S, B>. If you use uncurry, this is equivalent to a function of type Pair<A, S> -> Pair<S, B>.

Now, think about what an **impure** function is. It's a function whose body is an expression that is *not referentially transparent* because, when executed, it changes the state of the world outside the function body. This means it has a **side effect**, which breaks composition. But if a side effect is a change in the state of the world, the question now is: *Can you somehow represent the state of the world as the type S you use in a* State<S, T> *and encapsulate the side effect as a simple transformation?* In other words, if you define the type World as representing the current state of the world, can you use State<World, T> as a data type that encapsulates any possible side effects?

The answer to this question is *yes*, and the specific data type is IO<T>.

In this chapter, you'll learn:

- How to implement Hello World in a pure, functional way.

- What the IO<T> data type is.

- How to use IO<T> to **compose** functions with side effects.

- What **monad comprehension** is.

- How to use IO<T> in a practical example.

- How to use **suspendable functions** to solve basically the same problem IO<T> wants to solve.

This is an essential chapter, and now it's time to do some magic! :]

From State<S, T> to IO<T>

Hello World is probably the most popular application to implement when learning a new language. This is mainly because it's very simple and allows you to see how to execute some of the fundamental tasks in common between all applications, like compilation, execution, debugging and so on.

The app you'll implement here is a little bit different because it'll allow you to read a name from the standard input and then print a greeting message. Open **Greetings.kt** in the material for this chapter, and write the following code:

```
fun main() {
    print("What's your name? ") // 1
    val name = Scanner(System.`in`).nextLine() // 2
    print("Hello $name\n") // 3
}
```

In this code, you:

1. Print a message asking the user their name.

2. Use Scanner to read the name you type as input and save it to name.

3. Use name to format and print a greeting message.

Feel free to run it, and, after entering your name, you'll get an output like the one in Figure 16.1:

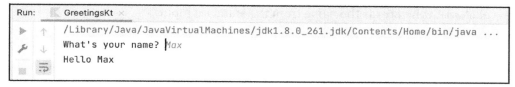

Figure 16.1: Running the greetings app

> **Note:** When you run the app, just put the cursor after the input message to insert your name, as shown in Figure 16.1. Then, type your name and press **Enter.**

The previous code works very well, but the expression in `main` is anything but pure. Using `Scanner`, you read the `name` from the standard input. Using `print`, you display the result on the standard output. They're both side effects: interaction with the rest of the world. So, how can you create the previous program but handle side effects in a pure and functional way?

The introduction of this chapter already gave you a hint. What if you think of the external world as a giant state you change when you *read* the `name` and *write* the greeting message?

You can follow this idea starting with the definition of a type you call `World`. Add the following in the **World.kt** file:

```
typealias World = Unit
```

Here, you define `World` as a simple alias for the `Unit` type. At this point, how you define the `World` type doesn't really matter. You'll see later if how you define `World` really matters or not. In the same file, add the following:

```
typealias SideEffect = (World) -> World
```

This is interesting because you're defining a `SideEffect` as any function from an initial state of the `World` to, probably, a different state of the same `World`. But here, something strange is happening. If you have a function of type `SideEffect` able to capture the whole `World` in input and return a different version of it, you've essentially eliminated the concept of a side effect because everything happens in the context of that function. In this case, all the functions would be pure.

To prove that you can modify the initial program as the composition of the function, you use:

- `readName`, which reads the name from the standard input.

- `printString`, which prints a `String` to the standard output.

`readName`'s type is `(World) -> Pair<String, World>` because it receives the `World` in input and provides the `String` for the name and a new version of the `World` in output. Add the following code to **Greetings.kt**:

```
val readName: (World) -> Pair<String, World> = { w: World ->
  Scanner(System.`in`).nextLine() to World
}
```

`printString`'s type is a little more interesting. It's `(String, World) -> World` because it receives the `String` to print and the current `World` in input, returning the new state for the `World`. In this case, you have two input parameters, but you can apply `curry`, getting the type `(String) -> (World) -> World`. With the previous definition of `SideEffect`, you can say that the type of `printString` is `(String) -> SideEffect`. In this way, you make the definition more explicit. Then, add the following code to the same **Greetings.kt** file:

```
val printString: (String) -> SideEffect = { str: String ->
  { a: World ->
    print(str) to World
  }
}
```

> **Note:** As you'll see later, a type like `(String) -> SideEffect` says something crucial. It says that `printString` doesn't execute a side effect but returns a description of it. This is the main reason it's a pure function now.

Now, test each of the previous functions by running the following code:

```
fun main() {
  // ...
  readName(World) pipe ::println // 1
  printString("Hello Max \n")(World) pipe ::println  // 2
}
```

In this code, you invoke:

1. readName, passing the current state of the World, printing in output the name you read from the standard input.

2. printString with a name, and then the function of type (World) -> World with the current state of the World.

After you insert the name in input, you'll get the output in Figure 16.2:

```
Run:        GreetingsKt  ×
  ▶    ↑    /Library/Java/JavaVirtualMachines/jdk1.8.0_261.jdk/Contents/Home/bin/java ...
  🔧   ↓    Max ①
            (Max, kotlin.Unit) ②
  ▦   ⇄    Hello Max ③
  📷   ⇲    kotlin.Unit ④
```

Figure 16.2: Testing readName and printString

In the image, you can see:

1. An example of a String input.

2. The output of readName, which is a Pair<String, Unit> of the String in input and the new state of the World you previously defined using Unit.

3. The output you get using print in printString.

4. The output of printString, which is again a Unit representing the new state of the World.

This is very interesting, but what you achieved now isn't actually what you need. You need a way to *compose* readName and printString as *pure functions* and get an app that works like the initial one.

Pure greetings

To accomplish your goal, you basically need to create askNameAndPrintGreetings, whose type is (World) -> World. The final state of the world is the one where you asked for a name and printed a greeting message.

Given readName and printString, you can add the following code to **Greetings.kt**:

```
fun askNameAndPrintGreetings(): (World) -> World = // 1
  { w0: World -> // 2
    val w1 = printString("What's your name? ")(w0) // 3
```

```
    val (name, w2) = readName(w1) // 4
    printString("Hello $name! \n")(w2) // 5
}
```

In this code, you:

1. Define `askNameAndPrintGreetings` as a function of type `(World) -> World`, which you can also refer to as `SideEffect` if you prefer.

2. Return a function with the input parameter `w0` of type `World`. With `w0`, you represent the initial state for the world.

3. Invoke `printString`, passing the message to ask the name along with the current state of the world, `w0`. Here, you get the new state of the world you store in `w1`.

4. Pass the current state of the world, `w1`, as an input parameter for `readName`, getting a `Pair<String, World>`. Using **destructuring**, you save the `String` in `name` and the new state of the world in `w2`.

5. Invoke `printString`, passing the greeting message to print along with the state of the world, `w2`, you got in the previous step. `printString` also returns the final state of the world you use as the return value for `askNameAndPrintGreetings`.

Test this code by running the following code:

```
fun main() {
    askNameAndPrintGreetings()(World) pipe ::println
}
```

Here, you invoke `askNameAndPrintGreetings`, passing the initial state of the world in input. When the function completes, you send the output to `println`.

After you insert a `String` in input, you'll get:

```
►   ↑   /Library/Java/JavaVirtualMachines/jdk1.8.0_261.jdk/Contents/Home/bin/java ...
🔧  ↓   What's your name? Max ①
            Hello  Max! ②
    ⇥   kotlin.Unit ③
```

Figure 16.3: Running askNameAndPrintGreetings

Here, you:

1. Provide a String as input.

2. Print the greeting message.

3. Print the output for askNameAndPrintGreetings, which is the Unit you used as the value representing the state of the world.

Besides the fact that askNameAndPrintGreetings works, you should also note these other crucial points:

- askNameAndPrintGreetings accepts the current state of the world as input and provides a new one.

- The code in askNameAndPrintGreetings's body looks like it's imperative. You invoke printString, readName and printString again, one after the other. This way of composing functions is called **monad comprehension**. It's the name for a programming idiom available in multiple languages, like JavaScript, F#, Scala or Haskell. Monad comprehension describes a way to compose sequential chains of actions in a style that feels natural for programmers used to procedural languages.

- At each step, you pass the current state of the world, getting the new state. You're not using World at all.

The last point is fundamental because it would be very useful to remove the requirement of passing the world ahead. This problem is similar to the one related to the State<S, T> monad you learned in Chapter 15, "Managing State".

Hiding the world

In Chapter 15, "Managing State", you implemented the State<S, T> monad as a data type encapsulating a StateTransformer<S, T> you defined like this:

```
typealias StateTransformer<S, T> = (S) -> Pair<T, S>
```

Note: You find the State<S, T> definition in the **State.kt** file in the **lib** sub-package in this chapter's material.

Here, you can follow the same process, defining the `WorldT` type like this in the **World.kt** file:

```
typealias WorldT<T> = (World) -> Pair<T, World>
```

Just be careful that `T` is a generic type parameter, but `World` is the actual type you defined earlier as a simple type alias of `Unit`. If you now look at the `readName` you defined in **Greetings.kt**, you can see that its type is exactly the same as `WorldT<String>`. You can add the following definition without any compilation errors in **Greetings.kt**:

```
val readNameT: WorldT<String> = readName
```

What about `printString`? Just remember that its type is `(String) -> (World) -> World`, which is basically equivalent to `(String)-> WorldT<Unit>`. This is a little bit more complicated, because it requires a little change. In **Greetings.kt**, add the following definition:

```
val printStringT: (String) -> WorldT<Unit> = { str: String ->
  { w: World ->
    Unit to printString(str)(w)
  }
}
```

Now, you need to solve a problem you're used to: *composition*. You need to compose `printStringT` with `readNameT` and `printStringT` again to implement your beautiful **Greetings** program in a pure, functional way.

Before doing that, it's useful to review the types of all the functions in play:

- `printStringT` has the type `(String) -> WorldT<Unit>`, which is `(String) -> (World) -> Pair<Unit, World>`.

- `readNameT` has the type `WorldT<String>`, which is `(World) -> Pair<String, World>`.

In the implementation for the **Greetings** app, you need to compose:

1. `printStringT` of type `(String) -> WorldT<Unit>` with

2. `readNameT` of type `WorldT<String>` with

3. `printStringT` again.

One way to do that is the definition of a function — you temporarily define `myOp` in **World.kt** with the following signature:

```
infix fun <A, B> WorldT<A>.myOp( // 1
  fn: (A) -> WorldT<B> // 2
): WorldT<B> = TODO() // 3
```

> **Note**: You'll find out the best name for `myOp` later. You might already know! :]

Here, you define `myOp`:

1. As an *infix* extension function of the `WorldT<A>` type. Remember that this is equivalent to having the receiver of type `WorldT<A>` as the first argument.

2. With an input parameter `fn` of type `(A) -> WorldT<B>`.

3. Returning a `WorldT<B>`.

This means that if you have a `WorldT<A>` and a function of type `(B) -> WorldT<B>`, you can use the `myOp` operator and get a `WorldT<B>`.

To make all the types explicit, write its type like the following:

```
    WorldT<A> // 1
-> (A) -> WorldT<B> // 2
-> WorldT<B> // 3
```

Remember that `WorldT<A>` is just an alias for the `(World) -> Pair<A, World>` type, which allows you to rewrite the previous definition like the following:

```
    (World) -> Pair<A, World> // 1
-> (A) -> (World) -> Pair<B, World> // 2
-> (World) -> Pair<B, World> // 3
```

Now, look at **2**. Remember that **uncurry** is a higher-order function that allows you to start with a function of type `(A) -> (B) -> C` and get an equivalent function of type `(A, B) -> C`. If you consider the equivalence between a function of two input parameters of type A and B, and a `Pair<A, B>`, you can write:

```
    (World) -> Pair<A, World> // 1
-> (Pair<A, World>) -> Pair<B, World> // 2
-> (World) -> Pair<B, World> // 3
```

This means you can compose the `WorldT<A>` in **1** with the uncurried version of `fn` at **2**. This allows you to write the implementation of `myOp` like the following, which you should write in **World.kt**:

```
infix fun <A, B> WorldT<A>.myOp(
  fn: (A) -> WorldT<B>
): WorldT<B> = this compose fn.uncurryP()
```

Note how you need to use `uncurryP`, a function you find in **Curry.kt** in the **lib** sub-package of this chapter's material. It uses `Pair<A, B>` as input in place of two parameters of types A and B, respectively.

```
fun <T1, T2, R> ((T1) -> (T2) -> R).uncurryP():
    Fun<Pair<T1, T2>, R> = { p: Pair<T1, T2> ->
  this(p.first)(p.second)
}
```

Now, it's time to use it.

A hidden greeting

The first implementation of `askNameAndPrintGreetings` you created forced you to carry the world on at each step.

```
fun askNameAndPrintGreetings(): (World) -> World =
  { w0: World ->
    val w1 = printString("What's your name? ")(w0)
    val (name, w2) = readName(w1)
    printString("Hello $name! \n")(w2)
  }
```

Now it's time to get rid of the world — *wow!* — and implement `askNameAndPrintGreetingsT`, like the following you can write in **Greetings.kt**:

```
fun askNameAndPrintGreetingsT(): WorldT<Unit> = // 1
  printStringT("What's your name? ") myOp { _ -> // 2
    readNameT myOp { name -> // 3
      printStringT("Hello $name! \n") // 4
    }
  }
```

In this code, you:

1. Define `askNameAndPrintGreetingsT` as a function returning a `WorldT<Unit>`, which is basically the world transformation encapsulating `Unit` as a value.

2. Invoke `printStringT` for printing a message. Remember that this returns a `WorldT<Unit>`. Using `myOp`, you compose `printStringT` with a lambda function that ignores the input parameter, which is of type `Unit`.

3. Use `readNameT`, which returns a `WorldT<String>`. To access the `String` it returns, you use `myOp` to compose `readNameT` with a function you define using a lambda expression with name in input.

4. Finally, use name to print the greetings using `printStringT`.

If you don't believe this works, just add this to **Greetings.kt**:

```
fun main() {
    askNameAndPrintGreetingsT()(World) pipe ::println
}
```

Here, you just invoke `askNameAndPrintGreetingsT`, getting the value of type `World<Unit>` you then use, passing `World` as a parameter. You'll get an output similar to the one you saw earlier:

```
  ▶  ↑   /Library/Java/JavaVirtualMachines/jdk1.8.0_261.jdk/Contents/Home/bin/java ...
  ⚲  ↓   What's your name? Max ①
  ▣  ⇥   Hello Max! ②
          (kotlin.Unit, kotlin.Unit) ③
```

Figure 16.4: Running askNameAndPrintGreetings

Here, you:

1. Enter your name after the "What's your name?" message.

2. Get the greeting in output.

3. See the output of `askNameAndPrintGreetingsT`, which is a `Pair<Unit, World>`. You get the double `Unit` because you represented `World` as `Unit` at the beginning of the chapter.

As you can see, you've got some good news and some bad news. The good news is that the `World` is now hidden. In the `askNameAndPrintGreetingsT` body, you don't have to receive any `World` and pass it on to the following methods.

The bad news is that you probably don't want to indent the code using all those {} and create many lambdas as arguments of myOp.

Don't worry. In the previous code, you definitely saw a lot of what you learned in Chapter 15, "Managing State". It's now time to follow the same process and define the IO<T> monad.

The IO<T> monad

So far, you've worked with WorldT<T>, which is an abstraction representing a World transformation. This World transformation is basically a side effect. It's not so different from StateTransformer<S, T> when you replace S with the type World.

Now, you need to:

1. Encapsulate WorldT<T> into a data type you'll call IO<T>.

2. Implement lift to encapsulate any WorldT<T> into an IO<T>.

3. Give IO<T> the *power* of a **functor**.

4. Extend IO<T> with the *power* of a **functor applicative**.

5. Give IO<T> the *superpower* of a **monad**.

6. Finally, you'll use IO<T> to solve the indentation problem you got with askNameAndPrintGreetingsT, implementing a sort of monad comprehension.

If you follow the same process you did for State<S, T>, replacing S with World, the first five points are simple. You could do them as an exercise or just follow along. :]

The IO<T> data type

In the **lib** sub-package in this chapter's material, you find all the files related to the State<S, T> monad. In **State.kt**, you find the following definition:

```
data class State<S, T>(
  val st: StateTransformer<S, T>
)
```

In the case of IO<T>, you just know that S in State<S, T> is the type World and that instead of StateTransformer<S, T>, you have WorldT<T>.

Knowing how these types relate to each other, open **IO.kt** and add the following definition:

```
data class IO<T>(val wt: WorldT<T>)
```

Congratulations! You just created the IO<T> data type. As you'll see, it's very simple *and* powerful. Now, it's time to add even *more* power, starting with the implementation of lift.

Implementing lift

As you know, lift is the function that allows you to get, in this case, an IO<T> from a WorldT<T>. Depending on the context, you might find the same function with a name like return or pure. Anyway, following the same approach you saw in the previous section, you implement it by replacing the existing code in **IO.kt** with the following:

```
data class IO<T>(val wt: WorldT<T>) {

  companion object { // 1
    @JvmStatic
    fun <S, T> lift(
      value: T // 2
    ): IO<T> = // 3
      IO { w -> value to w } // 4
  }
}
```

Here, you:

1. Implement lift as a *static function* in a companion object.

2. Define T as the input parameter type.

3. Set IO<T> as the type for the output.

4. Create the IO<T> using the default constructor, passing a lambda of type WorldT<T> that simply returns a Pair<T, World> in output.

To make the previous code simpler, the same way you did for State<S, T>, add the following code:

```
operator fun <T> IO<T>.invoke(w: World) = wt(w)
```

This allows you to apply the WorldT<T> transformation in IO<T> using the () operator directly.

IO<T> as a functor

The next step is to give IO<T> the power of a functor and provide an implementation of map. This is usually very easy, and this case is no different. Open **IO.kt**, and add the following code:

```
fun <A, B> IO<A>.map(
  fn: Fun<A, B>
): IO<B> =
  IO { w0 ->
    val (a, w1) = this(w0) // Or wt(w0)
    fn(a) to w1
  }
```

This is the classic implementation of map as an extension function of IO<A> accepting a Fun<A, B> as input and returning an IO<B> as output.

IO<T> as an applicative functor

Applicative functors are useful when you want to apply functions with multiple parameters. In the same **IO.kt**, add the following code:

```
fun <T, R> IO<T>.ap(
  fn: IO<(T) -> R>
): IO<R> =
  IO { w0: World ->
    val (t, w1) = this(w0)
    val (fnValue, w2) = fn(w1)
    fnValue(t) to w2
  }
```

You also add the infix version with this:

```
infix fun <A, B> IO<(A) -> B>.appl(a: IO<A>) = a.ap(this)
```

Again, you just started from the same functions for State<S, T>, replaced State with IO and removed S. In the implementation, you used wn instead of sn to represent the n-th state of the world.

IO<T> as a monad

Finally, you want to give IO<T> the superpower of a monad, adding the implementation of flatMap like this to **IO.kt**:

```
fun <A, B> IO<A>.flatMap(
  fn: (A) -> IO<B>
): IO<B> =
  IO { w0: World ->
    val (a, w1) = this(w0)
    fn(a)(w1)
  }
```

But, hey! You've seen this already, right? Earlier, you implemented myOp like this:

```
infix fun <A, B> WorldT<A>.myOp(
  fn: (A) -> WorldT<B>
): WorldT<B> = this compose fn.uncurryP()
```

Besides the fact that myOp is an extension function for WorldT<T> and flatMap for IO<A>, they both accept a function that reminds you of the Kleisli category.

The former accepts a function of type (A) -> WorldT<B> and the latter one of type (A) -> IO<B>. Yeah, they represent the same concept!

But how can you use all this magic? With a monadic greeting, of course!

Monadic greetings

In the previous sections, you implemented askNameAndPrintGreetingsT like this:

```
fun askNameAndPrintGreetingsT(): WorldT<Unit> =
  printStringT("What's your name? ") myOp { _ ->
    readNameT myOp { name ->
      printStringT("Hello $name! \n")
    }
  }
```

Using `printStringT` and `readNameT`, you implemented as:

```
val readName: (World) -> Pair<String, World> = { w: World ->
  Scanner(System.`in`).nextLine() to World
}

val readNameT: WorldT<String> = readName

val printStringT: (String) -> WorldT<Unit> = { str: String ->
  { w: World ->
    Unit to printString(str)(w)
  }
}
```

In this code, note how `readNameT` is just an alias for `readName` you used to make its type, `WorldT<String>`, explicit. In any case, now you need to work with `IO<T>`. To do this, write the following code in **IOGreetings.kt**:

```
val readNameM: IO<String> = IO(readNameT) // 1

val printStringM: (String) -> IO<Unit> =
  printStringT compose ::IO // 2
```

In this code, you define:

1. `readNameM` as a monadic version of `readNameT` you get just by encapsulating it into an `IO<String>`.

2. `printStringM` as a function accepting a `String` as input and returning an `IO<Unit>`. Because `readNameT` returns a `WorldT<Unit>`, you just need to compose it with the primary constructor of `IO<Unit>`.

Now, you have two functions working with `IO<T>` without exposing `WorldT<T>` anymore. If you look at `readNameM`, you realize it returns an `IO<String>` with the name you might've inserted during execution. Of course, you need to access that value. To do this, just add the following code to the same file:

```
fun <T> IO<T>.bind(): T = this(World).first
```

Because `IO<T>` represents a way to encapsulate a `WorldT<T>`, and because you have just one representation of the world, which is `World`, you can extract the value of type `T` by invoking the transformation with it to get a `Pair<T, World>`. Then, you get the `first` property of the `Pair<T, World>` and return it.

This is simple and powerful because you can finally write the following in
IOGreetings.kt:

```
fun askNameAndPrintGreetingsIO() : () -> Unit = { // 1
  printStringM("What's your name? ").bind() // 2
  val name = readNameM.bind() // 3
  printStringM("Hello $name! \n").bind() // 4
}
```

In this code, you:

1. Define `askNameAndPrintGreetingsIO` as the monadic version of the greeting
    app. Note how it returns a value of type `() -> Unit` you put as explicit here just
    to emphasize it.

2. Invoke `printStringM` with the input message. Remember how this returns an
    `IO<Unit>`. With bind, you actually extract the `Unit` value you don't even use.
    This means you could also avoid invoking `bind()`, but you invoke it here so all
    the instructions follow the same pattern.

3. Invoke `bind` on `readNameM` and assign the `String` you get to name. In this case,
    invoking `bind` is necessary because you need the `name` to pass to the next step.

4. Print the output using `printStringM`. In this case, invoking `bind()` allows you to
    return `Unit` from `askNameAndPrintGreetingsIO`. Without that, you'd have
    returned `IO<Unit>`.

This is great! You've learned some critical points. Here, you:

*   Don't explicitly pass the reference to the world ahead anymore.

*   Don't have all the indentations you had in `askNameAndPrintGreetingsT`.

*   Write your code in a way that's familiar to a procedural approach.

The only thing you need now is to test if it works. In the same **IOGreetings.kt** file,
add and run the following code:

```
fun main() {
  askNameAndPrintGreetingsIO().invoke()
}
```

And you'll get:

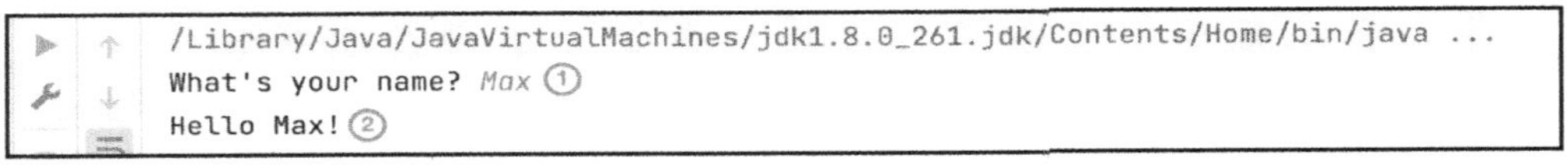

```
▶  ↑   /Library/Java/JavaVirtualMachines/jdk1.8.0_261.jdk/Contents/Home/bin/java ...
🔧  ↓   What's your name? Max ①
       Hello Max! ②
```

Figure 16.5: Running a monadic greeting

Here, you:

1. Type your name as input.

2. Print the greeting.

Just note how you don't have to pass any `World` to the `askNameAndPrintGreetingsIO`. The `IO<T>` monad does this all under the hood.

The meaning of IO<T>

The greeting example you've implemented so far is a great example of a practical use of `IO<T>`. However, in Chapter 14, "Error Handling With Functional Programming", you learned that sometimes things go wrong. For instance, you implemented `readNameM` like:

```
val readNameM: IO<String> = IO(readNameT)
```

Where:

```
val readNameT: WorldT<String> = readName

val readName: (World) -> Pair<String, World> = { w: World ->
    Scanner(System.`in`).nextLine() to World
}
```

What if `readName` fails for some reason? In that case, you should write a safe version of it. Open **Safe.kt**, and write the following code:

```
val safeReadName: (World) -> Pair<Result<String>, World> =
    { w: World -> // 1
        try {
            Result.success(Scanner(System.`in`).nextLine()) to World
        } catch (rte: RuntimeException) {
            Result.failure<String>(rte) to World
        }
    }
```

```
val safeReadNameError: (World) -> Pair<Result<String>, World> =
  { w: World -> // 2
    Result.failure<String>(
      RuntimeException("Something went wrong!")
    ) to World
  }

val safeReadNameT: WorldT<Result<String>> = safeReadName // 3
```

In this code, you define:

1. `safeReadName` as a function that returns the `String` you read from the standard input, encapsulated into a `Result<String>`.

2. `safeReadNameError`, which is a failing version of `safeReadName`.

3. `safeReadNameT` as a function of type `WorldT<Result<String>>`.

Now, add the following:

```
val safePrintStringT: (String) -> WorldT<Result<Unit>> =
  { str: String ->
    { w: World ->
      Result.success(Unit) to printString(str)(w)
    }
  }
```

This version of `printStringT` returns a `WorldT<Result<Unit>>` instead of a `WorldT<Unit>`. Now, you can create the monadic versions by adding the following code:

```
val safeReadNameM: IO<Result<String>> = IO(safeReadNameT) // 1

val safePrintStringM: (String) -> IO<Result<Unit>> =
  safePrintStringT compose ::IO // 2
```

In this case, you define:

1. `safeReadNameM` as encapsulating `safeReadNameT` into a `IO<Result<String>>`.

2. `safePrintStringM` as a function of type `IO<Result<Unit>>` encapsulating `safePrintStringT`.

Now, the version of the greeting app becomes the following:

```
fun safeAskNameAndPrintGreetingsIO(): () -> Result<Unit> = { //
1
  safePrintStringM("What's your name? ").bind() // 2
    .flatMap { _ -> safeReadNameM.bind() } // 3
    .flatMap { name ->
      safePrintStringM("Hello $name!\n").bind() // 4
    }
}
```

In this code, you:

1. Define `safeAskNameAndPrintGreetingsIO` as a function returning a `Result<Unit>`.

2. Invoke `safePrintStringM`, passing a message, and get the `Result<Unit>` using `bind`.

3. Use `flatMap`, passing a lambda that returns a `Result<String>` with the message in input or the error if something went wrong.

4. Invoke `flatMap` again, passing a lambda that invokes `safePrintStringM` with the greeting in output.

This function is pure and works perfectly. To test this, just run the following code:

```
fun main() {
  safeAskNameAndPrintGreetingsIO().invoke().fold(
    onSuccess = { _ ->
      // All good
    },
    onFailure = { ex ->
      println("Error: $ex")
    }
  )
}
```

Getting the usual output:

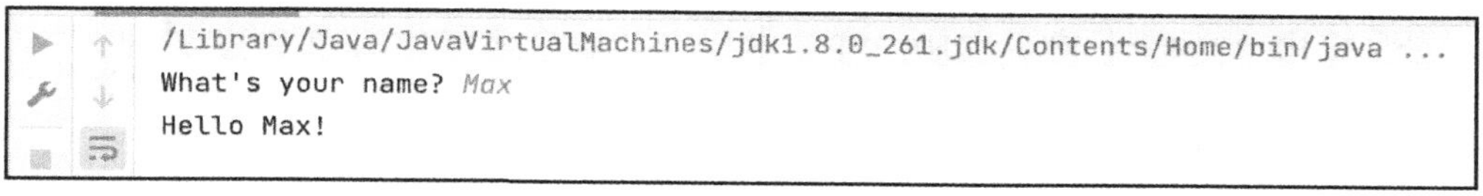

```
/Library/Java/JavaVirtualMachines/jdk1.8.0_261.jdk/Contents/Home/bin/java ...
What's your name? Max
Hello Max!
```

Figure 16.6: Running a monadic greeting with result

To test how this works in case of error, just replace safeReadName with safeReadNameError in the definition of safeReadNameT, like this:

```
val safeReadNameT: WorldT<Result<String>> = safeReadNameError
```

Run main again, and you'll get:

```
"/Applications/IntelliJ IDEA CE.app/Contents/jbr/Contents/Home/bin/java" ...
What's your name? Error: java.lang.RuntimeException: Something went wrong!
```

Figure 16.7: Running a monadic greeting with error

This is very good, but it might look complicated. This is why some frameworks like Arrow chose to use suspend functions instead of the IO<T> monad, which is an excellent decision.

Open **Coroutines.kt** and write the following code:

```
suspend fun readStringCo(): String = // 1
  Scanner(System.`in`).nextLine()

suspend fun printStringCo(str: String) = // 2
  print(str)

@DelicateCoroutinesApi
fun main() {
  runBlocking { // 3
    printStringCo("What's your name? ") // 4
    val name = async { readStringCo() }.await() // 5
    printStringCo("Hello $name!\n") // 6
  }
}
```

In this code, you:

1. Write the logic for reading the input `String` into `readStringCo`, which is a *suspendable* function. It's important to note how, in this case, the `suspend` is redundant, but it allows you to mark it as a function that has a side effect.

2. Do the same for `printStringCo` that just prints the input `String` to the standard output.

3. Just like `IO<T>`, a suspendable function allows you to wrap a side effect into a block. This is very important because when doing this, you're not actually running that code — you're just describing it. In this case, you're saying that there will *eventually* be some other component that runs that suspendable function. In this case, that component is a `Scheduler` in the `CoroutineContext` used by `runBlocking`.

4. Invoke `printStringCo` as a normal function.

5. Use `async` to wait for the input `String` you ask for.

6. Finally, use `printStringCo` to print the greeting message.

Coroutines also allow you to handle exceptions in a robust and easy way.

> **Note**: To learn more about coroutines, check out Kotlin Coroutines by Tutorials (https://www.raywenderlich.com/books/kotlin-coroutines-by-tutorials/).

Key points

- A **pure** function doesn't have any **side effects**.

- A side effect represents a change in the *state of the world*.

- The State<S, T> data type allows you to handle state transitions in a transparent and pure way.

- You can think of the state of the world as a specific type S in State<S, T> and consider StateTransformer<S, T> as a way to describe a transformation of the world.

- A transformation of the world is another way to define a side effect.

- Functions with IO operations are impure by definition.

- You can think of the IO<T> data type as a special case of State<S, T>, where S is the state of the world. In this way, all functions are pure.

- You can easily give IO<T> the superpowers of a **functor**, **applicative functor** and **monad**.

- The IO<T> data type is a way to decouple a side effect from its **description**.

- IO<T> contains the description of a side effect but doesn't immediately execute it.

- In Kotlin, a **suspendable function** allows you to achieve the same result as IO<T> in a more idiomatic and simple way.

Where to go from here?

Congratulations! With this chapter, you took another crucial step in the study of the main concepts of functional programming with Kotlin. State management with the IO<T> monad is one of the most challenging topics forcing you to think functionally. In the last part of the chapter, you saw how the IO<T> monad can be easily replaced with the use of coroutines. In the following chapter, you'll see even more about this topic and implement some more magic! :]

Chapter 17: Sequence & Flow

In Chapter 16, "Handling Side Effects", you learned how to use the IO<T> monad as a special case of the State<S, T> data type. You also learned that Kotlin provides **coroutines** to handle side effects as pure functions in a more idiomatic way. In this chapter, you'll learn everything you need to know about the following special Kotlin data types:

- Sequence<T>
- Flow<T>

You'll also have a quick overview of SharedFlow<T> and StateFlow<T>.

You'll learn how these data types work from a functional programming point of view. In particular, you'll answer the following questions for each of these:

- What is the **context** they provide?

- Are they a **functor**?

- Are they an **applicative functor**?

- Are they a **monad**?

> **Note**: If you don't know coroutines yet, Kotlin Coroutines by Tutorials (https://www.raywenderlich.com/books/kotlin-coroutines-by-tutorials) is the book for you.

This chapter is a big exercise that helps you take the concepts you've learned so far and apply them to the types you use every day in your job. It's time to have fun!

The Sequence<T> data type

In Chapter 9, "Data Types", you learned that List<T> is a data type with the **functor** and **monad** superpowers with the map and flatMap functions. In Chapter 4, "Expression Evaluation, Laziness & More About Functions", you also learned that **laziness** is one of the main characteristics of functional programming. To remind you what this means, open **ListDataType.kt** in this chapter's material and write the following code:

```
fun main() {
  listOf(1, 2, 3, 4, 5) // 1
    .filter(filterOdd.logged("filterOdd")) // 2
    .map(double.logged("double")) // 3
}
```

In this code, you:

1. Use listOf as a *builder* for a List<Int> with five elements of type Int.

2. Invoke filter, passing the reference to the logged version of filterOdd.

3. Use map to transform the filter's values using a logged version of double.

> **Note**: filterOdd and double are two very simple functions you find in **Util.kt** in the **lib** sub-package. logged is a utility higher-order function that decorates another function with a log message. Take a look at their simple implementation, if you want.

The interesting fact about the previous code happens when you run it, getting the following output:

```
filterOdd(1) = false
filterOdd(2) = true
filterOdd(3) = false
filterOdd(4) = true
filterOdd(5) = false
double(2) = 4
double(4) = 8
```

This happens because, in each line, you:

1. Create a List<Int> with five elements.

2. Invoke filter, which returns another List<Int> containing only the even values. It's crucial to see that filterOdd has been invoked for all the elements of the original List<Int>.

3. Use map, getting a new List<Int> with the double of the values in the previous List<Int>.

With this code, you basically created three lists without using any of the individual lists' values. What happens if you don't really need the values in the List<Int>? In this case, you started with a List<Int> of five elements. What if the list has a lot more elements? What if the elements in the List<T> are infinite?

Well, you don't have to blame the List<T> data type because its job is to contain an ordered collection of elements of type T. That's why it's been created that way. *That's its context*, or purpose, if you will. Another way to say it is that List<T> is **eager**.

If you don't want to keep all the possible values in a List<T>, Kotlin provides the Sequence<T> data type.

Open **SequenceDataType.kt** and write the following code:

```
fun main() {
    sequenceOf(1, 2, 3, 4, 5) // HERE
        .filter(filterOdd.logged("filterOddSeq"))
        .map(double.logged("doubleSeq"))
}
```

This code differs from the previous one because of the use of sequenceOf instead of listOf. More importantly, if you run the code, you'll get nothing as output. This is because Sequence<T> is **lazy**. If you want to actually consume the values in the Sequence<Int> you just created, you need to consume them using a **terminal operator**. To see how, add .count() to the end of the method chain. It should now look like this:

```
fun main() {
    sequenceOf(1, 2, 3, 4, 5)
        .filter(filterOdd.logged("filterOddSeq"))
        .map(double.logged("doubleSeq"))
        .count() // HERE
}
```

Here, you're just counting the elements in the sequence and, to do it, you need to consume all of them. This time, running the code, you'll get the following:

```
filterOddSeq(1) = false
filterOddSeq(2) = true
doubleSeq(2) = 4
filterOddSeq(3) = false
filterOddSeq(4) = true
doubleSeq(4) = 8
filterOddSeq(5) = false
```

Note how the order of the log messages is different from the one you got from the List<T>. In that case, each operator read the values from the input List<T>. Now, the chain of operators is called for each value you consume.

> **Note**: If you're curious and want to look at the definition of Sequence<T>, you'll find that it differs from the Iterable<T> interface in the use of the operator keyword, which allows its use in an enhanced form.

This clarifies the context for a Sequence<T> as a container that produces the values it contains *only when required*. That means it's **lazy**. But is Sequence<T> a functor?

Sequence<T> as a functor

Looking at the Sequence<T> documentation, you see the definition of map with the following signature:

```
public fun <T, R> Sequence<T>.map(transform: (T) -> R):
Sequence<R>
```

You used map in the example in the previous section. In this case, you want to do something more and use **property-based testing** to prove the functor laws for Sequence<T>.

> **Note**: You already used **property-based testing** in Chapter 12, "Monoids & Semigroups".

You want to prove that, given the two functions f and g and the identity i:

- `map(i) == i`

- `map(f compose g) == map(f) compose map(g)`

If you want to use property-based testing, you should define a way to generate random functions using a specific implementation of the following interface you find in **PropertyTest.kt** in the **lib** sub-package in this chapter's material:

```
fun interface Generator<T> {
    fun generate(n: Int): List<T>
}
```

As the first step, add the following to the **PropertyTestFun.kt** file:

```
fun <T, R> Generator<T>.map(fn: (T) -> R): Generator<R> = object
: Generator<R> {
    override fun generate(n: Int): List<R> =
    this@map.generate(n).map(fn)
}
```

This describes the map function for a Generator<T>. It's just a simple way to create a Generator<R> from a Generator<T> using a function of type (T) -> R or, using the typealiases in **Definitions.kt**, Fun<T, R>.

> **Note:** Be careful that Generator<T> isn't a functor because it's not even pure: It generates random values.

Now, you can get a Generator<Fun<A, B>> from a Generator<A> and Generator<B> with the following code you can add to the same **PropertyTestFun.kt**:

```
fun <A, B> funGenerator(bGen: Generator<B>): Generator<Fun<A,
B>> =
    bGen.map { b: B -> { b } }
```

Every Fun<A, B> describes a way to map values of type A into values of type B. The Fun<A, B> you'll get from funGenerator is a function that maps the same random value of type B to any values of type A you'll pass as input to the generated function. Because that return value is the same for all the input values, you can assume that the same would happen for a specific value you might generate during testing.

Open **SequenceDataTypeTest.kt** in the test build type, and add the following code:

```
@Test
fun `Identity Functor Law for Sequences`() {
  val intToStringFunGenerator =
    funGenerator<Int, String>(StringGenerator(5)) // 1
  val i = { s: String -> s } // 2
  100.times {   // 3
    val f = intToStringFunGenerator.one() // 4
    val seq = IntGenerator.generate(5).asSequence() // 5
    val list1 = seq.map(f compose i).toList() // 6
    val list2 = seq.map(f).toList()  // 7
    Truth.assertThat(list1).isEqualTo(list2) // 8
  }
}
```

Here, you:

1. Use `funGenerator` to generate a random function of type `Fun<Int, String>`. This function maps `Int`s to `String`s of length 5.

2. Provide the identity function `i`.

3. Iterate `100` times over the following commands.

4. Get a `Fun<Int, String>` from `intToStringFunGenerator` and store it in `f`.

5. Generate a sequence of 5 random elements in `seq`.

6. Apply the composition between `f` and `i` to `seq` using `map`.

7. In the same way, you apply only `f`.

8. Verify that the results are the same.

Run the test, and check that everything is successful. Now, you can be confident that the first law of `Sequence<T>` as a functor is valid.

The second law is very simple. Just add this code to the same file:

```
@Test
fun `Composition Functor Law for Sequences`() {
  val intToStringFunGenerator =
    funGenerator<Int, String>(StringGenerator(5))
  val stringToLongFunGenerator =
    funGenerator<String, Long>(LongGenerator) // 1
  100.times {
    val f = intToStringFunGenerator.one()
    val g = stringToLongFunGenerator.one() // 2
    val seq = IntGenerator.generate(5).asSequence()
```

```
        val list1 = seq.map(f compose g).toList() // 3
        val list2 = seq.map(f).map(g).toList() // 4
        Truth.assertThat(list1).isEqualTo(list2) // 5
    }
  }
```

The only difference here is that you:

1. Create a new Generator<Fun<String, Long>> in stringToLongFunGenerator.

2. Use intToStringFunGenerator and stringToLongFunGenerator to generate two different functions: f and g of type Fun<Int, String> and Fun<String, Long>, respectively.

3. Invoke map, passing the composition of f and g as a parameter.

4. Invoke map, first with f and then with g.

5. Compare the results of the two cases.

Now, just run the test and see that all the tests are successful. Great job!

Sequence<T> as an applicative functor

You just proved that the Sequence<T> data type is a functor because of the existing implementation of map. But what about applicative functors? Looking at the Kotlin documentation, you don't see any higher-order functions like your ap and app. No problem — you can do this!

Open **SequenceDataType.kt**, and add the following code:

```
fun <A, B> Sequence<A>.ap(
  fn: Sequence<(A) -> B>
): Sequence<B> = TODO()
```

This is the signature for the ap function for a Sequence<T>. It's an extension function on the type Sequence<A> and accepts an input parameter of type Sequence<(A) -> B> or Sequence<Fun<A, B>> if you use the type alias. The return type is Sequence<B>. Basically, you have two sequences. The first generates values of type A, and the second generates functions of type Fun<A, B>. The result, then, is a Sequence<B> of the value you get by applying the function in Sequence<Fun<A, B>> to the values in Sequence<A>. How would you implement ap?

> **Note:** Feel free to provide your implementation as a fun exercise if you want.

Now, replace the previous code with the following:

```kotlin
fun <A, B> Sequence<A>.ap(fn: Sequence<(A) -> B>): Sequence<B> =
  sequence { // 1
    val iterator = iterator() // 2
    while (iterator.hasNext()) {
      val fnIterator = fn.iterator() // 3
      val item = iterator.next()
      while (fnIterator.hasNext()) {
        yield(fnIterator.next().invoke(item)) // 4
      }
    }
  }
```

In this code, you:

1. Generate a Sequence<B> using the sequence builder.

2. Get the reference to the Iterator<A> from the Sequence<A> and iterate over it.

3. Get the reference to the Iterator<Fun<A, B>> from the Sequence<Fun<A, B>> you get as an input parameter and iterate over them.

4. Use yield to produce the value you get by applying the current function Fun<A, B> to the current value A.

To see how it works, start by adding the following utility function. It allows you to use ap as an infix operator, as you did with the other applicative functor implementations:

```kotlin
infix fun <A, B> Sequence<(A) -> B>.appl(a: Sequence<A>) =
  a.ap(this)
```

To see it working, replace the main implementation in **SequenceDataType.kt** with the following:

```kotlin
fun main() {
  data class User(  // 1
    val id: Int,
    val name: String,
    val email: String
  )

  val userBuilder = ::User.curry() // 2
  val userBuilderSeq = sequenceOf(userBuilder) // 3
  val idSeq = sequenceOf(10, 20, 30) // 4
  val nameSeq = sequenceOf("Minnie", "Donald", "Mickey") // 4
  val emailSeq =
    sequenceOf("aaaaaa@aaaaa.com", "bbbbb@bbbbb.com") // 4
```

```
    val userSeq =
      userBuilderSeq appl idSeq appl nameSeq appl emailSeq // 5

    userSeq.forEach(::println) // 6
}
```

In this example, you:

1. Create a `User` data class representing a user with `id`, `name` and `email` properties.

2. Use `curry` to get the `User` constructor as a function of type `(Int) -> (String) -> (String) -> User`.

3. Create a `Sequence<(Int) -> (String) -> (String) -> User>` using the `sequenceOf` builder.

4. Use `sequenceOf` for creating a `Sequence<Int>` for the ids, `Sequence<String>` for names and `Sequence<String>` for the emails.

5. Use `appl` to create a `Sequence<User>`.

6. Print all the values in the `Sequence<User>`.

When you run this code, you'll get $3 * 3 * 2 = 18$ different values, like the following:

```
User(id=10, name=Minnie, email=aaaaaa@aaaaa.com)
User(id=20, name=Minnie, email=aaaaaa@aaaaa.com)
// ...
User(id=20, name=Mickey, email=bbbbb@bbbbbb.com)
User(id=30, name=Mickey, email=bbbbb@bbbbbb.com)
```

Considering that the context of a `Sequence<T>` is to provide values of type T in a lazy way, applying a function with multiple parameters leads to a number of values, like in the previous example.

Sequence<T> as a monad

Is `Sequence<T>` finally a monad? Of course it is, because of the `flatMap` operation that Kotlin APIs provide with the following signature, similar to the Kleisli category:

```
fun <T, R> Sequence<T>.flatMap(
  transform: (T) -> Sequence<R>
): Sequence<R>
```

You can test how this works by running the following example:

```
fun main() {
  // ...
  val seqTo = { n: Int -> (1..n).toList().asSequence() }
  val seqOfSeq = sequenceOf(1, 2, 3, 4, 5).flatMap(seqTo)
  seqOfSeq.forEach { print("$it ") }
}
```

Getting an output like the following:

```
1 1 2 1 2 3 1 2 3 4 1 2 3 4 5
```

The Flow<T> data type

In Chapter 16, "Handling Side Effects", you learned that Kotlin allows you to achieve with suspendable functions what you can do with the IO<T> monad. In this chapter, you've already learned how to produce a *theoretically infinite* sequence of values in a lazy way. If the values you want to generate are the result of a suspendable function, the Flow<T> data type is what you need.

You can then say that the context of the Flow<T> data type is the generation of a sequence of values you create using a suspendable function which, as you know, allows you to handle side effects in a pure fashion.

As you'll see, a Flow<T> is very similar to a Sequence<T> in terms of functional programming concepts. So, the following sections are basically a good review of things you've already learned: *repetita juvant*, as the Romans used to say! :]

Flow<T> as a functor

To prove that Flow<T> is a functor, you could repeat the same process you did for Sequence<T> using property-based testing. In this case, you'll keep things easier, implementing some practical examples.

> **Note**: As an interesting exercise, you could use property-based testing for Flow<T> as well.

Open **FlowDataType.kt** and add the following code:

```
fun inputStringFlow(question: String = "") = flow { // 1
    val scanner = java.util.Scanner(System.`in`) // 2
    print(question) // 3
    while (scanner.hasNextLine()) { // 4
        val line = scanner.nextLine() // 4
        if (line.isNullOrEmpty()) { // 5
            break
        }
        emit(line) // 6
        print(question) // 3
    }
    scanner.close() // 7
}
```

In this code, you:

1. Define `inputStringFlow` as a function that returns a `Flow<String>` of the text you write as input using a `Scanner` reading from the standard input. This is a flow version of the effect you used in Chapter 16, "Handling Side Effects". You have a `question` parameter that allows you to print some text before the user enters anything.

2. Initialize the `Scanner` reading from the standard input.

3. Print the question.

4. Read all the input one line at a time.

5. Exit the cycle if the user enters an empty line.

6. Emit the value from the user as a value from the `Flow<String>`.

7. Close the `Scanner`.

As an example of a functor, add the following code to the same file:

```
fun main() {
    val strLengthFlow = inputStringFlow("Insert a word: ") // 1
        .map { str -> // 2
            str to str.length
        }
    runBlocking { // 3
        strLengthFlow.collect { strInfo -> // 4
            println("${strInfo.first} has length ${strInfo.second}")
        }
    }
}
```

In this code, you:

1. Use `inputStringFlow` to get a `Flow<String>` for the user input. Note that you run this outside any specific `CoroutineScope`. You're not executing anything — you're just stating you eventually might.

2. Invoke `map`, passing a lambda that returns a `Pair<String, Int>` of the input `String` and its length. It's important to note that the lambda here is executed as a suspendable block. This means that it has a scope, and it can contain invocations to other suspendable functions. In other words, using `map(String::length)` would give a compilation error because `String::length` isn't a suspendable function. In your context, this also means you can apply a transformation, `Fun<A, B>`, to the values you get from a `Flow<A, B>`, which is the consequence of a side effect.

3. Define a `runBlocking` block. This is because you'll *consume*, or better, *collect* what the `Flow<Pair<String, Int>>` produces, so the side effects you described will actually run.

4. Collect and print the output values of type `Pair<String, Int>` you get from the flow.

Now, you can run the code and get an output like the following:

```
/Library/Java/JavaVirtualMachines/jdk-12.jdk/Contents/Home/bin/java ...
Insert a word: Max
Max has length 3
Insert a word: supercalifragilisticexpialidocious
supercalifragilisticexpialidocious has length 34
Insert a word:

Process finished with exit code 0
```

Figure 17.1: Testing the flow data type

To answer the initial question, yes, `Flow<T>` is a functor, but remember that the transformation `Fun<A, B>` must be a suspendable function.

Flow<T> as an applicative functor

To see if the `Flow<T>` also behaves as an applicative functor, either repeat what you did for the `Sequence<T>` or just follow along. In **FlowDataType.kt**, add the following code:

```
fun <A, B> Flow<A>.ap(fn: Flow<(A) -> B>): Flow<B> = flow { // 1
  collect { a -> // 2
```

```
    fn.collect { f -> // 3
      emit(f(a)) // 4
    }
  }
}

infix fun <A, B> Flow<(A) -> B>.appl(
  a: Flow<A>
) = a.ap(this) // 5
```

Here, you:

1. Define ap with the usual signature as an extension function for Flow<A>.

2. Collect the value of type A from the Flow<A> you have as the receiver.

3. Collect the function f of type Fun<A, B> from the Flow<Fun<A, B>> or Flow<(A) -> B> you pass as the input parameter fn.

4. Apply the function f to the value a and emit the result.

5. As usual, define appl as an *infix* version of ap.

You can then test everything by adding the following code to the same file:

```
fun main() {
  val userBuilder = { id: Int ->
    { name: String ->
      { email: String -> User(id, name, email) }
    }
  }

  val userBuilderFlow = flowOf(userBuilder)
  val idFlow = listOf(10, 20, 30).asFlow()
  val nameFlow = listOf("Pippo", "Pippo2", "Pippo3").asFlow()
  val emailFlow = listOf(
    "pippo@pippo.com", "pippo2@pippo.com", "pippo3@pippo.com"
  ).asFlow()

  val userFlow =
    userBuilderFlow appl idFlow appl nameFlow appl emailFlow
  runBlocking {
    userFlow.collect(::println)
  }
}
```

This code shouldn't be a surprise anymore. When you run it, you'll get:

```
User(id=10, name=Pippo, email=pippo@pippo.com)
User(id=20, name=Pippo, email=pippo@pippo.com)
```

```
// ...
User(id=20, name=Pippo3, email=pippo3@pippo.com)
User(id=30, name=Pippo3, email=pippo3@pippo.com)
```

The same notes you learned for Sequence<T> are valid here.

Flow<T> as a monad

To answer the last question, you'll implement a more complex example using some of the code you already implemented in Chapter 14, "Error Handling With Functional Programming", that you can find in the material for this project. You basically want to use inputStringFlow to allow a user to insert some text to search for in the TV show database using the TVmaze API (https://www.tvmaze.com/api). Now, you're in the world of coroutines, so you should use their power. It's time for an interesting exercise to improve your *functional thinking*.

Imagine you have a basic function, like the following you can write in **Basic.kt**:

```
fun doSomeWork(name: String): Int = 10
```

It doesn't really matter what doSomeWork does. What's important is the type, which is (String) -> Int, and how the function achieves its goal. If it needs to do some hard work, you probably want to run it in the background, so in the context of a coroutine. You can do this with the following code, which you should add to the same file:

```
suspend fun doSomeBgWork(
  ctx: CoroutineContext,
  name: String
): Int = withContext(ctx) {
    doSomeWork(name)
}
```

This simple code has a few interesting things to note. doSomeBgWork:

• Is a **suspend** function.

• Accepts two parameters now. The first is of type CoroutineContext, and the second is the input for doSomeWork.

• Uses withContext to run doSomeWork in the CoroutineContext you provide as input.

• Has the return type Int.

You already know that in functional programming, you don't like functions with multiple parameters. No problem — you also know you can `curry` them, but with doSomeBgWork, there's a problem. You can see the problem by adding the following code:

```
fun main() {
   doSomeBgWork.curry()
}
```

You'll get the following error:

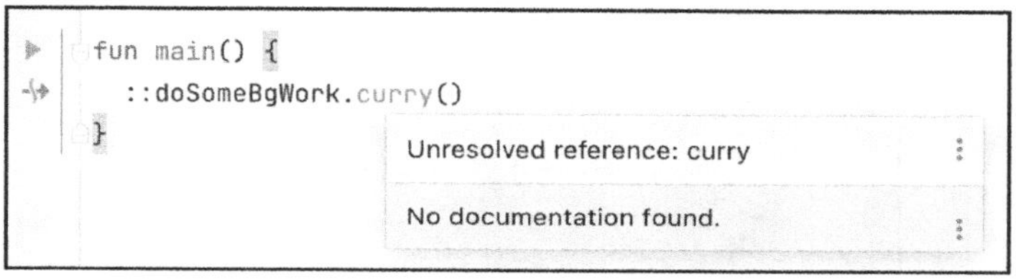

Figure 17.2: Unresolved reference: curry

The reason is very simple. When you set a function as `suspend`, you're basically changing its type. The Kotlin compiler adds implicit parameters of type `Continuation` that keep track of the state of the coroutine.

> **Note**: Look at the decompiled code, and you can see how the `Continuation` is used in a way that reminds you how you implemented the `State<S, T>` and `IO<T>` data types.

How can you then implement `curry` for a suspendable function? You already know that. In the same **Basic.kt** file, add the following definitions:

```
typealias SuspendFun<A, B> = suspend (A) -> B // 1
typealias SuspendFun2<A, B, C> = suspend (A, B) -> C // 2
typealias SuspendChain2<A, B, C> =
   suspend (A) -> suspend (B) -> C // 3
```

In this simple code, you define an alias for suspendable functions of:

1. One input parameter of type A and one output parameter of type B.

2. Two input parameters of type A and B and one output parameter of type C.

3. One input parameter of type A and a suspendable function of one input parameter of type B and output of type C.

These allow you to define `curry` for suspendable functions by adding the following code:

```
fun <A, B, C> SuspendFun2<A, B, C>.curry(): SuspendChain2<A, B,
C> =
  { a: A ->
    { b: B ->
      this(a, b)
    }
  }
```

Now, the previous code compiles successfully:

```
fun main() {
    ::doSomeBgWork.curry()
}
```

Figure 17.3: Curry for suspendable function

Implementing `curry` for suspendable functions is a kind of a warm-up. Going back to doSomeBgWork, you can say that the type of `::doSomeBgWork.curry()` is now `(String) -> (CoroutineContext) -> Int`. Umm, that's starting to ring a bell.

What really matters in functional programming is **composition**. What you did earlier is say that you can create a suspendable function from a non-suspendable one, providing a `CoroutineContext`, and this *carrying on* reminds you of something you already learned: the `State<S, T>` monad.

CoroutineContext as a state

To relate the `State<S, T>` monad to what you saw about suspendable functions, look again at doSomeBgWork, which you wrote in **Basic.kt**:

```
suspend fun doSomeBgWork(ctx: CoroutineContext, name: String):
Int =
  withContext(ctx) {
    doSomeWork(name)
  }
```

It has the type `(CoroutineContext, String) -> Int`. If the `CoroutineContext` is something you want to carry on, you can create doSomeMoreBgWork like the following:

```
suspend fun doSomeMoreBgWork(
  ctx: CoroutineContext,
```

```
    name: String
): Pair<CoroutineContext, Int> = withContext(ctx) {
    ctx to doSomeWork(name)
}
```

doSomeMoreBgWork has the type (CoroutineContext, String) ->
Pair<CoroutineContext, Int>. Applying curry, you can get a function of type
(String) -> (CoroutineContext) -> Pair<CoroutineContex, Int>.

> **Note**: Yes, the CoroutineContext and String types have different orders, but
> you already know how to implement flip, right?

Now, the analogy with State<S, T> is almost obvious. You just need to fix a problem
caused by the presence of the **suspend** modifier. No problem.

Open **SuspendState.kt** and add the following first definition:

```
typealias SuspendStateTransformer<S, T> =
    suspend (S) -> Pair<S, T>
```

Ring a bell now? Using this definition, the type of doSomeMoreBgWork is suspend
(String) -> SuspendStateTransformer<CoroutineContext, Int>.

You can now follow the same process you did for State<S, T>, keeping in mind
you're working with suspendable functions, and the state is a CoroutineContext.

In **SuspendState.kt**, add the following code:

```
data class SuspendableState<S, T>(
    val sst: SuspendStateTransformer<S, T>
) {

    companion object {
        @JvmStatic
        fun <S, T> lift(
            value: T
        ): SuspendableState<S, T> =
            SuspendableState { state -> state to value }
    }
}
```

Here, you define the SuspendableState data type using
SuspendStateTransformer.

You can now add the implementation for `map`:

```
fun <S, A, B> SuspendableState<S, A>.map(
  fn: SuspendFun<A, B>
): SuspendableState<S, B> =
  SuspendableState { s0: S ->
    val (s1, a) = this.sst(s0)
    s1 to fn(a)
  }
```

Finally, add the implementation for `flatMap` like this:

```
fun <S, A, B> SuspendableState<S, A>.flatMap(
  fn: suspend (A) -> SuspendableState<S, B>
): SuspendableState<S, B> =
  SuspendableState { s0: S ->
    val (s1, a) = this.sst(s0)
    fn(a).sst(s1)
  }
```

> **Note**: This time, you can't override the `invoke` operator as you did in a non-coroutine environment. To be useful, it should also be suspendable, and this wouldn't work.

How can you use this for your initial TV show problem? There's actually quite a bit more fun in store for you. :]

Back to the TV show

In the previous section, you created the `SuspendableState<S, T>` data type and implemented `lift`, `map` and `flatMap`. How can you use these for getting data about a TV show? In the **tools** sub-package in this chapter's material, you find `TvShowFetcher` and `TvShowParser` for, respectively, fetching and parsing data using the TVmaze API.

Look at the existing code, and you'll see that `TvShowFetcher` and `TvShowParser` don't actually handle exceptions. This is also why you used those objects in many different ways in Chapter 14, "Error Handling With Functional Programming".

Now, you want to run them as side effects in a suspendable function and handle errors. How can you do that?

Open **ShowSearchService.kt** and add the following code:

```
suspend fun fetchTvShowResult( // 1
  ctx: CoroutineContext,
  query: String
): Result<String> = // 2
  withContext(ctx) { // 3
    try {
      Result.success(TvShowFetcher.fetch(query)) // 4
    } catch (ioe: IOException) {
      Result.failure(ioe) // 5
    }
  }
```

This code should look familiar, even if it combines a few concepts. Here, you:

1. Define `fetchTvShowResult` as a suspendable function with a `CoroutineContext` as the first parameter and a `String` as the second. Note how the structure of this function is very similar to the one of doSomeMoreBgWork.

2. Set `Result<String>` as the return type. This is a little bit more complicated than a simple `String`. You'll need to do some more work because of this, as you'll see later.

3. Use the `CoroutineContext` you receive in `ctx` to create a coroutine.

4. Invoke `TvShowFetcher.fetch`, passing the `query` as input. In the case of success, you return the `String` wrapped in a `Result<String>`.

5. In the case of error, you encapsulate the `IOException` in a `Result<String>`. Yes, the value for the type parameter is `String`.

For `TvShowParser.parse`, you can follow the same pattern, adding this to the same file:

```
suspend fun parseTvShowResult(
  ctx: CoroutineContext,
  json: String
): Result<List<ScoredShow>> =
  withContext(ctx) {
    try {
      Result.success(TvShowParser.parse(json))
    } catch (e: Exception) {
      Result.failure(e)
    }
  }
```

This time, the resulting type is Result<List<ScoredShow>>, but the structure is the same.

So far, so good. Now, you have two functions:

1. fetchTvShowResult of type suspend (CoroutineContext, String) -> Result<String>.

2. parseTvShowResult of type suspend (CoroutineContext, String) -> Result<List<ScoredShow>>.

They look like the functions of type suspend (A) -> SuspendStateTransformer<CoroutineContext, B> you can compose using the flatMap implementation you created earlier for SuspendableState.

You can try to solve this problem by adding the following code:

```
val fetchSuspend: (String) -> SuspendableState<
  CoroutineContext, Result<String>> = { query ->
    SuspendableState { ctx: CoroutineContext ->
      ctx to fetchTvShowResult(ctx, query)
    }
  }

val parseSuspend: (String) -> SuspendableState<
  CoroutineContext, Result<List<ScoredShow>>> = { json ->
    SuspendableState { ctx: CoroutineContext ->
      ctx to parseTvShowResult(ctx, json)
    }
  }
```

Now:

1. fetchSuspend has type (String) -> SuspendableState<CoroutineContext, Result<String>>.

2. parseSuspend has type (String) -> SuspendableState<CoroutineContext, Result<List<ScoredShow>>>.

This is a problem because, in both cases, you have a SuspendableState<CoroutineContext, Result<T>>. This means a Result<T> data type encapsulates into a SuspendableState<S, T> data type. Composition, as defined in flatMap for SuspendableState, doesn't work. How can you fix it?

Composing SuspendableState<CoroutineContext, Result<T>>

To implement composition now is simpler than it seems. Open
SuspendableStateResult.kt, and add the following code:

```
typealias SuspendStateResultTransformer<S, T> =
  suspend (S) -> Pair<S, Result<T>> // 1

data class SuspendableStateResult<S, T>( // 2
  val sst: SuspendStateResultTransformer<S, T>
) {

  companion object {
    @JvmStatic
    fun <S, T> lift( // 3
      value: T
    ): SuspendableStateResult<S, T> =
      SuspendableStateResult { state ->
        state to Result.success(value)
      }
  }
}

fun <S, A, B> SuspendableStateResult<S, A>.map( // 4
  fn: SuspendFun<A, B>
): SuspendableStateResult<S, B> =
  SuspendableStateResult { s0: S ->
    val (s1, a) = this.sst(s0)
    s1 to a.fold(
      onSuccess = { Result.success(fn(it)) },
      onFailure = { Result.failure(it) }
    )
  }

fun <S, A, B> SuspendableStateResult<S, A>.flatMap( // 5
  fn: suspend (A) -> SuspendableStateResult<S, B>
): SuspendableStateResult<S, B> = SuspendableStateResult { s0 ->
  val (s1, res) = sst(s0)
  res.fold(onSuccess = { a: A ->
    fn(a).sst(s1)
  }, onFailure = { thowable ->
    s1 to Result.failure(thowable)
  })
}
```

It's a lot of code, but everything should be clear. In particular, you define:

1. `SuspendStateResultTransformer<S, T>` as a type of suspendable functions returning a `Pair<S, Result<T>>`.

2. `SuspendableStateResult<S, T>` as a data type encapsulating a `SuspendStateResultTransformer<S, T>`.

3. `lift` to create a `SuspendableStateResult<S, T>` from a value of type T.

4. `map` to apply a function of type `SuspendFun<A, B>` to a `SuspendableStateResult<S, A>` to get a `SuspendableStateResult<S, B>`.

5. `flatMap` to finally be able to compose functions returning `SuspendableStateResult<S, T>`.

Now, you're finally ready to access your TV show information.

Finally flatMap

It's finally time to put everything together so you can access the TVmaze database. Open **ShowSearchService.kt**, and add the following code:

```kotlin
val fetchSuspendResult: (String) -> SuspendableStateResult<
  CoroutineContext, String> = { query ->
    SuspendableStateResult { ctx: CoroutineContext ->
      ctx to fetchTvShowResult(ctx, query)
    }
  }

val parseSuspendResult: (String) -> SuspendableStateResult<
  CoroutineContext, List<ScoredShow>> = { json ->
    SuspendableStateResult { ctx: CoroutineContext ->
      ctx to parseTvShowResult(ctx, json)
    }
  }
```

Here, you create:

1. `fetchSuspendResult` of type `(String) ->`
   `SuspendableStateResult<CoroutineContext, String>`.

2. `parseSuspendResult` of type `(String) ->`
   `SuspendableStateResult<CoroutineContext, List<ScoredShow>>`.

You can now compose these functions. Just add the following code to the same file:

```
@OptIn(FlowPreview::class) // 1
suspend fun searchTvShow(ctx: CoroutineContext) = // 2
  withContext(ctx) {
    inputStringFlow("Search Your Show: ") // 3
      .flatMapConcat { query ->  // 4
        fetchSuspendResult(query)
          .flatMap(parseSuspendResult).sst(ctx) // 5
          .second.fold(
            onSuccess = { it.asFlow() }, // 6
            onFailure = { emptyFlow() }) // 7
    }
}
```

In this code, you:

1. Opt-in to the experimental Flow<T> API.

2. Define searchTvShow as a function accepting a CoroutineContext in input.

3. Invoke inputStringFlow, passing a String to use as a message.

4. Use the predefined flatMapConcat to compose inputStringFlow with the suspendable function you get by composing fetchSuspendResult and parseSuspendResult.

5. Pass the CoroutineContext you get as input to the function you get from the composition of fetchSuspendResult and parseSuspendResult.

6. Return the value in Result<List<ScoredShow>> as a Flow<ScoredShow> in case of success.

7. Return an empty Flow<ScoredShow> in case of error.

To test this, add the following code:

```
@OptIn(FlowPreview::class)
fun main() {
  runBlocking { // 1
    searchTvShow(Dispatchers.IO) // 2
      .collect { // 3
        println("Score: ${it.score}  " +
          "Name: ${it.show.name} " +
          "Genres: ${it.show.genres}") // 4
        println(it.show.summary)
        println("-----------------------------")
      }
  }
}
```

Here, you:

1. Use `runBlocking` to give some scope to `searchTvShow`.

2. Invoke `searchTvShow`, passing `Dispatchers.IO` as `CoroutineContext`. This allows your code to run in the background.

3. Collect all the results.

4. Print its content, if any.

Now, you can run the previous code and have some fun, like this:

```
/Library/Java/JavaVirtualMachines/jdk1.8.0_261.jdk/Contents/Home/bin/java ...
Search Your Show: Big Bang Theory
Score: 1.2618698  Name: The Big Bang Theory Genres: [Comedy]
<p><b>The Big Bang Theory</b> is a comedy about brilliant physicists, Leonard and Sheldon, who are the kind of "beautiful minds" that understand how the
  universe works. But none of that genius helps them interact with people, especially women. All this begins to change when a free-spirited beauty named
  Penny moves in next door. Sheldon, Leonard's roommate, is quite content spending his nights playing Klingon Boggle with their socially dysfunctional
  friends, fellow Cal Tech scientists Wolowitz and Koothrappali. However, Leonard sees in Penny a whole new universe of possibilities... including
  love.</p>
---------------------------
Search Your Show:
```

Figure 17.4: Querying the TVmaze API

Everything works as expected, and this has been a great exercise to understand how to:

*   Define the right abstraction.

*   Reuse what you learned in the previous chapters of the book.

*   Implement composition for the previous abstractions.

*   Think in a functional way.

Great job!

The SharedFlow<T> & StateFlow<T> data types

`SharedFlow<T>` and `StateFlow<T>` are two additional flavors the coroutines API provides for flows. In terms of data types and the functions they provide, you can think of `SharedState<T>` and `StateFlow<T>` as implementations of `Flow<T>` with specific behavior when collected by multiple collectors.

For this reason, all the concepts you've seen so far are also valid for `SharedState<T>` and `StateFlow<T>`.

Key points

- The List<T> data type allows you to store an ordered collection of elements of type T in an **eager** way.

- All the elements of a List<T>, which is immutable, are present at the moment you create it.

- The List<T> data type is a **functor** and **monad** because of the presence of map and flatMap. You can also make it an **applicative functor** by implementing ap.

- The Sequence<T> data type allows you to generate a sequence of values of type T in a **lazy** way.

- In a Sequence<T>, map and flatMapConcat are invoked when the values need to be collected and consumed.

- A Sequence<T> can work as a **functor**, **applicative functor** and **monad**.

- The Flow<T> data type is similar to Sequence<T> but in the context of a coroutine.

- **Suspendable functions** are an idiomatic and powerful tool to handle side effects in Kotlin.

- A Flow<T> allows you to generate a sequence, or flow, of values of type T that can be generated from suspendable functions.

- You can implement curry and composition for suspendable functions as you did for non-suspendable ones, just following the functional programming principles you learned in the previous chapters.

- You can repeat for SharedFlow<T> and StateFlow<T> the same process you followed for a Flow<T>.

Where to go from here?

Congratulations! In this chapter, you had the opportunity to apply concepts you learned in the previous chapter in a concrete example that allowed you to fetch information about your favorite TV shows. You've learned how to create Sequence<T> and how to use Flow<T> in an environment of concurrency. Finally, you've empowered your functional thinking by implementing abstractions for composing suspendable functions, returning a Result<T> monad. It's been a lot of work and also a lot of fun!

As mentioned previously, you can take a look at Kotlin Coroutines by Tutorials (https://www.raywenderlich.com/books/kotlin-coroutines-by-tutorials) to learn more about coroutines, `SharedFlow<T>` and `StateFlow<T>`. The following chapters will talk about a couple more libraries that embody functional programming principles.

Chapter 18: Mobius — A Functional Reactive Framework

In Chapter 15, "Managing State", you learned the importance of the concept of **state**. A state is usually defined as some value that can change over time. You also learned that what you consider a state defines **side effects**. A side effect is something that changes the *state of the world*, which is outside the context of a function.

Side effects aren't harmful as long as you can control them. In Chapter 16, "Handling Side Effects", you saw how important it is to separate the description of an effect from its actual execution.

These are all the fundamental principles used by Mobius (https://github.com/spotify/mobius), which is defined as: "a functional reactive framework for managing state evolution and side-effects, with add-ons for connecting to Android UIs and RxJava Observables. It emphasizes separation of concerns, testability, and isolating stateful parts of the code".

In this chapter, you'll learn:

- The main concepts Mobius is based on.

- What the Mobius loop is and how it works.

- What the Mobius workflow is, and how to apply it to a real case.

- How Mobius works with Android.

- How Mobius handles side effects.

You'll do this by creating a Mobius version of the RayTV app you met in Chapter 14, "Error Handling With Functional Programming". You'll call it **Raybius**. :]

> **Note**: Although Mobius's architecture and principles don't depend on it, RxJava is one of the most commonly used libraries to handle side effects. RxJava-specific concepts will be kept at a minimum, but if you want to learn all about it, Reactive Programming with Kotlin (https://www.raywenderlich.com/books/reactive-programming-with-kotlin) is the right place to go.

> **Note**: The Raybius app uses Dagger and Hilt. If you want to learn all about the Android dependency injection framework, Dagger by Tutorials (https://www.raywenderlich.com/books/dagger-by-tutorials) is the perfect book for you.

Mobius principles and concepts

To understand how Mobius works, just think about a typical mobile app. You have some UI that displays some information. You usually interact with the UI by pressing some buttons or providing some input. This triggers some actions to access, for instance, a server, fetch some data and show it in the UI. This might look like an overly simplified description of what usually happens, but the reality isn't far off. You can represent the flow like in Figure 18.1:

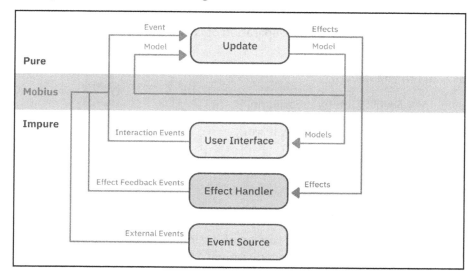

Figure 18.1: The Mobius loop

This image has numerous interesting concepts you can easily understand by following the flow described earlier.

When you launch your app, you can see a UI, which is usually a composition of *views*, like TextViews, Buttons and so on. You can think of a view as a way to represent some data. When the data changes, the UI usually changes. This is important because you can think of the data as the *current state* of the UI. The data you want to display with the UI is usually represented as the **model**.

As mentioned earlier, the user interacts with the UI by pressing some buttons or providing some data as input. Mobius represents these actions as **events**. An event is what makes an app interesting. Some events just update the UI, creating a new model to display. Others are more complicated because they trigger a request to the server or access to a database.

To handle both use cases, Mobius provides an **Update** function. It receives the current *model* and the input *event*, and returns the *new model* and an *optional description of a side effect*. It's crucial to see how the Update function lives in the **pure** section of the diagram. The Update function is *pure*. This is because:

- The new model just depends on the input *model/state* and *event*.

- It returns a *description of the side effects* you need to execute eventually.

This makes the Update function very easy to test. Not represented in Figure 18.1 is the Init function. Init is a version of Update that generates the first state and, optionally, the first set of effects to generate.

Now, Mobius sends the new model to the UI and the optional effects to some **effect handlers**. These are what actually execute the side effects, usually in a background thread. It's also interesting to see that effect handlers notify the outcome using *events* and how they go through the same flow you saw earlier for the events from the UI.

The Update function is invoked, and a new state/model is created along with other optional side effect descriptions.

This is an example of a **unidirectional flow**. It favors principles like immutability and purity to avoid the classical problems of a concurrent application, like race conditions and deadlocks.

Finally, an event source represents a generic component able to generate events even without a specific interaction from the user. Think about the events related to the battery level or your device going offline and then back online again.

The previous architecture is straightforward and gives each component a clear responsibility, as the **separation of concerns** principle suggests. This also allows the implementation of a process named the **Mobius workflow**.

The Mobius workflow

In the previous section, you learned that the main concepts in Mobius are:

- **Models**

- **Events**

- **Effects**

- **Init** functions

- **Update** functions

This implies that creating an app with Mobius means defining these same concepts in the domain of the app itself. This leads to a sequence of steps you can follow every time in the design and implementation of your app. This process has a name: the Mobius workflow. It consists of the following four steps:

1. **Model** or **MoFlow** (Short for "Mobius Flow")

2. **Describe**

3. **Plan**

4. **Build**

It's interesting now to see each of these in detail in the context of the Raybius app.

Model your app

Models in Mobius can represent different concepts like:

- The current state of the app.

- An event generated by a user action.

- An external event.

- An event result of a side effect's execution.

Usually, the steps are the following:

External events definition: In your case, the Raybius app doesn't handle any external events, but it could. For instance, you could display a message and disable the input if the device is offline and then restore that functionality when it reestablishes a connection. To track all the use cases, you create a table like the following. This is the MoFlow table.

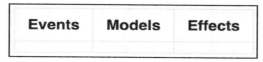

Events	Models	Effects

Figure 18.2: The initial MoFlow

Because you don't have external events, the table is initially empty. No problem! You deal with user interactions next.

Capture user interactions: These represent the possible events you can generate when the user interacts with the app. In your case, you can enter the name of a TV show in the EditField and tap the button to perform the search. This leads to the following events:

Events	Models	Effects
InputTextChanged		
SearchButtonClicked		

Figure 18.3: The MoFlow with user interaction events

When the user changes the text to use as input, the app generates an InputTextChanged with the new text. When the user clicks **SEARCH**, it triggers SearchButtonClicked.

Define effects: Here, you need to think about the effects the previous events can generate. In your case, you only have one effect — the one related to the request to the server for fetching the information about your TV show. Call this effect SearchTvShow, and add it to the table like this:

Events	Models	Effects
InputTextChanged		SearchTvShow
SearchButtonClicked		

Figure 18.4: Adding effects

Define your model: In this step, you need to define the model as a representation of your app's view. In Raybius, you enter text, so you probably want to disable the **SEARCH** button if the text field is empty or the text string is too short. So, the model should then contain some kind of property that enables or disables the **SEARCH** button. If you decide to handle the offline case, you also need a variable that disables all the features or displays some messages. For this, you can define TvShowModel, which makes your MoFlow table like the following:

Events	Models	Effects
InputTextChanged	TvShowModel	SearchTvShow
SearchButtonClicked		

Figure 18.5: Define models

As you'll see later, TvShowModel will contain different types of information, like:

• If you need to display a spinner.

• If you have some results.

• The current input text.

The view of your app will use all this data to render the information you need.

Define effects feedback events: Now, you have TvShowModel to keep track of the current state of the input text, and you know what events to generate when the user interacts with the app. You also know that you want the app to execute an effect for accessing the server to fetch the information about the input show. Hopefully, this effect will produce some results or — hopefully not — some errors. As you learned in Figure 18.1, effects notify some results using other events. In the case of Raybius, you can have a SearchSuccess containing the actual results and SearchFailure in case of errors. This leads to the following new version of the MoFlow table:

Events	Models	Effects
InputTextChanged	TvShowModel	SearchTvShow
SearchButtonClicked		
TvSearchSuccess		
TvSearchFailure		

Figure 18.6: Define effects feedback events

But what do you do in case of error? You probably need to display some error messages using, for instance, a Toast. To do this, you might need other events or, like in this case, a new effect. In case of success, you'll probably want to select an item from a list and display the details for the show. This leads to the ItemClicked event and the GetTvShowDetail effect, which then leads to the TvShowDetailSuccess and TvShowDetailFailure events. Moving from the list to the detail allows you to define the NavigateToDetail effect. When you get results, you probably want to hide the keyboard — you can do this with the HideKeyboard effect. The DetailViewResumed event is useful to trigger the GetTvShowDetail effect when the detail screen is displayed.

As you'll see later, the resulting MoFlow table is the following:

Events	Models	Effects
InputTextChanged	TvShowModel	SearchTvShow
SearchButtonClicked		DisplayErrorMessage
TvSearchSuccess		HideKeyboard
TvSearchFailure		NavigateToDetail
ItemClicked		GetTvShowDetail
DetailViewResumed		
TvShowDetailSucces		
TvShowDetailFailure		

Figure 18.7: Additional effects

Now, you have a clear understanding of what your app should do and how it should behave when different events are triggered. You'd usually do MoFlow on a whiteboard and with the help of your designer or other stakeholders.

Describe your app

When you have the MoFlow for your app, you can start implementing the Update function. Update is a pure function that receives the event and the current model as input and generates the new model and the set of effects as output. In Mobius, an instance of the Next class encapsulates this information.

To see how this is implemented in Raybius, open the starter project in this chapter's material in Android Studio, and run the app. You'll see the following screen:

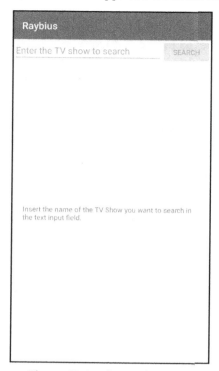

Figure 18.8: The Raybius app

Note how the **SEARCH** button is disabled. This is because the text field input is empty. When you insert a text string longer than three characters, you'll see the button enabled.

When you click it, you'll see the results in a list like this:

Figure 18.9: Some TV shows as results

Also, note how the keyboard is now hidden. At the moment, you can't select a show, but you'll implement that feature later in the chapter. Now, look at the existing code. Open **TvShowModel.kt** in the **raybius.mobius** package, and look at the current implementation for the model:

```
data class TvShowModel(
  val searchEnabled: Boolean = false, // 1
  val inputText: String = "", // 2
  val loading: Boolean = false, // 3
  val searchResults: List<ScoredShow> = emptyList(), // 4
  val error: Boolean = false // 5
)
```

This is a simple data class containing the properties that tells the view:

1. If the search button is enabled.

2. What the current input text is.

3. Whether the app is loading some data. This is useful for displaying a spinner.

4. What the existing results to display are.

5. If there's some error.

To see where this logic is actually used, open **FragmentSearchBindingExt.kt** in **raybius.ui**. This file contains extension functions for the FragmentSearchBinding class that the binding library creates for the **fragment_search.xml** layout file. In this file, you can see the following function:

```kotlin
fun FragmentSearchBinding.logic(model: TvShowModel) {
  if (model.loading) {
    showLoading()
  } else {
    hideLoading()
  }
  displayResults(model.searchResults)
  if (model.error) {
    errorMode()
  }
  searchButton.isEnabled = model.searchEnabled
}
```

This is quite simple and describes how the view changes when a new model needs to be rendered.

To see what happens when the user taps **SEARCH**, look at the initUI function in the same file.

```kotlin
fun FragmentSearchBinding.initUI(
  eventConsumer: Consumer<TvShowEvent>,
  onItemSelected: (Int) -> Unit
) {
  with(resultRecyclerView) {
    adapter = ScoredShowAdapter(onItemSelected)
    layoutManager = LinearLayoutManager(context)
    visibility = View.GONE
  }
  helpMessage.visibility = View.VISIBLE
  progressBar.visibility = View.GONE
  textUpdate { text ->
    eventConsumer.accept(InputTextChanged(text)) // 1
  }
```

```
    search {
      eventConsumer.accept(SearchButtonClicked) // 2
    }
  }
}
```

`TvSearchFragment` invokes this function to initialize the UI. It's basically UI code, but it uses an object of type `Consumer<TvShowEvent>` to generate Mobius events from the UI. Note how you use `eventConsumer` to fire:

1. `InputTextChanged` events when the user updates the text input.

2. `SearchButtonClicked` when the user taps **SEARCH**.

Later, you'll see where the `Consumer<TvShowEvent>` comes from, but for now, you can think of it as the tool to interact with the Mobius loop you saw in Figure 18.1.

To see the events, just open **TvShowEvent.kt** in **mobius**, and see they're very simple data classes or objects:

```
sealed class TvShowEvent
data class InputTextChanged(val text: String) : TvShowEvent()
object SearchButtonClicked : TvShowEvent()
data class TvSearchSuccess(
    val results: List<ScoredShow>
) : TvShowEvent()
data class TvSearchFailure(val ex: Throwable) : TvShowEvent()
```

Now, you've seen how to send events and how to change the UI based on the current model. But the core of the Mobius architecture is the `Update` function. Open **TvShowLogic.kt** in the **mobius** package, and look at the following code:

```
val tvShowLogic: TvShowUpdate = object : TvShowUpdate {
  override fun update(
    model: TvShowModel, event: TvShowEvent
  ): Next<TvShowModel, TvShowEffect> =
  when (event) {
    is InputTextChanged -> Next.next( // 1
      model.copy(
        searchEnabled = event.text.length >= 3,
        inputText = event.text
      )
    )
    is SearchButtonClicked -> Next.next( // 2
      model.copy(loading = true),
      setOf(SearchTvShow(model.inputText))
    )
    is TvSearchSuccess -> Next.next( // 3
      model.copy(
        searchResults = event.results,
```

```
            searchEnabled = true
        ), setOf(HideKeyboard)
    )
    is TvSearchFailure -> Next.next( // 4
      model.copy(
        error = true,
        searchEnabled = true
      ), setOf(
        HideKeyboard, DisplayErrorMessage(
          event.ex
        )
      )
    )
    else -> Next.noChange()
  }
}
```

This is a simple function that translates what you've designed in the MoFlow table into code. For instance, you can see that:

1. If you receive an `InputTextChanged` event, you check if the text in input has at least 3 characters and generate a new `TvShowModel` with the `searchEnabled` property set to `true` and the `inputText` with the new text. In this case, you don't trigger any effects.

2. When the user taps **SEARCH**, it generates a `SearchButtonClicked`. Here, you set the `loading` property to `true` and trigger a `SearchTvShow` effect.

3. If access to the server is successful, you receive a `TvSearchSuccess`. In this case, you update `SearchTvShow` with the results and trigger the `HideKeyboard` effect.

4. In case of error, you receive a `TvSearchFailure`, and you then trigger the `DisplayErrorMessage` effect to display an error message along with the `HideKeyboard` effect.

This function is easy to read and pretty straightforward to write. All good, but what about the effects?

Plan your app

In this step, you basically design how your app should do all the tasks you described in the `Update` function. The actual code should be part of the next step, but right now, you'll look at how different effects are executed. You already know that an effect is basically the description of an operation that changes the external world. The component responsible for actually executing an effect is called an **effect handler**. Mobius provides different ways to implement an effect handler.

In the case of the Raybius app, you have two of them. Open **TvShowEffect.kt** and look at the following effects' definitions:

```
sealed interface TvShowEffect
data class SearchTvShow(val query: String) : TvShowEffect
data class DisplayErrorMessage(
  val error: Throwable
) : TvShowEffect
object HideKeyboard : TvShowEffect
```

For each of them, you need to define an **effect handler**. Some are very simple and just need to consume the information into the effect class. Others are more complicated and need to generate some events as the result of the effect. DisplayErrorMessage is in the first category. Open **UIEffectHandlerImpl.kt** in **mobius.handlers**, and look at the following code:

```
override fun handleErrorMessage(effect: DisplayErrorMessage) {
  val errorMessage = effect.error.localizedMessage
    ?:
  activityContext.getString(R.string.generic_error_message)
    Toast.makeText(
      activityContext, errorMessage, Toast.LENGTH_SHORT
    ).show()
  }
```

Here, you just consume the DisplayErrorMessage and use the Context you inject to display a Toast.

An example of an effect that also generates some events is SearchTvShow. In this case, you need an RxJava transformer, like the following you find in **ApiRequestHandlerImpl.kt**.

```
override fun handleSearchTvShow(
  request: Observable<SearchTvShow>
): Observable<TvShowEvent> =
  request
    .flatMap { request ->
      fetchAndParseTvShowResult(request.query).fold( // 1
        onSuccess = {
          Observable.just(
            TvSearchSuccess(it.filter(removeIncompleteFilter))
          )
        }, // 2
        onFailure = {
          Observable.just(TvSearchFailure(it))
        } // 3
      )
    }
```

Note how you:

1. Use the `fetchAndParseTvShowResult` you implemented in the previous chapters.

2. Return an `Observable<TvSearchSuccess>` in the case of success.

3. Return an `Observable<TvSearchFailure>` in the case of failure.

Remember that `TvSearchSuccess` and `TvSearchFailure` are `TvShowEvents`. Mobius sends them to the Mobius loop when the effect has completed.

OK, but how do you tell Mobius what effect handler to use for every effect? In the Raybius app, this is done in **MobiusModule.kt** in **di** with the following code:

```
@Provides
fun provideEffectHandler(
  uiHandler: UIEffectHandler,
  apiRequestHandler: ApiRequestHandler
): TvShowEffectHandler =
  RxMobius.subtypeEffectHandler<TvShowEffect, TvShowEvent>()
    .addTransformer(
      SearchTvShow::class.java,
      apiRequestHandler::handleSearchTvShow
    ) // 1
    .addConsumer(
      DisplayErrorMessage::class.java,
      uiHandler::handleErrorMessage, // 2
      AndroidSchedulers.mainThread()
    )
    .addConsumer(
      HideKeyboard::class.java,
      uiHandler::handleHideKeyboardMessage,
      AndroidSchedulers.mainThread()
    )
    .build();
```

In this code, you bind:

1. The `SearchTvShow` event to the `apiRequestHandler::handleSearchTvShow` function.

2. `DisplayErrorMessage` to `uiHandler::handleErrorMessage`.

Besides some implementation details you can see directly in the project or the Mobius official documentation (https://github.com/spotify/mobius/wiki/Concepts), this is basically all you need to design and implement your app with Mobius. So, now it's time to implement some code yourself.

Build your app

In this step, you'll finish implementing the MoFlow table you described earlier. It's time for you to use Mobius to implement the feature to display TV show details.

Implementing the TvShowDetail feature

Now, you'll add the show detail feature. To do this, you need to:

1. Update the `TvShowModel` with the data you need to display the `ShowDetail`.

2. Create the events you need to display the `ShowDetail` information.

3. Define the effects you need to access the TV show detail.

4. *Update* the `Update` function (pun intended :]) to handle the new use case.

5. Implement the new effect handler.

6. Update UI-related code.

It's time to write some code!

Model update

Open **TvShowModel.kt**, and add the following constructor property:

```
val detailResult: ShowDetail? = null
```

This will contain a `ShowDetail`, which has the detailed information for a TV show.

Adding new events

Now, open **TvShowEvent.kt**, and add the following events:

```
data class DetailViewResumed(
  val id: Int
) : TvShowEvent() // 1
data class ItemClicked(
  val id: Int
) : TvShowEvent() // 2
data class TvShowDetailSuccess(
  val results: ShowDetail
) : TvShowEvent() // 3
data class TvShowDetailFailure(
  val ex: Throwable
```

```
) : TvShowEvent() // 4
```

This allows you to:

1. Trigger the request for the TV show detail.

2. Handle the selection of an item in the list result for the first query.

3. Handle a successful response for the detail.

4. Handle errors when accessing the detail information.

Adding effects

Add new effects. Open **TvShowEffect.kt**, and add the following code:

```
data class NavigateToDetail(val showId: Int) : TvShowEffect // 1
data class GetTvShowDetail(val showId: Int) : TvShowEffect // 2
```

These are the effects for:

1. Navigating to the detail fragment.

2. Triggering the request to the server to get the TV show detail.

Now, you need to bind all the logic together.

Update the update function

To bind events and effects together, you need to open **TvShowLogic.kt** and add the following code to the update when block:

```
is ItemClicked -> Next.next( // 1
  model, setOf(NavigateToDetail(event.id))
)
is DetailViewResumed -> Next.next( // 2
  model.copy(loading = true), setOf(GetTvShowDetail(event.id))
)
is TvShowDetailSuccess -> Next.next( // 3
  model.copy(loading = false, detailResult = event.results)
)
is TvShowDetailFailure -> Next.next( // 4
  model.copy(loading = false),
  setOf(DisplayErrorMessage(event.ex))
)
```

Here, you:

1. Trigger the `NavigateToDetail` effect when selecting an item in the list and then receive an `ItemClicked` event.

2. Launch a `GetTvShowDetail` effect when the `NavigateToDetail` completes and a `DetailViewResumed` is sent.

3. Update the `TvShowModel` with the detail information in the case of `TvShowDetailSuccess`.

4. Display an error message triggering a `DisplayErrorMessage` in the case of `TvShowDetailFailure`.

Now, you've defined some new effects and bound them to some events. At the moment, Mobius doesn't actually know how to execute them. It's time to implement the effect handlers.

Add new effect handlers

In the previous code, you defined the new `NavigateToDetail` and `GetTvShowDetail` effects. It's now time to tell Mobius how to execute them. They're both effects that need to generate some events as a result. Open **UIEffectHandler.kt**, and add the following definition to the interface:

```
fun handleNavigateToDetail(
    request: Observable<NavigateToDetail>
): Observable<TvShowEvent>
```

This operation defines how to execute a `NavigateToDetail`, generating a `TvShowEvent` as result. This is the interface, and you need to provide an implementation as well. Open **UIEffectHandlerImpl.kt**, and add the following code:

```
override fun handleNavigateToDetail(
    request: Observable<NavigateToDetail>
): Observable<TvShowEvent> = request
    .observeOn(AndroidSchedulers.mainThread())
    .map { request ->
      val activity = activityContext as AppCompatActivity
      activity.supportFragmentManager.beginTransaction()
        .replace(R.id.anchor, TvShowDetailFragment())
        .addToBackStack("Detail")
        .commit()

      DetailViewResumed(request.showId)
    }
```

Besides some implementation details related to the actual navigation, what's important here is the DetailViewResumed you send to the Mobius loop on the last line. This is to notify the workflow that the effect has been executed. Remember, this event triggers the GetTvShowDetail effect for access to the network to fetch the TV show details, which needs an effect handler. Open **ApiRequestHandler.kt**, and add the following definition:

```
fun handleTvShowDetail(
    request: Observable<GetTvShowDetail>
): Observable<TvShowEvent>
```

As before, you're just defining the operation for an effect handler that consumes a GetTvShowDetail and generates a TvShowEvent. For the implementation, open **ApiRequestHandlerImpl.kt**, and add the following code, which should be quite familiar:

```
override fun handleTvShowDetail(
    request: Observable<GetTvShowDetail>
): Observable<TvShowEvent> = request
    .flatMap { request ->
        fetchAndParseTvShowDetailResult(request.showId).fold(
            onSuccess =
{ Observable.just(TvShowDetailSuccess(it)) },
            onFailure = { Observable.just(TvShowDetailFailure(it)) }
        )
    }
```

Now, you've implemented the code for the new effect handlers, but Mobius doesn't know about them yet. Next, open **MobiusModule.kt**, and add the following transformers to provideEffectHandler below the existing transformer:

```
.addTransformer(
    GetTvShowDetail::class.java, // 1
    apiRequestHandler::handleTvShowDetail
)
.addTransformer(
    NavigateToDetail::class.java, // 2
    uiHandler::handleNavigateToDetail
)
```

In this code, you use `addTransformer` to tell Mobius what effect handler to execute for the effects:

1. `GetTvShowDetail`

2. `NavigateToDetail`

Now, you just need to update the UI logic for this new feature.

Update UI logic

You still need to do a few last things to handle user events and use the data you receive from the new effects. You basically need to:

- Enable the selection of an item in the list.

- Display `ShowDetail` in the `TvShowDetailFragment`.

Open **TvSearchFragment.kt**, and update the content of `onCreateView` to insert this code before the return statement:

```
searchBinding.initUI(eventConsumer) { showId ->
    eventConsumer.accept(ItemClicked(showId))
}
```

In this code, you use `eventConsumer` to send an `ItemClicked` event to the Mobius loop when the user selects an item in the result list.Now, you need to display the `ShowDetail` in the case of success.

Open **FragmentDetailBindingExt.kt**, and add the following to the bottom of `logic`:

```
if (model.detailResult != null) { // 1
    displayResult(model.detailResult) // 2
}
```

Here, you just:

1. Check if details are available.

2. Display them in the UI.

Now, you can build and run the app. When you select an item in the list of results, you can see how the detail screen is displayed, like in Figure 18.10:

Figure 18.10: The detail screen

Great job! As a last note, it's worthwhile to have a quick look at how you set up the Mobius loop in Android.

Mobius loop in Android

In Figure 18.1, you learned that Mobius's architecture is based on the creation of the Mobius loop, which is responsible for:

- Delivering the events to the Update function.

- Triggering the effects, invoking the configured effect handler.

- Helping with concurrency in the execution of side effects.

- Handling logging and monitoring.

Usually, there's an instance of the Mobius loop per surface when a surface is basically a screen of the app. You can decide to use a single Mobius loop or create multiple ones depending on the dimension of the app. In the case of Raybius, a single Mobius loop is shared between all the Fragments through the MainActivity class. To bind the lifecycle of the Mobius loop to the Activity one, Mobius provides a MobiusLoop.Controller. If you look at MainActivity, removing the unrelated things, you'll get the following:

```kotlin
@AndroidEntryPoint
class MainActivity :
  AppCompatActivity(), MobiusHost<TvShowModel, TvShowEvent> {

  @Inject
  lateinit var tvShowController: TvShowMobiusController // 1

  override fun onCreate(savedInstanceState: Bundle?) {
    // ...
    tvShowController.connect(::connectViews) // 2
    // ...
  }

  override fun onResume() {
    super.onResume()
    tvShowController.start() // 3
  }

  override fun onPause() {
    super.onPause()
    tvShowController.stop() // 4
  }

  override fun onDestroy() {
    super.onDestroy()
    tvShowController.disconnect() // 7
  }

  lateinit var eventConsumer: Consumer<TvShowEvent>

  private fun connectViews(
    eventConsumer: Consumer<TvShowEvent>
  ): Connection<TvShowModel> {
    this.eventConsumer = eventConsumer
    return object : Connection<TvShowModel> {
      override fun accept(model: TvShowModel) { // 5
        logic(eventConsumer, model)
      }

      override fun dispose() { // 6
      }
    }
  }
}
```

```
  var logic: (
    Consumer<TvShowEvent>, TvShowModel
  ) -> Unit = { _, _ -> }
  override fun injectLogic(
    logic: (Consumer<TvShowEvent>, TvShowModel) -> Unit
  ) { // 8
    this.logic = logic
  }
}
```

In this code:

1. You inject the object of type `TvShowMobiusController`, which is an alias for `MobiusLoop.Controller<TvShowModel, TvShowEvent>`.

2. You invoke `connect`, passing the reference to a function of type `(Consumer<TvShowEvent>) -> Connection<TvShowModel>`. This function returns an object of type `Connection<TvShowModel>`. The object `Connection<TvShowModel>` needs to override `accept` and `dispose`.

3. You start the Mobius loop, invoking `start` on the `TvShowMobiusController`. This happens in `onResume`.

4. You stop the Mobius loop, invoking `stop` on the `TvShowMobiusController`. This happens in `onPause`.

5. `accept` is invoked every time the Mobius loop needs to deliver a new model. This is where you bind the logic specific to your app.

6. `dispose` is invoked when you stop the loop.

7. `disconnect` removes the binding between the `MainActivity` and the `TvShowMobiusController` in `onDestroy`.

8. This is a function each `Fragment` can invoke to set its specific logic. This doesn't allow more `Fragments` to be visible at the same time, but for this app, this is an acceptable trade-off.

Key points

- **Mobius** is a functional reactive framework for managing state evolution and side effects, with add-ons for connecting to Android UIs and RxJava Observables.

- Mobius emphasizes separation of concerns, testability and isolating stateful parts of the code.

- Mobius is an example of unidirectional flow architecture.

- The **MoFlow** is a process that allows you to design your app in terms of **models**, **events** and **effects**.

- The **model** represents the current state of the UI.

- You can use **events** to represent a user interaction or the result of an effect.

- An **effect** is the description of a task that might change the state of the world.

- Models, events and effects are immutable.

- The Update function is a **pure** function, receiving the current model and the event as input, and returning the new model and the optional effects.

- The **purity** of the Update function makes it very easy to test.

- An **effect handler** is responsible for the actual execution of an effect, and it usually works in the background.

Where to go from here?

Congratulations! In this chapter, you learned how the Mobius framework works as an example of a unidirectional architecture that uses many of the principles you learned about functional programming. In the next — and final — chapter, you'll learn the most important concepts about a very important functional programming library in Kotlin: Arrow (https://arrow-kt.io/).

Chapter 19: Arrow

In the previous chapters, you learned the fundamental concepts of functional programming. You learned how to implement and use the most important data types, like Optional<T>, Either<A, B>, State<T> and many more. Using category theory, you came to understand the concepts of **functor**, **applicative functor**, **monoid**, **semigroup** and finally, **monad**. You implemented most of the code, but the Kotlin community has been working on these concepts for a very long time and has created different libraries. One of the most powerful libraries for functional programming in Kotlin is Arrow (https://arrow-kt.io/).

> **Note**: If you want to learn all about Arrow, read Arrow's official documentation (https://arrow-kt.io/), which is perfectly maintained by 47 Degrees (https://www.47deg.com/).

To cover all the features this library provides in a single chapter is impossible. For this reason, you'll focus on a specific problem: error handling. Using Arrow, you'll see how to handle errors in a functional way and learn what data types Arrow provides. This is the Arrow solution to what you did in Chapter 14, "Error Handling With Functional Programming".

In particular, you'll see:

- The Option<T> data type.

- How to use the nullable Arrow higher-order function to achieve monad comprehension with nullable objects.

- How to use `Either<A, B>` and achieve monad comprehension with `either`.

- What Arrow optics are and how you can use them to handle complex immutable objects easily.

It's time to have more fun! :]

Exceptions as side effects

In the previous chapters, you learned that exceptions aren't a great solution in the context of functional programming. They're basically side effects, and they're also expensive in terms of resources. Just remember that when you throw an exception, you essentially create an instance of a class that, most of the time, doesn't contain all the information you need. In Java — and Kotlin — you also have different types of exceptions that differ in name and not much more.

To see what tools Arrow provides for handling exceptions in a functional way, you'll start with the same code you wrote in Chapter 14, "Error Handling With Functional Programming", to fetch and parse data about some TV shows. Open the starter project in this chapter's material, and look at the code in the **tools** subpackages. In **TvShowFetcher.kt** in **tools.fetchers**, you'll find the following code:

```
object TvShowFetcher {
  fun fetch(query: String): String {
    val encodedUrl = java.net.URLEncoder.encode(query, "utf-8")
    val localUrl =
      URL("https://api.tvmaze.com/search/shows?q=$encodedUrl")
    with(localUrl.openConnection() as HttpURLConnection) {
      requestMethod = "GET"
      val reader = inputStream.bufferedReader()
      return reader.lines().toArray().asSequence()
        .fold(StringBuilder()) { builder, line ->
          builder.append(line)
        }.toString()
    }
  }
}
```

This is quite straightforward and allows you to query the TVmaze (https://www.tvmaze.com/api) database by passing a string as input and getting a JSON with the response as output. Run the previous method, executing the following `main`:

```
fun main() {
  fetch("Big Bang") pipe ::println
}
```

As output, you'll get a long JSON `String` like the following:

```
[{"score":1.1548387,"show":{"id":58514,"url":"https://
www.tvmaze.com/shows/58514/big-bang","name":"Big
bang","type":"Panel Show","language":"Norwegian","genres":
["Comedy"],"status":"Ended","runtime":60,"averageRuntime":60,
// ...
canine sidekick, Lil' Louis.</p>","updated":1628627563,"_links":
{"self":{"href":"https://api.tvmaze.com/shows/
10115"},"previousepisode":{"href":"https://api.tvmaze.com/
episodes/531559"}}}}]
```

You can also simulate a case where something goes wrong. Disconnect your machine from the network and run the `main` again — you'll get the following exception:

```
Exception in thread "main" java.net.UnknownHostException:
api.tvmaze.com
    at
java.net.AbstractPlainSocketImpl.connect(AbstractPlainSocketImpl
.java:196)
    at
java.net.SocksSocketImpl.connect(SocksSocketImpl.java:394)
    at java.net.Socket.connect(Socket.java:606)
```

What's important here is that you have a `TvShowFetcher` that provides `fetch` to query TVmaze about a TV show, and this can either succeed or fail.

Now, open **TvShowParser.kt** in **tools.parser**, and look at the following code:

```
object TvShowParser {

  private val jsonConfig = Json {
    ignoreUnknownKeys = true
  }

  /** Parses the json in input */
  fun parse(json: String): List<ScoredShow> = jsonConfig
    .decodeFromString<List<ScoredShow>>(
      ListSerializer(ScoredShow.serializer()), json
    )
}
```

This uses the Kotlin serialization library to parse the input JSON into a `List<ScoredShow>`. It can also either succeed or fail. To test the second case, simply run:

```
fun main() {
  TvShowParser.parse("Invalid JSON") pipe ::println
}
```

And get the output:

```
Exception in thread "main"
kotlinx.serialization.json.internal.JsonDecodingException:
Expected start of the array '[', but had 'EOF' instead
JSON input: Invalid JSON
    at
kotlinx.serialization.json.internal.JsonExceptionsKt.JsonDecodin
gException(JsonExceptions.kt:24)
```

Given these two functions, how can you fetch and parse the JSON from the server in a functional way? You already know the answer, but it's useful to see what Arrow provides.

Using Option<T>

A first possible solution to the previous problem is the Option<T> data type Arrow provides with the core library. Find it already added it to your project with the following definition in **build.gradle**:

```
def arrow_version = '1.0.1'
dependencies {
  // ...
    implementation "io.arrow-kt:arrow-core:$arrow_version"
}
```

> **Note**: Notice that the name for this data type is Option<T>, not Optional<T>.

To see how this works, open **TvShowOption.kt**, and add the following code:

```
fun fetchOption(query: String): Option<String> = try { // 1
  TvShowFetcher.fetch(query).some() // 2
} catch (ioe: IOException) {
  none() // 3
}

fun parseOption(
  json: String
): Option<List<ScoredShow>> = try { // 1
  TvShowParser.parse(json).some() // 2
} catch (e: Throwable) {
  none() // 3
}
```

In this code, you:

1. Define `fetchOption` and `parseOption` as `Option<T>` versions of `TvShowFetcher::fetch` and `TvShowParser::parse`, respectively.

2. Invoke the related function in a `try/catch` block. If the invocation is successful, you invoke the `some` extension function, which returns an `Option<T>`, and more precisely, an instance of `Some<T>`.

3. In the case of an exception, return `None`, invoking the `none` extension function.

If you look at `some` and `none` implementation, you find simple code like this:

```
public fun <A> A.some(): Option<A> = Some(this)

public fun <A> none(): Option<A> = None
```

Where `Some<T>` and `None` are specific definitions of the sealed class `Option<T>`, just as in the previous chapters. This is all quite simple.

Now, you need to fetch *and* parse the result while handling possible failure. You already know how to do it. Just add the following code to the same file:

```
fun fetchAndParseOption(
    query: StringBuilder
): Option<List<ScoredShow>> =
    fetchOption(query)
        .flatMap(::parseOption)
```

The `Option<T>` data type provides `flatMap` to compose functions the same way you did in the previous chapters.

To test everything together, use the following code:

```
fun main() {
  val searchResultOption = fetchAndParseOption("Big Bang") // 1
  if (searchResultOption.isDefined()) { // 2
    val searchResult =
      searchResultOption.getOrElse { emptyList() } // 3
    if (!searchResult.isEmpty()) {
      searchResult.forEach { // 4
        with(it.show) {
          println(
            "Name: ${name}  Genre: ${genres.joinToString()}"
          )
        }
      }
    }
  } else {
    println("No Results!") // 5
```

```
      }
    } else {
      println("Something went wrong!")   // 6
    }
  }
}
```

In this code, you:

1. Invoke `fetchAndParseOption`, passing the `String` you want to search. This will return an `Option<List<ScoredShow>>`.

2. Use `isDefined` to check if the `Option<T>` has a value and if it's a `Some<T>` or `None`.

3. Invoke `getOrElse`, which returns what's in the `Some<T>` if present, or the result of the lambda you pass as the parameter in the case of `None`. In this case, you already know you're in the `Some<T>` case, but `getOrElse` is the safe way to get a value of type `T` in any case.

4. Check that the result isn't empty, and display all the `ScoredShow` data as output, iterating over the resulting `List<ScoredShow>`.

5. Display a simple message if you get no results.

6. Print an error message if the initial result was `None`.

This is a pretty good solution if you're not interested in the specific reason for failure.

At this point, you might ask why you need `Option<T>` in Kotlin when you already have the opportunity to use optional types. This is an excellent question, and Arrow has an answer for it.

Handling null values

In the previous example, you created `fetchOption` and `parseOption` as versions of `TvShowFetcher::fetch` and `TvShowParser::parse`, respectively, returning an `Option<T>`. Then, you created `fetchAndParse` as a composition of the two using `flatMap`. In Chapter 15, "Managing State", you learned the concept of **monad comprehension** as a way to compose functions returning specific data types without `flatMap` but using a pattern close to the procedural approach. Well, this is what Arrow provides you for nullable types.

Open **TvShowNullable.kt**, and write the following code:

```
fun fetchNullable(query: String): String? = try { // 1
  TvShowFetcher.fetch(query) // 2
} catch (ioe: IOException) {
  null // 3
}

fun parseNullable(json: String): List<ScoredShow>? = try { // 1
  TvShowParser.parse(json) // 2
} catch (e: Throwable) {
  null // 3
}
```

As you can see here, you:

1. Define `fetchNullable` and `parseNullable` as versions of `TvShowFetcher::fetch` and `TvShowParser::parse`, respectively, returning a value of the optional type.

2. Return the actual result in the case of success.

3. Return `null` in the case of failure.

Using the `flatMap` implementation you find in **Nullable.kt** in the **lib** package, add the following:

```
fun fetchAndParseNullableFlatMap(query: String) =
  fetchNullable(query)
    .nullableFlatMap(::parseNullable)
```

Just remember to import `nullableFlatMap` like this to avoid conflicts with other `flatMap` extension functions:

```
import com.raywenderlich.fp.lib.flatMap as nullableFlatMap
```

Arrow provides you an alternative solution. In the same file, add the following code:

```
suspend fun fetchAndParseNullable(
  query: String
): List<ScoredShow>? = nullable {
  val json = fetchNullable("Big Bang").bind()
  val result = parseNullable(json).bind()
  result
}
```

This code has a few interesting things to note:

- `fetchAndParseNullable` is a suspendable function. This is because the `nullable` function, which is suspendable, allows `fetchNullable` and `parseNullable` to be suspendable functions as well. This is very useful, especially if you need to access the network, like in this case, or, in general, run tasks in a thread different from the main one.

- You invoke `fetchNullable` and `parseNullable` one after the other in the same way you would in a procedural case. The magic is provided by the `nullable` function but also by the `bind` you invoke on the result of each invocation. This is how Arrow handles `NullableEffect<T>`, which is an `Effect<T>` that can result in a `null` value.

- The result type is `List<ScoredShow>?`, and you explicitly wrote it in the previous code to make this clear, but it wouldn't have been necessary. This is the type of the last expression you write in the body of `nullable`.

To test this code, add the following to the same file:

```kotlin
suspend fun mainWithComprehension() { // 1
  val searchResultOption = fetchAndParseNullable("Big Bang") //
2
  if (searchResultOption != null) {
    printScoresShow(searchResultOption) // 3
  } else {
    println("Something went wrong!")
  }
}
```

Which isn't very different from the one you would've executed in the case of using `flatMap`, which is:

```kotlin
fun mainWithFlatMap() { // 1
  val searchResultOption = fetchAndParseNullableFlatMap("Big
Bang") // 2
  if (searchResultOption != null) {
    printScoresShow(searchResultOption) // 3
  } else {
    println("Something went wrong!")
  }
}
```

The differences are:

1. The one using `nullable` needs to be a suspendable function.

2. The function you invoke to get the optional type `List<ScoredShow>?`.

3. You use `printScoresShow`, which you find in **Util.kt**, to print the `List<ScoredShow>` content.

Finally, run the following `main`. This lets you check how the two implementations work basically the same — besides the need for a scope for the suspendable one:

```
fun main() {
  mainWithFlatMap()
  runBlocking {
    mainWithComprehension()
  }
}
```

Which one is the best? The answer is always the same: It depends! :] If you need to compose different functions that execute tasks in the background, the Arrow solution is probably the best.

In both cases, you get a nullable object that doesn't give you any information about what happens in the case of failure. You just get `null` without any other information. You've already met this problem in the previous chapters, and you already have a first solution: the `Either<A, B>` data type.

Using Either<A, B>

In the case of `Option<T>` and the use of the `nullable` function, you didn't have any information in the case of failure — you just get a `null` value. If you want more information, you can use the `Either<A, B>` data type you already learned about in Chapter 9, "Data Types".

Open **TvShowEither.kt**, and add the following code:

```
fun fetchEither(
  query: String
): Either<IOException, String> = try { // 1
  TvShowFetcher.fetch(query).right() // 2
} catch (ioe: IOException) {
  ioe.left() // 3
}

fun parseEither(
  json: String
```

```
): Either<Throwable, List<ScoredShow>> = try { // 1
  TvShowParser.parse(json  /* + "break" */).right() // 2
} catch (e: Throwable) {
  e.left() // 3
}
```

In this code, you:

1. Define fetchEither and parseEither as versions of TvShowFetcher::fetch
   and TvShowParser::parse, respectively, using the Arrow Either<A, B>
   implementation.

2. Use the right extension function, returning a Right<B> of the result in the case
   of success. Note how Either<A, B> is **right biased**, which means you
   conventionally use Right<B> as the success value and Left<A> for failure. This is
   important in the case of composition using flatMap. Note how the parameter for
   TvShowParser::parse has a commented code you can use to simulate a failure.

3. Use the left extension function on the exception in the case of an error.

Now, add the following code to the same file:

```
fun fetchAndParseEither(
  query: String
): Either<Throwable, List<ScoredShow>> =
  fetchEither(query)
    .flatMap(::parseEither)
```

Here, you simply use flatMap to compose the fetchEither and parseEither using
the mentioned right bias. To test this, just run the following code:

```
fun main() {
  fetchAndParseEither("Big Bang") // 1
    .fold( // 2
      ifRight = ::printScoresShow, // 3
      ifLeft = ::printException // 4
    )
}
```

Here, you:

1. Invoke fetchAndParseEither, passing the query in input.

2. Use fold to handle success cases, the right, as well as failure cases, the left.

3. Pass the reference to `printScoresShow` to the `ifRight` parameter in the case of `Right<B>`, which represents the successful case.

4. Pass the reference to `printException` in the case of `Left<A>`, which represents the failure case.

You can now simulate the failure of `fetchEither` by disconnecting your machine from the network. In that case, you'll get:

```
Error api.tvmaze.com
```

To simulate the failure of `parseEither`, just remove the comments from the code like here and, of course, restore your connection:

```
fun parseEither(json: String): Either<Throwable,
List<ScoredShow>> = try {
  TvShowParser.parse(json + "break").right() // HERE
} catch (e: Throwable) {
  e.left()
}
```

And you'll get:

```
Error Unexpected JSON token at offset 14069: Expected EOF after
parsing, but had b instead
JSON input: .....aze.com/episodes/531559"}}}}]break
```

This works exactly like the `Either<A, B>` data type you implemented in Chapter 9, "Data Types", but Arrow gives you the monad comprehension power as well. In this case, you can use the `either` function like this:

```
suspend fun fetchAndParseEitherComprehension( // 1
  query: String
): Either<Throwable, List<ScoredShow>> =
  either { // 2
    val json = fetchEither(query).bind() // 3
    val result = parseEither(json).bind() // 4
    result
  }
```

Here, you:

1. Define `fetchAndParseEitherComprehension` as a suspendable function.

2. Use the `either` function.

3. Invoke `bind` on the result of `fetchEither`.

4. Use the result you get from `fetchEither` as input for `parseEither` and invoke `bind` again.

To test this code, just repeat the previous scenarios on the following:

```
fun main() {
  runBlocking {
    fetchAndParseEitherComprehension("Big Bang")
      .fold(
        ifRight = ::printScoresShow,
        ifLeft = ::printException
      )
  }
}
```

You can easily verify that the results will be the same.

Arrow optics

One of the most important principles in functional programming is **immutability**. An object is immutable if it doesn't change its state after creation. A class is immutable if it doesn't provide the operation to change the state of its instances.

As you know, the state of an object is the set of values for all its properties. Immutable objects have many different advantages. For instance, different threads can safely share them without any risk of deadlock or race conditions.

Sometimes you need to "update" the state of an immutable object. *Wait, what?* Well, in Chapter 18, "Mobius — A Functional Reactive Framework", you saw that the `Update` function returns the *new state* and an optional set of effects, given the *current state* and the information about an *event*. Often, the new state has different values for some properties, leaving the remaining unchanged.

To solve problems like this, Arrow provides the **optics** library. It's an automatic DSL that allows users to use dot notation when accessing, composing and transforming deeply nested immutable data structures.

To understand how this works, open **Optics.kt**, and add the following code:

```
val bigBangTheory =
  ScoredShow(
    score = 0.9096895,
    Show(
```

```
      id = 66,
      name = "The Big Bang Theory",
      genres = listOf("Comedy"),
      url = "https://www.tvmaze.com/shows/66/the-big-bang-
theory",
      image = ShowImage(
         original = "", // HERE
         medium = "https://static.tvmaze.com/uploads/images/
medium_portrait/173/433868.jpg"
      ),
      summary = "<p><b>The Big Bang Theory</b> is a comedy about
brilliant physicists, Leonard and Sheldon...</p>",
      language = "English"
   )
 )
```

Here, you just create `bigBangTheory` with the values you get from the TVmaze database. To make the core more readable, you used named parameters and made the `summary` shorter. Now, imagine that when you got this data, the `original` version for the `image` wasn't available, as you can see with the empty value. Now that information *is* available, and you want to update `bigBangTheory` with the new value.

A solution is the following:

```
val updatedBigBangTheory = bigBangTheory.copy(
   show = bigBangTheory.show.copy( // 1
      image = bigBangTheory.show.image?.copy( // 2
         original = "https://static.tvmaze.com/uploads/images/
medium_portrait/173/433868.jpg" // 3
      )
   )
)
```

In this code, you use `copy` to update the:

1. `show` property of the `ScoredShow` with an updated version of `Show`.

2. `image` property of the `Show` with an updated version of `ShowImage`.

3. `original` property with the new value.

You can check that this works by running the following code:

```
fun main() {
   bigBangTheory pipe ::println
   updatedBigBangTheory pipe ::println
}
```

And check that the `original` property now has a value.

```
ScoredShow(score=0.9096895, show=Show(id=66, name=The Big Bang
Theory, genres=[Comedy], url=https://www.tvmaze.com/shows/66/
the-big-bang-theory, image=ShowImage(original=, medium=https://
static.tvmaze.com/uploads/images/medium_portrait/
173/433868.jpg), summary=<p><b>The Big Bang Theory</b> is a
comedy about brilliant physicists, Leonard and Sheldon...</p>,
language=English))
ScoredShow(score=0.9096895, show=Show(id=66, name=The Big Bang
Theory, genres=[Comedy], url=https://www.tvmaze.com/shows/66/
the-big-bang-theory, image=ShowImage(original=https://
static.tvmaze.com/uploads/images/medium_portrait/173/433868.jpg,
medium=https://static.tvmaze.com/uploads/images/medium_portrait/
173/433868.jpg), summary=<p><b>The Big Bang Theory</b> is a
comedy about brilliant physicists, Leonard and Sheldon...</p>,
language=English))
```

As mentioned, this works, but that's a lot of code for just updating a property of an immutable object. With Arrow, you can use **lenses**, which are provided with the optics library. A **lens** is exactly what its name suggests. It's a way to reach a property that might be very deep in a hierarchy of objects and basically *see it as if it were closer.*

> **Note**: The project is already configured to use optics. Please be careful if you want to update the library and plugin versions because they're strictly connected. A wrong version could cause the code to simply not work.

To use a lens, open **Show.kt** in **model**, and update all the data classes in it like this:

```
@optics // 1
@Serializable
data class ScoredShow(
  val score: Double,
  val show: Show
) {
  companion object // 2
}

@optics // 1
@Serializable
data class Show(
  val id: Int,
  val name: String,
  val genres: List<String>,
  val url: String,
  val image: ShowImage?,
```

```
    val summary: String?,
    val language: String
) {
    companion object // 2
}

@optics // 1
@Serializable
data class ShowImage(
    val original: String,
    val medium: String
) {
    companion object // 2
}
```

In this code, you:

1. Annotate each data class with @optics. This will cause the Arrow compiler to generate all the code you need.

2. Provide a companion object to each of the @optics classes. Arrow needs this to attach all the generated extensions functions.

Now, simply return to **Optics.kt**, and add the following code:

```
fun main() {
    val updateOriginalImageLens: Optional<ScoredShow, String> =
      ScoredShow.show.image.original // 1
    val updatedShow =
      updateOriginalImageLens.modify(bigBangTheory) { // 2
        "https://static.tvmaze.com/uploads/images/medium_portrait/
173/433868.jpg"
      }
    updatedShow pipe ::println // 3
}
```

Note: Make sure you rebuild the project and import the generated show and image properties to get this to compile.

Here, you:

1. Use the dot notation to get the reference of an object of type Optional<ScoredShow, String>. This function basically allows you to go from the original ScoredShow to the updated one in a single step. You save it in updateOriginalImageLens. If you consider Optional<S, T>, you can think of S as the original type and T as the type of the variable you want to update in S.

2. Invoke `modify` on `updateOriginalImageLens`, passing the original object and the new value of the property you want to update.

3. Finally, print the updated object, `updatedShow`, to verify that it actually worked.

Running the previous code, you'll get:

```
ScoredShow(score=0.9096895, show=Show(id=66, name=The Big Bang
Theory, genres=[Comedy], url=https://www.tvmaze.com/shows/66/
the-big-bang-theory, image=ShowImage(original=https://
static.tvmaze.com/uploads/images/medium_portrait/173/433868.jpg,
medium=https://static.tvmaze.com/uploads/images/medium_portrait/
173/433868.jpg), summary=<p><b>The Big Bang Theory</b> is a
comedy about brilliant physicists, Leonard and Sheldon...</p>,
language=English))
```

Note how the original property now has a value.

Arrow lenses

In the previous section, you learned that optics are basically abstractions that help you update immutable data structures in an elegant and functional way. A lens is an optic that can focus into a structure and **get**, **modify** or **set** the value of a particular property.

In terms of functional types, you can say that a `Lens<T, A>` is a way to aggregate a couple of functions:

*   `get` of type `(T) -> A`, which extracts the value of type `A` from the object of type `T`.

*   `setter` of type `(A) -> (T) -> T` which, given a value of type `A` for a property, provides the function you run to update the object of type `T`.

Given a `Lens<T, A>`, you call `T` the **source** of the lens and `A` its **target**.

Lenses can be seen as a pair of functions: a **getter** and a **setter**. A `Lens<S, A>` represents a getter: `get: (S) -> A`, and setter: `set: (A) -> (S) -> S`, where `S` is the source of the lens and `A` is the focus or target of the lens.

Open **Lens.kt**, and add the following code:

```
val addGenreLens: Lens<ScoredShow, List<String>> = Lens( // 1
  get = { scoredShow -> scoredShow.show.genres }, // 2
  set = { scoredShow, newGenres ->
    ScoredShow.show.genres.modify(scoredShow) { // 3
      scoredShow.show.genres + newGenres
    }
  }
)
```

In this code, you define:

1. addGenreLens as a lens of type Lens<ScoredShow, List<String>>, which wants to allow the addition of new genres to a given ScoredShow.

2. The get function using a lambda that simply accesses and returns the value of the genres property of the show for the ScoredShow in input.

3. The set function using a lambda receiving as input a ScoredShow and the List<String> for the genre to append. Note how you use the lenses Arrow already creates for you, as you learned above.

To use addGenreLens, simply add the following code to the same file:

```
fun main() {
  addGenreLens.set(
    bigBangTheory, listOf("Science", "Comic")
  ) pipe ::println
}
```

Run it, and you'll get the following output with the new genres added:

```
ScoredShow(score=0.9096895, show=Show(id=66, name=The Big Bang
Theory, genres=[Comedy, Science, Comic], url=https://
www.tvmaze.com/shows/66/the-big-bang-theory,
image=ShowImage(original=, medium=https://static.tvmaze.com/
uploads/images/medium_portrait/173/433868.jpg),
summary=<p><b>The Big Bang Theory</b> is a comedy about
brilliant physicists, Leonard and Sheldon...</p>,
language=English))
```

But lenses aren't just a way to write more concise code. Suppose you want to update the name for a given show. In the same file, add the following code:

```
val showLens: Lens<ScoredShow, Show> = Lens( // 1
  get = { scoredShow -> scoredShow.show },
  set = { scoredShow, newShow -> scoredShow.copy(show = newShow)
  }
)

val nameLens: Lens<Show, String> = Lens( // 2
  get = { show -> show.name },
  set = { show, newName -> show.copy(name = newName) }
)
```

Here, you define:

1. showLens as a lens to update the Show in a ScoredShow.

2. nameLens as a lens to update the name in a Show.

If you want to then update the name of a Show of a given ScoredShow, you can simply compose the previous lenses like this:

```
fun main() {
  // ...
  val updateName = showLens compose nameLens
  updateName.modify(bigBangTheory, String::toUpperCase)
  pipe ::println
}
```

Running this code, you'll get:

```
ScoredShow(score=0.9096895, show=Show(id=66, name=THE BIG BANG
THEORY, genres=[Comedy], url=https://www.tvmaze.com/shows/66/
the-big-bang-theory, image=ShowImage(original=, medium=https://
static.tvmaze.com/uploads/images/medium_portrait/
173/433868.jpg), summary=<p><b>The Big Bang Theory</b> is a
comedy about brilliant physicists, Leonard and Sheldon...</p>,
language=English))
```

As you can see, the name is now capitalized.

Key points

- **Arrow** is a library maintained by 47 Degrees that allows you to apply functional programming concepts to your Kotlin code.

- Arrow provides the implementation for the most important data types, like `Optional<T>`, `Either<A, B>`, `Monoid<T>` and many others.

- Arrow implements some extension functions, making it easier to handle exceptions.

- Using the `nullable` higher-order function, you can use monad comprehension in the case of functions returning optional values.

- Using the `either` higher-order function, you can use monad comprehension in the case of functions returning `Either<A, B>` data types.

- Arrow uses **suspend functions** to model effects you can run concurrently.

- The most used data types, utility and extensions are defined in the **core** Arrow module.

- Using the **optics** library, you can generate the code for reducing boilerplate in the case of handling immutable objects.

- A **lens** is an abstraction that helps you access properties and create new objects from existing immutable ones.

- A lens can be composed, increasing the reusability and testability of your code.

Where to go from here?

Wow, congratulations! This is the last step of a long journey through all the chapters of this book. Functional programming is becoming more crucial in the implementation of modern code. Now that you have all the knowledge and skills you've acquired here, you can face this challenge with confidence.

Conclusion

Congratulations! You've sure come a long way from the beginning of this book. You started with learning some of the very basic fundamentals of functional programming, all the way to discovering how to build on those fundamentals to manage state changes and error handling safely in your real-world applications. That's no small feat!

You stuck it out through some intense chapters. Maybe you read them and reread them. Or maybe you still feel you need to read them again — that's completely expected, by the way. These chapters each build on each other, so concepts you learned later in the book will help you when you return to earlier chapters. It's almost like a *Choose Your Own Adventure* book.

We hope you're inspired to use these functional programming concepts in your own application, be it as small as encouraging more pure functions or a complete functional programming overhaul. We promise that the more you use functional programming, the more you'll reap the benefits.

Toward the end of this book, you got a taste of how Kotlin coroutines can work with your functional code. To continue learning about coroutines, we recommend reading *Kotlin Coroutines by Tutorials*. While not strictly related, if you enjoyed this topic, you might also enjoy learning about the reactive programming paradigm in *Reactive Programming with Kotlin*.

If you have any questions or comments as you work through this book, please stop by our forums at https://forums.raywenderlich.com and look for the particular forum category for this book.

Thank you again for purchasing this book. Your continued support is what makes the books, tutorials, videos and other things we do at raywenderlich.com possible. We truly appreciate it!

– The *Functional Programming in Kotlin by Tutorials* team

Appendix

This book has many exercises and challenges throughout. In this appendix, you'll find solutions to all exercises and challenges, along with additional explanations about the answers.

Appendix A: Chapter 1 Exercise Solutions

Exercise 1.1

Implement the function sumInRange that sums the values in a List<String> within a given interval. The signature is:

```
fun sumInRange(input: List<String>, range: IntRange): Int
```

Exercise 1.1 solution

A possible solution is the following:

```
fun sumInRange(input: List<String>, range: IntRange): Int = // 1
    input
        .filter(::isValidNumber) // 2
        .map(String::toInt) // 3
        .filter { it in range } // 4
        .sum() // 5
```

In this code, you:

1. Define the sumInRange as requested.

2. Use filter with isValidNumber, which you defined in the chapter.

3. Invoke map, passing String::toInt to covert the String to Int.

4. Use filter again, passing a lambda that checks whether the value is in the range you pass in as input.

5. Invoke sum.

To test the previous code, run:

```
fun main() {
  println(sumInRange(listOf("1", "10", "a", "7", "ad2", "3"),
1..5))
}
```

Getting:

```
4
```

This is the sum of the values in List<String> that are valid Ints and in the range
1..5.

Exercise 1.2

Implement chrono, which accepts a function of type () -> Unit as input and
returns the time spent to run it. The signature is:

```
fun chrono(fn: () -> Unit): Long
```

Exercise 1.2 solution

A possible implementation for chrono is the following:

```
fun chrono(fn: () -> Unit): Long { // 1
  val start = System.currentTimeMillis() // 2
  fn() // 3
  return System.currentTimeMillis() - start // 4
}
```

In this code, you:

1. Define chrono as a function accepting a lambda as an input parameter and
   returning a Long.

2. Save the current time in milliseconds in the start variable.

3. Invoke the function fn you get as an input parameter.

4. Return the difference between the current time and the one in start.

One way to test this is:

```
fun main() {
  val waitOneSec = { Thread.sleep(1000) } // 1
  println(chrono(waitOneSec)) // 2
}
```

Here, you:

1. Define the `waitOneSec` lambda that waits at least `1000` milliseconds.

2. Invoke `chrono`, passing `waitOneSec` and printing the result.

When you run that code, you get something like:

```
1005
```

Note: Even if not strictly related to functional programming, it's useful to mention why the result isn't exactly `1000`. You might even get a different result every time you run the previous `main`. This is due to the `sleep` function of the `Thread` class. It asks the current thread to go to the `Wait` state for `1000` milliseconds. After the `1000` milliseconds, the task may or may not be the next to proceed. You only know that the thread will move from the `Wait` state to the `Runnable` state. When the thread will actually continue depends on the scheduler responsible for moving a thread from the `Runnable` state to the `Running` one. This is why you can never get a value less than `1000`.

Appendix B: Chapter 2 Exercise & Challenge Solutions

Exercise 2.1

Can you write an example of a function mapping distinct values in the domain to non-distinct values in the range, like **f(b)** and **f(c)** in Figure 2.2?

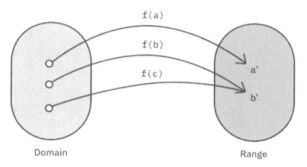

Figure 2.2: A function definition

Hint: Think of a possible way to group values you get as input. A very simple example is to return a Boolean that tells if the value in input is positive or not.

Exercise 2.1 solution

A simple example of a function mapping distinct values in the domain to non-distinct values in the range is:

```
fun isEven(x: Int): Boolean = x % 2 == 0
```

This function uses a modulo to determine if a number is even or not.

You can prove this by running the following code:

```
fun main() {
    println(isEven(2))
    println(isEven(-2))
    println(isEven(12))
    println(isEven(18))
    println(isEven(19))
    println(isEven(-3))
    println(isEven(1))
    println(isEven(-5))
}
```

This is the output:

```
true
true
true
true
false
false
false
false
```

Here, distinct values for the input are mapped to the same values in the output.

As you'll see in the rest of the book, a function mapping any type A to a Boolean is a Predicate. You can define all the predicates using the following typealias:

```
typealias Predicate<A> = Fun<A, Boolean> // (A) -> Boolean
```

Exercise 2.2

Can you write the inverse function of `twice`? What are the domain and range for the inverse function?

```
fun twice(x: Int) = 2 * x
```

Exercise 2.2 solution

This exercise isn't as easy as it looks. If `twice` has type `Fun<Int, Int>`, the inverse function should have the same type. This is because if a function has type `Fun<A,B>`, the inverse should have type `Fun<B,A>`. You get this by inverting the input type A with the output type B.

The following is a possible candidate as an inverse function of `twice`:

```
fun half(x: Int) = x / 2
```

The `half` type is still `Fun<Int, Int>` but, because of the division between `Int` values, `half` isn't invertible. This breaks the following required relation:

```
half after twice == twice after half
```

The first member is OK:

```
half after twice == half(twice(x)) == (2 * x) / 2 == x
```

But the second member isn't:

```
twice after half == twice(half(x)) == 2 * ( x / 2)
```

To prove that the last equation isn't valid, try giving it some values for `x`:

```
x = 0    2 * (x / 2) == 2 * (0 / 2) == 2 * 0 = 0 == x
x = 1    2 * (x / 2) == 2 * (1 / 2) == 2 * 0 = 0 != x
x = 2    2 * (x / 2) == 2 * (2 / 2) == 2 * 1 = 2 == x
x = 3    2 * (x / 2) == 2 * (2 / 2) == 2 * 1 = 2 != x
```

As you can see, this happens because `half` isn't invertible, so it can't be the inverse of `twice`. This is because if function `f` is the inverse of function `g`, then `g` must be the inverse of `f`. In this solution, `half`, *seems* to not work. *Seems* because if you consider `half` to be the inverse of `twice`, you shouldn't invoke it using odd input values. This is because they wouldn't be part of the range of `twice`. To be rigorous, the type of `twice` is `Fun<Int, EvenInt>`, where `EvenInt` is the type of all the even integer numbers. In that case, the inverse `half` would have the type `Fun<EvenInt, Int>`, and everything would be fine.

But how can you represent the `EvenInt` type? All the concepts are purposely being stressed a little bit here, but that's the topic for Challenge 3!

It's worth mentioning how, in practice, you usually come to compromises defining `twice` like this:

```
fun twice(x: Double): Double = 2 * x
```

Now, its type is `Fun<Double, Double>`, and the inverse function is:

```
fun half(x: Double): Double  = x / 2.0
```

Exercise 2.3

Can you prove that using Set*s as objects* and *"is a subset of" as morphisms* results in a category? In other words, a morphism from set A to set B would mean that A is a subset of B. In that case, what are the initial and terminal objects?

> **Hint**: Think of any objects in the category as a set of elements. A morphism from A to B means that A is a subset of B. Can this help you to prove composition, associativity and identity?

Exercise 2.3 solution

To prove some kinds of objects and morphisms define a category, you need to prove the three fundamental properties:

- Composition

- Associativity

- Identity

In this case, objects are sets, and morphisms define the relation of inclusion you represent with the $\subseteq$ symbol.

To prove composition, you need to prove that for every three sets A, B and C, if A is a subset of B and B is a subset of C, then it's also true that A is a subset of C. Visualizing the relation with a Venn diagram, like in Figure 2a.1, helps to prove composition:

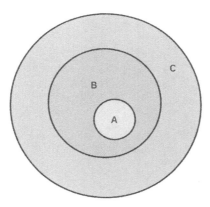

Figure 2a.1: Composition of sets

From the definition of category, to prove associativity, you need to prove that:

$(h \circ g) \circ f \ = \ h \circ (g \circ f).$

A similar Venn diagram helps to prove associativity:

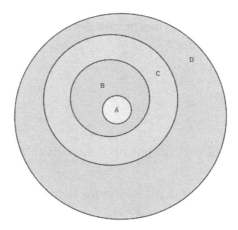

Figure 2a.2: Associativity of sets

Using the following morphisms:

- f = A is a subset of B

- g = B is a subset of C

- h = C is a subset of D

You can break it down like this:

- (h∘g) = B is a subset of D

- (g∘f) = A is a subset of C

- (h∘g)∘f = A is a subset of D

- h∘(g∘f) = A is a subset of D

Identity has a simple proof because each set contains itself, so A is a subset of A.

This proves that sets and the morphism "is a subset of" create a category.

What about the initial and terminal objects? Again, the definition comes to the rescue. The initial point is an object with outgoing arrows to all other objects in the category. In terms of sets, what set is the subset of all the other sets?

The terminal object is an object with unique incoming morphisms from all other objects in the category. What, then, is a set containing all the other sets? It has a name: **superset**.

The problem, in this case, is that the superset isn't easy to represent in practice. Think of the set of all the subsets of integer values. This doesn't exist because, for any candidate you find, there's always another one containing it with some other integer values not included in the initial candidate. For this reason, the category of sets and the morphism "is a subset of" doesn't have a terminal object. Categories using some kind of ordering relation like the one in this exercise don't have terminal objects.

Exercise 2.4

In this chapter, you defined `after`, which allows you to write expressions like:

```
val formatTwice = g after f
```

Can you write `compose` instead, which would allow you to implement the same expression as:

```
val formatTwice = f compose g
```

Exercise 2.4 solution

In this case, you need to consider f as the receiver of the function and write the following code:

```
inline infix fun <A, B, C> Fun<A, B>.compose(
  crossinline g: Fun<B, C>
): Fun<A, C> =
  { a: A ->
    g(this(a))
  }
```

As you can see:

- The receiver of the function is Fun<A, B>.

- The parameter of compose is a function g of type Fun<B, C>.

- In the body, you invoke the f receiver first and then pass the result to the function g.

To test `compose`, use the following code with `twice` and `format`, which you created in the previous exercises.

```
fun main() {
  val f: Fun<Int, Int> = ::twice
  val g: Fun<Int, String> = ::format
  val formatTwice = f compose g // HERE
  println(formatTwice(37))
}
```

Note how the previous `g after f` is now `f compose g`.

Exercise 2.5

Can you write an example of an isomorphic function `f` and its inverse `g` and prove they always compose to `identity`?

Exercise 2.5 solution

The following is an example of a function and its inverse:

```
fun addOne(x: Int) = x + 1

fun removeOne(x: Int) = x - 1
```

To prove `addOne` and `removeOne` are the inverse of each other, you need to prove that:

```
addOne after removeOne = removeOne after addOne = identity
```

This is equivalent to proving that:

```
(x - 1) + 1 = 1 + (x - 1) = x
```

This is identity, so `addOne` and `removeOne` are the inverse of each other. They're both **isomorphic** functions.

Challenge 1: Functions and sets

How would you represent a specific `Set` using a function? For instance, how would you represent the set of even numbers with a function? After that, how would you print all the values in the set?

Challenge 1 solution

A `Set` is something more than a bunch of things because it has some structure. An object can be in the set or not. If an object is in the `Set`, it must be unique. You can't have the same object in a `Set` twice.

The type for a function describing a `Set` is then `Fun<A, Boolean>`. `Boolean` is an interesting type because you associate it with a set with just two elements: `true` or `false`. A function of type `Fun<A, Boolean>` is a **predicate**, and you can add the following definition to the **Aliases.kt** file in the project for this chapter:

```
typealias Predicate<A> = Fun<A, Boolean>
```

To represent the `Set` of even `Int` numbers, write:

```
val evenIntSet: Predicate<Int> = { a: Int -> a % 2 == 0}
```

To check if a value is in the `Set` of even numbers, you just invoke `evenIntSet`. For instance:

```
fun main() {
    println(" 0  is even?  ${evenIntSet(0)}")
    println(" 9  is even?  ${evenIntSet(-9)}")
    println(" 10 is even?  ${evenIntSet(10)}")
    println(" 3  is even?  ${evenIntSet(3)}")
}
```

Running the previous code, you'll get:

```
0  is even?  true
9  is even?  false
10 is even?  true
3  is even?  false
```

Representing a set with a function allows you to check if a value is in the set or not. To actually print all the values in the set, you need to scan the whole domain and print the ones whose predicate function returns true.

For the previous example, do the following:

```
(Int.MIN_VALUE..Int.MAX_VALUE)
  .filter(evenIntSet)
  .forEach { println(it) }
```

Challenge 2: Functions and set again

How would you represent the intersection and union of two sets using functions? The intersection is the set of objects that belong to set A and set B, and the union is the set of all objects that belong to set A or set B.

Challenge 2 solution

Suppose you have the following functions for two different sets:

```
/** The set of all the odd Ints */
val oddIntSet: Predicate<Int> = { a: Int -> a % 2 != 0 }

/** The set of all multiples of 37 */
val multipleOf37: Predicate<Int> = { a: Int -> a % 37 == 0 }
```

You would define the union like this:

```
/** The union of the two sets */
fun <A> union(
  set1: Predicate<A>,
  set2: Predicate<A>
): Predicate<A> = { a: A ->
  set1(a) || set2(a)
}
```

And the intersection like this:

```
/** The intersection of the two sets */
fun <A> intersection(
  set1: Predicate<A>,
  set2: Predicate<A>
): Predicate<A> = { a: A ->
  set1(a) && set2(a)
}
```

It's interesting to note how the union and intersection sets are also `Predicate<A>`, and therefore functions of the same type as the ones you had as parameters.

You can test out your functions with the following:

```
val oddMultipleOf37Union =
    union(oddIntSet, multipleOf37)
val oddMultipleOf37Intersection =
  intersection(oddIntSet, multipleOf37)

println("1    is in union ${oddMultipleOf37Union(1)}")
println("37   is in union ${oddMultipleOf37Union(37)}")
println("74   is in union ${oddMultipleOf37Union(74)}")
println("100 is in union ${oddMultipleOf37Union(100)}")

println("1    is in intersection $
{oddMultipleOf37Intersection(1)}")
println("37   is in intersection $
{oddMultipleOf37Intersection(37)}")
println("74   is in intersection $
{oddMultipleOf37Intersection(74)}")
println("100 is in intersection $
{oddMultipleOf37Intersection(100)}")
```

Challenge 3: The right domain

Consider the following function:

```
fun oneOver(x: Int): Double = 1.0 / x
```

What's the domain and the range for this function? When you invoke `oneOver(0)`, you get an exception.

How can you be sure you only pass values in the domain as an input parameter?

Challenge 3 solution

You probably know from your math in school that the function 1/x doesn't exist for x = 0. This means that the domain of `oneOver` is the set represented by all the `Int` values without 0.

The question now is: How would you represent the type of all the `Int` values without 0? If the related type was `NonZeroInt`, the previous function would become:

```
fun oneOver(x: NonZeroInt): Double = 1.0 / x
```

And, as said earlier, it would return a value for every input in its domain.

A possible option would be to define NonZeroInt like this:

```
@JvmInline
value class NonZeroInt private constructor(val value: Int) {
  companion object {
    operator fun invoke(value: Int): NonZeroInt? {
      return when (value) {
        0 -> null
        else -> NonZeroInt(value)
      }
    }
  }
}
```

In this case, you can create a NonZeroInt only using a value that isn't 0. However, you have a problem. Try running the following code to understand what the problem is:

```
fun main() {
  println("1/3 = ${oneOver(NonZeroInt(3))}") // ERROR
}
```

This doesn't compile because of what IntelliJ is telling you here:

```
fun main() {
  println("1/3 = ${oneOver(NonZeroInt( value: 3))}"
}
                                    Type mismatch.
                                    Required: NonZeroInt
                                    Found:    NonZeroInt?
```

2.16 - Type Mismatch. Required: NonZeroInt. Found: NonZeroInt?

oneOver is expecting a NonZeroInt and not the nullable version NonZeroInt?. As a shortcut, you might use the !! operator. In that case, the code compiles but throws an exception in case of 0: NonZeroInt(0).

```
fun main() {
  println("1/3 = ${oneOver(NonZeroInt(3)!!)}") // COMPILES
}
```

A better idea is moving the error to the creation of the NonZeroInt object itself, replacing the previous implementation of NonZeroInt with:

```
@JvmInline
value class NonZeroInt(val value: Int) {
  init {
    require(value != 0) { "0 is not a value for this type!" }
  }
}
```

In this case, you can change main like this:

```
println("1/3 = ${oneOver(NonZeroInt(3))}")
```

When you run, you get the following output:

```
1/3 = 0.3333333333333333
```

Using the following code:

```
println("1/3 = ${oneOver(NonZeroInt(0))}")
```

You'll get the following output instead:

```
Exception in thread "main" java.lang.IllegalArgumentException: 0
is not a value for this type!
```

In both cases, as you'll learn in the following chapters, this isn't a very functional way to handle this problem. One more reason to keep reading this book! :]

Appendix C: Chapter 3 Exercise & Challenge Solutions

Exercise 3.1

Is inc a pure function?

```
var count = 0

fun inc(x: Int): Int = ++count + x
```

Exercise 3.1 solution

In this case, inc is *not* a pure function because it increments a global variable that's part of the external world. Incrementing count is a **side effect**. The function also doesn't return the same value with the same input value, as you can verify by executing the following code:

```
fun main() {
   println(inc(1))
   println(inc(1))
   println(inc(1))
   println(inc(1))
}
```

Here, you invoke `inc` with the same value in input, but you get different values in output, as you can see in the following logs:

```
2
3
4
5
```

Exercise 3.2

Is `inc2` a pure function?

```
val count = 0

fun inc2(x: Int): Int = x + count + 1
```

Exercise 3.2 solution

This function isn't so obvious, but it *is* pure because it always returns the same value in output for the same value in input. It uses `count`, which is part of the universe, but it's a `val`, so it never changes. You can see `count` as part of the universe's state but, because it's immutable, it can't be the consequence of any side effect, and it wont change the output.

Exercise 3.3

Is `expr3`:

```
val expr3 = 42
val (a1, a2) = expr3 to expr3
```

The same as the following?

```
val (a1, a2) = 42 to 42
```

Exercise 3.3 solution

Yes, in this case, `expr2` is referentially transparent. You can prove this by running the following code without any exceptions:

```
fun main() {
  // Expr3 is referentially transparent, as you can see here
  val expr3 = { 42 }
  val (a1, a2) = expr3() to expr3()
  val expr3Eval = expr3()
  val (a1Eval, a2Eval) = expr3Eval to expr3Eval
  assertOrThrow("expr3 is not RT") {
    a1 == a1Eval && a2 == a2Eval
  }
}
```

Additionally, `expr3` doesn't have any side effects.

Exercise 3.4

Suppose you have the following code:

```
val CounterIterator = object : Iterator<Int> {

  private var count = 0

  override fun hasNext(): Boolean = true

  override fun next(): Int = count++
}
```

Is the following expression referentially transparent?

```
val expr4 = { CounterIterator.next() }
```

Exercise 3.4 solution

In this case, expr4 is *not* referentially transparent because the expression has a side effect.

You can prove this with the following code:

```
fun main() {
  // Expr4 is not referentially transparent, as you can see here
  val expr4 = { CounterIterator.next() }
  val (a1, a2) = expr4() to expr4()
  val expr4Eval = expr4()
  val (a1Eval, a2Eval) = expr4Eval to expr4Eval
  assertOrThrow("expr4 is not RT") {
    a1 == a1Eval && a2 == a2Eval
  }
}
```

Run the code, and you'll get:

```
Exception in thread "main" java.lang.AssertionError: expr4 is
not RT
```

Every time you evaluate expr4, you change the internal state of CounterIterator, which is part of the external universe and, for the same reason, you get a different output value.

Exercise 3.5

The Writer<A, B> data type you defined earlier is a very important concept in functional programming. If you use types as objects and the functions Writer<A, B> as morphisms, you get a very special category: the **Kleisli category**.

Can you prove that by using types as objects and Writer<A, B> as morphisms, you get a category?

```
typealias Writer<A, B> = (A) -> Pair<B, String>
```

Exercise 3.5 solution

In Chapter 2, "Function Fundamentals", you learned that some **objects** with arrows between them, known as **morphisms**, form a category if all the following rules are true:

1. **Composition**

2. **Associativity**

3. **Identity**

In this exercise, you basically need to prove these rules for every type A and every function you represent as Writer<A, B>.

Proving composition

In this case, you have to prove that for every morphism f from the objects A to B, and g from B to C, there's always a morphism g ∘ f from A to C, which is the composition of f with g.

You've actually already proved this composition in this chapter, Chapter 3, "Functional Programming Concepts", with the following higher-order function:

```
infix fun <A, B, C> Writer<B, C>.after(
    w: Writer<A, B>
): Writer<A, C> = { a: A ->
    val (b, str) = w(a)
    val (c, str2) = this(b)
    c to "$str\n$str2\n"
}
```

As you did in Chapter 2, "Function Fundamentals", you might also define compose with the following code:

```
infix fun <A, B, C> Writer<A, B>.compose(
    w: Writer<B, C>
): Writer<A, C> = w after this
```

With these two functions, you prove composition.

Proving associativity

To prove associativity for `Writer<A, B>`, you basically need to prove that:

```
(h after g) after f == h after (g after f)
```

Where:

```
f: Writer<A, B>
g: Writer<B, C>
h: Writer<C, D>
```

A possible way of doing this is applying the substitution model, but there's a simpler way. Look at how composition works in the previous paragraph, and you'll notice that associativity is true if it's true for both the `first` and `second` properties of the resulting `Pair`s of `Writer`s. For `first`, you're applying the normal composition of functions `Fun<A, B>`. For `second`, you're basically concatenating `String`s. Because you already know that associativity is true for function `Fun<A, B>`, you basically need to also prove that `String` concatenation is associative. Given three `String`s — `str1`, `str2` and `str3` — you can easily prove that:

```
(str1 + str2) + str3 == str1 + (str2 + str3)
```

This proves that, using the composition you defined in the previous paragraph, associativity for `Writer<A, B>` is also true.

Proving identity

In this case, you need to prove that for every type A, there's always a morphism `Writer<A, A>` called identity `id<A>`, such that, for every f of type `Writer<A, B>` the following is true:

```
f after id == id after f == f
```

In this chapter, Chapter 3, "Functional Programming Concepts", you met the function:

```kotlin
fun <A, B> Fun<A, B>.liftW(
  log: (A, B) -> String
): Writer<A, B> =
  { a: A ->
    val b = this(a)
    b to log(a, b)
  }
```

This function suggests what the identity might be. Just imagine starting from the identity for Fun<A, B>, which is:

```
fun <A> identity(a: A) = a
```

And apply liftW() using the empty String. What you'll get is simply:

```
fun <A> id(): Writer<A, A> = { a -> a to "" }
```

Now, you need to prove that, whatever f of type Writer<A, B> is, the following rule is true:

```
f after id == id after f == f
```

To prove this, you need to start with the implementation of composition for Writer<A, B>. Then, use id<A> both as the receiver and as the parameter w.

```
infix fun <A, B, C> Writer<B, C>.after(
  w: Writer<A, B>
): Writer<A, C> = { a: A ->
  val (b, str) = w(a)
  val (c, str2) = this(b)
  c to "$str\n$str2\n"
}
```

If you want to reduce the first part, you start from:

```
f after id
```

You can write the definition of composition assuming that w is id<A>, getting:

```
fun <A, C> Writer<A, C>.after(): Writer<A, C> = { a: A ->
  val (b, str) = id<A>()(a)
  val (c, str2) = this(b)
  c to "$str\n$str2\n"
}
```

In the above:

```
str = ""
b = a
c = f(b) = f(a)
"$str\n$str2\n" = "$str2\n"
```

The result is then:

```
f(a) to "$str2\n"
```

Which is exactly what you'd get from f of type Writer<A, B>.

Now, you need to prove that you get the same result starting from:

```
id after f
```

Doing the same substitution, you'll get:

```
infix fun <A, C> Writer<A, C>.after(
  w: Writer<A, C>
): Writer<A, C> = { a: A ->
  val (b, str) = w(a)
  val (c, str2) = id<C>()(b)
  c to "$str$str2\n"
}
```

Which becomes:

```
val (b, str) = f(a)
c = id(b) = b to "$str\n"
```

Which is, again, what you'd get from f.

```
f(a) to "$str\n"
```

Just note that in this case, the decoration of f is str and not str2, like in the previous case.

This proves that by using types as objects and Writer<A, B> as morphisms, you get a category that's actually very important: the **Kleisli category**!

Challenge 1: Pure or impure?

Is inc3 a pure function? Why or why not?

```
var count = 0
fun inc3(x: Int): Int {
  val result = x + ++count + 1
  println("Res: $result") // WHAT IF YOU REMOVE THIS?
  --count
  return result
}
```

What if you remove the println() with the comment?

Challenge 1 solution

The answer, in this case, isn't so obvious. Every time you invoke inc3, you calculate a result incrementing count, a global variable. You then print the result and decrement the global variable count before returning the result. println makes this function impure.

But what if you remove the println? Is the function still impure? The function *is* still impure because it changes the values of count while executing. If you invoke another function in another thread accessing the same count variable, a race condition might cause some unexpected results.

Challenge 2: Pure or impure?

Is output a pure function? Why or why not?

```
fun output(x: Int): Unit = println("x = $x")
```

Challenge 2 solution

This function always provides the same output, Unit, for the same input. The problem is that it logs messages, so it has side effects. Because of this, output is *not* a pure function.

Challenge 3: Pure or impure?

Is randomAdd a pure function? Why or why not?

```
fun randomAdd(a: Int, b: Int): Int = a + b + Random.nextInt()
```

Challenge 3 solution

This function doesn't provide the same output for the same input values because of the Random component. What about side effects? Even if it's not directly visible, this function has a side effect: It changes the state of the Random object.

Appendix D: Chapter 4 Exercise & Challenge Solutions

Exercise 4.1

Can you write a lambda expression that calculates the distance between two points given their coordinates, x1, y1 and x2, y2? The formula for the distance between two points is $distance = \sqrt{(x2-x1)^2+(y2-y1)^2}$.

Exercise 4.1 solution

You can approach this problem in different ways. Assuming you pass all the coordinates as distinct parameters, you can write the following code:

```
val distanceLambda = { x1: Double, y1: Double, x2: Double, y2:
Double -> // 1
    val sqr1 = (x2 - x1) * (x2 - x1) // 2
    val sqr2 = (y2 - y1) * (y2 - y1) // 2
    Math.sqrt(sqr1 + sqr2) // 3
}
```

In this example, you:

1. Define a lambda expression with four Double parameters for each set of coordinates.

2. Calculate the square of the distances between coordinates x and y.

3. Produce the final return result with the last expression of the lambda.

You can get the same result in other ways. Here's one using the `Point` typealias:

```
typealias Point = Pair<Double, Double>

val distanceLambdaWithPairs = { p1: Point, p2: Point ->
  val sqr1 = Math.pow(p1.first - p2.first, 2.0)
  val sqr2 = Math.pow(p1.second - p2.second, 2.0)
  Math.sqrt(sqr1 + sqr2)
}
```

You can then test your lambdas with the following code:

```
fun main() {
  println(distanceLambda(0.0, 0.0, 1.0, 1.0))
  println(distanceLambdaWithPairs(0.0 to 0.0, 1.0 to 1.0))
}
```

When you run, you get:

```
1.4142135623730951
1.4142135623730951
```

Exercise 4.2

What's the type for the lambda expression you wrote in Exercise 4.1?

Exercise 4.2 solution

The type of `distanceLambda` is:

```
val distanceLambda: (Double, Double, Double, Double) -> Double
```

The type of `distanceLambdaWithPairs` is:

```
val distanceLambdaWithPairs: (Point, Point) -> Double
```

Or:

```
val distanceLambdaWithPairs: (Pair<Double, Double>, Pair<Double,
Double>) -> Double
```

Exercise 4.3

What are the types of the following lambda expressions?

```kotlin
val emptyLambda = {} // 1
val helloWorldLambda = { "Hello World!" } // 2
val helloLambda = { name: String -> "Hello $name!" } // 3
val nothingLambda = { TODO("Do exercise 4.3!") } // 4
```

Can you write an example of a lambda expression of the following type?

```kotlin
typealias AbsurdType = (Nothing) -> Nothing
```

In this case, can you show how to invoke it?

Exercise 4.3 solution

You start by looking at:

```kotlin
val emptyLambda = {}
```

This is a lambda expression with no input parameters and no return value. Well, that's not quite true in Kotlin. The expression is actually returning something: Unit. Its type is then:

```kotlin
val emptyLambda: () -> Unit
```

The type for:

```kotlin
val helloWorldLambda = { "Hello World!" }
```

Is:

```kotlin
val helloWorldLambda: () -> String
```

A little bit different is the type of:

```kotlin
val helloLambda = { name: String -> "Hello $name!" }
```

Which is:

```kotlin
val helloLambda: (String) -> String
```

Finally, you have something else a little different, like:

```
val nothingLambda = { TODO("Do exercise 4.3!") }
```

In this case, the return type is Nothing. The return type would also be Nothing if you throw an exception. The type nothingLambda is then:

```
val nothingLambda: () -> Nothing
```

Nothing and lambda

Given the type:

```
typealias AbsurdType = (Nothing) -> Nothing
```

You can write a function like the following:

```
val absurd: AbsurdType = { nothing -> throw Exception("This is
Absurd") }
```

As you learned in Chapter 2, "Function Fundamentals", the problem with the absurd lambda expression is that you need a value of type Nothing for its invocation. You might write:

```
fun main() {
    absurd(TODO("Invoked?"))
}
```

Because Kotlin uses strict evaluation, it evaluates the expression you pass as a parameter of absurd before the absurd itself. In this case, TODO doesn't complete, so the absurd will never be invoked. The same happens with:

```
fun main() {
    absurd(throw Exception("Invoked?"))
}
```

Now, isn't that absurd!

Exercise 4.4

Can you implement a function simulating the **short-circuit and** operator with the following signature without using &&? In other words, can you replicate the short-circuiting behavior of left && right:

```
fun shortCircuitAnd(left: () -> Boolean, right: () ->
Boolean): Boolean
```

Can you also write a test to prove that right evaluates only if left is false?

Exercise 4.4 solution

In Kotlin, if is an expression, so you can implement shortCircuitAnd like this:

```
fun shortCircuitAnd(
  left: () -> Boolean,
  right: () -> Boolean
): Boolean = if (left()) {
  right()
} else {
  false
}
```

In this lambda, right will only evaluate if left is true.

To test its behavior, you can use the following main:

```
fun main() {
  val inputValue = 2
  shortCircuitAnd(
    left = { println("LeftEvaluated!"); inputValue > 3 },
    right = { println("RightEvaluated!"); inputValue < 10 },
  )
}
```

Running this with inputValue = 2, you get:

```
LeftEvaluated!
```

Change inputValue = 10, and you get:

```
LeftEvaluated!
RightEvaluated!
```

This proves that shortCircuitAnd evaluates right only if left is true.

Exercise 4.5

Can you implement the function myLazy with the following signature, which allows you to pass in a lambda expression and execute it just once?

```
fun <A: Any> myLazy(fn: () -> A): () -> A // ???
```

Exercise 4.5 solution

myLazy accepts a lambda expression of type () -> A as an input parameter. It's also important to note that A has a constraint, which makes it non-null. This makes the exercise a little bit easier, because you can write something like:

```
fun <A : Any> myLazy(fn: () -> A): () -> A {
  var result: A? = null // 1
  return { // 2
    if (result == null) { // 3
      result = fn() // 4
    }
    result!! // 5
  }
}
```

In this function, you:

1. Use result as a local variable that tells you whether the lambda expression fn has been evaluated, and the value of type A can't be null because of the constraint.

2. Return a lambda of the same type, () -> A, as the input parameter.

3. Check if result is null. This means fn hasn't been evaluated yet.

4. Evaluate fn and store the value in result, which now isn't null anymore.

5. Return result, which is always of type A.

To test myLazy, write:

```
fun main() {
  val myLazy = myLazy { println("I'm very lazy!"); 10 }
  3.times {
    println(myLazy())
  }
}
```

Run it, and you get:

```
I'm very lazy!
10
10
10
```

This proves the lambda expression is actually evaluated only once, and the result is simply reused.

You can remove the not nullability constraint in Challenge 4.1. See you there! :]

Exercise 4.6

Create a function fibo returning the values of a Fibonacci sequence. Remember, every value in a Fibonacci sequence is the sum of the previous two elements. The first two elements are 0 and 1. The first values are, then:

```
0  1  1  2  3  5  8  13  21 ...
```

Exercise 4.6 solution

The following is a possible implementation for the Fibonacci sequence using lambda evaluation:

```
fun fibo(): () -> Int {
    var first = 0
    var second = 1
    var count = 0
    return {
        val next = when (count) {
            0 -> 0
            1 -> 1
            else -> {
                val ret = first + second
                first = second
                second = ret
                ret
            }
        }
        count++
        next
    }
}
```

To test the previous code, you can use:

```
fun main() {
  val fiboSeq = fibo()
  10.times {
    print("${fiboSeq()} ")
  }
}
```

Run it, and you get:

```
0  1  1  2  3  5  8  13  21  34
```

Challenge 4.1

In Exercise 4.5, you created myLazy, which allowed you to implement memoization for a generic lambda expression of type ()-> A. Can you now create myNullableLazy supporting optional types with the following signature?

```
fun <A> myNullableLazy(fn: () -> A?): () -> A? // ...
```

Challenge 4.1 solution

To remove the constraint, you just need to use an additional variable, like this:

```
fun <A> myNullableLazy(fn: () -> A?): () -> A? {
  var evaluated = false // HERE
  var result: A? = null
  return { ->
    if (!evaluated) {
      evaluated = true
      result = fn()
    }
    result
  }
}
```

To test `myNullableLazy`, you can write:

```
fun main() {
  val myNullableLazy: () -> Int? =
    myNullableLazy { println("I'm nullable lazy!"); null }
    3.times {
      println(myNullableLazy())
    }
}
```

Run it, and you get:

```
I'm nullable lazy!
null
null
null
```

Challenge 4.2

You might be aware of **Euler's number e**. It's a mathematical constant of huge importance that you can calculate in very different ways. It's an irrational number like **pi** that can't be represented in the form n/m. Here you're not required to know what it is, but you can use the following formula:

$$e = \sum_{n=0}^{\infty} \frac{1}{n!} = 1 + \frac{1}{1} + \frac{1}{1 \cdot 2} + \frac{1}{1 \cdot 2 \cdot 3} + \cdots$$

Figure 4.2: Euler's formula

Can you create a sequence that provides the sum of the n terms of the given formula?

Challenge 4.2 solution

A possible implementation of the Euler formula is:

```
fun e(): () -> Double {
  var currentSum = 1.0 // 1
  var n = 1

  tailrec fun factorial(n: Int, tmp: Int): Int = // 2
    if (n == 1) tmp else factorial(n - 1, n * tmp)

  return {
    currentSum += 1.0 / factorial(n++, 1).toDouble() // 3
    currentSum
  }
}
```

This basically translates the formula in Figure 4.2 into code. Here, you:

1. Initialize currentSum to the first value, which is 1.

2. Implement factorial, which provides the factorial of a given number n. A factorial is the product of the number from 1 to n. For example 3 factorial would be 1 * 2 * 3.

3. Return a lambda expression of type () -> Double, updating and returning currentSum.

Write and run the following code:

```
fun main() {
  val e = e()
  10.times {
    println(e())
  }
}
```

You get the following output:

```
2.0
2.5
2.6666666666666665
2.708333333333333
2.7166666666666663
2.7180555555555554
2.7182539682539684
2.71827876984127
2.7182815255731922
2.7182818011463845
```

The last value is 2.7182818011463845, which is a good approximation of Euler's number.

Looking at the previous code, you can see an additional optimization. In fact, you calculate the factorial every time.

Why not also make it a sequence? In this case, you can write:

```
fun factSeq(): () -> Int {
  var partial = 1
  var n = 1
  return {
    partial *= n++
    partial
  }
}
```

This allows you to implement e in a better way, like this:

```
fun fastE(): () -> Double {
  var currentSum = 1.0
  val fact = factSeq()
  return {
    currentSum += 1.0 / fact().toDouble()
    currentSum
  }
}
```

You can then write and run the following code when you use `fastE` instead of `e`:

```
fun main() {
  val e = fastE() // HERE
  10.times {
    println(e())
  }
}
```

The output is exactly the same, just more performant:

```
2.0
2.5
2.6666666666666665
2.708333333333333
2.7166666666666663
2.7180555555555554
2.7182539682539684
2.71827876984127
2.7182815255731922
2.7182818011463845
```

Appendix E: Chapter 5 Exercise & Challenge Solutions

Exercise 5.1

Kotlin provides you with `first`, which returns the first element of `Iterable<T>` for which a predicate you provide as an input evaluates to `true`. Remember that `Iterable<T>` is the abstraction of all the collections providing an `Iterator<T>` implementation.

```
public interface Iterable<out T> {
    public operator fun iterator(): Iterator<T>
}
```

`Iterator<T>` allows you to iterate over all the elements of a collection in a way that doesn't depend on the collection implementation itself:

```
public interface Iterator<out T> {

    public operator fun next(): T

    public operator fun hasNext(): Boolean
}
```

The current `first` signature is:

```
public inline fun <T> Iterable<T>.first(predicate: (T) ->
Boolean): T
```

Kotlin doesn't allow you to override the current extension function on `Iterable<T>`. So, how would you implement `first` on `Array<T>`?

The current implementation of `first` throws an exception if the collection is empty, so there's no first T. How would you implement the function `firstOrNull` on Array<T> returning `null` in such a case?

Exercise 5.1 solution

As mentioned, Kotlin doesn't allow you to override the extension function on Iterable<T> so, for this exercise, you need to implement `first` on Array<T>. A possible solution is:

```kotlin
public inline fun <T> Array<T>.first(
  predicate: (T) -> Boolean
): T { // 1
  for (item in this) { // 2
    if (predicate(item)) { // 3
      return item // 4
    }
  }
  throw NoSuchElementException("Array contains no element
matching the predicate.") // 5
}
```

The code is quite simple. In it, you:

1. Define `first` as an extension function for Array<T>, accepting a predicate as an input parameter and returning a value of type T.

2. Iterate over the values in Array<T>.

3. Evaluate the predicate on the current `item`.

4. Return the value for which `predicate` evaluates to `true`.

5. Throw a `NoSuchElementException` if `predicate` never evaluates to `true`.

Test `first` with the following code:

```kotlin
fun main() {
  val input = arrayOf(1, 2, 3, 4, 5)
  println(input.first {
    it > 3  // 1
  })
  println(input.first {
    it > 10 // 2
  })
}
```

When you run the previous code, you get:

```
4
Exception in thread "main" java.util.NoSuchElementException:
Array contains no element matching the predicate.
```

Note how:

1. Passing the predicate `{ it > 3}`, you get the value 4.

2. Using `{ it > 30}`, you get `NoSuchElementException`.

What if you don't want to throw an exception but implement `first` in a more functional way without `NoSuchElementException` as a side effect?

A possible solution is the following `firstOrNull` implementation:

```
public inline fun <T> Array<T>.firstOrNull(
  predicate: (T) -> Boolean
): T? { // 1
  for (item in this) {
    if (predicate(item)) {
      return item
    }
  }
  return null // 2
}
```

The code isn't very different from the `first` one. Here, you:

1. Have the optional `T?` as a return type.

2. Return `null` if there's no `value` for the given predicate.

Test `firstOrNull` by running the following code:

```
fun main() {
  val input = arrayOf(1, 2, 3, 4, 5)
  println(input.first {
    it > 3
  })
  println(input.firstOrNull { // HERE
    it > 10
  })
}
```

In the previous code, you use `firstOrNull` instead of `first`. Run this code, and you get:

```
4
null
```

Exercise 5.2

The command pattern (https://en.wikipedia.org/wiki/Command_pattern) is another important design pattern that defines abstractions like `Command` and `CommandExecutor`. `Command` abstracts every possible operation that `CommandExecutor` can run. In other words, a `Command` represents a task and you can pass a `Command` to a `CommandExecutor` to run it. How would you represent them in a functional way?

Optionally, can you also provide a way to "redo" the most recent `Command`?

Exercise 5.2 solution

`Command` is basically a way to abstract the concept of a task. To represent it in a functional way, write:

```
typealias Command = () -> Unit
```

`CommandExecutor` is the component responsible for the execution of `Command`. A simple way to represent it is:

```
typealias CommandExecutor = (Command) -> Unit
```

You can create a possible implementation like the following:

```
class MyCommandExecutor : CommandExecutor { // 1

  val commandHistory = mutableListOf<Command>() // 2

  override fun invoke(command: Command) { // 3
    command.run {
      commandHistory.add(this)
      this()
    }
  }

  fun redo() { // 4
    commandHistory.lastOrNull()?.let {
```

```
        it()
      }
    }
  }
```

In the previous code, you:

1. Define `MyCommandExecutor` as an implementation of `CommandExecutor`.

2. Initialize `commandHistory`, which will contain the history of all the commands you execute. This isn't necessary, but usually, the command pattern allows you to run `Command` multiple times.

3. Override `invoke`, passing `Command` as a parameter. In the body, you simply invoke `Command` after saving its reference in `commandHistory`.

4. Provide `redo()` as a chance to execute the last command again.

Usually, the command pattern also allows you to undo `Commands`, but that's out of the scope of this book.

Exercise 5.3

Can you implement the following `Reader` interface as a functional interface? How would you test it?

```
interface Reader {
  fun readChar(): Char?
  fun readString(): String {
    TODO("Call readChar() until it returns null")
  }
}
```

Exercise 5.3 solution

The `TODO` in the problem description's code gives you a hint about a possible solution. One option is the following:

```
fun interface Reader {
  fun readChar(): Char?
  fun readString(): String {
    val result = StringBuilder()
    do {
      val nextChar = readChar()
      if (nextChar != null) {
```

```
          result.append(nextChar)
        }
    } while (nextChar != null)
    return result.toString()
  }
}
```

In this code, you're basically implementing readString using StringBuilder appending Char, which you get from readChar until you get null. In that case, you return what's in StringBuilder by invoking toString.

So far, so good! But how do you test it? Does making Reader a functional interface help? Actually, it doesn't.

To test Reader, use the following implementation:

```
class MyReader(val str: String) : Reader { // 1
  var pos = 0 // 2
  override fun readChar(): Char? =
    if (pos < str.length) str[pos++] else null // 3
}
```

Here, you:

1. Create MyReader as a simple implementation of Reader, receiving String as an input parameter.

2. Initialize pos to 0, which is the position of the first Char you want to return from readChar.

3. Check if pos is in the boundary of the String provided as input. If so, you return the Char in it and increment pos. Otherwise, you return null.

To test how this works, just run the following code:

```
fun main() {
  val input = MyReader("This is a String!")
  println(input.readString())
}
```

Getting:

```
This is a String!
```

The initial question remains: What advantage do you have by making `Reader` a functional interface? It gives you two advantages:

1. You can use the handy `Type { /* lambda */}` syntax.

2. You can pass a `Reader` implementation instance using a simple lambda expression as an input parameter of another function. In that case, Kotlin would infer the right type.

You could test the first case with the following code:

```
fun main() {
  val inputString = "This is a String!"
  var pos = 0
  val input = Reader {
    if (pos < inputString.length) inputString[pos++] else null
  }
  println(input.readString())
}
```

In this case, the `Reader` implementation captures the value of `pos`, which basically represents its own state. What if you had the following code instead?

```
fun main() {
  val inputString = "This is a String!"
  var pos = 0
  val input = Reader {
    if (pos < inputString.length) inputString[pos++] else null
  }
  val input2 = Reader {
    if (pos < inputString.length) inputString[pos++] else null
  }
  println(input.readString())
  println(input2.readString())
}
```

Only the first `println` would actually print something. To make things work, you'd need a second variable for the state of `Reader` for `input2`, like this:

```
fun main() {
  val inputString = "This is a String!"
  var pos = 0
  var pos2 = 0
  val input = Reader {
    if (pos < inputString.length) inputString[pos++] else null
  }
  val input2 = Reader {
    if (pos2 < inputString.length) inputString[pos2++] else null
  }
```

```
    println(input.readString())
    println(input2.readString())
}
```

This method is confusing and error-prone.

You'd have the same problem, even if you pass Reader as an input parameter of another function, like this:

```
fun consumeReader(reader: Reader) {
  println(reader.readString())
}

fun main() {
  var pos = 0
  val inputString = "This is a String!"
  consumeReader({
    if (pos < inputString.length) inputString[pos++] else null
  })
}
```

The only advantage here is that you don't need to specify the Reader type before the lambda because the Kotlin compiler infers it for you.

So, what's the lesson here? As you learned in the chapter, typealias allows you to give a name to an existing type. In the case of function types, you can assume they already exist somewhere, and typealias is a tool to reduce the quantity of code you have to write, especially for generic types. Types like (T)-> Boolean, (T,T) -> T and so on already exist, even if you don't declare them explicitly.

The type you define using a functional interface is a new type, and the implementations must specify the name explicitly. They don't exist before that, even if they basically define an existing type. As proved in the chapter, consider the functional interface:

```
fun interface SinglePredicate<T> {
  fun accept(value: T): Boolean
}
```

This is basically equivalent to (T)-> Boolean, but it's a completely different type. The extension function you define for SinglePredicate<T> doesn't work for (T)-> Boolean, and vice versa. If you have a parameter of type SinglePredicate<T>, you can't pass a lambda expression of type (T)-> Boolean.

As a last note, remember that typealiases aren't visible from Java, but functional interfaces are.

Exercise 5.4

Implement an extension function `isEqualsPredicate` on the generic type T that returns a predicate that tests if a given value is equal to the same T. The signature should be the following:

```
fun <T> T.isEqualsPredicate(): (T) -> Boolean //
```

How would the same function be different if you use the following functional interface?

```
fun interface SinglePredicate<T> {
    fun accept(other: T): Boolean
}
```

Exercise 5.4 solution

A possible solution to the initial problem is the following:

```
fun <T> T.isEqualsPredicate(): (T) -> Boolean =
    { value -> this == value }
```

Test this with the following code:

```
fun main() {
    listOf(1, 2, 3, 4, 4, 5, 6, 7, 8, 8)
        .filter(4.isEqualsPredicate())
        .forEach(::println)
}
```

Run it, and you get:

```
4
4
```

If you use the functional interface `SinglePredicate<T>`, you have:

```
fun <T> T.isEqualsIPredicate(): SinglePredicate<T> =
    SinglePredicate<T> { value -> this == value }
```

Note how the name of the extension function isn't `isEqualsPredicate`. This avoids conflicts with the previous one because they're both acting on the same receiver, T, and not because of the different return type.

Exercise 5.5

Can you implement the same logic for implementing the example in the **Imperative vs. declarative approach** section using the definitions of Predicate1<T> and filterWithPredicate? Given a list of email addresses, you need to:

- Filter the valid email addresses.

- Filter the email addresses with the right length.

- Take the first five of them.

Exercise 5.5 solution

Using the definitions of Predicate1<T> and filterWithPredicate you have in **Predicates.kt** and what's in **Imperative.kt** and **Declarative.kt**, you can write:

```
val isValidEmail: Predicate1<String> = // 1
  Predicate1 { value -> EMAIL_REG_EX.matches(value) }

fun isLongerThan(length: Int): Predicate1<String> = // 2
  Predicate1 { value -> value.length > length }

fun main() {
  emails
    .filterWithPredicate(isValidEmail and isLongerThan(10)) // 3
    .take(5) // 4
    .forEach(::println) // 5
}
```

In this code, you:

1. Define isValidEmail as a Predicate1<String> that checks the validity of email addresses.

2. Create isLongerThan as a function returning a Predicate1<String> that checks the length of String.

3. Use filterWithPredicate, passing in as input the logic and between isValidEmail and isLongerThan.

4. Take the first 5 successful email addresses.

5. Print the result.

Running the previous code, you get:

```
email@emmmaail.com
mike@mcarli.it
first.second@ggg.com
test@test.co.uk
fp_is_great@funprog.com
```

Challenge 5.1: Mapping is important

In the chapter, you learned how to implement different types of higher-order functions, and in the next chapter, you'll see many more. A very important one is called map. This is a function that applies a given function fn of type (A) -> B to all the elements of a collection of items of type A, getting a collection of items of type B.

Can you implement the function map for the Array<A> type with the following signature?

```
fun <A, B> Array<A>.map(fn: (A) -> B): Array<B>
```

When you run this code:

```
fun main() {
  val square = { a: Int -> a * a }
  val toString = { a: Int -> "This is $a" }
  arrayOf(1, 2, 3)
    .map(square)
    .forEach(::println)
  arrayOf(1, 2, 3)
    .map(toString)
    .forEach(::println)
}
```

You should get:

```
1
4
9
This is 1
This is 2
This is 3
```

Challenge 5.1 solution

A possible implementation of map for Array<A> is the following:

```
inline fun <A, reified B> Array<A>.map(fn: (A) -> B): Array<B> =
    Array(this.size) { fn(this[it]) }
```

This simply uses the constructor for Array to initialize all the values after applying fn to all the elements in the original array.

Note the use of reified for the type B. This is because the Kotlin compiler needs to retain some information about the type B to properly initialize Array in output.

Running main in the challenge, you get the expected output:

```
1
4
9
This is 1
This is 2
This is 3
```

Challenge 5.2: Prime number filtering

Write a higher-order function all returning a new array containing all the values in an Array<T> for which a given Predicate1<T> is true. You can find the Predicate1<T> definition in **Predicates.kt**.

```
fun <T> Array<T>.all(predicate: Predicate1<T>) : Array<T>
```

Then, use it to return all the positive prime values in Array<Int>. A number is prime if it's not evenly divisible with any number other than 1 and itself.

Challenge 5.2 solution

You can implement all in many different ways. One of them is:

```
inline fun <reified T> Array<T>.all(
    predicate: Predicate1<T>
): Array<T> = filter { predicate.accept(it) }.toTypedArray()
```

You leverage the existing `filter`, adapting `Predicate1<T>` to the type `(T) ->` `Boolean` it requires. Then, you use `toTypedArray()` to make the `List<T>` an `Array<T>`. This requires more type information and is the reason for the `reified` keyword.

The following is a possible implementation of `Predicate1<Int>` testing if a given `Int` is a prime number:

```
val isPrime = Predicate1<Int> { value ->
  if (value <= 3) value > 1
  else if (value % 2 == 0 || value % 3 == 0) false
  else {
    var i = 5
    while (i * i <= value) {
      if (value % i == 0 || value % (i + 2) == 0)
        return@Predicate1 false
      i += 6
    }
    true
  }
}
```

This predicate tests if the `Int` is a prime number or not.

Finally, you can test it with:

```
fun main() {
  arrayOf(1, 45, 67, 78, 34, 56, 89, 121, 2, 11, 12, 13)
    .all(isPrime)
    .forEach(::println)
}
```

Running the previous code, you get:

```
89
2
11
13
```

Appendix F: Chapter 6 Exercise & Challenge Solutions

Exercise 6.1

In this section, you learned it's useful to avoid creating multiple instances of immutable classes because they represent the same value. Given the following immutable class Id:

```
class Id(val id: Int)
```

How would you change it to prevent any client from creating multiple instances of Id for the same id?

When you run this code:

```
fun main() {
    val id1 = // Create Id for id = 1
    val id2 = // Create Id for id = 1
    val id3 = // Create Id for id = 2
    val id4 = // Create Id for id = 2
    println("${id1 === id2}")
    println("${id1 === id2}")
    println("${id1 === id3}")
    println("${id3 === id4}")
}
```

You get:

```
true
true
false
true
```

Exercise 6.1 solution

In *Effective Java* — the book by Joshua Bloch mentioned earlier in the chapter — "Item 1" states: "Consider using **static factory methods** instead of constructors". This is because they allow you to control the way an instance of a class is created. In this case, "controlling" means:

- Deciding whether or not to allow the creation.

- Returning instances of different classes depending on some criteria. For example, returning a different implementation of the sort algorithm depending on the number of items.

- Reusing the same instance if it's an option.

The last point is the one you'll use to do the exercise. Consider, for instance, the following code:

```
class Id private constructor(val id: Int) { // 1
  companion object { // 2
    private val ids = mutableMapOf<Int, Id>() // 3
    fun of(id: Int): Id { // 4
      var existingId = ids[id]
      if (existingId == null) { // 5
        existingId = Id(id)
        ids[id] = existingId
      }
      return existingId // 6
    }
  }
}
```

In this code, you:

1. Define a class `Id` with a private constructor. With this, no client can directly create an instance of `Id` — only a method of the same `Id` class can.

2. Create a `companion` object so you can invoke the factory method without an instance of `Id`.

3. Define `ids` as a `MutableMap<Int, Id>` to store all the `Id` instances you create for a given `id`.

4. Implement the static factory method `of`, which allows you to create an instance of Id using the simple instance `Id.of(1)`.

5. Check if you already have an instance of Id for a given id. If you don't have an existing Id for the given id, you create a new one and save it in ids.

6. Return the new or recycled Id.

The `main` in the exercise becomes:

```
fun main() {
    val id1 = Id.of(1)
    val id2 = Id.of(1)
    val id3 = Id.of(2)
    val id4 = Id.of(2)
    println("${id1 === id2}")
    println("${id1 === id2}")
    println("${id1 === id3}")
    println("${id3 === id4}")
}
```

Run it, and you get what you expect:

```
true
true
false
true
```

Exercise 6.2

What happens if the Id class in Exercise 6.1 is a data class?

Exercise 6.2 solution

To see what happens when Id is a data class, you just need to add `data` to the class declaration:

```
data class Id private constructor(val id: Int) {
    // ...
}
```

This compiles fine but, if you look carefully, IntelliJ gives you the warning in Figure 6a.1:

```
33    data class Id private constructor(val id: Int) {
34      companion object    Private primary constructor is exposed via the generated 'copy()' method of a 'data' class.    ⋮
35        private val ids
36        fun of(id: Int): Id {
37    💡   var existingId : Id?  = ids[id]
38          if (existingId == null) {
39            existingId = Id(id)
40            ids[id] = existingId
41          }
42          return existingId
43        }
44      }
45    }
```

Figure 6a.1: Private primary constructor is exposed via the generated 'copy()' method of a 'data' class.

This means that with data classes, you can always create a copy of a class through the copy method. It's also important to note how the value you get with copy is an object with its own identity.

You can prove this by running the following code:

```
fun main() {
  val id1 = Id.of(1)
  val id2 = id1.copy()
  println("${id1 == id2}") // 1
  println("${id1 === id2}") // 2
}
```

The output is:

```
true
false
```

The value you get with copy is:

1. **Structurally equal** to the original one.

2. **Referentially equal** to the original one.

Unfortunately, there's nothing you can do to fix this. To understand why, look at the decompiled code:

```java
public final class Id {
    // ...
    private Id(int id) { // 1
        this.id = id;
    }

    @NotNull
    public final Id copy(int id) { // 2
        return new Id(id);
    }

    // $FF: synthetic method
    public static Id copy$default(Id var0, int var1, int var2,
Object var3) {
        if ((var2 & 1) != 0) {
            var1 = var0.id;
        }

        return var0.copy(var1);
    }
    // ...
}
```

In this code, note that the:

1. Id constructor is `private`.

2. copy invokes the `Id` constructor, making de facto public.

The potential Kotlin value classes (https://github.com/Kotlin/KEEP/blob/master/notes/value-classes.md) should solve these kinds of problems.

Exercise 6.3

The Tower of Hanoi (https://en.wikipedia.org/wiki/Tower_of_Hanoi) is a classic example of a recursive function. It is a famous game consisting of three rods and a set of n disks of different radii. At the beginning, all the disks are stacked on the first rod. You need to move all the disks from the first rod to the third, following some rules.

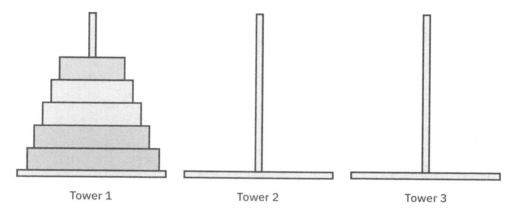

Figure 6a.2: Hanoi Towers

- Only one disk may be moved at a time.

- Each move consists of taking the top disk from one of the stacks and placing it on top of another stack or on an empty rod.

- No disk may be placed on top of a disk that's smaller than it.

Can you implement this in Kotlin?

Exercise 6.3 solution

To solve this problem, remember that:

1. You have three rods.

2. You must follow the rules for moving each disk.

3. When moving disks from rod 1 to rod 3, you can use rod 2 as an intermediate step.

4. For moving n disks from rod 1 to rod 3, you need to move n−1 disks from rod 1 to rod 2 using rod 3. Then, move the remaining from rod 1 to rod 3. Finally, you move the remaining n−1 from rod 2 to rod 3 using rod 1. You can see a visualization for this on Wikipedia (https://en.wikipedia.org/wiki/ Tower_of_Hanoi).

Following these steps, you end up writing code like this:

```
fun moveDisk(disks: Int, from: Int, to: Int, using: Int) {
   if (disks > 0) {
      moveDisk(disks - 1, from, using, to)
      println("Moving $disks from $from to $to")
      moveDisk(disks - 1, using, to, from)
   }
}
```

In this code, you represent the number of disks with a number, as well as each rod. The parameters include what disk you're currently trying to move, the rod you're moving from, the rod you're moving to, and the rod you're using as the intermediary.

You recursively start by moving the disks above the current one from the from rod to the using rod. You can then move them from the using rod to the to rod and work your way down the stack.

To test this, run:

```
fun main() {
    moveDisk(disks = 4, from = 1, to = 3, using = 2)
}
```

The output is:

```
Moving 1 from 1 to 2
Moving 2 from 1 to 3
Moving 1 from 2 to 3
Moving 3 from 1 to 2
Moving 1 from 3 to 1
Moving 2 from 3 to 2
Moving 1 from 1 to 2
Moving 4 from 1 to 3
Moving 1 from 2 to 3
Moving 2 from 2 to 1
Moving 1 from 3 to 1
Moving 3 from 2 to 3
Moving 1 from 1 to 2
Moving 2 from 1 to 3
Moving 1 from 2 to 3
```

You can change the number of disks as well and watch the result.

Exercise 6.4

Tail-recursive functions usually provide better performance. Can you prove this using the chrono function in **Util.kt**?

```
/** Utility that measures the time for executing a lambda N
times */
fun chrono(times: Int = 1, fn: () -> Unit): Long {
    val start = System.nanoTime()
    (1..times).forEach({ fn() })
    return System.nanoTime() - start
}
```

Exercise 6.4 solution

In the chapter, you encountered different recursive implementations for the factorial of a number n:

```
fun recursiveFactorial(n: Int): Int = when (n) { // 1
    1 -> 1
    else -> n * recursiveFactorial(n - 1)
}

tailrec fun tailRecFactorial(n: Int, fact: Int = 1): Int = when
(n) { // 2
    1 -> fact
    else -> tailRecFactorial(n - 1, n * fact)
}
```

These are:

1. Recursive, but not a tail-recursive implementation recursiveFactorial.

2. A tail-recursive implementation tailRecFactorial using the **tailrec** keyword.

For the sake of this exercise, you also create noTailRecFactorial as a version of tailRecFactorial but without the **tailrec** keyword:

```
fun noTailRecFactorial(n: Int, fact: Int = 1): Int = when (n)
{ // 2
    1 -> fact
    else -> noTailRecFactorial(n - 1, n * fact)
}
```

To measure the performance of the three different implementations, run the following code:

```kotlin
fun main() {
  val times = 1000000
  println("recursiveFactorial ${chrono(times) {
    recursiveFactorial(50)
  }}") // 1
  println("tailRecFactorial    ${chrono(times) {
    tailRecFactorial(50)
  }}") // 2
  println("noTailRecFactorial ${chrono(times) {
    noTailRecFactorial(50)
  }}") // 3
}
```

The output will be something like:

```
recursiveFactorial 92446751
tailRecFactorial    8587841
noTailRecFactorial 50125777
```

Of course, your values will probably be different, but what matters here is the comparison. As you can see:

- `recursiveFactorial` is the slowest.

- `tailRecFactorial` is the fastest.

- `noTailRecFactorial` is faster than `recursiveFactorial` but slower than `tailRecFactorial`.

This suggests that tail-recursive implementations, when possible, are the best in terms of performance.

Challenge 6.1: Immutability and recursion

In "Immutability and recursion", you implemented `recAddMulti5` as a recursive function. Is the `loop` internal function tail recursive?

Challenge 6.1 solution

Yes, you can write `recAddMulti5` like this, adding **tailrec** to `loop`:

```
fun recAddMulti5(list: List<Int>): Int {
    tailrec fun loop(i: Int, sum: Int): Int = when { // HERE
        i == list.size -> sum
        list[i] % 5 == 0 -> loop(i + 1, sum + list[i])
        else -> loop(i + 1, sum)
    }
    return loop(0, 0)
}

fun main() {
    val list = listOf(1, 5, 10, 12, 34, 55, 80, 23, 35, 12, 80)
    println(recAddMulti5(list))
}
```

Challenge 6.2: Tail-recursive Fibonacci

Fibonacci is one of the most famous sequences you can implement using recursion. Remember, the nth Fibonacci number is the sum of the two previous Fibonacci numbers, starting with 0, 1, 1.... Can you implement it as a tail-recursive function? Can you prove the tail-recursive function has better performance than the non-tail-recursive companion?

Challenge 6.2 solution

You can implement a function that provides the nth value in the Fibonacci sequence with a tail-recursive function like this:

```
tailrec fun tailRecFib(n: Int, a: Int = 0, b: Int = 1): Int =
when (n) {
    0 -> a
    1 -> b
    else -> tailRecFib(n - 1, b, a + b)
}
```

The non-tail-recursive version is:

```
fun noTailRecFib(n: Int): Int = when (n) {
    0 -> 0
    1 -> 1
    else -> noTailRecFib(n - 1) + noTailRecFib(n - 2)
}
```

To compare the performance of the two implementations, run the following code:

```
fun main() {
    println(chrono {
        noTailRecFib(40) // 1
    })
    println(chrono {
        tailRecFib(40) // 2
    })
}
```

The output will be something like:

```
527457813 // 1
12316 // 2
```

This proves huge performance improvements when using tail-recursive functions.

Appendix G: Chapter 7 Exercise & Challenge Solutions

Exercise 7.1

Implement the extension function isEmpty(), which returns true if FList<T> is empty and false otherwise.

Exercise 7.1 solution

You can solve this exercise a few different ways. The first uses what you implemented in the chapter and the size function.

```
fun <T> FList<T>.isEmpty(): Boolean = size() == 0
```

Here, you just return true if the size is 0 and false otherwise.

Another solution uses the same size logic like this:

```
fun <T> FList<T>.isEmpty(): Boolean = match(
  whenNil = { true },
  whenCons = { _, _ -> false }
)
```

Here, you simply return:

1. true if the receiver is Nil.

2. false if the receiver is FCons<T>.

Verify the usage by running the following code:

```
fun main() {
  println(FList.empty<Int>().isEmpty())
  println(FList.of(1).isEmpty())
  println(FList.of(1, 2, 3).isEmpty())
}
```

And you get the following output:

```
true
false
false
```

Exercise 7.2

Implement the extension function `tail()`, which returns the `tail` of a given `FList<T>`.

Exercise 7.2 solution

You can easily implement the `tail` function like this:

```
fun <T> FList<T>.tail(): FList<T> = match(
  whenNil = { FList.empty() },
  whenCons = { _, tail -> tail }
)
```

In this case, you simply return:

1. The empty list `List.empty()` if the receiver is `Nil`.

2. The `tail` property if the receiver is `FCons<T>`.

Verify the usage by running the following code:

```
fun main() {
  println(FList.empty<Int>().tail())
  println(FList.of(1).tail())
  println(FList.of(1, 2, 3).tail())
}
```

You'll get something similar to the following output:

```
com.raywenderlich.fp.Nil@27c170f0
com.raywenderlich.fp.Nil@27c170f0
FCons(head=2, tail=FCons(head=3,
tail=com.raywenderlich.fp.Nil@27c170f0))
```

Exercise 7.3

Kotlin provides `forEachIndexed` for the `Iterable<T>` interface, which accepts as input a lambda of type `(Int, T) -> Unit`. The first `Int` parameter is the index of the item `T` in the collection. To test `forEachIndexed`, run the code:

```
listOf("a", "b", "c").forEachIndexed { index, item ->
  println("$index $item")
}
```

Getting the following output:

```
0 a
1 b
2 c
```

Can you implement the same for `FList<T>`?

Exercise 7.3 solution

The solution, in this case, is a little more complicated because you need to keep track of the index for the current element. The following implementation is a possible option:

```
fun <T> FList<T>.forEachIndexed(fn: (Int, T) -> Unit) { // 1

  fun FList<T>.loop(i: Int = 0): Unit = match( // 2
    whenNil = {}, // 3
    whenCons = { head, tail ->
      fn(i, head) // 4
      tail.loop(i + 1) // 5
    }
  )

  loop() // 6
}
```

In this code, you:

1. Define forEachIndexed as an extension function for FList<T>, accepting a lambda of type (Int, T) -> Unit as input.

2. Implement loop as an internal extension function that takes the current element's index as input. The default value for the index i is 0.

3. Do nothing if the receiver is Nil because you completed the iteration on the list.

4. Evaluate the input lambda fn, passing the current index and the current element otherwise.

5. Invoke the same forEachIndexed on tail, passing the next index value as input.

6. Invoke loop, using its default input parameter, 0, to start the iteration.

When you run this code:

```
fun main() {
  FList.of("a", "b", "c").forEachIndexed { index, item ->
    println("$index $item")
  }
}
```

You'll get the following output:

```
0 a
1 b
2 c
```

Exercise 7.4

Another option to implement forEachIndexed is to make FList<T> an Iterable<T>. How would you do that? To make all the code coexist in the same codebase, call the Iterable<T> version IFList<T> with INil and ICons<T>.

Exercise 7.4 solution

As mentioned in the problem statement, start the exercise with the existing
FList<T> definition in **FList.kt** and rename it in IFList<T> along with INil and
ICons<T>. A possible solution could be:

```
sealed class IFList<out T> : Iterable<T> { // 1

  companion object {
    @JvmStatic
    fun <T> of(vararg items: T): IFList<T> {
      val tail = items.sliceArray(1 until items.size)
      return if (items.isEmpty()) {
        empty()
      } else {
        ICons(items[0], of(*tail))
      }
    }

    @JvmStatic
    fun <T> empty(): IFList<T> = INil
  }
}

private object INil : IFList<Nothing>() { // 2
  override fun iterator(): Iterator<Nothing> =
    object : Iterator<Nothing> {
      override fun hasNext(): Boolean = false
      override fun next(): Nothing =
        throw NoSuchElementException()
    }
}

private data class ICons<T>(
  val head: T,
  val tail: IFList<T> = INil
) : IFList<T>() {

  override fun iterator(): Iterator<T> =
    object : Iterator<T> { // 3
      var current: IFList<T> = this@ICons // 4
      override fun hasNext(): Boolean = current is ICons<T> // 5

      override fun next(): T {
        val asICons = current as? ICons<T> ?:
          throw NoSuchElementException() // 6
        current = asICons.tail // 7
        return asICons.head // 8
      }
    }
}
```

In this code, after copying the content of **FList.kt** and renaming FList<T> to IFList<T>, Nil to INil and FCons<T> to ICons<T>, you:

1. Make IFList<T> implement Iterable<T>. This requires you to implement iterator in both INil and IFList<T>.

2. Implement Iterable<Nothing> in INil. Here, the list is empty, so hasNext always returns false and next throws a NoSuchElementException.

3. Make ICons<T> implement Iterator<T>, which requires some state.

4. Define current as the current state of the iterator, pointing initially to the ICons<T> receiver itself.

5. Implement hasNext, checking whether the current element is an ICons<T>. In this case, it has something to iterate over. Otherwise, it's Nil, so there's nothing more.

6. Access the current element in next, casting it to ICons<T>. Usually, clients invoke next after hasNext, so you're assuming the cast will be successful. If this isn't true, you throw another NoSuchElementException. Save the value in the local constant asICons.

7. Move the cursor ahead, assigning the value of tail to current.

8. Return the value of asICons.

Now, test the code by running this:

```
fun main() {
  IFList.of(1, 2, 3).forEach {
    println(it)
  }
}
```

You then get the following output:

```
1
2
3
```

Exercise 7.5

Implement addHead, which adds a new element at the head of an existing FList<T>.

Exercise 7.5 solution

The addHead function is very simple:

```
fun <T> FList<T>.addHead(newItem: T): FList<T> =
  FCons(newItem, this)
```

You just create a new FCons<T> object by passing the new value as head and using the current receiver as the tail.

To test the previous code, run:

```
fun main() {
  val initialList = FList.of(1, 2)
  val addedList = initialList.addHead(0)
  initialList.forEach {
    print("$it ")
  }
  println()
  addedList.forEach {
    print("$it ")
  }
}
```

You'll get the output:

```
1 2
0 1 2
```

Exercise 7.6

Kotlin defines the take function on Iterable<T> that allows you to keep a given number of elements.

For instance, running the following code:

```
fun main() {
    listOf(1, 2, 3, 4, 5, 6, 7, 8, 9, 10)
        .take(3)
        .forEach { print("$it ") }
}
```

You'd get:

```
1 2 3
```

Can you implement the same take function for FList<T>?

Exercise 7.6 solution

A possible implementation of the take function for FList<T> is the following:

```
fun <T> FList<T>.take(n: Int): FList<T> = match( // 1
    whenNil = { FList.empty() }, // 2
    whenCons = { head, tail ->
        if (n > 0) {
            FCons(head, tail.take(n - 1)) // 3
        } else {
            FList.empty() // 4
        }
    }
)
```

In this code, you:

1. Define take using match.

2. Return the empty list if the receiver is Nil.

3. Check the parameter n that indicates how many elements you have to take. If this isn't 0, you return a new FList<T> containing the head and, as the tail, what you get invoking take for n − 1 elements.

4. Return no more elements if n is 0.

Test the solution by running this code:

```
fun main() {
  FList.of(1, 2, 3, 4, 5)
    .take(0) // 1
    .forEach { print("$it ") }
  println()
  FList.of(1, 2, 3, 4, 5)
    .take(1) // 2
    .forEach { print("$it ") }
  println()
  FList.of(1, 2, 3, 4, 5)
    .take(5) // 3
    .forEach { print("$it ") }
  println()
  FList.of(1, 2, 3, 4, 5)
    .take(6) // 4
    .forEach { print("$it ") }
}
```

The output is:

```
            // 1
1           // 2
1 2 3 4 5   // 3
1 2 3 4 5   // 4
```

These are the values for:

1. take(0).

2. take(1).

3. Taking all the elements in FList<T>.

4. Taking more elements than the available ones.

Exercise 7.7

Kotlin defines the takeLast function on Iterable<T> that allows you to keep a given number of elements at the end of the collection. For instance, running the following code:

```
fun main() {
   listOf(1, 2, 3, 4, 5, 6, 7, 8, 9, 10)
      .takeLast(3)
      .forEach { print("$it ") }
```

You'd get:

```
8 9 10
```

Can you implement the same takeLast function for FList<T>?

Exercise 7.7 solution

This exercise is a little more complicated than the previous one. A first implementation could be the following:

```
fun <T> FList<T>.takeLast(n: Int): FList<T> = match( // 1
   whenNil = { FList.empty() }, // 2
   whenCons = { head, tail ->
      if (tail.size() >= n) {
         tail.takeLast(n) // 3
      } else {
         FCons(head, tail) // 4
      }
   }
)
```

Here, you:

1. Define `takeLast` as an extension function of `FList<T>`, accepting an input parameter `n` of type `Int` representing the number of elements you want to take at the end of the list.

2. Return the empty list if the receiver is `Nil`.

3. Check the value of `n`. If it's greater than the current `size`, you return the result of invoking `takeLast` on the `tail`. This is because it means you still have elements to skip at the beginning of the list.

4. Return a new `FCons<T>` using the current head and `tail` if the `size` is equal to or smaller than `n`.

Run this code to test the previous code:

```
fun main() {
  (0..6).forEach {
    println("takeLast $it")
    FList.of(1, 2, 3, 4, 5)
      .takeLast(it)
      .forEach { print("$it ") }
    println()
  }
}
```

It allows you to test `takeLast` with different values for the size of the input. You get:

```
takeLast 0

takeLast 1
5
takeLast 2
4 5
takeLast 3
3 4 5
takeLast 4
2 3 4 5
takeLast 5
1 2 3 4 5
takeLast 6
1 2 3 4 5
```

The previous code is simple, but it uses the function `size` you implemented in the chapter, which has complexity **O(N)**. This makes the complexity of `takeList` **O(N^2)**. The usual question is: Can you do better? Of course you can!

Look at `takeLast` as another way to say:

1. Your `Flist<T>` has length M.

2. You need to keep n elements.

3. So, just return what you have when you skip M–n elements.

Following this idea, you could implement the `skip` function like this:

```
fun <T> FList<T>.skip(n: Int): FList<T> = match( // 1
  whenNil = { FList.empty() }, // 2
  whenCons = { head, tail ->
    if (n > 0) {
      tail.skip(n - 1) // 3
    } else {
      FCons(head, tail) // 4
    }
  }
)
```

Here, you:

1. Define `skip` as an extension function of `FList<T>`, accepting an input parameter n of type `Int` representing the number of elements you want to skip at the beginning of the list.

2. Return the empty list if the current receiver is `Nil`.

3. Invoke `skip` on the `tail`, passing n - 1 as parameter value if there are other values to skip.

4. Return the current receiver if there's nothing else to skip. This happens when n <=0.

Again, run the following code to test the behavior of `skip`:

```
fun main() {
  // ...
  (0..6).forEach {
    println("Skipping $it")
    FList.of(1, 2, 3, 4, 5)
      .skip(it)
      .forEach { print("$it ") }
    println()
  }
}
```

You get:

```
Skipping 0
1 2 3 4 5
Skipping 1
2 3 4 5
Skipping 2
3 4 5
Skipping 3
4 5
Skipping 4
5
Skipping 5

Skipping 6
```

Now, write `takeLast2` as a second version of `takeLast`, like this:

```
fun <T> FList<T>.takeLast2(n: Int): FList<T> = // 1
    skip(size() - n) // 2
```

Here, you:

1. Define `takeLast2` as an extension function of `FList<T>`, accepting an input parameter `n` of type `Int` representing the number of elements you want to take at the end of the list.

2. Invoke `size` to get the length of the receiver, and invoke `skip` to skip the values in excess.

Run this code to test how this works:

```
fun main() {
  (0..6).forEach {
    println("takeLast2 $it")
    FList.of(1, 2, 3, 4, 5)
      .takeLast2(it)
      .forEach { print("$it ") }
    println()
  }
}
```

Getting the following output:

```
takeLast2 0

takeLast2 1
5
takeLast2 2
```

```
4 5
takeLast2 3
3 4 5
takeLast2 4
2 3 4 5
takeLast2 5
1 2 3 4 5
takeLast2 6
1 2 3 4 5
```

Because you invoke `size` only once, the complexity of `takeLast2` is `O(N)`.

Challenge 7.1

Kotlin provides the functions `first` and `last` as extension functions of `List<T>`, providing, if available, the first and last elements. Can you implement the same for `FList<T>`?

Challenge 7.1 solution

The implementation of `first` for `FList<T>` is simple because it's exactly the same as head, which you implemented in the chapter.

```
fun <T> FList<T>.first() = head()
```

The implementation of `last` is also simple if you use the functions `skip` and `size` that you implemented earlier.

```
fun <T> FList<T>.last() = skip(size() - 1).head()
```

Run the following code to get the value of `first` and `last` in some specific edge cases:

```
fun main() {
    println(FList.empty<Int>().first())
    println(FList.empty<Int>().last())
    println(FList.of(1).first())
    println(FList.of(1).last())
    println(FList.of(1, 2).first())
    println(FList.of(1, 2).last())
}
```

And you get:

```
null
null
1
1
1
2
```

Challenge 7.2

Kotlin provides an overload of first for Iterable<T> that provides the first element that evaluates a given Predicate<T> as true. It also provides an overload of last for List<T> that provides the last element that evaluates a given Predicate<T> as true. Can you implement firstWhen and lastWhen for FList<T> with the same behavior?

Challenge 7.2 solution

A very simple first implementation for firstWhen is:

```
fun <T> FList<T>.firstWhen(predicate: Predicate<T>): T? =
    filter(predicate).first()
```

Here, you just use filter to get the FList<T> of all the values for the given predicate, and then you take the first element.

You might notice that in this case filter creates a complete FList<T> of all the values that evaluate the predicate as true, but you just need the first. A possible better implementation is the following:

```
fun <T> FList<T>.fastFirstWhen(predicate: Predicate<T>): T? =
  match(
    whenNil = { null },
    whenCons = { head, tail ->
      if (predicate(head)) {
        head
      } else {
        tail.fastFirstWhen(predicate)
      }
    }
  )
```

In this code, you search for the first element that evaluates the `predicate` to `true`. You do this by testing the `head` and continue to the `tail` if it evaluates to `false`.

Use the same approach as `firstWhen` with the following implementation of `lastWhen`:

```kotlin
fun <T> FList<T>.lastWhen(predicate: Predicate<T>): T? =
  filter(predicate).last()
```

Here, the only difference is that you take the last element of the one you got, invoking `filter` first.

Note how a `fast` version of `lastWhen` doesn't make sense because you always need to evaluate all the elements in `FList<T>` to find the last one.

Run this code to test `firstWhen` and `lastWhen`:

```kotlin
fun main() {
  val isEven: Predicate<Int> = { a: Int -> a % 2 == 0 }
  println(FList.of(1, 2, 3, 4, 5, 6).firstWhen(isEven))
  println(FList.of(1, 2, 3, 4, 5, 6).lastWhen(isEven))
  println(FList.of(1, 2, 3, 4, 5, 6).fastFirstWhen(isEven))
}
```

You get:

```
2
6
2
```

Challenge 7.3

Implement the function `get` that returns the element at a given position `i` in `FList<T>`. For instance, with this code:

```kotlin
fun main() {
  println(FList.of(1,2,3,4,5).get(2))
}
```

You get:

```
3
```

Because 3 is the element at index 2. Consider 0 the index of the first element in `FList<T>`.

Challenge 7.3 solution

Creating a set of reusable functions is a very powerful tool and allows you to implement a complete library. A possible solution for the get function is the following:

```
fun <T> FList<T>.get(i: Int): T =
    skip(i).head() ?: throw ArrayIndexOutOfBoundsException()
```

You basically skip i values and take the head. If the head doesn't exist, you throw an ArrayIndexOutOfBoundsException. This allows you to run the following code:

```
fun main() {
    val list = FList.of(1, 2, 3)
    println(list.get(0))
    println(list.get(1))
    println(list.get(2))
    println(list.get(3))
}
```

And get:

```
1
2
3
Exception in thread "main"
java.lang.ArrayIndexOutOfBoundsException
```

Of course, accessing the value at index 3 throws an ArrayIndexOutOfBoundsException.

To make things fancier, just use the **operator** keyword like this:

```
operator fun <T> FList<T>.get(i: Int): T =
    skip(i).head() ?: throw ArrayIndexOutOfBoundsException()
```

Now, you can use the [] syntax:

```
fun main() {
    val list = FList.of(1, 2, 3)
    println(list[0])
    println(list[1])
    println(list[2])
    println(list[3])
}
```

And get the same output.

Appendix H: Chapter 8 Exercise & Challenge Solutions

Exercise 8.1

In this chapter, you implemented the generic `curry` function that basically maps a function of type `(A, B) -> C` in a function of type `(A) -> (B) -> C`. Can you now implement the `uncurry` function, which does the inverse? It's a function that maps a function of type `(A) -> (B) -> C` in a function of type `(A, B) -> C`.

Exercise 8.1 solution

The implementation of the `uncurry` function is:

```
fun <A, B, C> ((A) -> (B) -> C).uncurry(): (A, B) -> C =
  { a: A, b: B ->
    this(a)(b)
  }
```

This is an extension function of the `(A) -> (B) -> C` type that returns a function of two input parameters, a and b, of type A and B, respectively. In the body, you just invoke the receiver function first with a and then the resulting function with b.

It's interesting to note how, if you apply uncurry to the curry version of a function, you get the function itself. To prove this, run the following code:

```
fun main() {
  val sum = { a: Int, b: Int -> a + b }
  println(sum(2, 3))
  val sum2 = sum.curry().uncurry()
  println(sum2(2, 3))
}
```

Which gives you:

```
5
5
```

Exercise 8.2

Implement a higher-order function `flip` that maps a function of type `(A, B) -> C` in the function `(B, A) -> C`, flipping the order of the input parameters.

Exercise 8.2 solution

The `flip` function is very interesting and useful. Given you already have `curry` and `uncurry`, you can implement `flip` like this:

```
fun <A, B, C> ((A, B) -> C).flip(): (B, A) -> C =
  { b: B, a: A ->
    this(a, b)
  }
```

As you can see:

- `flip` is an extension function on the type `(A, B) -> C`.

- The return type is `(B, A) -> C`.

- It returns a function of the parameters b and a of types B and A, respectively.

- In the body, you just invoke the receiver, passing the parameters in the right order.

As a first example of the usage of this function, you can use the following:

```
fun append(a: String, b: String): String = "$a $b"
```

Now, run this:

```
fun main() {
  val flippedAppend = ::append.flip() // 1
  println(append("First", "Second")) // 2
  println(flippedAppend("First", "Second")) // 3
}
```

In this code, you:

1. Define `flippedAppend` as the function you get by invoking `flip` on `::append`.

2. Print the result of `append`, passing `"First"` and `"Second"` as input values.

3. Print the result of `flippedAppend` with the same parameters in the same order.

You'll get:

```
First Second
Second First
```

Which proves `flip` is working.

Sometimes, using `flip` with `curry` is useful. Consider, for instance, the following function:

```
fun runDelayed(fn: () -> Unit, delay: Long) { // 1
    sleep(delay) // 2
    fn() // 3
}
```

In this code, you:

1. Define `runDelayed` as a function with two input parameters. The first is a lambda of type `() -> Unit` and the second is a `Long` that represents the time you have to wait before invoking the previous lambda.

2. `sleep` for the `delay` time.

3. Invoke `fn`.

To use this code, just run:

```
fun main() {
    // ...
    runDelayed({
        println("Delayed")
    }, 1000)
}
```

You'll see the program wait one second and then print `Delayed`. This is code you can improve because you pass the lambda expression as the first parameter and the interval as the second. Of course, you could use named parameters, but you can do something better instead.

Just run the following code:

```
fun main() {
  // ...
  val runDelayed1Second =
    ::runDelayed.flip() // 1
      .curry() // 2
      .invoke(1000L) // 3
  runDelayed1Second { // 4
    println("Delayed")
  }
}
```

In this code, you:

1. Define `runDelayed1Second` as a function that allows you to run a given lambda after a one-second delay. First, you invoke `flip`, getting a function with `Long` as the first parameter and the lambda as the second.

2. Invoke `curry()`, getting a function of type `(Long) -> (() -> Unit) -> Unit`.

3. Invoke the curried function with `1000L` as an input parameter for the delay. This makes `(() -> Unit) -> Unit` the type of `runDelayed1Second`.

4. Use `runDelayed1Second`, passing the lambda expression you want to run, but delayed by 1 second.

Using composition in this way makes the code more reusable and simpler to write.

Exercise 8.3

The `curry` function maps a function of type `Fun2<A, B, C>` to a function of type `(A) -> (B) -> C`. How would you define an overload of `curry` for functions of three, four, five or, in general, n parameters?

Exercise 8.3 solution

To make the code easier to read, start by writing a `typealias` for each function type with a specified number of parameters, from 3 until 5 like this:

```
typealias Fun3<I1, I2, I3, O> = (I1, I2, I3) -> O
typealias Fun4<I1, I2, I3, I4, O> = (I1, I2, I3, I4) -> O
typealias Fun5<I1, I2, I3, I4, I5, O> =
  (I1, I2, I3, I4, I5) -> O
```

You can also do the same for the output types for the curry functions, like this:

```
typealias Chain3<I1, I2, I3, 0> = (I1) -> (I2) -> (I3) -> 0
typealias Chain4<I1, I2, I3, I4, 0> =
  (I1) -> (I2) -> (I3) -> (I4) -> 0
typealias Chain5<I1, I2, I3, I4, I5, 0> =
  (I1) -> (I2) -> (I3) -> (I4) -> (I5) -> 0
```

In the case of three parameters, you can then write the following curry overload:

```
fun <I1, I2, I3, 0> Fun3<I1, I2, I3, 0>.curry():
    Chain3<I1, I2, I3, 0> = { i1: I1, i2: I2 ->
  { i3: I3 ->
    this(i1, i2, i3)
  }
}.curry()
```

How can you consider a function with three parameters as a function with two parameters returning another function? Basically, you consider the type:

```
(I1, I2, I3) -> 0
```

As the following:

```
(I1, I2) -> ((I3) -> 0)
```

This allows you to reuse the curry overload you implemented for N−1 parameters for a function of N parameters. Now, you can do the same for functions with four and five parameters, like this:

```
fun <I1, I2, I3, I4, 0> Fun4<I1, I2, I3, I4, 0>.curry():
    Chain4<I1, I2, I3, I4, 0> = { i1: I1, i2: I2, i3: I3 ->
  { i4: I4 ->
    this(i1, i2, i3, i4)
  }
}.curry()
```

And:

```
fun <I1, I2, I3, I4, I5, 0>
    Fun5<I1, I2, I3, I4, I5, 0>.curry():
    Chain5<I1, I2, I3, I4, I5, 0> =
  { i1: I1, i2: I2, i3: I3, i4: I4 ->
    { i5: I5 ->
      this(i1, i2, i3, i4, i5)
    }
  }.curry()
```

As an example, run the following code:

```kotlin
fun main() {
  val sum = { a: Int, b: Int, c: Int, d: Int, e: Int ->
    a + b + c + d + e // 1
  }
  val curriedSum = sum.curry() // 2
  println(curriedSum(1)(2)(3)(4)(5)) // 3
}
```

In this code, you:

1. Implement a simple function, `sum`, that calculates the sum of the five input parameters.

2. Define `curriedSum`, invoking `curry` on `sum`. The type of `curriedSum` is `Chain5<I1, I2, I3, I4, I5, O>`.

3. Invoke `curriedSum` and print the result. Note how you pass the input parameters using `()`.

Of course, you'll get the result:

```
15
```

In the previous example, you met the expression:

```
curriedSum(1)(2)(3)(4)(5)
```

As stated already, functional programmers don't like parentheses and try, whenever possible, to avoid them. You also already met the `pipe` function. One possible option might be this:

```kotlin
fun main() {
  val sum = { a: Int, b: Int, c: Int, d: Int, e: Int ->
    a + b + c + d + e
  }
  val curriedSum = sum.curry()
  val result = 5 pipe 4 pipe 3 pipe 2 pipe 1 pipe curriedSum //
HERE
  println(result)
  println(curriedSum(1)(2)(3)(4)(5))
}
```

Unfortunately, this code doesn't compile. The reason is the associativity priority between the `pipe` infix functions, which is left to right. This means that the compiler tries to execute `5 pipe 4` first, which doesn't exist.

To use `pipe`, you need to use parentheses in another way, like this:

```
val result = 5 pipe (4 pipe (3 pipe (2 pipe (1 pipe
curriedSum))))
```

You basically just moved the same parentheses to another place. There's a trick, though. Simply add the following code:

```
infix fun <A, B> Fun<A, B>.epip(a: A): B = this(a)
```

The `epip` function is basically the `pipe` reversed, but it allows you to completely remove parentheses. Just replace the previous code with the following:

```
fun main() {
  val sum = { a: Int, b: Int, c: Int, d: Int, e: Int ->
    a + b + c + d + e
  }
  val curriedSum = sum.curry()
  val result = curriedSum epip 1 epip 2 epip 3 epip 4 epip 5 //
HERE
  println(result)
}
```

And everything will be fine!

Feel free to play with these `curry` overloads and the `flip` function you implemented in this exercise to change the order of your functions as you like.

Exercise 8.4

How would you apply the previous pattern for `Array<T>`? Basically, you need a way to compose functions of type:

```
typealias ToArray<A, B> = (A) -> Array<B>
```

In other words, if you have two functions:

```
val fun1: (A) -> Array<B>
val fun2: (C) -> Array<C>
```

Can you implement `compose` so that the following will compile and `fun2` is applied to all elements resulting from `fun1`?

```
fun1 compose fun2
```

Exercise 8.4 solution

First, you need to understand what composing functions of type ToArray<A, B> means. The first is a function receiving an input value of type A and returning an Array<B>. The second receives an input of type B and returns an Array<C>.

The composition should then be something that gets an Array<B> from the first function and applies the second function to all the elements. A possible implementation is:

```
inline infix fun <A, B, reified C> ToArray<A, B>.compose(
  crossinline g: ToArray<B, C> // 1
): ToArray<A, C> = { a: A -> // 2
  val bArray = this(a) // 3
  val cArray = mutableListOf<C>() // 4
  for (bValue in bArray) {
    cArray.addAll(g(bValue))
  }
  cArray.toTypedArray() // 5
}
```

In this code, you:

1. Define compose as an infix extension function of the ToArray<A, B> type, accepting an input parameter of type ToArray<B, C>. Of course, the return type is ToArray<A, C>.

2. Return a function of the input parameter a of type A.

3. Invoke the received on a getting an Array<B> you save in bArray.

4. Create a MutableList<C> you fill with the values you get by invoking g on each element of bArray.

5. Return the Array<C> version of MutableList<C>. This is the reason the type C requires reified.

Now you can create your own example to test how this works. For instance, write the following:

```
val fibo = { n: Int -> // 1
  tailrec fun fiboHelper(a: Int, b: Int, fiboN: Int): Int =
    when (fiboN) {
      0 -> a
      1 -> b
      else -> fiboHelper(b, a + b, fiboN - 1)
    }
  fiboHelper(1, 1, n)
```

```
    }

fun main() {
    val counter = { a: Int -> Array(a) { it } } // 2
    val fiboLength = { n: Int -> Array(n) { fibo(it) } } // 3
    val counterFibo = counter compose fiboLength // 4
    counterFibo(5).forEach { print("$it ") } // 5
}
```

Here, you:

1. Define a utility function, `fibo`, that returns the nth value in the Fibonacci sequence.

2. Create `counter` as a function that, given an `Int`, returns an `Array<Int>` of values from 0 to n−1.

3. Define `fiboLength` as a function that, given an `Int`, returns an `Array<Int>` of the first n values of the Fibonacci sequence.

4. Create `counterFibo` as composition of `counter` and `counterFibo`.

5. Invoke `counterFibo` and print the values of the resulting `Array<Int>`.

Running the previous code, you get:

```
1 1 1 1 2 1 1 2 3
```

To understand this output a bit better, walk through what it's doing:

1. First, `counter` is invoked with 5, resulting in the array `[0,1,2,3,4]`.

2. Then, for each item in that resulting array, `fiboLength` is invoked, creating a list of the first n Fibonacci numbers. So, on the first element, 0, the result is `[]`. The second, 1, results in `[1]`. This pattern continues until you reach the element 4, which results in `[1,1,2,3]`.

3. The results of each of these interations are combined into the final resulting list that you see printed at the end.

In Chapter 12, "Monoids & Semigroups", you'll learn how to use a very important function called `fold`. If you already know how to use it, a possible alternate solution is:

```
inline infix fun <A, B, reified C> ToArray<A,
B>.composeWithFold(
    crossinline g: ToArray<B, C>
): ToArray<A, C> = { a: A ->
```

```
    this(a).fold(mutableListOf<C>()) { acc, item ->
      for (bValue in g(item)) { // HERE
        acc.add(bValue)
      }
      acc
    }.toTypedArray()
}
```

As you'll learn, to use `fold`, you need to define what it means for a type to be *composable*. To test this implementation, just add and run this code:

```
fun main() {
  // ...
  val counterFiboWithFold = counter composeWithFold fiboLength
  counterFiboWithFold(5).forEach { print("$it ") }
}
```

Which gives you the same output:

```
1 1 1 1 1 2 1 1 2 3
```

Challenge 1: Callable stuff

In the chapter, you learned how to implement the `compose` function in different scenarios following a common pattern. Consider, now, the following function type:

```
typealias WithCallable<A, B> = Fun<A, Callable<B>>
```

How would you implement `compose` for `WithCallable<A, B>`? This is using `java.util.concurrent.Callable` (https://docs.oracle.com/javase/8/docs/api/java/util/concurrent/Callable.html) defined as:

```
interface Callable<V> {
  @Throws(Exception::class)
  fun call(): V
}
```

Challenge 1 solution

Following the same pattern you learned in the chapter, you can implement `compose` like this:

```
infix fun <A, B, C> WithCallable<A, B>.compose( // 1
  g: WithCallable<B, C>
```

```
): WithCallable<A, C> = { a: A -> // 2
  Callable<C> { // 3
    g(this(a).call()).call() // 4
  }
}
```

Here, you:

1. Define `compose` as an infix extension function for `WithCallable<A, B>`.

2. Return a function of the input parameter a of type `A`.

3. Return a new `Callable<C>` from the inner function.

4. Get the body of the returning `Callable<C>` invoking `call` on the receiver and then `call` again on the `Callable<B>` you get in the first place.

Test the previous code with:

```
fun main() {
  val waitAndReturn = { a: Int -> // 1
    Callable {
      sleep(1000)
      a
    }
  }
  val comp = waitAndReturn compose waitAndReturn  // 2
  chronoMs {
    comp(2).call() // 3
  } pipe ::println
}
```

Here:

1. `waitAndReturn` is a function that returns a `Callable<Int>` that waits about 1 second and then returns the same value you pass as input.

2. You compose `waitAndReturn` with itself.

3. Using the `chrono` function in `Util.kt`, you check that by invoking `call`, you're actually invoking the `call` on the `WithCallable<A, B>` you're composing.

The output will be something like:

```
2053
```

> **Note:** Remember that sleep doesn't allow you to wait a specific amount of time but rather a minimum amount of time. This is because it guarantees that the thread scheduler puts the current thread in a runnable state for the time you pass as an input parameter. A thread in a runnable state is a candidate to run, but this doesn't mean it'll run soon. This is also why the previous output isn't exactly 2000 but a little bit more.

Challenge 2: Parameters or not parameters?

Suppose you have the following functions:

```
val three = { 3 } // 1

val unitToThree = { a: Unit -> 3 } // 2
```

In this code:

1. three is a function of type () -> Int, returning 3.

2. unitToThree is a function of type (Unit) -> Int, also returning 3.

They look like the same function, but they're actually not. This is because you need a Unit to invoke unitToThree. This also has consequences when you compose. Consider the following code:

```
fun main() {
  val double = { a: Int -> a * 2 } // 1
  val comp2 = unitToThree compose double // 2  COMPILE
  val comp1 = three compose double // 3  DOESN'T COMPILE
}
```

Here, you:

1. Define a simple double function.

2. Compose unitToThree with double. This compiles.

3. Try to compose three with double. This doesn't compile.

The reason is that you don't have any compose overload with the type () -> T as a receiver. The type (Unit) -> T instead falls into Fun<A, B>.

Can you implement a higher-order function, addUnit, that converts a function of type () -> T in the equivalent (Unit) -> T and removeUnit that does the opposite? Using these functions, how would you fix the code in the previous main?

Challenge 2 solution

The solution to this challenge is very simple. You just need to define the following functions:

```
fun <A> (() -> A).addUnit() = { unit: Unit -> this() }

fun <A> ((Unit) -> A).removeUnit() = { this(Unit) }
```

The previous example becomes:

```
fun main() {
    val double = { a: Int -> a * 2 }
    val comp2 = unitToThree compose double
    val comp1 = three.withUnit() compose double // HERE
```

Invoking withUnit on three makes it composable with double.

Appendix I: Chapter 9 Exercise & Challenge Solutions

Exercise 9.1

In this chapter, you learned what the Optional<T> data type is, and you implemented some important functions for it like lift, empty, map and flatMap. Kotlin defines its own optional type represented by ?. How would you implement the lift, empty and getOrDefault functions for it?

Exercise 9.1 solution

You can implement the previous functions like this:

```
fun <T : Any> T.lift(): T? = this // 1

fun <T : Any> T.empty(): T? = null // 2

fun <T : Any> T?.getOrDefault(defaultValue: T): T =
    this ?: defaultValue // 3
```

In this code, you define:

1. lift as an extension function of the type T. Note that the receiver type T isn't optional because of the constraint T: Any. The important thing here is that lift returns the same receiver but as a reference of the optional type T?.

2. empty as an extension function of the not-optional type T, returning null, but as the value of a reference of type T?.

3. `getOrDefault` also as an extension function of the optional type T?. Note how the return type is the not-optional type T. In the body, you just check if `this` is `null`, returning `defaultValue` if it is.

Run the following code for a better understanding of how all this works:

```
fun main() {
    val optStr = "10".lift() // 1
    optStr pipe ::println
    val empty = String.empty() // 2
    empty pipe ::println
    optStr                       // 3
        .getOrDefault("Default")
        .pipe(::println)
    empty                        // 4
        .getOrDefault("Default")
        .pipe(::println)
}
```

And you get the output:

```
10        // 1
null      // 2
10        // 3
Default   // 4
```

Here, you use:

1. `lift` to convert a `String`, `"10"`, into an optional `String?` you then print.

2. `empty` to get `null` through a reference of type `String?` you also print.

3. `getOrDefault` on `optStr`, getting `10` as the result.

4. `getOrDefault` on `empty`, getting the default value `Default` you pass as a parameter.

Exercise 9.2

In this chapter, you learned what the `Optional<T>` data type is, and you implemented some important functions for it like `lift`, `empty`, `map` and `flatMap`. Kotlin defines its own optional type represented by ?. How would you implement the `map` and `flatMap` functions?

Exercise 9.2 solution

A possible implementation of map for the Kotlin optional type is:

```
fun <A : Any, B : Any> A?.map(fn: Fun<A, B>): B? =
    if (this != null) fn(this).lift() else null
```

This code has several important details:

1. map is an extension function for the optional type A?.

2. map accepts a single parameter of type Fun<A, B>.

3. You return null if the receiver is null.

4. If the receiver isn't null, you pass it as an input parameter of the function fn and return the lifted result of type B?.

A possible implementation of flatMap for the Kotlin optional type is:

```
fun <A : Any, B : Any> A?.flatMap(fn: Fun<A, B?>): B? =
    if (this != null) fn(this)?.lift() else null
```

In this case, you note that flatMap:

1. Is an extension function of the optional type A?.

2. Accepts a single parameter of type Fun<A, B?>. It's important to note the optional B? as a return type for the function, which differs from map.

3. Returns null if the receiver is null or if fn returns null.

4. Returns the result of invoking fn if the receiver isn't null.

Exercise 9.3

How would you replicate the example you implemented in **OptionalTest.kt** using T? instead of Optional<T>? Use the solutions of Exercise 9.1 and Exercise 9.2 to implement this example.

Exercise 9.3 solution

You can test the code you created in Exercise 9.1 and Exercise 9.2 by running the
following code:

```kotlin
fun strToInt(value: String): Int? = // 1
  try {
    value.toInt().lift()
  } catch (nfe: NumberFormatException) {
    null
  }

fun <T : Any> T?.getOrDefault(defaultValue: T): T = // 2
  if (this == null) defaultValue else this

fun main() {
  "10" // 3
    .lift()
    .flatMap(::strToInt)
    .map(::double)
    .getOrDefault(-1)
    .pipe(::println)

  "10sa" // 4
    .lift()
    .flatMap(::strToInt)
    .map(::double)
    .getOrDefault(-1)
    .pipe(::println)
}
```

In this code, you:

1. Define strToInt as a function that converts a String into the Int it contains, if
   possible. If that isn't possible, it returns null. This is a function of type
   Fun<String, Int?> you can pass as input to flatMap.

2. Create getOrDefault, checking the receiver's value and returning defaultValue
   if it's null.

3. Use the same structure you used with Optional<T> with a valid String.

4. And again, use the same structure with an invalid String.

The output is:

```
20
-1
```

Exercise 9.4

Implement a function that reverses a `String` using one of the folding functions you've implemented in this chapter.

Exercise 9.4 solution

A `String` is just an array of `Char`s. This means that a possible implementation for the `reverse` function is:

```
fun reverse(str: String) =
  str.toCharArray().toList() // 1
    .declarativeFoldRight(StringBuilder()) { c, acc -> // 2
      acc.append(c) // 3
      acc
    }.toString() // 4
```

In this code, you:

1. Convert the `String` passed as input to a `List<Char>`.

2. Invoke `declarativeFoldRight`, passing a `StringBuilder` as the initial state for the accumulator.

3. Append the character to the previous accumulator state in the combination function.

4. Return the content of `StringBuilder` as a `String`.

To test the previous code, just run the following code:

```
fun main() {
  reverse("supercalifragilisticexpialidocious") pipe ::println
}
```

Getting:

```
suoicodilaipxecitsiligarfilacrepus
```

Exercise 9.5

In this chapter, you implemented `declarativeFold` and `declarativeFoldRight` as extension functions for `List<T>`. How would you implement them for `Iterable<T>`?

Exercise 9.5 solution

The folding functions work for any ordered collection of items, so what really matters is the ability to iterate over them. A possible implementation for declarativeFold on Iterable is:

```
fun <T, S> Iterable<T>.iterableFold(
  start: S,
  combineFunc: (S, T) -> S
): S { // 1
  tailrec fun helper(iterator: Iterator<T>, acc: S): S { // 2
    if (!iterator.hasNext()) { // 3
      return acc
    }
    return helper(iterator, combineFunc(acc,
iterator.next())) // 4
  }
  return helper(iterator(), start) // 5
}
```

In this code:

1. You create iterableFold as an extension function for Iterable<T>. The name is different from your previous implementations, so there are no conflicts.

2. You define helper as a function accepting an Iterator<T>. In fact, you just need to check if you're at the end of the Iterator<T> or not, which you do with hasNext.

3. If you're at the end of the Iterator<T>, you just return acc.

4. Otherwise, you recursively call helper, passing the same iterator and the result you get combining acc with the next element.

5. You start everything, invoking helper with the Iterator<T> you get from iterator. This is possible because the receiver is an Iterable<T>.

Using the same approach, you can also implement iterableFoldRight like this:

```
fun <T, S> Iterable<T>.iterableFoldRight(
  start: S,
  combineFunc: (T, S) -> S
): S {
  fun helper(iterator: Iterator<T>): S {
    if (!iterator.hasNext()) {
      return start
    }
    return combineFunc(iterator.next(), helper(iterator))
```

```
    }
    return helper(iterator())
}
```

To test how they work, run the following code:

```
fun main() {
    "supercalifragilisticexpialidocious".asIterable()
        .iterableFoldRight(StringBuilder()) { item, acc ->
        acc.append(item)
        acc
    } pipe ::println
    "supercalifragilisticexpialidocious".asIterable()
        .iterableFold(StringBuilder()) { acc, item ->
        acc.append(item)
        acc
    } pipe ::println
}
```

Getting:

```
suoicodilaipxecitsiligarfilacrepus
supercalifragilisticexpialidocious
```

Challenge 9.1: Filtering

How would you implement a `filter` function on a `List<T>` using `fold` or `foldRight`? You can name it `filterFold`. Remember that given:

```
typealias Predicate<T> = (T) -> Boolean
```

The `filterFold` function for a `List<T>` should have this signature:

```
fun <T> List<T>.filterFold(predicate: Predicate<T>): List<T> {
    // Implementation
}
```

Challenge 9.1 solution

You know that `fold` allows you to basically recreate a collection of items. If you add an item after the evaluation of a predicate, you basically implement the `filter` function. One possible solution is:

```
fun <T> List<T>.filterFold(predicate: Predicate<T>): List<T> =
```

```
fold(mutableListOf()) { acc, item -> // 1
  if (predicate(item)) { // 2
    acc.add(item) // 3
  }
  acc
}
```

In this code, you:

1. Invoke `fold` using a `MutableList<T>` as a starting value.

2. Evaluate the predicate against the current value.

3. Add the element if the predicate evaluates to `true`.

To test the previous code, simply run:

```
fun main() {
  listOf(1, 2, 3, 4, 5, 6, 7, 8, 9, 10)
    .filterFold { it % 2 == 0 }
    .forEach(::println)
}
```

And the output is:

```
2
4
6
8
10
```

Challenge 9.2

How would you implement the `length` function for a `List<T>` that returns its size using `fold` or `foldRight`?

Challenge 9.2 solution

A possible implementation is:

```
fun <T> List<T>.length(): Int =
  fold(0) { acc, _ ->
    acc + 1
  }
```

In this case, you don't care about the items, but you increment `acc` for each of them. To test how this works, just run the following code:

```
fun main() {
    val list = List<Int>(37) { it }
    list.length() pipe ::println
}
```

And you get:

```
37
```

In this case, using `fold` or `foldRight` doesn't make any difference.

Challenge 9.3: Average

How would you implement the `avg` function for a `List<Double>` that returns the average of all the elements using `fold` or `foldRight`?

Challenge 9.3 solution

The solution here is simple, and is basically the implementation of the definition of average: the sum of all the elements divided by the number of elements:

```
fun List<Double>.average(): Double =
    fold(0.0) { acc, item -> acc + item } /
        fold(0.0) { acc, _ -> acc + 1 }
```

Run this code to test the solution:

```
fun main() {
    val list = List<Int>(37) { it }
    list.average() pipe ::println
}
```

You get:

```
18.0
```

Challenge 9.4: Last

How would you implement the `lastFold` function for a `List<T>` that returns the last element using `fold` or `foldRight`? What about `firstFold`?

Challenge 9.4 solution

One possible implementation is:

```
fun <T> List<T>.lastFold(): T? =
  fold(null as T?) { _, item -> item }
```

In this case, it's curious to see how the initial value matters only if the receiver is empty. Otherwise, only the last item matters. To test how it works, run this code:

```
fun main() {
  val list = List<Int>(37) { it }
  list.lastFold() pipe ::println
  val empty = emptyList<Int>()
  empty.lastFold() pipe ::println
}
```

Getting:

```
36
null
```

Note that to get the first element, you just need to use `foldRight` instead, like this:

```
fun <T> List<T>.firstFold(): T? =
  foldRight(null as T?) { item, acc -> item }
```

To test this, just run this code:

```
val list = List<Int>(37) { it }
list.firstFold() pipe ::println
```

And you get:

```
0
```

Appendix J: Chapter 10 Exercise Solutions

Exercise 10.1

What's the cardinality of the following type?

```
typealias Triplet = Triple<UByte, Boolean, Unit>
```

Exercise 10.1 solution

As you learned in the chapter, the cardinality of Triplet is the product of the cardinalities of UByte, Boolean and Unit, which are:

```
UByte * Boolean * Unit = 256 * 2 * 1 = 512
```

This is because:

- **UByte** is an unsigned 8-bit integer with ranges from 0 to 255.

- **Boolean** can be true or false.

- **Unit** represents a singleton.

The total number of possible values you can represent with Triplet is then **512**.

Exercise 10.2

What's the cardinality of the following type?

```
typealias Unique = Pair<Unit, Unit>
```

Is this isomorphic with Unit?

Exercise 10.2 solution

Of course, the cardinality of Unique is exactly 1 because Unit is the only existing value of type Unit. Because of this, Unique is isomorphic to Unit.

Exercise 10.3

What's the cardinality of the following type?

```
typealias MultiEither = Either<UByte, Either<Boolean, Triage>>
```

Is MultiEither isomorphic with MultiEither2, which you define in the following way?

```
typealias MultiEither2 = Either<Either<UByte, Boolean>, Triage>
```

Exercise 10.3 solution

In the chapter, you learned that Either<A, B> is a way to represent addition. For this reason, you can represent the previous definition like:

```
UByte + (Boolean + Triage) = 256 + (2 + 3) = 256 + 5 = 261
```

Repeat the exercise with MultiEither2, and you'll get:

```
(UByte + Boolean) + Triage = (256 + 2) + 3 = 256 + 5 = 261
```

They're the same because addition is associative. You can find a function that maps each value in MultiEither to each value in MultiEither2 and vice versa. Because of this, the two types are isomorphic.

Appendix K: Chapter 12 Exercise Solutions

Exercise 12.1

Can you find an example of a monoid whose operation isn't commutative?

Exercise 12.1 solution

A typical example of a monoid in programming that isn't commutative is:

- A set of `Strings`

- Concatenation

Concatenation is associative because:

```
a + (b + c) = (a + b) + c
```

But it's commutative because:

```
a + b != b + a
```

You can easily verify this with the following code:

```
fun main() {
    val str1 = "Hello"
    val str2 = " World!"

    println(str1 + str2)
    println(str2 + str1)
}
```

When you run it, you get:

```
Hello World!
  World!Hello
```

What about the **unit** element? Of course, this is the empty String. To test this, just add and run the following code:

```
fun main() {
  // ...
  val unit = ""
  println(str1 + unit)
  println(unit + str1)
}
```

Getting as output:

```
Hello
Hello
```

Exercise 12.2

Can you prove that the set of integer values and multiplication define a monoid? In this case, what would the **unit** element be?

Exercise 12.2 solution

To prove that the set of integer values and multiplication form a monoid, you have to prove that:

- Multiplication is associative.

- There's a unit element.

The first property is obvious because:

```
a * (b * c) = (a * b) * c
```

In this case, of course, the **unit** element is **1** because:

```
a * 1 = a
1 * a = a
```

You can get a better idea of this with some simple code:

```kotlin
fun main() {
    val a = 3
    val b = 7
    val c = 13
    val res1 = a * (b * c)
    val res2 = (a * b) * c

    println(res1)
    println(res2)

    val unit = 1
    val res3 = a * unit
    val res4 = unit * a

    println(res3)
    println(res4)
}
```

When you run the code above, you get:

```
273
273
3
3
```

Exercise 12.3

How would you implement the monoid `MonoidIntMult` for `Int` and *multiplication*?

Exercise 12.3 solution

The implementation of `MonoidIntMult` is simple because it's similar to `MonoidIntAdd`, which you saw in the chapter. Follow that pattern, and you can implement `MonoidIntMult` like this:

```kotlin
object MonoidIntMult : Monoid<Int> { // 1
    override val unit: Int
        get() = 1 // 2
    override val combine: Int.(Int) -> Int
        get() = Int::times // 3
}
```

In this case, you define:

1. MonoidIntMult as an object implementing Monoid<Int>.

2. 1 as the unit for the *multiplication*.

3. combine using Int::times, which is of type Int.(Int) -> Int.

Exercise 12.4

How would you implement the monoid MonoidStringConcat for String and String *concatenation*?

Exercise 12.4 solution

As mentioned in the chapter, String concatenation is an example of a monoid with an operation that isn't commutative. The implementation of MonoidStringConcat isn't so different from MonoidIntAdd. A possible implementation is:

```
object MonoidStringConcat : Monoid<String> { // 1
  override val unit: String
    get() = "" // 2
  override val combine: String.(String) -> String
    get() = String::plus // 3
}
```

In this code, you define:

1. MonoidStringConcat as an object implementing Monoid<String>.

2. The empty String "" as the unit for the String *concatenation*.

3. combine using String::plus, which is of type String.(String) -> String.

Exercise 12.5

In the chapter, you proved that *addition* is different from *multiplication* using op(op(a, 1), 1) and op(a, 2). The two expressions are equal for any Int a if op is addition, but the same isn't true if op is multiplication. Can you implement a Property<Int> implementation for this rule and use it to create a new test?

Exercise 12.5 solution

Following the pattern you used previously in the chapter, a possible implementation is the following:

```
class DoubleIncrementProperty : Property<Int> { // 1
    override fun invoke(
        gen: Generator<Int>,
        fn: (List<Int>) -> Int
    ): Boolean { // 2
        val randomValue = gen.generate(1)[0] // 3
        val res1 = fn(listOf(fn(listOf(randomValue, 1)), 1)) // 4
        val res2 = fn(listOf(randomValue, 2)) // 5
        return res1 == res2 // 6
    }
}
```

In this code, you:

1. Define DoubleIncrementProperty as a Property<Int> implementation.

2. Override invoke, using Int as a value for the type parameter T.

3. Use the Generator<Int> to get a random Int value.

4. Invoke fn, passing 1 as the second parameter and then using the result to invoke fn again.

5. Invoke fn, using 2 as the second parameter.

6. Verify the two results are equal.

A possible test with `DoubleIncrementProperty` is:

```
class PropertyTestTest {

  @Test
  fun `Exercise 5 solution`() {
    100.times {
      val additionProp =
        CommutativeProperty<Int>() and
            DoubleIncrementProperty() and
            IdentityProperty(0)
      val evaluation = additionProp(IntGenerator) {
        sum(it[0], it[1])
      }
      Truth.assertThat(evaluation).isTrue()
    }
  }
}
```

As you see, this is very similar to the test you implemented in the chapter using `DoubleIncrementProperty` in place of `AssociativeProperty`.

Appendix L: Chapter 13 Exercise Solutions

Exercise 13.1

How would you make the Optional<T> data type you created in Chapter 9, "Data Types", a monad?

Exercise 13.1 solution

In Chapter 9, "Data Types" you implemented the Optional<T> type like this:

```
sealed class Optional<out T> {
  companion object {
    @JvmStatic
    fun <T> lift(value: T): Optional<T> = Some(value)

    @JvmStatic
    fun <T> empty(): Optional<T> = None
  }
}

object None : Optional<Nothing>()
data class Some<T>(val value: T) : Optional<T>()
```

To give Optional<T> the monad superpowers you initially need to make it a functor by adding the map function, implement it like this:

```
fun <A, B> Optional<A>.map(fn: Fun<A, B>): Optional<B> =
  when (this) {
    is Some<A> -> Some(fn(this.value))
    is None -> None
  }
```

In the chapter, you learned that you can implement the `fish` operator starting from the implementation of the `optionalFlatten` function, which is a function of type `(Optional<Optional<T>>) -> Optional<T>`. After that, you just need to implement `optionalBind` and then `optionalFish` in the same way you saw in the chapter.

A possible implementation for `optionalFlatten` is:

```
fun <T> Optional<Optional<T>>.optionalFlatten(): Optional<T> =
when (this) {
  is Some<Optional<T>> -> when (this.value) {
    is Some<T> -> Optional.lift<T>(this.value.value)
    is None -> Optional.empty()
  }
  is None -> Optional.empty()
}
```

Here, you just return `Some<T>` if both the `Optional`s are `Some`.

Now, you can implement `optionalBind` like this:

```
infix fun <B, C> Optional<B>.optionalBind(
  g: Fun<B, Optional<C>>
): Optional<C> =
  map(g).optionalFlatten()
```

Finally, you can implement `optionalFish` like this:

```
infix fun <A, B, C> Fun<A, Optional<B>>.optionalFish(
  g: Fun<B, Optional<C>>
): Fun<A, Optional<C>> = { a: A ->
  this(a).optionalBind(g)
}
```

Exercise 13.2

What's the relation between the fish operator, >=>, and flatMap? Can you express the latter in terms of the former for Optional<T>?

Exercise 13.2 solution

The >=> operator for Optional<T> has type:

```
((A) -> Optional<B>, (B) -> Optional<C>) -> (A) -> Optional<C>
```

The flatMap has type (Optional<A>, (A) -> Optional<B>) -> Optional<B>.

A possible way to implement flatMap is the following:

```
fun <A> Optional<A>.lift(value: A): Optional<A> =
  Optional.lift(value) // 1

fun <A, B> Optional<A>.flatMap(fn: Fun<A, Optional<B>>):
Optional<B> =
  map(::lift optionalFish fn).optionalFlatten() // 2
```

In this code, you:

1. Define lift as an extension function of Optional<A>. Here, you simply invoke the lift you defined as a static function.

2. Implement flatMap using optionalFish for creating a function composing lift of type (A) -> Optional<A> and g of type (A) -> Optional<B>, getting a function of type (A) -> Optional<B>. If you use the function as a parameter for map, you get a value of type Optional<Optional<B>> that you know how to flatten using optionalFlatten.

Appendix M: Chapter 14 Exercise Solutions

Exercise 14.1

ResultAp<E, T> is very similar to Either<E, T>. Can you implement flatMap for it as well?

Exercise 14.1 solution

A possible flatMap implementation for ResultAp<E, T> is the following:

```
fun <E : Throwable, B, D> ResultAp<E, B>.flatMap(
  fn: (B) -> ResultAp<E, D>
): ResultAp<E, D> = // 1
  when (this) {
    is Error<E> -> ResultAp.error(error) // 2
    is Success<B> -> { // 3
      val result = fn(value)
      when (result) {
        is Error<E> -> ResultAp.error(result.error) // 4
        is Success<D> -> ResultAp.success(result.value) // 4
      }
    }
  }
```

In the code, you replaced:

1. `Either<E, T>` with `Result<E: Throwable, T>`.

2. `Left<E>` with `Error<E>`

3. `Right<T>` with `Success<T>`.

4. `left` with `error` and `right` with `success`.

As a quick note, notice that this `flatMap` implementation uses the fail fast approach.

Exercise 14.2

In the previous paragraphs, you implemented a simple system to fetch and parse data using both `Optional<T>` and `Either<E, T>`. Can you do the same using `ResultAp<E, T>`?

Exercise 14.2 solution

In this case, you have to follow the same process you did in the chapter. Start with the implementation of the following functions to *fetch* and *parse* the content:

```
fun fetchTvShowResultAp(
  query: String
): ResultAp<IOException, String> = try {
  ResultAp.success(TvShowFetcher.fetch(query))
} catch (ioe: IOException) {
  ResultAp.error(ioe)
}

/** Invokes the parser returning a ResultAp<E, T> */
fun parseTvShowResultAp(
  json: String
): ResultAp<SerializationException, List<ScoredShow>> = try {
  ResultAp.success(TvShowParser.parse(json))
} catch (e: SerializationException) {
  ResultAp.error(e)
}
```

Here, you just do the same replacements you did in Exercise 14.1.

The next step is the composition of fetchTvShowResultAp and parseTvShowResultAp, like this:

```
fun fetchAndParseTvShowResultAp(query: String) =
   fetchTvShowResultAp(query)
     .flatMap(::parseTvShowResultAp)
```

Finally, you can run the following code to test your solution:

```
fun main() {
   fetchAndParseTvShowResultAp("Big Bang Theory")
     .errorMap {
       println("Error: $it")
       it
     }
     .successMap {
       println("Result: $it")
     }
}
```

Just note that Throwable as an upper bound forces you to return a Throwable from errorMap. Again, feel free to remove that limitation if this bothers you.

Made in the USA
Monee, IL
22 May 2022

96662208R20367